WORKING WORDS

WORKING WORDS

Punching the Clock and Kicking Out the Jams

Edited and introduced
by M. L. Liebler

FOREWORD BY BEN "RIVETHEAD" HAMPER

COFFEE HOUSE PRESS
MINNEAPOLIS 2010

Coffee House Press books are available to the trade through our primary distributor, Consortium Book Sales & Distribution, www.cbsd.com or (800) 283-3572. For personal orders, catalogs, or other information, write to: info@coffeehousepress.org.

Coffee House Press is a nonprofit literary publishing house. Support from private foundations, corporate giving programs, government programs, and generous individuals helps make the publication of our books possible. We gratefully acknowledge their support in detail in the back of this book.

To you and our many readers around the world,
we send our thanks for your continuing support.

LIBRARY OF CONGRESS CIP INFORMATION
Liebler, M. L.
Working words : literature of labor / M.L. Liebler.
p. cm.
Includes bibliographical references and index.
ISBN 978-1-56689-248-3 (alk. paper)
1. Working class writings, American.
2. Labor—Literary collections.
3. Work—Literary collections.
4. Working class—Literary collections.
I. Title.

PS508.W73L54 2010
810.9'352623—dc22

2010023932

PRINTED IN THE UNITED STATES
1 3 5 7 9 8 6 4 2
FIRST EDITION | FIRST PRINTING

WORKING WORDS

1. LABOR POEMS AND SONGS

2. SHORT FICTION

3. NON-FICTION, HISTORIES, AND MEMOIRS

Foreword

BEN "RIVETHEAD" HAMPER

Admittedly, it was an odd vigil, yet one I couldn't abandon. I'd become convinced that one of these days, on one of these vapid, faceless shifts, my line-
mates would eventually burst into a spontaneous musical number. It would
go down just like *The Music Man* or *West Side Story*. All I asked was to be on
hand. It was one big reason why I rarely missed work. Can you imagine playing hooky on the day that such an event took place?

I had nothing but time, so I decided to wait them out. I waited for days.
I waited for weeks. When the wait would bore me, I'd do other things—spot
weld, read a newspaper, install a pencil rod, have a smoke. None of us were
going anywhere. If need be, I could probably have waited for years.

It wasn't like these musical eruptions didn't occur now and then. It happened in *Oklahoma!* It happened on the west side of New York City. It happened in River City, Iowa, of all places. Documentation does exist. They have
countless videos available that you can purchase or rent, all of them showing
ordinary folk lunging out of their mundane circumstances and headlong into
marvelous song and dance. Beautiful lyrics. Sensational stepping. Three minutes or so of synchronized melodic glee—then right on back to the nothingness
of their lackluster Now. Just like nothing of significance had taken place, as if
they had merely taken a break to jiggle a toilet handle or stir a pot of beans.

Well shit, I figured. If it could happen in rural Oklahoma, or out in the
cornpone prairies of Iowa, it could just as easily occur right here in the cab
shop of the massive GM Truck & Bus Plant in Flint, Michigan. Surely those
schmoes from the aforementioned productions didn't have *that* much of an
advantage on us. We had talent too. For instance, I knew one guy over in
Trim who used to play drums for the Box Tops, and the woman on the door-
latch job sang Supremes songs so gorgeously that grown men were frequently
seen using their hankies for something other than dabbing up residual malt
liquor beads. I swear—even *I* could carry a tune as well as Rod Steiger, and
probably a whole lot better than Paul Lynde.

All it was going to take was that first plucky working stiff to jumpstart
the number. Some exultant dreg whose monotony meter lolled so deeply into
the red that an explosion of artistic impulse might be the last real recourse

available. Art born entirely of an heroically pure instinct to find another level—a level of true self-expression, a level of strenuous survival where something actually happened . . . if only for three minutes.

I'd already ruled myself out for this role. After all, this was about spontaneity, and I was already too invested in the whole expectation of the event to be eligible for that. A voyeur's role was to merely observe and experience. That role became rudely compromised if the voyeur attempted to manipulate or assist in the achievement of the action.

Of course, I only realized this notion after a few of my own flimsy attempts at "spontaneous" song imploded on the runway, resulting in nothing more than odd glances from my coworkers. The most dubious failure occurred when I decided to use my spot-welder cable as a load-bearing jungle vine and proceeded to hoist myself up on the highline track that ran through our department. Once situated, I launched into some awkward Goulet-esque scat that went something like, "The hills are alive with . . . fuck, it's so *hot* in here." My only review came in the form of a verbal reprimand from our dullard supervisor.

With me out of the picture (and, most likely, the soundtrack), that left approximately forty good men and women to ignite the musical. At $12.82 an hour—decent dough for the late seventies—I resumed my role as a bored yet well-compensated voyeur.

I watched and I waited. I watched and I waited. Every now and then it seemed like it was about to go down. I'd see some guy jump off the mig-welding platform with a brazing rod in his hand and immediately imagine him to be our Harold Hill, baton poised to strike up those seventy-six trombones. Or I'd look up in the rafters and spot a pipefitter feeding down new hose to an air gun, quickly assuming he'd soon take flight and swoop above us like Mary Martin en route to Neverland. It got to the point where a guy couldn't warble along to "Iron Man" on the radio without me whipping my head out of a wheel-well like some skittish, art-craving bloodhound.

I guess it was a little over five years into my wait when I realized that my linemates just weren't into it. Who knows why—perhaps they were all under contract somewhere else. I can't say that I was angry with any of them. Maybe I'd been asking too much. Lord knows attaching doors and truck beds and tailgates to steady-paced body frames was a lot of work unto itself. It didn't leave much time or energy for leaping into song, perfecting pirouettes, or squeezing art from thin, gruesome air.

But that didn't mean I quit searching for something. I just tempered my expectations a bit. By the time I transferred down to the rivet line, I was becoming keenly aware that the seeds of art were all around me. Something that drifted through the rafters and lurked amongst the bins. Poems and elegies. Comedies and dramas. Tall tales and short stories featuring invisible bylines and universal rights. They may not have had a discernible rhythm to them, or resembled anything that would soon be splashed along Broadway, but they were there. They had always been there. It was only a matter of escorting them out of the shadows.

I hadn't really written anything since high school, and the only reason I wrote back then was to impress a few hippie girls I knew. Other than that, the whole notion of writing wasn't very attractive. It seemed like a lot of hard work—You had to have something to say. You had to know things. And I didn't know much outside of the fact that it would be nice to have sexual relations with a hippie girl.

Perhaps I was still haunted by an earlier failure I'd had with literature. A few years before, my brother Bob and I had decided to write our own Hardy Boys books, being too poor to buy new volumes and feeling confident that we'd figured out Franklin W. Dixon's winning formula. We hunkered down in our bedroom one summer afternoon, Bob writing on the bed, me at the desk. No doubt about it, this was hard work. Now and then, Bob and I would switch spots, remaining speechless, too locked into our fantastic yarns to disturb the muse.

Finally, Bob asked if I'd take a look at what he'd come up with. His book was titled *The Mystery of the Flying Robot*. Hmm . . . I had to hand it to him, that title sure had a lot of the zing we were after. The text read precisely as follows: "Frank and Joe were walking down the street with their girlfriends. Suddenly, they looked up in the sky and saw a flying robot!" I reread it and tilted my head in thought. "Well . . . well?" my brother said. I didn't know much about writing, but it occured to me that Bob may have given away the plotline a bit prematurely. When I mentioned this to him, he became quite irate, demanding to see what I'd come up with. He grabbed my blank sheet of paper and scoffed. "At least I came up with something," he said. The whole ordeal left a sour taste in our mouths, and we vowed never to write again.

I kept my word for twenty-five years, until the rivet line presented itself to me—an unlikely muse clumsily disguised as just another indoor meadow of dread and drear. It would come in bursts—quotes, notions, theories, riddles— slammed down on the back of stock tags and paper towels. I'd bring them home in my back pocket and peck out paragraphs on an old typewriter I found in my mother's basement. Suddenly, going to work was no longer this auto- matic eight-hour death sentence for the soul. There were new considerations and a daily parade of possibilities. There were leading men and bit players and reoccurring heavies. They still didn't sing or dance in any organized pattern, but that hardly mattered anymore.

I couldn't say that writing about my job made assembly-line labor appealing, but it did supply me with a purpose, an introduction to another part of me, and, most importantly, it gave me something meaningful to do. On a General Motors assembly line, it was crucial to kill time before it had a chance to kill you. I'd seen it happen to members of my own family—that lazy spiral of boredom and regret that often winnowed its way through the whiskeyman's till. That paystub sure looked fine, but it didn't act as much of a salve against one's lack of purpose and placement.

I've always felt that work, unto itself, was only a noble concept in one of those absurd bromides that mothers are fond of reciting. The notion that work builds strong character strikes me as a defeatist's consolation, as intrinsically daft as believing bombs build good peace. Like anything else, work is what you make of it. In this way, all workers are artists, sworn to an ingenuity that they must create for themselves.

In the words that follow in this collection, we see and feel those who have made their move toward the understanding of work—seeking more than bromides, wanting far more than any paystub can provide. We move with them. We uphold their struggles and embrace their celebrations. We achieve more.

Let's keep moving. Let's want more. Let's see where the work song takes us. Eventually we'll become the singers, and we'll become the dancers, that our dreams flung dares at.

—Suttons Bay, Michigan
October 2010

Introduction

M. L. LIEBLER

"You work. You work, Buddy. You work."

These first words from one of my favorite working-class poems, "Grandfather's Breath," by Ohio poet Ray McNiece, sum up the first life lesson I remember being taught by my factory-worker grandfather and working-class grandma, who raised me in the shadow of the Dodge Main & Detroit. These words have always been my attitude and mantra, and I have kept them in my mind throughout my entire life and certainly while editing this anthology.

In compiling *Working Words: Punching the Clock and Kicking Out the Jams,* I had two goals in mind. First, I wanted to let American writers tell their uniquely American stories of work, labor, and class through their poems, songs, stories, and memoirs. To that end, I looked for some of the finest representations of late nineteenth-century through early twenty-first-century working-class literature by writers from a variety of backgrounds, cultures, and communities within the American experience. Second, my most sincere intent was to pay homage in the most inclusive and diverse way to the uniqueness of working-class cultures and to my own working-class roots, which have taught me everything I know about this world and about work. *"You work. You work, Buddy."*

The idea of an entire anthology about the working class and labor may seem an odd choice of subject matter to some readers, largely because the working class has long been seen as "nonacademic" and undereducated. The truth, however, is that art and creative writing have long played important roles in the everyday lives of America's working class and the working poor. While there is some official historical record of the relationship between the arts and the working class, it has only in recent years become interesting to academics and book publishers; Coffee House Press is one of the first to make such a major commitment to this type and style of literature in a multi-genre text. The neglect of working-class literature is particularly surprising, given that the connection between labor and art has had such a rich and long history in the United States. My Wayne State colleague David Sprague Herreshoff corroborates this in his insightful study *Labor into Art: The Theme of Work in Nineteenth-Century American Literature* (Wayne State University Press, 1991). He explains that a close examination of the work of Henry David Thoreau, Herman Melville, Emily Dickinson, Frederick Douglass, and Walt Whitman reveals that "when engaged with the theme of work, their poetry, essays and fiction penetrate and judge what making a living felt like as they took in and imagined the experience." (page 1)

The lack of academic awareness or interest in the creative activities and arts within working-class communities does not lessen its importance, its relevance, or its connection to working people in America. Working-class people don't need no professors to signify their existence; we have always relied on our own storytelling, music, songwriting, plays, cartooning, and mural art to express ourselves and to tell of our experiences, struggles, and dispossession by the powerful, who control all of the nation's wealth, politics, and educational systems.

Working-class Americans have always had their homemade art. Sometimes it took the form of creatively told versions of family stories. Our family's old, familiar story was about how Uncle Andy rose to the top of his profession as a Detroit garbageman and became, as we told it, "the best damn garbageman ever in the history of Detroit." At other times, we expressed ourselves in song, like the kind we used to sing in our old Dodge Polara while driving to Aunt Ruth's cottage in the heat of a Michigan summer. This may not have been what academia would refer to as "high art," but this was the way our creativity manifested itself in our daily lives. Our creativity has always been informed by our relationship to labor and class. These unique forms of creative expression offered us some pleasure, some relief in hard times, something to dream about as we looked forward to a better tomorrow, and, at times, it represented the joy of being alive in this hard, hard world.

Working-class art is folksy, down to earth, and real, and it is an important and constant aspect of our daily lives. Working people don't necessarily need a museum to validate their art (that's what the toolshed, the basement, or the garage is for). However, it is important to note that one of the great working-class pieces of public art, *Detroit Industry,* has been on display in the Detroit Institute of Arts since the early thirties. This famous public mural was painted by the great Diego Rivera; ironically, it was funded and supported by Henry Ford's family. So I guess it is safe to say that museums, basements, and toolsheds all have a special place in the working-class reality and aesthetic.

As for working-class literature, it doesn't necessarily need to be published in books to remind us of how hard life can be, because we have each other to keep these stories, songs, and art alive forever by passing them from one generation to the next in the good old-fashioned way of the "oral tradition."

Sometimes working-class literature is even written on the backs of credit-card bills, or in the simple way words are ordered on the family grocery list. In addition, much public working-class art can be seen on buildings, subways, and expressway overpasses from New York to Detroit to Los Angeles. In this sense, the world becomes the working classes' museum, canvas, and exclusive publisher. Still, there have always been, and there continue to be, working-class artists whose work makes it into print, onto recordings, into theaters, and sometimes even onto the walls of museums. While these artists may not make up the majority of those who have their work presented in various public forums, all of their works are, nonetheless, important in telling the "real" story of how "real people" built America.

Part of telling the story of art and the working class involves clarifying the historical significance of the arts and their continuous intersection with labor throughout the history of the United States. One of the most important public benchmarks in the American labor arts movement is the bestselling (even to this day) *Little Red Songbook* of the Industrial Workers of the World Union (IWW). The IWW was the first union to be inclusive of all working people when many other unions exclusively served and represented "skilled laborers." In addition to this historic and popular songbook, the IWW, along with Greenwich Village artists like John Reed, Dorothy Day, and Eugene O'Neill, put together the now famous 1913 Paterson Strike Pageant at Madison Square Garden in New York City. Together, creative artists, writers, actors, musicians, union leaders, and strikers organized a march from Paterson, New Jersey's Silk Mills to New York, culminating in a widely attended program that saw the strikers perform skits about their situation and their struggle to have a union. The performance was their attempt at dealing with their all too familiar and constant conflicts with capitalist employers over fair treatment in exchange for their hard and important labor. As historians have noted, "nothing like it had been known before in the history of labor agitation" (Joyce Kornbluh, *Rebel Voices: An I.W.W.* Anthology [University of Michigan Press, 1964], 212).

The event was one of the first times labor activists and union organizers used public art as a tool for labor agitation and pro-union propaganda. Public use of art continued in the working class into the twenties with the American adaptation of agitprop (a portmanteau of agitation propaganda), a form of street-style theater originating in Russia in the early twentieth century. This theatrical genre was used to help convince people by agitating their minds with highly emotional language; it was occasionally employed by working-class movements to alert workers to what company owners were really up to when they opposed their organizing attempts. By the late twenties, due to FDR's New Deal public funding, the Federal Writers' Project and the Federal Theatre Project were developed. These programs helped put artists (writers, actors, musicians, and so on) back to work by hiring them to produce theater programs like the Living Newspaper and free public presentations of classic, modern, and original plays that were performed for working-class audiences in public places such as parks, local theaters, schools, and church basements.

The Living Newspaper was one of the early undertakings of the Federal Theatre Project. Playwrights, in collaboration with local artists acting as a central research and editorial committee, created public performances featuring topics that were relevant to the local political, social, or cultural issues of each community involved. Later, the Federal Theatre Project produced plays by "local writers immersed in the life and problems of farm workers and immigrant working-class communities" (Paul Sporn, *Against Itself: The Federal Theatre and Writers' Projects in the Midwest* [Wayne State University Press, 1995], 45). During this time, the program also began to create and produce theater written and performed by artists who would have normally been ignored, including American foreign-language writers and artists as well as African Americans and Latinos, among others.

Original plays such as *Turpentine, Big White Fog, 200 Were Chosen,* and *The Tailor Becomes a Shopkeeper,* as well as classics by writers such as Molière, Shakespeare, and Marlowe were produced and performed for predominately working-class audiences. It was during this period that Clifford Odet's plays; novels such as Michael Gold's *Jews Without Money* (1930) and Langston Hughes's *Not Without Laughter* (1930); and *Songs and Stories of the Anthracite Industry,* the Federal Writers' Project's 1927 anthology, appeared (ibid., 55). Also significant was the publication of several novels about a series of strikes in the South: Mary Heaton Vorse's *Strike!* (1930), Grace Lumpkin's *To Make My Bread* (1932), Sherwood Anderson's *Beyond Desire* (1932), William Rollins's *The Shadow Before* (1934), Albert Halper's *The Foundry* (1934), and the well-known James T. Farrell's Stud Lonigan trilogy (1932, 1934, and 1935). Much of this working-class literature did indeed reach larger audiences, who responded favorably to its labor-related themes and their representations of working-class life.

As the twentieth century moved into the forties and the fifties, working-class themes were still being presented in important works by Richard Wright, William Attaway, John Steinbeck, Upton Sinclair, Henry Roth, Zora Neale Hurston, Nelson Algren, Tillie Olsen, and others. In the sixties and seventies, stories of work and the working class were occasionally presented, notably in such works as Charles Bukowski's *Post Office* and Hurbert Selby, Jr.'s *Last Exit to Brooklyn;* these novels seem to be more popular now in the twenty-first century than they were in their own time.

Music played an even larger role in working-class self-expression. Well-known musicians, including Woody Guthrie, Huddie Ledbetter, and Pete Seeger, and many singers and songwriters who are unknown nationally, played a very important role in creating working-class art through their original songs and public performances in support of workers. Detroit boasts one of the best examples of the interconnection and impact of art with and upon the working class, via the figurative and literal assembly line, in Berry Gordy, Jr.'s creation of Motown Records. After closely observing how the assembly line worked at Detroit's Ford Rouge Plant, Berry Gordy translated the process for the recording industry, creating a record company now known around the world as Motown Records—"The Sound of Young America." Motown Records was not only developed from the assembly-line process, but many of its stars were working-class teens from various Detroit public high schools. The Motown story is a quintessential working-class tale right down to its later downsizing and outsourcing of jobs when Gordy decided in 1972 to move the company, unannounced, to Los Angeles. Like many companies these days, he posted a simple sign on the Hitsville Studio doors saying, "There will be no work today—Motown has moved its operation to Los Angeles." Many of the label's recording artists found themselves, once again, out of work, displaced and back on the unemployment line just like their counterparts at the auto plant.

Like Berry Gordy, and some of Motown's artists, earlier blues and jazz legends like John Lee Hooker, Hank Ballard, Bobo Jenkins, and Little Willie John also came to Detroit to work on assembly lines for the Big Three. In the late sixties, five working-class kids, the sons of Downriver factory workers, formed the now influential and legendary pre-punk Motor City Five (also known as the MC 5); this anthology's subtitle is borrowed from one of their famous songs, "Kick Out the Jams." Many of their working-class counterparts, like Bob Seger, Iggy Pop, and others from industrial America, also went on to become Rock and Roll Hall of Fame inductees who have influenced the direction of rock in the late twentieth century into the twenty-first century. Even in the early twenty-first century, the working-class communities in Detroit were still spawning new waves of musical art with artists like Emimem, the White Stripes (both included here), and the invention of the globally popular techno music that was inspired by the constant beat of factory machines.

In addition to influencing current popular music, working-class artists involved with slam poetry have brought poetry to the forefront as public art in the last two decades. Slam poetry is a term and movement created by Chicago construction worker turned poet (a là Carl Sandburg) Marc Kelly Smith. His desire was to bring poetry to the people through the oral tradition. Since he started this new literary genre in the early eighties, in a neighborhood bar in Chicago's barrio, it has gone national and now international; it is an art form that attracts poets of all ages and cultural backgrounds. Today, young poets write, read, and perform their own original works everywhere, from union halls to coffee houses to colleges and universities, and even in classrooms in elementary, middle, and high schools across the United States. While the art form is open to all ages and all backgrounds, it is primarily practiced by young people inspired by working-class, social, and political populism. Slam poetry is a genuine art form that returns poetry to the days of Vachel Lindsay and Carl Sandburg in the early twentieth century, when poets traveled the country to read to "regular folks" wherever people gathered.

Detroit has also had its own working-class poetry movement in recent years. In 1998, I helped develop, with Sam Stark of the United Auto Workers of America (UAW) Union, the now well-known and annual Worker Writers' Festival. Since its inception the event, known to worker-artists around Motown, has been going strong for over ten years. This annual literary arts festival features factory workers and other union members reading and performing their poetry and songs before a large, supportive audience in a local metro-area union hall. Other cities like Chicago, Pittsburgh, and Milwaukee have developed similar events. A particularly impressive program is the annual labor arts event sponsored by the Labor Heritage Foundation in Washington, DC. This organization has been holding the annual and very inclusive Great Labor Arts Exchange at the George Meany Center for Labor Studies in Silver Spring, Maryland, for almost thirty years. The event brings together labor writers, songwriters, musicians, muralists, and performers for a week's worth of collaboration and fellowship centered upon using all the arts as organizing tools for workers. Each year the event affords the opportunity for working-class artists to meet like-minded colleagues concerned with labor issues.

So, from storytelling around the backyard grill to sing-alongs in the family car to the blues, jazz, and rock music, to worker writer festivals, to slam poetry and theater by and for the working class, we can easily start to understand the very important role that art plays, and has played, in the working class throughout the twentieth century and continuing now into the twenty-first century.

It is my hope that readers will think about this rich history as they experience the stories, poems, songs, and essays in this anthology. Spanning the late nineteenth century to the early twenty-first century, the anthology includes a variety of works offering a multitude of perspectives on the working-class experience. Readers will find many important literary pieces about physical labor—from depictions of life in the auto plants, the mines, and the mills across the United States of the past and present to representations of the hard work that waitresses, child laborers, and slave laborers have done over the past two centuries. Other literature included in this collection deals more generally with working-class family life by detailing relationships between husbands and wives, children and parents, and friends and neighbors.

In addition to chronological breadth, the collection has geographical variety—it includes selections by American writers from the South, West, East, and North. By including the widest possible range of works and writers, I hope to highlight the lives of American workers as they are depicted in literature from every conceivable working-class point of view.

Some of the pieces discuss such sensitive and controversial subjects as domestic abuse and violence (as witnessed in Chris Leland's short story "The Old West," or in Stephen Crane's late nineteenth-century work *Maggie: A Girl of the Streets*). The hardships of the working poor and the unemployed are also depicted here, for example in Willa Cather's "Paul's Case," a study of a young man who commits suicide after being pressured by his father, who wants his son to rise above his family's working-class status. I also wanted literature that featured humor and moments of tenderness, as in the excerpt from Bill Harris's fiction piece "Just Like in the Movies," where the characters are always looking for possible symbols in their lives that can be translated into winning picks in the daily numbers racket. Their constant hope is to be free of their working-class conditions, to move up in society. There are many examples of this side of the working-class lifestyle, including stories like Jim Daniel's "No Pets" and poems by Sue Doro and Michael Casey.

It is important for readers of working-class literature to have access to pieces that take a closer look at the hardships, struggles, and often unrecognized contributions of American working women of all races. To that end, I have included important and enlightening poems by Dorianne Laux, Diane Wakoski, Maggie Anderson, Wanda Coleman, Frances E. W. Harper, and fiction and creative non-fiction by excellent and diverse writers like Jeanne Bryner, Lolita Hernandez, Rebecca Harding Davis, Jennifer Gillan, Dorothy Day, and others. Stories and poems by these writers from diverse backgrounds and experiences shed light on the important role women have always played, and continue to play, in the working-class experience.

In the working class, it is often said that "we laugh to keep from crying." I wanted to include pieces that demonstrate this important aspect of life. A great example of working-class humor and the unique way the working class lightens their daily burdens is seen in Bonnie Jo Campbell's "Selling Manure." This story was one of many where I found myself laughing out loud each time I read it. Campbell writes, "There is no vocation more honest than selling manure. Consider what most people do for a living. They go to work where they build crap or sell crap or move crap. . . . When I deliver manure to someone's garden, the customer and I are both upfront about what we're dealing with. All I have to ask is, 'Where do you want this shit?'"

Also consider the humor in Milwaukee poet Antler's hilarious poem "Written after Learning Slaves in Ancient Greece and Rome Had 115 Holidays a Year." This poem compares the working life of today to that of the Greek and Roman slaves. Antler writes:

Instead of a higher standard of living
    why not a higher standard of loving?
Why not a higher standard
    of getting high?
. . . .
Slaves in Ancient Greece and Rome
    had 115 holidays a year!
Hey, wait a minute, that makes us
    more slaves than them!

I have included some songs, like Woody Guthrie's "1913 Massacre," Bob Dylan's "Union Sundown," Eminem's "Lose Yourself," Jack White's "The Big Three Killed My Baby," and Joe Henry's "Our Song," because they seem important as works that uniquely address the working-class experience, and speak the truth about the sadness and desperation of the human condition in the same way that a poem like Vietnam vet and poet Lamont B. Steptoe's "Day Worker" does. Steptoe's poem is a moving account of the hard times endured by his mother in Philadelphia. He writes that "much of her life would be spent on her knees in white folks kitchens . . . momma . . . momma . . . after all those cold winters, after all those hot summers, after all those years of your life you gave to those white people for our sake, how can it be that you could teach us how to be gentle?"

For a satiric and irreverent look at the working class, I have included the hysterical (but painfully true) view of factory work presented in Ben Hamper's working classic *Rivethead: Tales from the Assembly Line* (Warner Books, 1992). To offer a more realistic look at our capitalist system, I have included Michael Moore's biting commentary "Horatio Alger Must Die," from his book *Dude, Where's My Country?* (Warner Books, 2003).

In this anthology, readers will find familiar labor and working-class authors from different generations and communities throughout the USA, but I also have included newer, up-and-coming writers like Michael Shay, Matthew Olzmann, and Vievee Francis, who will likely be discovered by readers for the first time in these pages.

When thinking of how readers, students, and teachers could use this anthology for discussion groups at union halls, in college or high-school class-rooms, or in individual study groups, I recalled the basic ideas and philosophy offered by the late Peter Maurin, cofounder of the Catholic Worker Movement. Maurin believed that workers should engage in continual and progressive "round table discussions" related to all issues and topics concerning the working and laboring classes. Maurin felt that by holding regular, open discussions, workers could teach each other in a collective and collaborative learning environment. He further believed that this was the tool workers needed to educate themselves and to help them on their first steps toward independence and parity with those who would otherwise keep them under control. Maurin's main idea was simple and to the point: "make all scholars workers and all workers scholars." He knew that with knowledge, awareness, and education, workers would never again be under their bosses' thumbs or lulled by the false sense of security offered by big corporations that unfortunately direct most areas of American society (witness the 2010 health care debate, and how huge insurance corporations influence the average working-class American's life). When workers become educated, they inevitably learn how to take charge of the means of production. This always spells trouble for the companies and their big boss men, who would like nothing better than to keep workers under a close watch. This anthology was designed for working-class people and anyone else who is interested in better understanding the thoughts, realities, dreams, and hopes of the people who are involved in doing work for the benefit of all in our society.

The great writer Wallace Stegner (author of *Joe Hill*) said this about literature as an art form: "let me learn to respect human differences, human privacy, human dignity, human pain. And then let me find the words to say it so it can't be overlooked and can't be forgotten." This is exactly what

I am looking for in this anthology. I want to let people see, feel, smell, taste, and truly understand what working-class life is all about, and I think the best way to do this is through the art and literature of working-class and labor writers.

For more than twenty years, I have taught a labor studies course entitled "Labor through the Arts" at Wayne State University. I've also recently taught the class in Munich, Germany, at the Ludwig Maximillian University's Amerika-Institut, the University of Stuttgart, Novosibirsk State University in Russia, and other locations around the world. I have yet to find a complete anthology dedicated solely to all genres of literature dealing *exclusively* with the working-class experience. My intention with this collection is to fill this obvious void and to pay homage to my own working-class roots. This book is "payback" to the community that raised me, nurtured me, and taught me strong values and the importance of work. I felt it both urgent and important, through this literature, to provide some much-deserved and overdue dignity, honor, and presence to the voiceless many who bear the workload of this country.

I approached this project with the idea of presenting engaging, vivid, and entertaining literary works for all citizens of the world, regardless of class, to read, enjoy, and discuss. Readers will not need a Ph.D. in English literature to get at the heart and soul of these pieces. The work in this anthology is serious and dimensional literature, but it is also accessible.

Finally, it should be noted that all of the writers included in this anthology have given freely of their art to enhance, pay homage to, and support the spirit of the working class. I am grateful, humbled, and honored to count those included as good friends of mine and real friends to the working class in America.

This is an anthology for all Americans to read to better understand the plight, the successes, the humor, and the generous spirit of this country's working class. Use this anthology to get to the heart of "what work is," to borrow a phrase from Pulitzer Prize-winning poet Philip Levine. For me and countless others in the working class, Ray McNiece's words still ring true: *"You work. You work, Buddy. You work."*

The literature in this book presents our stories, and they tell what is at the very core of our working-class lives as we all continue with our daily struggles and continued attempts at "making it right!"

—Wayne State University, Detroit, Michigan
April 2010

1

LABOR POEMS AND SONGS

Spitting in the Leaves

MAGGIE ANDERSON

In Spanishburg there are boys in tight jeans,
mud on their cowboy boots and they wear huge hats
with feathers, skunk feathers they tell me.
They do not want to be in school, but are.
Some teacher cared enough to hold them. Unlike
their thin disheveled cousins, the boys on Matoaka's
Main Street in October who loll against parking meters
and spit into the leaves. Because of them, someone
will think we need a war, will think the best solution
would be for them to take their hats and feathers,
their good country manners and drag them off somewhere,
to Vietnam, to El Salvador. And they'll go.
They'll go from West Virginia, from hills and back roads
that twist like politics through trees, and they'll fight,
not because they know what for but because what they know
is how to fight. What they know is feathers,
their strong skinny arms, their spitting
in the leaves.

Closed Mill

MAGGIE ANDERSON

I'm not going to tell you everything,
like where I live and who I live with.
There are those for whom this would be
important, and once perhaps it was to me,
but I've walked through too many lives
this year, different from my own,
for a thing like that to matter much.
All you need to know
is that one rainy April afternoon,
exhausted from teaching six classes
of junior high school students,
I sat in my car at the top of a steep hill
in McKeesport, Pennsylvania, and stared
for a long time at the closed mill.

"Death to Privilege," said Andrew Carnegie,
and then he opened up some libraries,
so that he might "repay his deep debt,"
so that light might shine on Pittsburgh's poor
and on the workers in the McKeesport Mill.
The huge scrap metal piles below me
pull light through the fog on the river
and take it in to rust in the rain.
Many of the children I taught today
were hungry. The strong men who are
their fathers hang out in the bar
across the street from the locked gates
of the mill, just as if they were still
laborers with lunch pails, released
weary and dirty at the shift change.

Suppose you were one of them?
Suppose, after twenty or thirty years,
you had no place to go all day
and no earned sleep to sink down into?
Most likely you would be there too,
drinking one beer after another,
talking politics with the bartender,
and at the end of the day
you'd go home, just as if you had
a paycheck, your body singing
with the pull and heave of imagined
machinery and heat. You'd talk mean
to your wife who would talk mean back,
your kids growing impatient and arbitrary,
way out of line. Who's to say you would not
become your father's image, the way any of us
assumes accidental gestures,
a tilt of the head, hard labor,
or the back of his hand.

From here the twisted lines of wire
make intricate cross-hatchings against
the sky, gray above the dark razed mill's red
pipe and yellow coals, silver coils of metal
heaped up and abandoned. Wall by wall,
they are tearing this structure down.
Probably we are not going to say
too much about it, having as we do
this beautiful reserve, like roses.

I'll say that those kids were hungry.
I would not dare to say the mill won't
open up again, as the men believe.
You will believe whatever you want to.
Once, philanthropy swept across our dying cities
like industrial smoke, and we took everything
it left and we were grateful, for art
and books, for work when we could get it.
Any minute now, the big doors buried under

scrap piles and the slag along this river
might just bang open and let us back inside
the steamy furnace that swallows us
and spits us out like food, or heat
that keeps us warm and quiet
inside our little cars in the rain.

from Factory

ANTLER

I

The machines waited for me.
Waited for me to be born and grow young,
For the totempoles of my personality to be carved,
    and the slow pyramid of days
To rise around me, to be robbed and forgotten,
They waited where I would come to be,
    a point on earth,
The green machines of the factory,
    the noise of the miraculous machines of the factory,
Waited for me to laugh so many times,
    to fall asleep and rise awake so many times,
    to see as a child all the people I did not want to be,
And for suicide to long for me as the years ran into the mirror
    disguising itself as I grew old
    in eyes that grew old
As multitudes worked on machines I would work on,
    worked, ceased to exist, and died,
For me they waited, patiently, the machines,
    all the time in the world,
As requiems waited for my ears
    they waited,
As naked magazines waited for my eyes
    they waited,
As I waited for soft machines like mine
    time zones away from me, unknown to me,
    face, flesh, all the ways of saying goodbye,
While all my possibilities, like hand over hand on a bat
    to see who bats first, end up choking the air—
While all my lives leap into lifeboats
    shrieking—"You can't afford to kill time
    while time is killing you!"

5

Before I said *Only the religion whose command before all others*
    is Thou Shalt Not Work shall I hosanna,
Before I said *Not only underground are the minds of men*
    eaten by maggots,
Before I said *I would rather be dead*
    than sweat at the work of zombies,
The machines waited.

Now the factory imagines I am there,
The clock keeps watching me while it works
    to see how much time it has left.
How much does it get paid? Are coffins the safes
    where it keeps its cash?
I see my shadow working on the shadow of a machine.
Everywhere I look I am surrounded by giant machines—
Machines that breathe me till I become stale
    and new windows of meat must be opened.
Each year of my name they ran, day and night,
Each time I kissed, each time I learned a new word,
    or name of a color, or how to spell boy,
Night, day, without stopping, in the same place running,
Running as I learned how to walk, talk, read, count, tell time
    and every time I ever ran alone
    pretending to be a wild black stallion,
They ran as I thought never (my eyes in the clouds)
    would my future corpse need to be buried
    premature in slavery of exchange to contemplate
    the leisure vacations of photosynthesis and limnology
    and the retirement of tombstone inscriptions
    into veils that veronica the earth,
They ran, and I never heard them,
    never stopped to hear them coming,
All the times walking to school and back,
All the times playing sick to stay home and have fun,
All the summers of my summer vacations
I never once thought I'd live to sacrifice my dwindling fleshbloom
    packaging the finishing touches on America's decay
For money to earn me so I can write in the future
    about what I am now, then am no longer,

Shortening the lifespan of planet for 6¢ a minute
    so I can elegize the lifespan of beauty and my life,
So I can say before my parents ever met
    machines were blaring the same hysterical noise,
So I can say they were waiting for me
    every mouthful of food I swallowed,
So I can say they were waiting for me
    every time paper eyes of paper nakedness
    watched my hands perform the ritual of dreams,
So I can say each second so many die so many are born,
    like rapid snapping of fingers, snap, snap,
    snap you live, snap you die, snap you live and die again!

Each day of my life is my life!
So, winding my watch before work
    with the galaxies of my fingerprints—
    each twist of my lifeline a dungeon of ticks—
I wondered was it for this
    my hide'n'seek Huckleberryhood?
And pondered how each day goes to its grave single file
    without the corpse of what I might have been,
Yet the hour hand is so slow
    no one will ever see it move.

Each of the great works never written
By those who work in factories so they can write words,
    what they say will be great words,
Does not care, does not wait to be written—
At the end of a day's work he who left his mind
    eight hours at his writing desk for the repugnance
    of metal on metal, noise on noise,
Sits down with his pen as if he had already written
    the great words of his dreams.
His feet feel like nursing homes for wheelchairs,
His ears an inferno of crickets,
And he says—"I feel like the grave of someone I loved"
And dreams of being hired to hammock-drowse
    outside where workers work
    to contemplate the utopias of sleep

Or to conduct tours of the plant reciting by heart
      the godliest glossolalias of divine frenzy.
Each day, those reaching the cliff of their last words
      waterfall into the gorges of night, wondering
How much do corpses get paid for working underground?
How much should they receive for urging their eyes to become
      the eyes on butterfly wings, peacock tails, and potatoes?
How much to package their innards into the innards of trees
      and leaves that creep down shirtfronts of children
      hiding in them?
How much to coax their hearts into the eight hearts
      of the hermaphroditic nightcrawler or into the pink stars
      that are the noses of moles?
What union do corpses join? How do they feel, more segregated
      than old people, when we keep them from humans that live—
      as if their bodies weren't the bodies we loved
      and called by the names we loved them by—
      and cut the dandelions from their faces?

Perhaps I have never left the factory.
Perhaps I'm made to dream the 16 hours my identity flees.
It's the drug in the water that does it, remarkable.
To think I'll work here forever thinking I go home and return
      and do all sorts of things in between,
      like writing this poem
Of course I'm not writing this poem!
I'm on the machine now packaging endless ends of aluminum
      for the tops and bottoms of cans.
Our foreman laughed—"You'll wake up in the middle of the night
      as if you're working. It's so easy
      you can do it in your sleep."
And I know that in one day owning this place
I'd make more than if my life worked my lifetime here.
In my lifetime I'd make more than all the workers combined.
Then I could envy those who make a million a second—
To them the prostitutes must be most beautiful
      and pornography a religion that is never disbelieved.
To those, this memo, dashed during breaks in slavery
      whose chains regenerate faster than tails of salamanders

or penis's reengorgement.
To my soul wondering if I have a body or not: Huck, Huck,
    look down at your funeral from lofts of the barn o' blue,
Look down at me dreaming my deathbed in factory,
    machines gone berserk, drowning in a sea of lids,
Dying where no one could hear my last whisper
    for industries of scholars to unhieroglyph—
Where the noise is so loud that if I screamed louder than I can
    no one would hear me, not even myself,
Where the bathroom stalls are scratched with the multiplication
    of men's lives in money, the most begging graffiti,
Where it is not I who wrote this tomb, but a machine,
    and the earplugs, and the timeclock
Waiting so many times to pick up the card that tells me my name,
Where metal cries louder than human yearning to return
    under earth,
And the first shift can't wait to go home,
And the second shift can't wait to go home,
And the third shift can't wait for the millions
    of alarmclocks to begin ringing
As I struggle with iron in my face,
Hooked fish played back and forth to work
    by unseen fisherman on unseen shore,
Day after day my intestines unwinding around me
Until I am a mountain of waste
From whose depths all that is left of me,
    a penis and a mouth,
Dreams of reaching the peak of all I contained,
Dreams of jerking that fisherman from the earth
    and dragging him to the pearls
    in the jaws of the giant clams of the sky. . . .

II

"All you have to do is stand here
    and package lids as they come from the press
    checking for defects every so often.
Shove enough lids in the bag like this,
Stand the filled bag on end like this,
Fold over the top like this,

9

Pull enough tape off
  and tape it like this,
Then stack 'em like this on the skid."

How many watching me watch the woman
  teach me my job
Remembered *their* first day on the job,
Remembered wondering what the woman felt
  teaching them in a minute
  the work she'd done all her life,
Showing them so fast all they needed to know?
How many could still remember who they were in search of a living—
Name, address, telephone, age, sex, race,
Single, married, children, parents, what they do or why they died,
Health record, police record, military record, social security #,
  how far in school, everywhere worked, why quit or fired,
  everything written here is true, signature, interview,
  the long wait, the call "you're hired"—
Could still see themselves led through the factory
  to the spot they would work on,
  strange then and now so familiar?

This is the hall big as a football field.
Here are the 24 presses chewing can lids
  from hand-fed sheets of aluminum.
Here are the 10 minsters chomping poptops
  nonstop into lids scooped into their jaws.
Machines large as locomotives,
  louder than loudest rockgroup explosions,
Screeching so loud you go deaf without earplugs,
  where the only way to speak is to gesture,
Or bending to your ear as if I were telling a secret
  the yell from my cupped hands less than a whisper.

Now the film of myself each day on the job begins.
I see myself enter the factory, led to the spot I will work on.
I see myself adjusting the earplugs to stopper the deluge of sound.
I see the woman who showed me the job
  she'd done her whole life in a minute
Let me take over, and the minute she left how I fumbled,

how the lids gushed all over the floor
And when the foreman rushed over and I hollered—
    "Something's wrong! It's too fast!
    No one can work at this speed!"
How he stared and the stares of the others
    who couldn't hear what I said but could tell.
And I gulped, This "Beat the Clock" stunt
    must be performed *eight hours*
    before the lunatic buzzer itself
    becomes consolation prize.

Yet sooner than I thought, I mastered the rhythms,
    turned myself into a flywheel dervish,
And can't deny being thrilled by the breakthrough
    from clumsy to graceful—
Though old-timers scowled as if it took years
    to learn all the fine points.
But long after my pride in doing such a good job
    turned into days crossed off the calendar
    each night before pulling out the alarm
        I woke to push in,
    up, eat, go, work, eat, work, back, eat, sleep,
All the days I would work stared
    ahead of me the line of machines,
    behind me the line of machines,
Each with a worker working as I work,
    doing the same job that I do,
Working within sight of the wall clock
    whose second hand is still moving.

III

Thus as the foreman watched me from the corner of his eye
    as I watched him from the corner of mine
    pretending to be doing my best
        as if I didn't know I was under inspection,
I relished the words I would write
    intoned in this factory where no one could hear them,
    swallowed in the shrill-greased ecstasy of machines
        as I led processions of naked acolytes

11

sopranoing Athenian epitaphs, candles in their hands.

To write this poem, to bring the word beautiful into Factory
You must never forget when the lids first come from the press
    they are hot, they are almost slippery.
You must never forget since each tube holds 350 lids
    and each crate holds 20 tubes and each day I fill 40 crates
From my work alone 280,000 lids each day—
    huge aluminum worm wriggling one mile long
    into the cadaver of America.
You must never forget 14 million cans each day
    from a single factory!
5,110,000,000 cans each year from a single factory!
More throwaway cans each year than human beings on this planet!
Every high, every heartbeat of your life
    the machines have been running.
Every time you heard a pianissimo
    the earsplitting machines have been running.
You've already spent more time working here
    than making love,
More time working here than lying on hills
    looking at the sky.
Each of your favorite books you must pilgrimage here to age,
    to absorb and exude wisdom,
To think of those who worked here before you
    and those who will work here after you.
You must say to yourself—"If I don't work here
    this poem won't be able to write me."
And asked—"What's that smell?" you must remember
    on your clothes, on your skin, in your lungs
    and when the breeze is just right through your bedroom window
        the smell of the factory.
You must brainstorm machines and workers are like poets and readers:
    the poets eat sheets of steel and press them into words
        that are the ends of containers,
The reader stands in one place shifting from foot to foot,
    crating and crating,
Searching for defects so the noisemaker can be shut down
    and while white-coated mechanics scurry to fix it

like doctors around a sick president, he can take a break,
get a drink, take a crap, unwrap some butterscotch to suck on,
    glimpse a glimpse of second-shift sunset,
    watch the guard lower the flag.

To birth this womb, to do for Continental Can Company
    what Walt Whitman did for America,
You must celebrate machine-shop rendezvous!
You must loafe observing a disc of aluminum!
You must sing the security of treadmills
    remembering where you are today
        you were yesterday
        you will be tomorrow.
So, after suicide invites you through the naked mirror
    and poetry dares you to dive headfirst into the sky,
After memorizing the discovery of fire, tools, speech,
    agriculture, industry,
And all the inventors, inventions and dates
    of the last 10,000 years you got a 100 on in History,
And after the ceaseless history of human war
    reads the eyes in your face,
Faced with the obituary of man,
Caught in the deathrattle of the world,
    from the deathblows of pollution,
    from the deathknells of overpopulation,
    from factories which are the deathbeds of Nature
        and the seedbeds of bombs,
After contemplating the graveyard of elegies,
    the immortality of maggots
    and the immolation of the sun,
Then, Antler, or whatever your name is,
Enjoy returning prodigal to your machine
    to forget the view from the skyscrapers of money,
    to forget the hosts of human starvations
        belly-bloated or brainwashed in Mammon,
    to forget the sign over the entrance to Auschwitz
        WORK MAKES MAN FREE,
    to forget that working here you accomplice
        the murder of Earth,

to forget the birds that sing eight hours a day
    daydreaming the salaries of worms,
to forget how old you must be
    to be rich and young before you die,
to forget your mother waking you
    from this nightmare
    is only a dream—
So nothing called life can torment you with undertakings
    and your only responsibility toward mankind
    is to check for defects in the ends of cans.

IV

All I have to do is stand here
    and do the same thing all day.
But the job requiring five steps repeated over and over
    eight hours every day
    is not monotonous.
Only the body and mind finding such work monotonous
    is monotonous.
Those who gripe work is boring
    gripe they are boring.
Yet if I work hours and the clock says
    only five minutes has gone by,
If the last hour working seems longer
    than the seven before it,
Won't my last day on the job seem longer
    than all the months that preceded it?
Could I have been here more in one day
    than someone who's put in ten years?
Or has he learned how to punch in and out
    fast as a punching bag?
Don't we both know the way
    to the prong of our alarm in the dark?
How long could I work without looking up at the clock?
How long before I was watching its hands
    more than watching my own package lids? . . .

Written after Learning Slaves in Ancient Greece and Rome Had 115 Holidays a Year

ANTLER

Instead of creating better murder weapons
    to "protect" ourselves,
Better create loving boys and girls
    who become loving women and men.
Instead of a higher standard of living
    why not a higher standard of loving?
Why not a higher standard
    of getting high?
No more brainwashed robot zombies!
No more socialization lobotomies!

Thoreau could live a whole year
    on money from working 6 weeks.
We canned ourselves in concentration camps
    called cities
And in buildings and rooms where we work.
We have become hermetically sealed containers.
The can of today is the wilderness that was.
The can-to-be is the wilderness that is.

As Oscar Wilde said: "Work is the curse
    of the drinking man."
As Stan Jones said: "It's not what the machine makes,
    but what the machine makes you."
As Virgil said: Deus nobis haec otia fecit:
    "A god has granted us this idleness."
As Lessing said: "Let us be lazy in everything
    except in loving and drinking,
    except in being lazy."

Should cans stop being made?
Should all factories immediately close down?
What solution do you provide? If everyone's a poet
        and no one works, how do we survive?
The way St. Theresa survived on Light?
Love becomes a full-time job?
But where do we get the money
        to pay people not to work?

Slaves in Ancient Greece and Rome
        had 115 holidays a year!
Hey, wait a minute, that makes us
        more slaves than them!

Migration Scene c. 1939

ALBERT AUBERT

boy, that old cracker said to me, what the hell
you doin' sitting down in my shade?
i was real young and must not've known
any better so i said to him,
your shade, bossman? i wasn't
so young as not to know i was
supposed to call him bossman, though.
yeah, nigger, he said, my shade.
that's my trees you sittin' under
on my land so that makes it my shade.
now once i got started it seemed
i couldn't stop so i asked him
what makes the shade, the sun or the tree?
i must've caught him off guard 'cause
he answered me almost civil like
he said, the sun's got a part in it
but his civilness didn't last all
that long. now you sass me one more
time, nigger, he said, and you see
that big limb right there over
your head? bet that limb'll hold
a fat rope just fine, t'other end
fitted right tight 'round your black neck.
well, after that it seems like i just
couldn't shut my mouth so i said to him,
the sun's yourn too, bossman? that's
when he pulled out this pistol long
as my two feet set end on end and it
was then i heard a voice sayin' run
for your life and i headed off into
the wind. i outrun the first piece
of lead he sent flyin' my way so you

know the other pieces ain't stood
a chance and that's how i ended up
here in detroit.

A Poem Some People Will Have to Understand

AMIRI BARAKA

Dull unwashed windows of eyes
and buildings of industry. What
industry do I practice? A slick
colored boy, 12 miles from his
home. I practice no industry.
I am no longer a credit
to my race. I read a little,
scratch against silence slow spring
afternoons.

    I had thought, before, some years ago
that I'd come to the end of my life.

    Watercolor ego. Without the preciseness
a violent man could propose.

    But the wheel, and the wheels,
won't let us alone. All the fantasy
    and justice, and dry charcoal winters
All the pitifully intelligent citizens
    I've forced myself to love.

We have awaited the coming of a natural
phenomenon. Mystics and romantics, knowledgeable
workers
of the land.
But none has come.
(Repeat)
    but none has come.
Will the machinegunners please step forward?

My Father Teaches Me to Dream

JAN BEATTY

You want to know what work is?
I'll tell you what work is:
Work is work.
You get up. You get on the bus.
You don't look from side to side.
You keep your eyes straight ahead.
That way, nobody bothers you—see?
You get off the bus. You work all day.
You get back on the bus at night. Same thing.
You go to sleep. You get up.
You do the same thing again.
Nothing more. Nothing less.
There's no handouts in this life.
All this other stuff you're looking for—
it ain't there.
Work is work.

Poetry Workshop at the Homeless Shelter

JAN BEATTY

So I'm the white teacher reading
some Etheridge Knight poems to the four
residents who showed: *For Black Poets*
Who Think of Suicide—thinking
these guys have seen it all and want
something hard-core, when a black man
named Tyrone raises his hand:
These poems offend me.
They do? I say. *Yes. I was raised*
not to curse, and I don't see why
a poem has to use those words.

What poems do you like?
Langston Hughes.
Yeah, someone says, *Jean Toomer, man.*
Tyrone says, *Let's talk about calculating a poem.*
Pardon me, I say—
You know, cipherin a poem—
Why don't you show me?
Tyrone draws this two-dimensional
image of this three-dimensional grid, based
on numerology, he says, in which each letter
of the alphabet corresponds to a number.

Look, it's like you start
with a 13, 25, then go to 8, 5, 1, 18, 20—
that's the start of the first line:
"My heart opens to the new world"—*See?*
I am stunned by it all—strange genius
or just strange? *How long*
have you been writing this way?
All my life, but nobody understands it,

21

I got boxes in my room filled with calculations,
I got plays and soap operas, and one day
I'll sell them.

I'm looking into Tyrone's eyes, beautiful
savant, wondering what to say:
I'm standing here in my new Levis and
Chuck Taylors, knowing I don't understand
either, and his desire humbles me.
Class is ending so I ask him to bring
more next week, but he has to see
his caseworker about his bad leg,
jammed up in a streetbeating in Philly.

Now I'm walking out of the shelter,
my white skin reminding me how wrong
I am most days, thinking about his sweet
numbers, his poems luminous with industry.
I'm opening the door to my car, counting
vowels: 13, 25, 85, 5, 1, 18, 20, my heart
stirring in the new world.

Mad River

JAN BEATTY

Two dollars and sixty-five cents
at the Hot Spot Take-Out Shack
for one chili dog and a Coke,
Birmingham, Alabama, 1979.
I kissed a Greyhound bus driver
too many times so I could eat,
I got one chili dog, I wanted two,
thought I'd get two. Lucky I'm not dead.
I asked him about his children, his
fourteen-year-old daughter saved my life,
pulled up his rotten conscience like
regurgitation, black bile memory—I said
How old is your daughter, afraid he'd want
more for his money, and in the slant light
of his dark Chevy he saw a slice
of my young girl face and said,
She's fourteen, I better get you back
to the depot, and the black stench
of his twisted conscience wanted one more
kiss, one more kiss to get me back
to the bus station and my long ride home,
to wanting to spit up the dark beans,
their reddish bodies staining my insides
like a dead baby, like a blood spill,
my heart pumping its mad river with
sixty cents in my pocket and twenty-six
hours till home, I prayed for rain,
I prayed for morning.

A Waitress's Instructions on Tipping or Get the Cash Up and Don't Waste My Time

JAN BEATTY

Twenty percent minimum as long as the waitress doesn't inflict bodily harm.
If you're two people at a four top, tip extra.
If you sit a long time, pay rent.
Double tips for special orders.
Always tip extra when using coupons.
Better yet, don't use coupons.
Never leave change instead of bills, no pennies.
Never hide a tip for fun.
Overtip, then tip some more.
Remember, I am somebody's mother or daughter.
No separate piles of change for large parties.
If people in your party don't show up, tip for them.
Don't wait around for gratitude.
Take a risk. Don't adjust your tip so your credit card total is even.
Don't ever, ever pull out a tipping guide in public.
If you leave 10% or less, eat at home.
If I call a taxi for you, tip me.
If I hang up your coat for you, tip me.
If I get cigarettes for you, tip me.
Better yet, do it yourself.
Don't fold a bill and hand it to me like you're a big shot.
Don't say, *There's a big tip in it for you if* . . .
Don't say, *I want to make sure you get this,* like a busboy would steal it.
Don't say, *Here, honey, this is for you*—ever.
If you buy a $50 bottle of wine, pull out a ten.
If I serve you one cocktail, don't hand me 35 cents.
If you're just having coffee, leave a five.

Prayer from a Picket Line

DANIEL BERRIGAN

Bring the big guardian
angels or devils in black
jackets and white casques
into the act at last. *Love, love at the end.*

The landholders withholding
no more; the jails springing
black and white Easter men;
truncheons like lilies, hoses
gentle as baby pee. *Love, love at the end.*

Bishops down in the ranks
mayors making it too.
Sheriff meek as a shorn lamb
smelling like daisies, drinking dew.
Love, love at the end.

My Son Is Worried about Me

LAURA BOSS

My son is worried about me
He worries that I'll grow to have no money
& then no place to rent without money
& then no food without money (reinforcing his image
    of me starving & gaunt)
& then with no food—
a homeless mother—
a few shopping bags (probably ancient
    ones from Annie Sez and Bloomingdales)
her smelling of urine—
her with dirty orange streaked hair
her a worse embarrassment to him than ever
And so, he declares to her on the phone, he's going to help
her get a *condominium*—going to erase the possibility of a
homeless, reeking of urine, shopping bagcart mother for
all his friends to see—
for his conscience to wrestle with—
And also after I die, I will
will it to him, he tells me—
& if he dies first—I can barely write that—he
will leave his half to me but meantime he'll pay half
the mortgage—but I should mail him my check early so
his credit won't be ruined by my careless ways
And if he gets married—it's understood
this imagined wife will never be able to get
his half—or would I then if they get divorced
have to live here with her—the two of us—
divorced women—living as divorced women do—
& me thinking if he doesn't like her
& can't live with her
then how will I ever be able
to live with this unknown woman

whom he will divorce and give his half
of this condominium to—Is she worth
my living in this condominium my son
wants me to have—
& I hear him silently saying
remember never to embarrass me after
the mortgage goes through—

Oh, darling son, I promise you,
my son, not ever to embarrass
you, except perhaps in my poems

The League of Defense

MELBA JOYCE BOYD

—for Attorney Kenneth V. Cockrel (1938–1989)

when revolutionaries
are sent
the time to move
is meant.
there is no reproach
in manner,
no hesitation
in diction.
your style
engaged the elegance
of the gazelle.

against the rich
profiting from
our life imprisonment,
and their politicians
petitioning
for the narcotic
incarceration of generations
policed under
STRESS,
you argued
for the defense
for the resurrection
of soldiers
in the factories,
in the streets,
in the churches,
holding court
for the people
in one
long
breath.

The Year of No Snow

MELBA JOYCE BOYD

my grandfather's ghost
guards the peace circle
around the children's
open window,
while i think
under a dim,
cracked lamp,
grateful for luck,
the tendril
of my fortune.
like the homeless,
i too,
carry space
between my footsteps.
so,
inside the warmth
of a rented rectangle
i craft common sense
and creative resistance
into oval,
beaded
compositions.

yesterday,
there was no winter
here,
no reports
of frozen women
or children
interrupted sardonic
consensus
through which

gray prayers
lifted the president's
veil,
revealing a crooked
smile, the
right-angled deletion
of reagan reasons.

you see,
contrary to
popular poles,
the macaw still flies
over tropical regions,
and magic does
restore color
to damaged skies
and dismembered
dreamers.

The Company Pool

MICHAEL CASEY

ya want ta be in our pool?
I was gonna axk ya sooner
but I didn't know
if ya wanted ta
I'll show ya how it works
ya pay a dollar an a quarter
ya givit ta me
but you'll haf ta start next week
the dollar goes inta the home run pool
and ya don't haf ta pay the quarter
unless if ya want ta
we use The Record
and we check out the runs column
on the sports page
not that this paper's always right
in fact it usually aint right
but this is the paper we use anyway
ya gotta use something ta go by
the team with the most runs
at the end a the week
the guy with that team wins the pool
the quarter is for the thirteen run pool
if ya team gets exactly thirteen runs
ya win that
that don't happen too often
Alfred over there
made thirty bucks last week winning that
so if ya want ta
ya can be in that one too
ya see we pick the team from this can
every week
so one guy don't get stuck

with the same shitty team
the tricky thing is
that the week for the pool
starts on Thursday and for the paper
it starts on Monday
so we just carry it over
y'understand this?

Cement

HAYAN CHARARA

—for J.D.

When construction workers
smoothed out the parking lot,
I carved my name into the concrete
with a stick, and beside that,
a dash, then the letters
that belong to my sister.
Stray dogs pissed on each syllable,
summertime weeds hid them,
the cement cracked.

My father worked 16 years
until midnight, checking IDs,
swearing at teenagers
trying to buy six packs
or cigarettes, then went home,
smells of Budweiser, Pabst,
and sweat lingering on his clothes.

I would like that day back,
to keep my name from vanishing.

The store's sold, and where
soda pop bottles were stacked to the ceiling,
chickens are slaughtered,
livers and gizzards packaged.
My father doesn't work anymore.
When I ask about the names,
he says he forgets.
It was a long time ago.
I was eight years old,

too young to realize that my name
was a gift, that I could
rub my fingers over each letter, and
this much was much.

Working for Profit

ANDREI CODRESCU

i grow not old not tall smiling
at the unserviceable idea of self
which is not my self to which my self
serves as a tool for undoing the locks on the mysterious
language capsules whose timers are ticking
in the drawers of the state a self of enclosure
a fossil dreaming of becoming the animal it once was
by employing me to recreate every detail
of its destroyed world & smiling because
i am not recreating i am playing in the mud
with a new body

Drone

WANDA COLEMAN

i am a clerk
i am a medical billing clerk
i sit here all day and type
the same type of things all day long
insurance claim forms
for people who suffer chronic renal failure
fortunately these people i rarely see
these are hardcore cases
most of them are poor, black or latin
they are cases most other doctors refuse
they are problem cases
some of them have complications like heroin abuse
some of them are very young
most of them have brief charts
which means they died within a year of beginning treatment
sometimes a patient gets worried about his or her
coverage and calls the office
i refer them to the dialysis unit caseworker
a few of the patients do bad things. for instance
some of them might refuse treatment as scheduled
sometimes they get drunk and call up
the nurses or attendants and curse them out
sometimes they try to fight the attendants
because they feel neglected/afraid
sometimes they wait until the last minute
to show up and it is the last minute
most of the patients, good patients,
quietly expire
i retire their charts to the inactive file
a few more claims i won't be typing up anymore
they are quickly replaced by others black, latin or poor
i make out crisp new charts

and the process starts all over again
the cash flows and flows and flows
so that the doctors can feed their racehorses
and play tennis and pay the captains of their yachts
and keep up their children's college tuition and
trusts and maintain their luxury cars
for this service i am paid a subsistence salary
i come in here each morning
and bill the government for the people by the people
for these patients
i sit here and type
is what i do and that's very important
day after day/adrift in the river of forms
that flows between my desk and the computer that
prints out the checks
there are few problems here. i am a very good clerk
i sit here all day and type
i am a medical billing clerk
i am a clerk
i clerk

Accounts Payable

WANDA COLEMAN

i've been reduced to rubber-tipped fingers
shuffling tons of invoices
a debt that remains unpaid
the auditors have arrived
and the ledger of my sweat, closed
appeals to accounting
go unrecognized among the columns
and day after day the figure i seek to identify avoids tally
at the bank they whisper when they see me enter the line
another withdrawal
my days here are numbered

One Black Mark

DAVID CONNOLLY

At 14, I delivered groceries to the neighborhood;
it was a real job, in the retail clerk's union
and I did a good job for them and my neighbors,
proud of being a union man.

At 16, I was hired as a regular in the store, throwing stock,
a member of the same union, got a letter of commendation
for crashing through the front door
with the escaping thief I tackled.

At 18, the phone company hired me
to climb poles and string wire
for Ma Bell, my neighbors and the IBEW.
My brothers on the job voted me their union steward.

At 48, I left the company to retirement
to look back on a life spent as a working man,
mostly in the city of my birth,
and found just one black mark.

See, when I was 19 and 20, I had a non-union job,
the only one I ever had,
in the Infantry of the U.S. Army.
And my job, killing Vietnamese, I did well.

But the medals and the badges they gave me
didn't make what I did right
and without a union card in my pocket
I should have known better.

Requiem for 'Two Dago Reds'

CARLOS CORTEZ

Tu Nicola,
Non sei morto,
E tu Bartolo,
Non sei morto,

Just because they didn't like your ideas
    They hung a rap on you,
    These good upright people
    Of the Commonwealth of Massachusetts.
    They tried to tell the World
    That you the fish peddler
    And you the shoe cobbler
    Pulled a heist,

Ma chi era i brigandi?

    They pulled every dirty trick in the book,
    These upright citizens.
    They really stacked the cards
    Against you two
    Who only wanted to sell fish
    And make shoes
    And tell your fellow workingmen
    Of a better world.

    The best legal minds in the country
    Showed where they were wrong
    But the judge kept a deaf ear.
    The Portygee hood who was in the pokey
    With you two
    Who said he didn't care for guinea radicals
    Saw your families come to visit you

And the little kids who wondered
When their Daddy would come out
And play with them again,
Broke down and told the cops
And told the lawyers
How you two couldn't have pulled the heist
But the Judge wouldn't listen.

Questo vecchio scarpone Thayer,

He hated foreigners, especially radical ones
And by the living god of Massachusetts
And all that was holy
He was going to see you two burn.
That's what he boasted as he was playing golf
While you the fish peddler
And you the shoe cobbler
Were sitting in prison
Away from your families
And away from the children
And away from the fellow workingmen
Whom you loved so well.

No Nicola, non sei morto
E tu Bartolo, non sei morto
Ma quant' genti ricordan' il vecchio Thayer?

They had their way,
These scions of the witch burners
And betrayers of the Indians
Who saved them from starvation,
These sons of Cotton Mather.
They shaved your heads
And strapped you in the chair.
They placed the metal plates on your heads
And the bands on your limbs
And turned on the voltage
And watched you burn!

Chi eta i brigandi?
Chi era i scorponi!

> These men who adjusted the bands,
> Who threw the switch,
> Who took you from your homes and people
> And from the World.
> This old man
> Who in the name of the Commonwealth of Massachusetts
> Pounded that gavel for the last time.
> How many remember their names?
> But you, fish peddler
> And you, shoe cobbler
> The World will not forget you,
> > *Nostri Fratelli,*
> > *Nuestro Hermanos,*
> > *Unsere Brüder,*
> > *Adelfia Mas.*
> Whatever languages, wherever workingmen
> Who dream of a better World come together
> Your names live on in their hearts.

No Nicola. No
Bartolo, Questo
e certo, Non sei
morto!

Three Spirits (Frank Little, Wesley Everest, Joe Hill)

CARLOS CORTEZ

From the wide-belted windswept plains
    where the imperceptible sobs of the dead tribesmen
    are lost on the ears of the speeding motorist
    bound on his way toward some intangible oblivion
And over the hump-backed backbone of a continent
    whose deep-throated canyons and serpentine roadways
    are a strain on the nerves of the speeding motorist
    bound on his way toward some intangible oblivion

To the salt-sprayed meadows and tall evergreen forests
    whose rocky-shored ocean is only another obstacle
    in the path of the speeding motorist
    bound on his way toward some intangible oblivion

The shadows of all the long-gone spirits drift endlessly
    unnoticed by those who are destined to become spirits
    but notice everything including the speeding motorist
    bound on his way toward some intangible oblivion

And occasionally these spirits stop drifting
    long enough to come together in small groups
    to reminisce of days gone by before they
    become part of the spirit-World
And somewhere on a high scrub-timbered mountain slope
    overlooking a sprawling, growing West-country metropolis
    three spirits come together for a short while
    to reminisce of days gone by before they
    became part of the spirit-World
One of them a limping battered half-Indian who in Montana
    entered the spirit-World at the hands of a mob
    who continued to drag his body over the ground
    long after the breath of life passed out of it,

another of a soldier from the first great war
who had been told he was fighting for the freedom
of all men and because he continued to fight for
the freedom of all men in his civilian life
he entered the spirit-World in Washington
hanging from a trestle with his genitals cut off
and the third an immigrant who wrote songs
to inspire the Working men he helped to organize
and had entered the spirit-World in a Utah prison
facing a firing squad
and these three who lived the same hard life and
died the same violent death for all the same cause,
this half-breed, this veteran and this Swede,

From their vantage point among the scrub timber
      look down upon the sprawling sea of a city with all of
      its factories and its railyards and its supermarkets and
      its apartments and its tenements and homes and the streets
      and freeways where run the speeding motorist
      bound on his way toward some intangible oblivion
And they see all the homes of the working men with
      the television aerials and new cars parked in front
      with all the modern labor-saving devices inside
      and they reflect on how much has been done since they
      became part of the spirit-World

And they also see these working men and their wives
      putting in extra hours of work to keep up the payments
      on luxuries that their Grandsires never dreamed of
      while many of their sons go to die in far-off jungles
      and they see how much has yet to be done before many more
      become part of the spirit-World

For the time is getting shorter and shorter for this
      slumbering Humanity who have yet so far to travel
      and they hope they won't have to welcome too many
      more spirits who are only trying to open all men's eyes
      including the myopic eyes of the speeding motorist
      bound on his way toward some intangible oblivion

44

But they linger no longer as their restless destinies
    preordain them to drift ever on without end
    and shortly after on the very spot they had rested, a bit
    of hard packed mountain soil trembles ever so slightly
    to break open where a small green shoot slowly emerges
    to gasp hungrily at the clean Mountain air
    high above the thoughts
    and beyond the eyes of the speeding motorist
    bound on his way toward some intangible oblivion

I Got the Blue-Ooze 93

JAYNE CORTEZ

I got the blue-ooze
I got the fishing in raw sewage blue-ooze
I got the toxic waste dump in my backyard blue-ooze
I got the contaminated drinking water blue-ooze
I got the man-made famine blue-ooze
I got the HIV AIDS epidemic blue-ooze
I got the dead house dead earth blue-ooze
I got the blue-ooze
I got the living in a drain-pipe blue-ooze
I got the sleeping in a cardboard box waiting for democracy to hit blue-ooze
I got the 5 hundred year black hostage colonialism never never stops blue-ooze
I got the Francophone anglophone alementiphone lusophone telephone blue-ooze
I got this terminology is not my terminology
    these low standards are not my standards
    this religion is not my religion and
    that justice has no justice for me blue-ooze
I got the blue-ooze
I got the gangbanging police brutality blue-ooze
I got the domestic abuse battered body blue-ooze
I got the ethnic conflict blue-ooze
I got the misinformation media penetration blue-ooze
I got the television collective life is no life to live
    and this world is really becoming
    a fucked up crowded place to be blue-ooze
    I got to find a way out this blue-ooze
    because the blue-ooze
    will make you sorry
    that you ever had
    the blue-oo-oo-ooze
    I got the blue-ooze
    I got the blue-oo-oo-ooze

We Don't Wanna Peso Much

CARLOS CUMPIÁN

"Let's make this Thanksgiving completely different,"
some big shot musta' said, on a slow news day
full of state-wide layoffs and wallet-bruising deficits,
"Let's privatize the immigration department
and allow every patriot to become a migra agent.
Rush this idea over the airwaves,
Lord knows we need more involved voters."

Meanwhile, fiery-eyed *Superbarrio*
in front of his tiny tele in Tenochtitlan,
watches helplessly as the u.s. Border Patrol
and National Guard units seal off the roads
leading to occupied Mexico, home of the real Pep Boys.

"The turkeys finally got their way,
though both sides will suffer when it's over,
no one is getting through Tijuana/San Diego,
Juarez/EI Paso, the two Laredos or even
Piedras Negras/Eagle Pass without a hassle,
every ride is stopped twenty minutes of the river,
often it's an hour before you can either drive ahead
or expect to be dragged away in chains,
instead of heading off free toward Arizona, California,
New Mexico, and Texas. Now they got an army of troopers busy
twisting concertina wire and singing, 'Light up the border,'
while blabbing about new Blazers, baseball pennants,
and burritos as big as their heads chased by beer
colder than an Alaskan whore's bed."
Superbamo from miles away can hear the gabas say,
"Just where are those busboys, dishwashers and cooks?
Got any idea where the gardeners and groundskeepers are hiding?
We can't make Mexican food without the ingredients or from a book,

has anyone seen Armando, Mario, Justo or Beto?
Those guys should be here by now, filling bags of groceries.
Mr. Franklin, we got a ton of letters to get out this week, and
Irma, Maria, Luz and the new girl from Michoacán didn't come in.
Kind of quiet in the barrio for a Saturday night, ain't it
    Sergeant O'Malley?
Last week my school bus was half empty.
    What happened to the Latino kids,
they all started eating Jimson weed or something?"
From burning beaches where ice blue raspas are shaved into cones,
to the dark apple orchards after the fall dumps its lonely pickers,
to the gravel pits of sorrow, where ruined bruised backs
    once gathered,
is there no one conducting an underground railroad to save targeted
people, who lack the empire's proper papers for staying this side
    of the fence.

Black and white Los Angeles rejects
millions of dollars in sales and taxes,
handing over to soldiers an entire football stadium of
    Spanish-speakers,
the radio warns, "A battalion of barrio Brown Berets are blocking
all roads to East L.A.," and what's worse Los Lobos canceled
    their concert.

"Good morning, did you hear the Gov has ordered extra police
helicopters to flank suburban commuters headed downtown.
This is live drive-time talk radio with Richard Byrd,
we're taking your calls on the immigration troubles."

"Hello, this is Herb, all I'm saying is we Anglos are sick and tired
of the sneaky Mexican take over. Back in 1992, that writer guy,
    Carlos Fuentees,
bragged on PBS how Mexican women are like Trojan Horses
    bringing in their bellies new partisans
for their slow demographic reconquest of the American Southwest."

"Herb, sounds like you're worried about white folks'
zero population growth and losing your parking
space to a guy named Pancho buying his kid pampers."

"Hey, think what you want Dickey-bird,
the Mexies are pushing
for a permanent shift in our values,
and I'll guarantee it's about more than greasy menudo, corn-on-the-cob
sold as elotes, and tacos full of green runny nopales. You want your kids
    growing up eating all that?
Look, they want to take back all our golf courses."

"Let's take another call, this time from Dallas.
    Hi Jack, what's on your mind?"

"Dickey, I'm calling on a cellular phone, it's hard to hear your show
from this grassy knoll because of the snipers.
Let me call you back later, to explain myself after all's well."
(click)

Juan ate seven slices of pizza (delivered by his illegal primo),
Juan ate seven hot hamburgers (served, at minimum wages),
Juan ate seven heads of lettuce (sprayed with poisonous pesticides),
Juan ate seven sun-ripe tomatoes (with turtle-shell durability),
Juan ate seven bowls of corn flakes (a gift from the Hopis),
Juan ate seven hard-boiled eggs (someone crack a window),
Juan ate seven sour dough loaves (made by gay Frisco bakers),
Juan ate seven buttery pancakes (git yr own syrup, I ain't ja mama),
Juan ate seven bags of zoo peanuts
    (Animal Liberationists freed the monkeys),
Juan ate seven rolls of Californian sushi
    (green wasabe hotter than hades).

Juan will be eating the fruits of his labor when la migra
deports him out of the state that tilts to the ocean,
oyes Juan as they proposition you to leave,
diles que ya es muy tarde, it's already too late,
Chicago has been renamed Chicano, Illinois,
y la majority of Americanos use
more hot salsa que ketchup,
in fact tortillas are overtaking space
once reserved for white sliced bread,
while Spanish songs sink roots inside 35 million heads.

Juan, after you're safely across the border,
ten cuidado can ese gordito el media freak Superbarrio,
Mexico's masked righter of wrongs
(no relation to subcomandante Marcos)
is going to greet you and hold your trembling mano,
to pose for fotas en La Jomada, Uno Mas Uno y tal vez
High Performance, pero tu sabes, it's going to take more than
a December pilgrimage to nuestra Tonantzin, Guadalupe or
any one woman or man in a flabby wrestler's mask and outfit
to prevent greedy Kens and Barbies
from La Jolla to Mount Shasta from attacking
the weakest immigrant links in
America's chain of command.

Soon It's Robots

CARLOS CUMPIÁN

Smokers huddle at a thousand doors,
withdrawing 12 minutes every day
from the new-world mirage,
no one inhales the same anymore,
as mosquito-mean bosses look for blood in
every dollar, expecting us to laugh to forget our stress.
Ya don't call in "sick" or expect a raise, so fragile are
job guarantees these days, that pink slips
are sent without a two-week notice or regrets
for your IDS and keys.

It's about to rain fiscal ill-will when auditors
show up in green rubber boots and umbrellas,
they'll purge the place for pro-bono fame,
to contribute to the mayor's re-election bid,
fully expecting his guano-covered ship to win.

Every Christmas your debts throb hangover hard,
followed by numb New Year reruns, waking to dark
cold coffee, back to shuffling papers and
leaving three phones unanswered.
Pete, another colleague, has gone seeking
precarious temp employment
somewhere up the street.

What don't you believe? That you'll be sacrificed
by greedy priests serving the one-eyed money moloch?
If you're smart, you won't light another match,
even if it's the white man's most ingenious planetary gift,
you see, the company is watching,
checking conversations, wastebaskets, and computer screens,
I'd say you're better off eating that damn cigarette
when your file is so thick.

Over in a glass building reflecting like a highway patrolman's
mirrored shades, manicured applause flutter
across a board room, followed by discriminating cigars
and brandy poured into crystal goblets, they close with pithy
toasts in celebration of profits after reduction in personnel.

We haven't moved a muscle but we're ripped,
hopes down-sized, and for our loyalty we're shown
the bottom line, and soon it's robots and our exit time,
to look for that phosphorus head of luminous
full-time commitment, amid crushed butts
and ashes at our feet.

The White Heat

EMILY DICKINSON

Dare you see a Soul at the White Heat?
Then crouch within the door—
Red—is the Fire's common tint—
But when the vivid Ore

Has vanquished Flame's conditions,
It quivers from the Forge
Without a color, but the light
Of unanointed Blaze.

Least Village has its Blacksmith
Whose Anvil's even ring
Stands symbol for the finer Forge
That soundless tugs—within—

Refining these impatient Ores
With Hammer, and with Blaze
Until the Designated Light
Repudiate the Forge—

The Red Pocket Knife

GERI DIGIORNO

i remember my father
cutting into the white
flesh of an apple
the red skin spiraling down
like new years streamers
he did the same with oranges
the thick rind winding upward
toward the glint of steel
you could take the empty peel
in your cupped hands
and reform it
back to its original shape
he did the same with pencils
trimming the soft wood
into perfect points
with perfect scalloped edges
and one time i remember
when our car broke down
somewhere between reno and sacramento
the night dead black like coal
and daddy whittling a wooden plug
for the engine
we kids sat at bare tables
in an empty café watching my father
shivering in the pale glow
of a single electric bulb
casting an eerie spell
on him and the men helping
their voices floating
in the dark half-light
voices soft like the lighted wood
flying around my father's fingers

Revolutionary Letter #19
(for The Poor People's Campaign)

DIANE DI PRIMA

if what you want is jobs
for everyone, you are still the enemy,
you have not thought thru, clearly
what that means

if what you want is housing,
industry
    (G.E. on the Navaho
    reservation)
a car for everyone, garage, refrigerator,
TV, more plumbing, scientific
freeways, you are still
the enemy, you have chosen
to sacrifice the planet for a few years of some
science fiction utopia, if what you want

still is, or can be, schools
where all our kids are pushed into one shape, are taught
it's better to be 'American' than black
or Indian, or Jap, or PR, where Dick
and Jane become and are the dream, do you
look like Dick's father, don't you think your kid
secretly wishes you did

if what you want
is clinics where the AMA
can feed you pills to keep you weak, or sterile
shoot germs into your kids, while Mercke & Co
grows richer

if you want
free psychiatric help for everyone
so that the shrinks
pimps for this decadence, can make
it flower for us, if you want
if you still want a piece
a small piece of suburbia, green lawn
laid down by the square foot
color TV, whose radiant energy
kills brain cells, whose subliminal ads
brainwash your children, have taken over
your dreams

degrees from universities which are nothing
more than slum landlords, festering sinks
of lies, so you too can go forth
and lie to others on some greeny campus

THEN YOU ARE STILL
THE ENEMY, you are selling
yourself short, remember
you can have what you ask for, ask for
everything

Assembly Room Women

SUE DORO

blue net caps on heads
bent over tables
covered with trays
of wire springs

thousands
of tiny copper coils

curling in piles
near hundreds of
boxes of metal brushes
endless numbers
of little two-inch

squares
each needing
a wire spring
attached
each needing soldering
needing counting
needing boxing
needing the

assembly room women
to complete
their
creation

Ours

SUE DORO

they can't take the sky away
we know it's outside
though eyes see only
metal work pieces
going round and round
in the machines we run
and daylight filters in
through dark blue slits
of wired windows

they can't take the wind away
we know it's still there
flying across the parking lot
though the only breeze we feel
is our own air blowing
from lower lips
onto sweaty faces
as we work the line

they can't take the land away
it waits for us here under the bricks
of this factory building
owned by sick old dinosaurs
heaving their last stinking breaths

we are like the sky and the wind
watching over our land
making plans to bury the dinosaurs
we are this poem that
cannot be taken away
that cannot
be taken
away

Tiny Griefs

SEAN THOMAS DOUGHERTY

1

Mist
    ghosting over the peaks
        of West Virginia.

2

Into the coal-mining dawn,
    I stumbled bleary-eyed
        from cheap Motels

to roadside diners: toast, grits,
    eggs asked, *how-you-want-em,*
        honey? By the waitresses

named Bobbie, Anne-Louise, or Mabel,
    as miners lifted stark, white cups
        with dust, darkened hands.

3

What to say of hope
    I wondered that first week
        in towns where no one worked,

or mined the earth for ore?
    I spoke teacher to those men
        who asked in every bar;

they understood
    I saw their children
        running in their eyes,

& more than once they offered,
    "Have a beer on me then, friend."
        Before walking away, quietly,

into the safe talk of the mines.

4

In the schools
    I saw those men
        in the face

of every child,
    and still I sometimes dream
        of that tiny third-grade girl

who lifted her head
    to drawl so softly
        I almost couldn't hear,

"This is a poem for my daddy
cause I loved him.'
(then she cleared her throat)
'His skin was dust

when he came home.
He never hugged me

before he washed his hands.
The bible says I know

that when we die
we go to dust.'

(she looked right up at me)
It makes me think of him."

Then she gave a little bow.
    I reached to touch her palm,
        and she shook my hand.

5

That evening I drove toward
    another dying town;
        the glare of headlights

caught the rain
    of insects
        against the glass

like tiny griefs
    we seldom feel.
        My hands,

still shaking,
    gripped
        the wheel.

Last Thoughts on Woody Guthrie

BOB DYLAN

When yer head gets twisted and yer mind grows numb
When you think you're too old, too young, too smart or too dumb
When yer laggin' behind an' losin' yer pace
In a slow-motion crawl or life's busy race
No matter what yer doing if you start givin' up
If the wine don't come to the top of yer cup
If the wind's got you sideways with one hand holdin' on
And the other starts slipping and the feeling is gone
And yer train engine fire needs a new spark to catch it
And the wood's easy findin' but yer lazy to fetch it
And yer sidewalk starts curlin' and the street gets too long
And you start walkin' backwards though you know that it's wrong
And lonesome comes up as down goes the day
And tomorrow's mornin' seems so far away
And you feel the reins from yer pony are slippin'
And yer rope is a-slidin' 'cause yer hands are a-drippin'
And yer sun-decked desert and evergreen valleys
Turn to broken down slums and trash-can alleys
And yer sky cries water and yer drain pipe's a-pourin'
And the lightnin's a-flashing and the thunder's a-crashin'
And the windows are rattlin' and breakin' and the roof tops a-shakin'
And yer whole world's a-slammin' and bangin'
And yer minutes of sun turn to hours of storm
And to yourself you sometimes say
"I never knew it was gonna be this way
Why didn't they tell me the day I was born"
And you start gettin' chills and yer jumping from sweat
And you're lookin' for somethin' you ain't quite found yet
And yer knee-deep in dark water with yer hands in the air
And the whole world's a-watchin' with a window-peek stare
And yer good gal leaves and she's long gone a-flying
And yer heart feels sick like fish when they're fryin'

And yer jackhammer falls from yer hands to yer feet
And you need it badly but it lays on the street
And yer bell's bangin' loudly but you can't hear its beat
And you think yer ears mighta been hurt
Or yer eyes've turned filthy from the sight-blindin' dirt
And you figured you failed in yesterday's rush
When you were faked out an' fooled while facing a four flush
And all the time you were holdin' three queens
And it's makin' you mad, it's makin' you mean
Like in the middle of *Life* magazine
Bouncin' around a pinball machine
And there's something on yer mind that you wanna be saying
That somebody someplace oughta be hearin'
But it's trapped on yer tongue and sealed in yer head
And it bothers you badly when you're layin' in bed
And no matter how you try you just can't say it
And yer scared to yer soul you just might forget it
And yer eyes get swimmy from the tears in yer head
And yer pillows of feathers turn to blankets of lead
And the lion's mouth opens and yer staring at his teeth
And his jaws start closin' with you underneath
And yer flat on yer belly with yer hands tied behind
And you wish you'd never taken that last detour sign
And you say to yerself just what am I doin'
On this road I'm walkin', on this trail I'm turnin'
On this curve I'm hanging
On this pathway I'm strolling, in the space I'm taking
In this air I'm inhaling
Am I mixed up too much, am I mixed up too hard
Why am I walking, where am I running
What am I saying, what am I knowing
On this guitar I'm playing, on this banjo I'm frailin'
On this mandolin I'm strummin', in the song I'm singin'
In the tune I'm hummin', in the words that I'm writin'
In the words that I'm thinkin'
In this ocean of hours I'm all the time drinkin'
Who am I helping, what am I breaking
What am I giving, what am I taking
But you try with yer whole soul best

Never to think these thoughts and never to let
Them kind of thoughts gain ground
Or make yer heart pound
But then again you know why they're around
Just waiting for a chance to slip and drop down
'Cause sometime you hear 'em when the night time comes creeping
And you fear that they might catch you a-sleeping
And you jump from yer bed, from yer last chapter of dreamin'
And you can't remember for the best of yer thinking
If that was you in the dream that was screaming
And you know that it's somethin' special you're needin'
And you know that there's no drug that'll do for the healin'
And no liquor in the land to stop yer brain from bleeding
And you need something special
Yeah, you need something special all right
You need a fast flyin' train on a tornado track
To shoot you someplace and shoot you back
You need a cyclone wind on a steam engine howler
That's been banging and booming and blowing forever
That knows yer troubles a hundred times over
You need a Greyhound bus that don't bar no race
That won't laugh at yer looks
Your voice or your face
And by any number of bets in the book
Will be rollin' long after the bubblegum craze
You need something to open up a new door
To show you something you seen before
But overlooked a hundred times or more
You need something to open yer eyes
You need something to make it known
That it's you and no one else that owns
That spot that yer standing, that space that you're sitting
That the world ain't got you beat
That it ain't got you licked
It can't get you crazy no matter how many
Times you might get kicked
You need something special all right
You need something special to give you hope
But hope's just a word

64

That maybe you said or maybe you heard
On some windy corner 'round a wide-angled curve
But that's what you need man, and you need it bad
And yer trouble is you know it too good
'Cause you look an' you start getting the chills
'Cause you can't find it on a dollar bill
And it ain't on Macy's window sill
And it ain't on no rich kid's road map
And it ain't in no fat kid's fraternity house
And it ain't made in no Hollywood wheat germ
And it ain't on that dimlit stage
With that half-wit comedian on it
Ranting and raving and taking yer money
And you think it's funny
No you can't find it in no night club or no yacht club
And it ain't in the seats of a supper club
And sure as hell you're bound to tell
That no matter how hard you rub
You just ain't a-gonna find it on yer ticket stub
No, and it ain't in the rumors people're tellin' you
And it ain't in the pimple-lotion people are sellin' you
And it ain't in no cardboard-box house
Or down any movie star's blouse
And you can't find it on the golf course
And Uncle Remus can't tell you and neither can Santa Claus
And it ain't in the cream puff hair-do or cotton candy clothes
And it ain't in the dime store dummies or bubblegum goons
And it ain't in the marshmallow noises of the chocolate cake voices
That come knockin' and tappin' in Christmas wrappin'
Sayin' ain't I pretty and ain't I cute and look at my skin
Look at my skin shine, look at my skin glow
Look at my skin laugh, look at my skin cry
When you can't even sense if they got any insides
These people so pretty in their ribbons and bows
No you'll not now or no other day
Find it on the doorsteps made outta paper mâché
And inside it the people made of molasses
That every other day buy a new pair of sunglasses
And it ain't in the fifty-star generals and flipped-out phonies

Who'd turn yuh in for a tenth of a penny
Who breathe and burp and bend and crack
And before you can count from one to ten
Do it all over again but this time behind yer back
My friend
The ones that wheel and deal and whirl and twirl
And play games with each other in their sand-box world
And you can't find it either in the no-talent fools
That run around gallant
And make all rules for the ones that got talent
And it ain't in the ones that ain't got any talent but think they do
And think they're foolin' you
The ones who jump on the wagon
Just for a while 'cause they know it's in style
To get their kicks, get out of it quick
And make all kinds of money and chicks
And you yell to yourself and you throw down yer hat
Sayin', "Christ do I gotta be like that
Ain't there no one here that knows where I'm at
Ain't there no one here that knows how I feel
Good God Almighty
THAT STUFF AIN'T REAL"

No but that ain't yer game, it ain't even yer race
You can't hear yer name, you can't see yer face
You gotta look some other place
And where do you look for this hope that yer seekin'
Where do you look for this lamp that's a-burnin'
Where do you look for this oil well gushin'
Where do you look for this candle that's glowin'
Where do you look for this hope that you know is there
And out there somewhere
And your feet can only walk down two kinds of roads
Your eyes can only look through two kinds of windows
Your nose can only smell two kinds of hallways
You can touch and twist
And turn two kinds of doorknobs
You can either go to the church of your choice
Or you can go to Brooklyn State Hospital

You'll find God in the church of your choice
You'll find Woody Guthrie in Brooklyn State Hospital

And though it's only my opinion
I may be right or wrong
You'll find them both
In the Grand Canyon
At sundown

Union Sundown

BOB DYLAN

Well, my shoes, they come from Singapore,
My flashlight's from Taiwan,
My tablecloth's from Malaysia,
My belt buckle's from the Amazon.
You know, this shirt I wear comes from the Philippines
And the car I drive is a Chevrolet,
It was put together down in Argentina
By a guy makin' thirty cents a day.

Well, it's sundown on the union
And what's made in the USA
Sure was a good idea
'Til greed got in the way.

Well, this silk dress is from Hong Kong
And the pearls are from Japan.
Well, the dog collar's from India
And the flower pot's from Pakistan.
All the furniture, it says "Made in Brazil"
Where a woman, she slaved for sure
Bringin' home thirty cents a day to a family of twelve,
You know, that's a lot of money to her.

Well, it's sundown on the union
And what's made in the USA
Sure was a good idea
'Til greed got in the way.

Well, you know, lots of people complainin' that there is no work.
I say, "Why you say that for
When nothin' you got is U.S.-made?"
They don't make nothin' here no more,

You know, capitalism is above the law.
It say, "It don't count 'less it sells."
When it costs too much to build it at home
You just build it cheaper someplace else.

Well, it's sundown on the union
And what's made in the USA
Sure was a good idea
'Til greed got in the way.

Well, the job that you used to have,
They gave it to somebody down in El Salvador.
The unions are big business, friend,
And they're goin' out like a dinosaur.
They used to grow food in Kansas
Now they want to grow it on the moon and eat it raw.
I can see the day coming when even your home garden
Is gonna be against the law.

Well, it's sundown on the union
And what's made in the USA
Sure was a good idea
'Til greed got in the way.
Democracy don't rule the world,
You'd better get that in your head.
This world is ruled by violence
But I guess that's better left unsaid.
From Broadway to the Milky Way,
That's a lot of territory indeed
And a man's gonna do what he has to do
When he's got a hungry mouth to feed.

Well, it's sundown on the union
And what's made in the USA
Sure was a good idea
'Til greed got in the way.

The Lonesome Death of Hattie Carroll

BOB DYLAN

William Zanzinger killed poor Hattie Carroll
With a cane that he twirled around his diamond ring finger
At a Baltimore hotel society gath'rin'.
And the cops were called in and his weapon took from him
As they rode him in custody down to the station
And booked William Zanzinger for first-degree murder.
But you who philosophize disgrace and criticize all fears,
Take the rag away from your face.
Now ain't the time for your tears.

William Zanzinger, who at twenty-four years
Owns a tobacco farm of six hundred acres
With rich wealthy parents who provide and protect him
And high office relations in the politics of Maryland,
Reacted to his deed with a shrug of his shoulders
And swear words and sneering, and his tongue it was snarling,
In a matter of minutes on bail was out walking.
But you who philosophize disgrace and criticize all fears,
Take the rag away from your face
Now ain't the time for your tears.

Hattie Carroll was a maid of the kitchen.
She was fifty-one years old and gave birth to ten children
Who carried the dishes and took out the garbage
And never sat once at the head of the table
And didn't even talk to the people at the table
Who just cleaned up all the food from the table
And emptied the ashtrays on a whole other level,
Got killed by a blow, lay slain by a cane
That sailed through the air and came down through the room,
Doomed and determined to destroy all the gentle.
And she never done nothing to William Zanzinger.

But you who philosophize disgrace and criticize all fears,
Take the rag away from your face.
Now ain't the time for your tears.

In the courtroom of honor, the judge pounded his gavel
To show that all's equal and that the courts are on the level
And that the strings in the books ain't pulled and persuaded
And that even the nobles get properly handled
Once that the cops have chased after and caught 'em
And that the ladder of law has no top and no bottom,
Stared at the person who killed for no reason
Who just happened to be feelin' that way without warnin'.
And he spoke through his cloak, most deep and distinguished,
And handed out strongly, for penalty and repentance,
William Zanzinger with a six-month sentence.
Oh, but you who philosophize disgrace and criticize all fears,
Bury the rag deep in your face
For now's the time for your tears.

Visiting My Parents' Grave

W. D. EHRHART

If you had told me thirty years ago
I'd miss this town, I'd have told you
—well, you know what I'd have said,
so smug it was, so self-content,
its point of view so narrow one could
get a better field of vision peering
through the barrel of a shotgun.
I, at seventeen, could see that much
and so much more I couldn't wait
to leave. It didn't help, of course,
that I was who I was:
the preacher's and the teacher's son,
blow my nose the whole town knew,
anonymous a word I used
to stare at in the dictionary,
wishing it were me. Yet here I am,
thirty years later, back again.

I've come at night because I know
in daylight I could walk these streets
from dawn to dusk, meeting no one
who would know my name, or even yours.
Peter Shelly's house lies buried under
Nockamixon Lake, the Bryan's dairy farm's
a shopping mall, tract housing's crowded
out the sledding run near Callowhill;
Jeff Apple's gone to Melbourne Beach,
Larry Rush went schizophrenic
paranoid, and just about the only
thing that hasn't changed is Larry's mom,

who's still convinced he'll come out right
if only he'll repent and turn to God.

Me, I'm pretty well convinced that she's
the reason Larry's nuts, but that's
the only thing I'm sure of anymore.
I've been to the other side of world,
said what I've thought, hedged no bets, had
no use for comfortable hypocrisies
or delicate interpretations
meant to keep the world the way it is.
I've quit every job I've ever had
for something else, for this or that, or else
because someone's always screwing someone
else, and silence to injustice
large or small is simply cowardice.

Which may be true, but what I've got
for all my years is unemployed
and unemployable, a dozen books
that no one reads, a wife who works
to earn what I cannot, a daughter
I have trouble looking in the eye
because I fear she'll recognize
her father for the failure he's become.
That's the worst of it: I don't trust
my own judgment anymore. What used
to seem so obvious has vanished
in the glare of consequences
prudent people manage to avoid.
So here I am: sitting on your gravestone
on a hill above this town I couldn't
wait to get as far away from
as the moon, and though I know it's only
an illusion, here's the moon just rising
over Skyline Drive so huge it looks
as if I'd only need to reach
my fingers out to touch it,

just like sitting here at night
makes the town appear like nothing's changed,
as if at any moment Jeff and Larry
might appear on bikes, wave to me, and shout,
"Let's chase the cows at Bryan's farm!"
As if the years might fall away
and let me start again.

The Farmer

W. D. EHRHART

Each day I go into the fields
to see what is growing
and what remains to be done.
It is always the same thing: nothing
is growing; everything needs to be done.
Plow, harrow, disc, water, pray
till my bones ache and hands rub
blood-raw with honest labor—
all that grows is the slow
intransigent intensity of need.
I have sown my seed on soil
guaranteed by poverty to fail.
But I don't complain—except
to passersby who ask me why
I work such barren earth.
They would not understand me
if I stooped to lift a rock
and hold it like a child, or laughed,
or told them it is their poverty
I labor to relieve. For them,
I complain. A farmer of dreams
knows how to pretend. A farmer of dreams
knows what it means to be patient.
Each day I go into the fields.

Lose Yourself

EMINEM

Look, if you had one shot, or one opportunity
To seize everything you ever wanted—one moment
Would you capture it or just let it slip?

His palms are sweaty, knees weak, arms are heavy
There's vomit on his sweater already, mom's spaghetti
He's nervous, but on the surface he looks calm and ready
To drop bombs, but he keeps on forgettin'
What he wrote down, the whole crowd goes so loud
He opens his mouth, but the words won't come out
He's choking, how everybody's joking now
The clock's run out, time's up over, bloah!
Snap back to reality, oh, there goes gravity,
Oh, there goes Rabbit, he choked
He's so mad, but he won't give up that
Easy, no
He won't have it, he knows his whole back's to these ropes
It don't matter, he's dope
He knows that, but he's broke
He's so stagnant that he knows
When he goes back to his mobile home, that's when it's
Back to the lab again yo
This this whole rhapsody
He better go capture this moment and hope it don't pass him

[Hook:]
You better lose yourself in the music, the moment
You own it, you better never let it go
You only get one shot, do not miss your chance to blow
This opportunity comes once in a lifetime yo

The soul's escaping, through this hole that it's gaping

This world is mine for the taking
Make me king, as we move toward a new world order
A normal life is boring, but superstardom's close to post-mortem
It only grows harder, only grows hotter
He blows us all over these hoes is all on him
Coast to coast shows, he's known as the globetrotter
Lonely roads, God only knows
He's grown farther from home, he's no father
He goes home and barely knows his own daughter
But hold your nose cause here goes the cold water
His hoes don't want him no mo, he's cold product
They moved on to the next schmoe who flows
He nose dove and sold nada
So the soap opera is told and unfolds
I suppose it's old partner, but the beat goes on
Da da dum da dum da da

[Hook]

No more games, I'ma change what you call rage
Tear this motherfucking roof off like two dogs caged
I was playing in the beginning, the mood all changed
I been chewed up and spit out and booed off stage
But I kept rhyming and stepwritin' the next cypher
Best believe somebody's paying the pied piper
All the pain inside amplified by the fact
That I can't get by with my nine to five
And I can't provide the right type of life for my family
Cause man, these goddamn food stamps don't buy diapers
And it's no movie, there's no Mekhi Phifer, this is my life
And these times are so hard and it's getting even harder
Trying to feed and water my seed, plus
Teeter totter caught up between being a father and a prima donna
Baby mama drama's screaming on and
Too much for me to wanna
Stay in one spot, another day of monotony
Has gotten me to the point, I'm like a snail
I've got to formulate a plot 'fore I end up in jail or shot
Success is my only motherfucking option, failure's not

Mom, I love you, but this trailer's got to go
I cannot grow old in Salem's lot
So here I go is my shot.
Feet fail me not cause maybe the only opportunity that I got

[Hook]

You can do anything you set your mind to, man

Have You Been to Jail for Justice?

ANNE FEENEY

Was it Cesar Chavez? Maybe it was Dorothy Day
Some will say Dr. King or Gandhi set them on their way
No matter who your mentors are it's pretty plain to see
That, if you've been to jail for justice, you're in good company

Have you been to jail for justice? I want to shake your hand
Cause sitting in and lyin' down are ways to take a stand
Have you sung a song for freedom? or marched that picket line?
Have you been to jail for justice? Then you're a friend of mine

You law-abiding citizens, come listen to this song
'Cause laws were made by people, and people can be wrong
Once unions were against the law, but slavery was fine
Women were denied the vote and children worked the mine
The more you study history the less you can deny it
A rotten law stays on the books 'til folks like us defy it

The law's supposed to serve us, and so are the police
And when the system fails, it's up to us to speak our peace
It takes eternal vigilance for justice to prevail
So get courage from your convictions
Let them haul you off to jail!

Notes from a Slave Ship

EDWARD FIELD

It is necessary to wait until the boss's eyes are on you
Then simply put your work aside,
Slip a fresh piece of paper in the typewriter,
And start to write a poem.

Let their eyes boggle at your impudence;
The time for a poem is the moment of assertion,
The moment when you say I exist—
Nobody can buy my time absolutely.

Nobody can buy me even if I say, Yes I sell.
There I am sailing down the river,
Quite happy about the view of the passing towns,
When I find that I have jumped overboard.

There is always a long swim to freedom.
The worst of it is the terrible exhaustion
Alone in the water in the darkness,
The shore a fading memory and the direction lost.

Harder Options *(Hamtramck, Michigan)*

VIEVEE FRANCIS

I live here
and invite you
over and over,
the harder option
where sacrifice is
the mainstay,
the bed with broken springs
and a painful lull in the middle.
I should have chosen another
city with a less thin veneer
and nature
if I wanted to lapse
into the easy sleep
of convenience,
of clean air.
This sky bears no stars
so looking out is futile.
There is the factory
and the smudged cathedral
whose bells are off several minutes.
There are the gray rows
of houses and their tenants
sitting for dinners of sausages
and doughy children.
The television is on.
Nothing is remarkable.
Grace is a quick word
or two.
I wait for your heavy hands
and their smell of oil and habit.

Found in Juarez

VIEVEE FRANCIS

—for the women whose murders have not been solved

There's talk of her on the American side of the border
Dulcisima siempre Virgin Maria

de la Merced . . . she was my second cousin,
my father's uncle's daughter . . . they found her breast under a tree

a Guadalupe palm . . . the killer rested in its shade . . .

Is everything O.K.? The waitress asks, but doesn't smile,
just re-fills mugs with chicory—the specialty.

. . . she just wanted to work,
to feed her family. What threat?

From El Paso to Palenque there are families of women
who favor each other by hair, nose, teardrop faces,

wearing jeans and men's shirts—stained by oil, by sweat,
by the blood of their breasts,

Virgen de Guadalupe, Madrey . . .

wearing cotton skirts edged by embroidered roses—
outlined in red.

By the broom closet . . . *Sweet, always Virgin, Mary of Mercy . . .*
glass candles line the shelf—prayers for the Mother.

Cars clop on cobblestones down the narrow side track,
otherwise the cantina is quiet

with common talk of cousins and killers,
in the dust of a mid-afternoon.

The Auto Trade

STEWART FRANCKE

When he sleeps my father dreams of cars,
Thunderbirds and Mustangs he sold to football stars
There was music in the corner bars—Sinatra, Ella and sad old Johnny Ray;
We'd race soapbox at the Fairgrounds Saturdays.

They came out of that great good war, my father's friends and brothers
and their promise to this world.
When he'd walk me across that showroom floor, there was glass & steel & rubber;
the fenders shone like pearls, and he'd say "Son that's the way they do it in Detroit."

Young men grow old in the auto trade.
Stories are told as we're handed down our names.
The winters are cold, but the summers remain the same . . .
that's the way we do it in Detroit.

I pray my work is not in vain;
I worry that my time here will live up to my name.
There's a faith found deep down in my brother's eyes,
It says we love the work far more than the prize.

Young men grow old in the auto trade.
Stories are told as we're handed down our names.
The winters are cold, but the summers remain the same . . .
that's the way we do it in Detroit.

Lucky Man Cafe

CYNTHIA GALLAHER

Noon and the men sitting here
on Milwaukee Avenue
feel lucky,
eating at the Lucky Man Cafe,
maybe that's why they
strolled in anyway.

Lucky, in this city
of Polish promise,
second only to Warsaw,
where on every lunch plate,
each pierogi appears a pillow
of back-home comfort,
a savory springboard to another chance
for men steps from the port of entry.

And lucky, me,
the only woman,
in this bright place,
with patrons polite and
respectful as uncles,
the owner asks
for my order in Polish
as if I were family.

Lucky, how he still sees a pastoral Poland
my grandparents broke root from,
now planted somewhere behind my eyes,
dished visions and forcefed
high-speed culture
from both coasts,
tumbled together in a Midwest stew.

Lucky, maybe this is the lucky hour,
for men who bear names of cabbages,
who won't ever become kings,
but perhaps artists.

Lucky, when two strong arms can
join limber legs not only
in night club desirable dances,
but flex profitable in daylight hours
at tomorrow's worktables.

Lucky, when illegal.
to find friendly streets of familiars,
and multi-blocks of mixtures
to get lost in,
who won't ask questions;
while trusting those who know answers
to keep silent in your own language.

Lucky, to those of
underground reputation as
hard workers, good mechanics,
with diamond-in-the-rough handyman skills
that fire up when
factory chimneys cool,
to renovate and rent three flats.

Lucky, even when you don't yet own
a coat to cover your thick-sweatered back,
to own a seat for an hour,
in a place you might dream
in slices of tomorrow,
in a place with lots of elbow room
for new notions
and plenty of ears to share
uncharted and singular chantings
together as one,
to own a seat for an hour,
to warm your world for an hour,
in a place that says it all,
lunch at the Lucky Man.

Daddy, We Called You

MARIA MAZZIOTTI GILLAN

"Daddy" we called you, "Daddy"
when we talked to each other in the street,
pulling on our American faces,
shaping our lives in Paterson slang.

Inside our house, we spoke
a southern Italian dialect
mixed with English
and we called you "Papa"

but outside again, you became Daddy
and we spoke of you to our friends
as "my father"
imagining we were speaking
of that *Father Knows Best*
TV character
in his dark business suit,
carrying his briefcase into his house,
retreating to his paneled den,
his big living room and dining room,
his frilly-aproned wife
who greeted him at the door
with a kiss. Such space

and silence in that house.
We lived in one big room—
living room, dining room, kitchen, bedroom,
all in one, dominated by the gray oak dining table
around which we sat, talking and laughing,
listening to your stories,
your political arguments with your friends.

Papa, how you glowed in company light,
happy when the other immigrants
came to you for help with their taxes
or legal papers.

It was only outside that glowing circle
that I denied you, denied your long hours
as night watchman in Royal Machine Shop.
One night, riding home from a date,
my middle-class, American boyfriend
kissed me at the light; I looked up
and met your eyes as you stood at the corner
near Royal Machine. It was nearly midnight.
January. Cold and windy. You were waiting
for the bus, the streetlight illuminating
your face. I pretended I did not see you,
let my boyfriend pull away, leaving you
on the empty corner waiting for the bus
to take you home. You never mentioned it,

never said that you knew
how often I lied about what you did for a living
or that I was ashamed to have my boyfriend see you,
find out about your second-shift work, your broken English.

Today, remembering that moment,
still illuminated in my mind
by the streetlamp's gray light,
I think of my own son
and the distance between us,
greater than miles.

Papa,
silk worker,
janitor,
night watchman,
immigrant Italian,
I honor the years you spent in menial work

while your mind, so quick and sharp,
longed to escape,
honor the times you got out of bed
after sleeping only an hour,
to take me to school or pick me up;
the warm bakery rolls you bought for me
on the way home from the night shift,

the letters
you wrote
to the editors
of local newspapers.

Papa,
silk worker,
janitor,
night watchman,
immigrant Italian,
better than any "Father Knows Best" father,
bland as white rice,
with your wine press in the cellar,
with the newspapers you collected
out of garbage piles to turn into money
you banked for us,
with your mousetraps,
with your cracked and calloused hands,
with your yellowed teeth.

Papa,
dragging your dead leg
through the factories of Paterson,
I am outside the house now,
shouting your name.

Growing Up Italian

MARIA MAZZIOTTI GILLAN

When I was a little girl,
I thought everyone was Italian,
and that was good. We visited
our aunts and uncles,
and they visited us.
The Italian language smooth
and sweet in my mouth.

In kindergarten, English words fell on me,
thick and sharp as hail. I grew silent,
the Italian word balanced on the edge
of my tongue and the English word, lost
during the first moment
of every question.

It did not take me long to learn
that olive-skinned people were greasy
and dirty. Poor children were even dirtier.
To be olive-skinned and poor was to be dirtiest of all.

Almost every day
Mr. Landgraf called Joey
a "spaghetti bender:"
I knew that was bad.
I tried to hide
by folding my hands neatly
on my desk and
being a good girl.

Judy, one of the girls in my class,
had honey-blonde hair and blue eyes.
All the boys liked her. Her parents and

grandparents were born in America.
They owned a local tavern.
When Judy's mother went downtown
she brought back coloring books and candy.
When my mother went downtown, she brought back
one small brown bag with a towel or a sheet in it.

The first day I wore my sister's hand-me-down coat,
Isabelle said, "That coat looks familiar. Don't
I recognize that coat?" I looked at the ground.

When the other children brought presents
for the teacher at Christmas, embroidered silk
handkerchiefs and "Evening in Paris" perfume,
I brought dishcloths made into a doll.

I read all the magazines that told me
why blondes have more fun,
described girls whose favorite color was blue.
I hoped for a miracle that would turn my dark skin light,
that would make me pale and blonde and beautiful.

So I looked for a man
with blond hair and blue eyes
who would blend right in,
and who'd give me blond, blue-eyed children
who would blend right in
and a name that could blend right in
and I would be melted down
to a shape and a color
that would blend right in,
till one day, I guess I was forty by then,
I woke up cursing
all those who taught me
to hate my dark, foreign self,

and I said, "Here I am—
with my olive-toned skin
and my Italian parents,

and my old poverty,
real as a scar on my forehead,"
and all the toys we couldn't buy
and all the words I didn't say,
all the downcast eyes
and folded hands
and remarks I didn't make
rise up in me and explode.

onto paper like firecrackers
                    like meteors
and I celebrate
                    my Italian American self,
rooted in this, my country, where
all those black/brown/red/yellow
olive-skinned people
soon will raise their voices
and sing this new anthem:

Here I am
     and I'm strong
     and my skin is warm in the sun
     and my dark hair shines,

and today, I take back my name
and wave it in their faces
like a bright, red flag.

The Herald News Calls Paterson a "Gritty City"

MARIA MAZZIOTTI GILLAN

When I walk out of Passaic County Community College at dusk,
the sky is the most amazing color—deep violet and luminous,
like an old woman who smiles suddenly and looks young.
The courthouse dome is outlined against the sky,
the rococo arches of the old post office,
the clock tower of the new federal building,
starkly simple, and the clock tower of city hall,
ornate and elegant.

I love the voice of this city, the eyes
of its people, the whooshing sound of the Great Falls,
the old mill that has become a museum,
its brick work shining in sunlight.

I see the old men sleeping in the dumpster,
the prostitute resting against the walls of St. Paul's
Church, the empty crack vials
in the gutter, the transvestites on the corner,
but under the gritty surface, a fresh energy rises,
and it is the heart of the city—
it beats in the shinny copper of the fountain
in Cianci Street park, in the old men in the Roma Club
shrewd and wary, squinting against cigarette smoke,
playing Italian card games and drinking espresso.

It bears in the chests of the new immigrants—
Iranians and Columbians, Cubans and Syrians
Dominicans and Indians, carting their hopes to this city
and dreaming, and in the young men with the gangsta pants,
their underwear showing, and in the bravado
of the girl with the braids and the yellow barrettes
and her starched dress and in the little boy

with his torn sneakers and his jean jacket
and the handsome clean lines of his face.
I sing this song for them, for all of them,
the saved and the lost, the ones who will survive
and the ones who will not. I sing for the Jamaican family
and their new restaurant and their hard work
and the young Cuban woman who wants to make money
from her poetry, and for those who will find
the city's heart beating under grit
and who will hear its music
and sing along.

After School on Ordinary Days

MARIA MAZZIOTTI GILLAN

After school on ordinary days we listened
to the tabletop radio and *The Lone Ranger*
and a program where a woman with a husky voice
read fairy tales, and we gathered around
the radio that was always kept on the china cabinet
built into the wall in that tenement kitchen,
a china cabinet that held no china, except
cups and saucers, thick and white
and utilitarian, poor people's cups
from the 5 & 10 cents store.

My mother was always home
from Ferraro's Coat factory
by the time we walked in the door
after school on ordinary days,
and she'd give us milk with Bosco in it
and cookies she'd made that weekend.
the three of us would crowd around the radio,
listening to the voices that brought a wider world
into our Pateson apartment. Later

we'd have supper at the kitchen table,
the house loud with our arguments
and laughter. After supper, on ordinary
days, we'd play Monopoly or gin rummy
after we did our homework, the kitchen
warmed by the huge coal stove, the wind
outside rattling the loose old windows.

we inside, tucked in, warm and together,
on ordinary days that we didn't know
until we looked back across a distance
of forty years would be captured for us
like fossils preserved in amber
that would glow and shimmer
in memory's flickering light.

Boys

MARIELA GRIFFOR

A torturer does not redeem himself through suicide. But it does help.
—Mario Benedetti

The boys from the neighborhood, some of them,
stay behind the mud and the rain.

I ask myself what has become of
Romero, Quezada, Coleman?
Did their bodies and souls
escape deterioration?

Did they go into the army
to do their duty as soldiers
of the fatherland, the ones
who protect us from hate and
foreign tyrants?

Did they climb like the General
by usurping through disloyalty,
lies, secret codes and
finally through money?

Did they have families and
continue living in the city
as if nothing had happened?

Or did they sell their modest houses,
move to another neighborhood where
no one knows anything about them?

There they will come in the evening and
will wash the remnants of dried blood
from their fingers.

Will they look for their wives,
give them a kiss, touch their bodies
with those same hands?

Will their daytime nightmares
be cast upon those who
know nothing of where they
come at the end of the night?

Will they return their heads,
smashed by the memories they left
in the cells, streets, apartments to a soft warm
pillow that washes away their sacrileges?

What happened to the men
I knew and never saw again?

Did they turn themselves into
men hungry for justice or did
they leave little by little in silence?

Did they put on their clothes
in the morning without knowing
whether they would return in
the evening to their dear ones?

Did they learn to kill in clandestine training or
did they become more men with the
passing of these hard times?

Did they love like those
pure men
I met on those evenings
when to play was
all our universe?

1913 Massacre

WOODY GUTHRIE

Take a trip with me in nineteen thirteen
To Calumet, Michigan, in the copper country.
I'll take you to a place called Italian Hall
Where the miners are having their big Christmas ball.
I'll take you through a door, and up a high stairs.
Singing and dancing is heard everywhere,
I will let you shake hands with the people you see.
And watch the kids dance round that big Christmas tree.
You ask about work and you ask about pay;
They'll tell you that they make less than a dollar a day,
Working the copper claims, risking their lives,
So it's fun to spend Christmas with children and wives.
There's talking and laughing and songs in the air,
And the spirit of Christmas is there everywhere,
Before you know it, you're friends with us all
And you're dancing around and around in the hall.
Well, a little girl sits down by the Christmas tree lights,
To play the piano, so you gotta keep quiet.
To hear all this fun you would not realize
That the copper-boss thug-men are milling outside.
The copper-boss thugs stuck their heads in the door;
One of them yelled and he screamed, "There's a fire!"
A lady, she hollered, "There's no such a thing!
Keep on with your party, there's no such a thing."
A few people rushed, and it was only a few.
"It's only the thugs and the scabs fooling you."
A man grabbed his daughter and carried her down;
But the thugs held the door and he could not get out.
And then others followed, a hundred or more,
But most everybody remained on the floor.
The gun-thugs they laughed at their murderous joke,
While the children were smothered on the stair by the door.

Such a terrible sight I never did see.
We carried our children back up to their tree.
The scabs outside still laughed at their spree.
And the children that died there were seventy-three.
The piano played a slow funeral tune,
And the town was lit up by a cold Christmas moon;
The parents they cried and the miners they moaned,
"See what your greed for money has done."

Bury Me in a Free Land

FRANCES E. W. HARPER

Make me a grave where'er you will,
In a lowly plain, or a lofty hill,
Make it among earth's humblest graves,
But not in a land where men are slaves.

I could not rest if around my grave
I heard the steps of a trembling slave;
His shadow above my silent tomb
Would make it a place of fearful gloom.

I could not rest if I heard the tread
Of a coffle gang to the shambles led,
And the mother's shriek of wild despair
Rise like a curse on the trembling air.

I could not sleep if I saw the lash
Drinking her blood at each fearful gash,
And I saw her babes torn from her breast,
Like trembling doves from their parent nest.

I'd shudder and start if I heard the bay
Of bloodhounds seizing their human prey,
And I heard the captive plead in vain
As they bound afresh his galling chain.

If I saw young girls from their mother's arms
Bartered and sold for their youthful charms,
My eye would flash with a mournful flame,
My death-paled cheek grow red with shame.

I would sleep, dear friends, where bloated might
Can rob no man of his dearest right;

My rest shall be calm in any grave
Where none can call his brother a slave.

I ask no monument, proud and high,
To arrest the gaze of the passers-by;
All that my yearning spirit craves,
Is bury me not in a land of slaves.

Walker Evans Photograph:
Factory Street, Amsterdam, New York, 1930

STEPHEN HAVEN

I used to walk here with my friends
when the second shift went home,
the curbs worn by people who were gone,
the old mills crowding the road.
We'd brush the sawdust from our pants
and shirts, blow it from our nostrils,
the hush of stopped circular saws
ringing as we took the shortcut down
to the house where I was born.
The alleys were thatched, are thatched,
with wires, derricks and poles,
and lined by the barred, the broken
and green-tinted windows.
But Evans never
worked here, his ears covered
with headphones, never slept
ten minutes stretched out on skids
of particle board, the evening shift's
second buzzer finally rousing him
up to cut and stack the wood.
That day he drove along route 67
the looms were still running full,
the early morning shift begun,
a muffled hum spilling down
the empty, cobbled road. I don't know
why he stopped here, where he'd
been, where he was going,
but only that he parked his car
and walked, climbed the nearby
cemetery hill, angled

his camera down, the Mohawk Carpet Co. clock
just short of eight in the photograph.

Evans knew the looms would soon be still.
The din of that morning, and this narrow
tunnel-like street, must have pulled him
back, if only he were listening,
to horse-drawn wagons cutting past
the loading docks and down
the mill yard's antebellum roads,
the drivers heading their teams beyond
anything I know. He must have read
the scarred brick with his fingertips,
and the stone, then climbed the ladder down
to the Chuctanunda, the creek, even then,
forever dumping dye into the river.

Someone should have scared him off
or told him as he put his tripod away
he got it wrong, heard only his own
echo, saw only his own
image in the darkened windows.
If he'd ever worked here, if he'd lived
this livelihood, the *Slow
Keep Right*, the traffic post,
might have brought back for him
some laughter lifting from the rows
of unseen triple-decker homes,
the sign pointing past the factories
and up the distant hill
to where the sidewalks meet
at a crop of elm. Just short
of eight, he caught it: the apparent
permanence of things, the absence
of human beings, the crystals,
the cataracts of white and grey and black.

Putting Up Beans

ALLISON ADELLE HEDGE COKE

My cotton-covered lap aproned for canning,
summers ago, I snapped green beans for an old lady.
Green beans far from French-styled,
not even French Canadian,
more Huron I suppose, Tsa la gi on the southern side.
Holding hard with indexes, thumbs, double-handed
popping apart plump green strings
fresh from leafy hills in the fields.
Bristling with bees and dirt wasps.
Slightly rubbery, slightly sweet
enough bushel baskets to put away winter hunger
for about another year.

I remember the first time I canned in the barns,
tobacco barn burners gassed up blue,
I filled four steel washtubs with seventy pint jars each—
forty if they were quart-sized Masons.
The barn itself layered in rafters
for hanging sticks
filled with great leaves of tobacco, green as beans.
Though soon to be gold and brown-cured.
Now nowhere near Winston or Salems.
Not even close to American Spirit.
More likely Bull Durham and Drum.

Full flavor sticks hung all through the entire shingle barn,
above my head where I set gas to boil beans and
waited outside underneath the tin shade
resting on poles which were only sideways logs.

A wasp landed near my shoulder
and died.

Maybe it got cured inside the loft.
It was huge, black, hard, and shiny, so
large the only dime in my pocket
barely marked its half trunk.

I remember ant lions tossing dust
up over the dead wasp
like a funeral.

And the funeral for the grandma down the road

how she'd spent so much time making this apron
I remember on my lap.
In a time where women don't wear
aprons much anymore.

Off-Season

ALLISON ADELLE HEDGE COKE

—for fieldworkers and framers like me

Early, on grayest morning, when we
nettled deep in between rows,
tobacco and sweet potato,
both two seasons away from planting,
you reasoned I belonged there,
flowing like creek water
below our bright leaf fields,
then snowing only golden stubble and root.
You said I'd never make it
swinging hammers and teething
saws for Inland Construction.
I raised my back wings, those muscles
wrought from priming rows, muscles
which cradled my ribs and sides. I
chucked tools in the flatbed, headed
north, to the city sprawled out like
scattered masonry and split rails, Raleigh,
smoked factory winds and speakeasy halls.

A white chicken fell off a Tyson rig,
just a bit ahead of me on Saunders Street.
I called her "Hooker"
from walking down the red-light street.
The Inland guy hiring was big and red,
sat behind a door laid flat for a desk on cinder block.
He chuckled much like you
at the sight of me, but the fields and breaking horses,
justified my ninety pounds of lean.
Next day he had me start out on a crew full of men.
Men who'd never seen a woman work
that way in town, first

time I had chance to operate a backhoe,
first time I got to frame, and when I swung the hammer
full leverage, three pounds drove in sixteenpennys straight.
In six weeks, I made foreman.
Just before I drove back to you.
"Hooker" almost got pecked to death
by our bantams—citified as she was.

I laid out so much money, I beat
what you pulled in for fall, We settled in
for the long freeze. You ate ridicule and haste.
We never were the same,
until spring when the fields reclaimed
us as their own and we returned
to what we *both* knew and belonged to.
The off-season only an off-shoot
in what we were meant to be.
You never did know this part
of what I am, Fieldworker, or framer,
I only showed you what you said I couldn't be.

Our Song

JOE HENRY

I saw Willie Mays
at a Scotsdale Home Depot
looking at garagedoor springs
at the the far end of the fourteenth row

his wife stood there beside him
she was quiet and they both were proud
I gave them room but was close enough
that I heard him when he said outloud

this was my country
and this was my song
somewhere in the middle there
though it started badly and it's ending wrong

this was my country
this frightful and this angry land
but it's my right if the worst of it
might still somehow make me a better man

the sun is unforgiving
and there's nobody who would choose this town
but we've squandered so much of our good will
that there's nowhere else will have us now

we push in line at the picture show
for cool air and a chance to see
a vision of ourselves portrayed
as younger and braver and humble and free

this was our country
this was our song

somewhere in the middle there
though it started badly and it's ending wrong

this was our country
this frightful and this angry land
but it's my right if the worst of it
might still somehow make me a better man

I've started something I just can't finish
and I barely leave the house it's true
I keep a wrap on my sores and joints
but yes I've had my blessings too

I've got my mother's pretty feet
and the factory keeps my house in shape
my children they've both been paroled
and we get by on the piece we've made

I feel safe so far from heaven
from towers and their ocean views
from here I see a future coming across
what soon will be beaches too

but that was him, I'm almost sure,
the greatest center fielder of all time
stooped by the burden of endless dreams
his and yours and mine

he hooked each spring beneath his feet
he leaned over then he stood upright
testing each against his weight
for one that had some play and some fight

he's just like us I wanna tell him
and our needs are small enough
something to slow a heavy door
something to help us raise one up

and this was my country
this was my song
somewhere in the middle there
though it started badly and it's ending wrong

well this was God's country
this frightful and this angry land
but if it's his will the worst of it
might still somehow make me a better man

if it's His will
the worst of it might still
somehow make me
a better man

Samuella's Fufu

LABAN CARRICK HILL

—for Rose Blankson-Austin

Maame Rose knows. She cuts
cassava in block chunks.
Splits plantains, opens
dark veins concealed
beneath pale, sweet meat.

Maame Rose does it this way, stokes a fire
with coal, tosses in skins.
They curl in on themselves like small hands
closing into fists. The iron pot sits there
like a hungry chief, swallowing

cassava and plantains into boil. Listen
to Maame Rose. She will not steer
you wrong. She says pound
that cooked fruit in a dahuoma mortar,
hard as your ancestor's teeth.

Yes, the pestle is heavy, she says. Take this essan trunk,
thick as your arm, tall as your eyes.
Look at the way it mushrooms out
at its base, soft and pliant
like a good brush, like your tongue.

It must be that way, Maame Rose says, so it works
the fruit as you pound and pound.
You should smile because it is hard.
Everyone tires, she says, but it is the ones
who pound cassava and plantain

until their hearts ache, until they
have forgotten their children's names,
until their ghosts show them
how to hold the stick with two hands.
Do it this way, Maame Rose says,

and you see she is right and pound
that cassava, that plantain until the tough fiber
is broken down, until the whole village
has pushed you up that coconut tree
and you never meet your grandmother's corpse.

—Cape Coast, Ghana

The Sweatshop Poem

EDWARD HIRSCH

There are thirty-one shallow graves in August
with thirty-one swollen coffins, waiting.

During the day I work in a sweatshop
sewing the pink slips and cotton dresses,
the cashmere skirts and thick tweeds
of winter. During the day my fingers
hum with needles, the needles slide
through patches of steaming cloth.
I am preparing the hottest iron.
I am preparing the warmest clothes
for the beautiful thighs of young models
and the sweating hips of new mannequins.
All day I am prepared for leaving.

And at night the factory is silent.
My tired face dims in the window, my
shadow paces through the empty corridors,
alone. At night the cloth in my hands
never whispers with other men's dreams
or purrs with other women's secrets.
My exhausted body is too heavy for clothes.
All night the heavy tongue of summer repeats
its one heavy syllable, its one drooling
syllable of stupor; the crystal glass
of another night asks me to drink.
And I do drink, deeply.
And later I lie in the naked sheets
without sleeping, without breaking the door
or plunging into the river. Without screaming.

But sometimes I move through the house, slowly.
Sometimes I sit in the dark kitchen
or stand at the swollen bathroom window
to watch the glistening blue worm,
the invisible needle of moonlight
sewing a dark shroud for my body.

Second-Story Warehouse

EDWARD HIRSCH

(Summer 1966)

Come with me to the second-story warehouse
where I filled orders for the factory downstairs,
and commanded the freight elevator, and read
high in the air on a floating carpet of boxes.

I could touch the damp pipes in the ceiling
and smell the rust. I could look over
the Puerto Rican workers in the parking lot,
smoking and laughing and kidding around

in Spanish during their break, especially Julia,
who bit my lower lip until it bruised and bled,
and taught me to roll cigarettes in another language,
and called me her virgin boy from the suburbs.

All summer I read Neruda's *Canto General*
and took lessons from Juan, who trained me
to accept orders with dignity—dignidad—
and never take any shit from the foreman.

He showed off the iron plate in his skull
from a bar fight with a drunken supervisor,
while the phone blinked endlessly from Shipping
& Handling, and light glinted off the forklift.

I felt like a piece of wavy, fluted paper
trapped between two sheets of linerboard
and disliked the industrial A-flutes and the 565
stock cartons that we carried through the aisles

while downstairs a line of blue collars fed
slotting, gluing, and stitching machines.
Juan taught me about mailers and multidepths,
and praised the torrential rains of childhood,

the oysters that hid in the bloody coral,
their pearls shimmering in rock,
green stones polished by furious storms
and coconut palms waving at twilight.

He praised the sun that floats over the island
like a bell ringed with fire, or a sea rose,
and the secret torch that burns
inside us, a beacon no one can touch.

Come with me to the second-story warehouse
where I learned the difference between
RSC, FOL, die-cuts and five-panel folders,
and saw the iron shine inside a skull.

Every day at precisely three in the afternoon
we delivered our orders to the loading dock.
We may go down dusty and tired, Juan said,
but we come back smelling like the sea.

The Last Wobbly

MIKHAIL HOROWITZ

In McKees Rocks Pennsylvania back in 1908
When the Pressed Steel Car workers walked out
I seen a mounted trooper try to club a little girl
So I broke seven teeth in his mouth
    I'm the last damn Wobbly I'm a hundred-and-five
    The fatcats are flummoxed that I'm still alive
    But I'm strong and I'm spry and I don't intend to die
    'Til the world is One Big Union
We were sewer hogs and bindlestiffs, splinter bellies too
From Chicago we answered the call
The 1-double-w give us the slogan
A hurt to one boys that's a hurt to all
    I'm the last of the Wobblies I'm a hundred-and-five
    The fatcats are damned that I'm still alive
    From the mill to the mine I'll keep walkin' that line
    'Til the world is One Big Union
Well I tossed a few stones to defend Mother Jones when
the goons tried to take her away
I was knocked on my ass by the bulls in Lawrence, Mass.
But my ass was back on strike the same day
    I'm the last damn Wobbly I'm a hundred-and-five
    The fatcats are flustered that I'm still alive
    But I'll spit in their eye, because I don't intend to die
    'Til the world is One Big Union

    Yeah I'm the last Wobbly, one-hundred-and-five
    The fatcats are damned that I'm still alive
    But I'll piss in their eye, because I don't intend to die
    'Til the world is One Big Union

Jobs

MIKHAIL HOROWITZ

Joe operates bulldozers; Steve
Juggles orange boxes; Spencer
Jones orders building supplies;
John organizes ballplayers; Sarah
Jigsaws odd blocks; Simon
Junks ornery Buicks; Stanley
Jones outfits buckaroos; Sam
Jointly oversees bank stuff;
Jane owns book stall;
Jeremiah officiates; Bill services
Jets; Oliver bead-strings
Jade; Ophelia's beauty shop
Jazzes old bags; Susan
Jars olives; Barry sells
Jackets; Otis breeds schipperkes;
Jim opens bundles; Samantha's
Journalism occasionally brings someone
Justice; Olivia baby-sits;
Jorge ornaments beams; Sherman
Jams on Beale Street;
Jackson oils bricks. Sans
Job, Oscar begs; Sidney
Jumps off bridge; Stella
Johnson ossifies; Bobby slices
Jugular; Oswald's breath stinks;
Joan overdoses; Bart starves.

Detroit Addendum

MURRAY JACKSON

—*for Philip Levine*

Not Virgil, not Beatrice.
You, Philip, took us on slick city streets
to the pimped belch of Detroit

DODGE MAIN WYANDOTTE CHEMICAL FORD ROUGE CHEVROLET GEAR & AXLE
in one unbroken line.

Riverrun past burning moat, round
sanguine cauldrons, ending and beginning over again
in a coke-oven shake-out.

From fiery epicenters, black faces,
white faces, glow red. *We stare* through words
into fire until our eyes are also fire.

Things passed from hand to hand in darkness
that we, like machines, cannot see.

King Henry's table, seating in split shifts,
neck bones 'n' ribs, corned beef on rye
with mustard, kielbasa and raw onions.

Philip, I do remember a black man,
the Old Boy who danced all night
at Ford Highland Park—my father.

What Work Is is work.

Gifts

MURRAY JACKSON

I.

I stood in the tunnel warehouse
holding hands with my brother and Dad,
with our Red Flyer wagon that the Goodfellows left.
We came for potatoes, salt pork, beans, and flour.
The lines were long, but we had to stay. Strangers
waited with us, against the flush of winter.

II.

Lunch at the Book Cadillac, second basement.
Our uncle worked in the Kay Danzer Flower Shop.
He took roses to the stadium ticket window.
We got to see the Tigers play the Yankees.
Greenberg hit one out onto Cherry Street.

III.

I had a report due in Social Science.
Finished it while Mom did the dishes.
I washed my safety-patrol belt every Monday.
Mr. Loving expected them to be spotless.
I brushed, scrubbed, and soaked it.
Mom suggested table salt. It glowed.

Prayer to a Farm Worker

VICTOR JARA, translated by Mariela Griffor

Rise up and look at the mountain, from
where the wind, the sun, the water come.
Thou, who determines the course of
rivers, thou who scatters the flight of
your soul.
Rise up and look at your hands. Join
hands with your brothers, together
in blood we go. Now is the time that
can be tomorrow. Tomorrow.
Deliver us from the men of
misery. Take us to your kingdom of justice and
justice. Blow like the wind the gorge's flower.
Clean the fire
in the barrel of my gun.
Thy will be done
here on Earth. Give us your strength and
your courage in combat.
Blow like the wind the field's daffodil.
Clean fire in the barrel of my gun.

Rise up and look at your hands. Join
hands with your brothers, together
in blood we live,
now and at the hour of
our death. Amen. We live. Amen.

Talking Dust Bowl Blues

X. J. KENNEDY

Old cow's almost dry now, her hooves scrape hard dirt.
Where's the man going to pay me what I'm worth?
Forty acres played out, soil like the corn meal low in the can
Reminds me of a woman holding back on a man.
Nights, hot nights I walk by the warped board fence
Hoping to find a fresh water breakthrough or some sense.
Seeing my kids run round in washed-out flour bags
Makes my heart move like a man with one lame foot that drags,
Sending 'em to bed before sundown every night
So they won't run around and work up an appetite.
Hearing my kids whine in the dark through their bunk room door,
We only had nine stew beans, can't we have some more?
Had my fill of hanging around this town
Like a picture on a nail waiting to be took down.
Seen my name writ ten times on the same yellow pad,
Don't mean a damn, they don't send for you, makes a man mad.
Stalk of corn can grub its roots deep, find iron in dry ground.
Let a man try, he can't go deep—where's food to be found?
Shoes wearing thin not from plowing, not from working a road,
Just from tromping back and forth carrying their same old load.
Beth used to wear her hair in a neat combed braid,
Now she lets it fall any old way down her forehead.
Black topsoil used to roll off from the eye straight north,
Nothing now but wind towing dust clouds back and forth.
No more point in hanging around this town.
Going to fix me an old Ford, lay those patched tires round and round,
Going to head due west where the oranges hang low,
Let my kids pick too, eat red pears right off of the bough,
Furry peach bending the branch, and its stem thumb-thick,
Shrinking back from your hand like a young cunt from a prick.
Dust clouds bearing down now, dust stretching from pole to pole.
No use staying here till I'm dried in the long dust bowl.

Comin' Back in a Cadillac

AL KOOPER

Right now I don't have a dime
most folks say the way I live is a crime
my telephone it don't get no calls
I guess I don't amount to too much at all
but I know that one day everything will be okay
just you wait and see

You might say I don't live high on the hog
I'm unemployable
no one will front me a job
I live from day to day on a handout or two
and I can't say a word when someone asks me what's new
But I know pretty soon that I might hang the moon
Just you wait and see

Hey I'll be coming back
in a Cadillac
Living in some mansion not some shotgun shack
I'll be coming back
sure nuff in a Cadillac
I don't own no suit, no fancy dress shirt
anything I wear is usually covered with dirt
I don't have a woman or a girlfriend to love
All I have is faith in the creator above
But I know that one day everything will be okay
Just you wait and see

Hey I'll be coming back in a Cadillac
right from the direction of the right side of the tracks
I'll be coming back
sure nuff in a Cadillac
all right now
all right now

Get down now
make ya moan for love now
make ya moan for love now

Continental tire,
you know my license won't expire
wire-wheeled convertible Cadillac

make ya moan for love baby
make ya moan for love now

I want to get you in the back of my Cadillac, baby
make ya moan for love now
make ya moan for love
want to hear you say
want to hear you say
mmmmmmmmmm

I bet there's some girls in Notodden tonight
could make some noises like that
mmmmmmmmmm
well you know I would like to try something here
I wonder if you could help us out by clapping your hands or stomping your feet
ah, that's good

You know over in America, in the USA
on Sunday morning in church
they do a thing called soul clapping
You know anything about soul clapping?
I'm going to teach you real quick about soul clapping
clap, clap, clap, clap, clap, clap, clap
But don't speed up, cause we're teachers up here
And we'll keep you after the show
Okay now keep that nice and tight
cause we're just going to turn it over to you for a few bars

clap, clap, clap, clap
ah, that's good
you are doing it

now can you yell out while you're doing that
at the same time
I thought you could
yeah

mmmmmmmmmmmmm
they kept going the whole time
yeah

you get an "A", "A+"
gotta go now
gotta go now
but I'm going to come back
in a Cadillac
You ain't seen nothng like me
And when I come back
I'm going to get you in the back of my Cadillac
Make ya moan for love now
ahhhhhhh
Make ya moan for love
Get down

The Shipfitter's Wife

DORIANNE LAUX

I loved him most
when he came home from work,
his fingers still curled from fitting pipe,
his denim shirt ringed with sweat,
smelling of salt, the drying weeds
of the ocean. I'd go to where he sat
on the edge of the bed, his forehead
anointed with grease, his cracked hands
jammed between his thighs, and unlace
the steel-toed boots, stroke his ankles
and calves, the pads and bones of his feet.
Then I'd open his clothes and take
the whole day inside me—the ship's
gray sides, the miles of copper pipe,
the voice of the foreman clanging
off the hull's silver ribs. Spark of lead
kissing metal. The clamp, the winch,
the white fire of the torch, the whistle,
and the long drive home.

from The Cleaving

LI-YOUNG LEE

He gossips like my grandmother, this man
with my face, and I could stand
amused all afternoon
in the Hon Kee Grocery,
amid hanging meats he
chops: roast pork cut
from a hog hung
by nose and shoulders,
her entire skin burnt
crisp, flesh I know
to be sweet,
her shining
face grinning
up at ducks
dangling single file,
each pierced by black
hooks through breast, bill,
and steaming from a hole
stitched shut at the ass.
I step to the counter, recite,
and he, without even slightly
varying the rhythm of his current confession or harangue,
scribbles my order on a greasy receipt,
and chops it up quick.

Such a sorrowful Chinese face,
nomad, Gobi, Northern
in its boniness
clear from the high
warlike forehead . . .

Of Love and Other Disasters

PHILIP LEVINE

The punch-press operator from up north
met the assembler from West Virginia
in a bar near the stadium. Friday, late,
but too early to go home alone. Neither
had anything in mind, so they conversed
about the upcoming baseball season
about which neither cared. We could
be a couple, he thought, but she was
all wrong, way too skinny. For years
he'd had an image of the way a woman
should look, and it wasn't her, it wasn't
anyone he'd ever known, certainly not
his ex-wife who'd moved back north
to live with her high school sweetheart.
About killed him. I don't need that shit,
he almost said aloud, and then realized
she'd been talking to someone, maybe
to him, about how she couldn't get
her hands right, how the grease ate
so deeply into her skin it became
a part of her, and she put her hand,
palm up, on the bar and pointed
with her cigarette at the deep lines
the work had carved. "The life line,"
he said, "which one is that?" "None,"
she said, and he noticed that her eyes
were hazel flecked with tiny spots
of gold, and then—embarrassed—looked
back at her hand, which seemed tiny
and delicate, the fingers yellowed
with calluses but slender and fine.
She took a paper napkin off the bar,

spit on it and told him to hold still
while she carefully lifted his glasses
off, leaving him half blind, and wiped
something off of just above his left
cheekbone. "There," she said, handing
him back his glasses, "I got it," and even
with his glasses on what she showed
him was nothing he could see, maybe
only make believe. He thought, better
get out of here before it's too late, but
suspected too late was what he wanted.

Arrival and Departure

PHILIP LEVINE

Arriving in December on a Greyhound
from Paducah, you saw the usual sun
rising on your right over the bowed houses
of Dearborn as a wafer of moon descended
on your left behind the steaming rail yards
wakening for work. "Where are we?" you asked.
In 1948 people still talked
to each other even when they had something
to say, so of course I answered. I wasn't
innocent exactly, nor experienced
either, just a kid; "Downtown," I said,
as the bus with its cargo of bad breath
pulled in behind the depot just off
Washington Boulevard. Had you been
a woman, even one with crooked teeth,
a tight smile, and no particular charm,
I would have offered you a place to stay,
but at 6'-2" and 185
with your raw Indian features and hands
twice the size of mine, you got only advice,
in the long run not very good advice.
I should have said, "Go home, this town
will break your heart," but what did I know
about your home on a hillside tobacco farm
in North Carolina? What do I know now
except the forests as you climb higher,
dotted here and there with weathered shacks
the color of lead, and the rising silence
of winter as the snow descends unstained
into the early dusk. There was snow here, too,
speckled with cinders, piss yellowed, tired,
and the smell of iron and ashes blowing

in from Canada, and you and I waiting
for a streetcar that finally arrived
jammed with the refuse of the nightshift
at Plymouth Assembly. I should have seen
where we were headed; even at twenty
it was mine to know. Like you I thought
2.35 an hour was money, I thought
we'd sign on for afternoons and harden
into men. Wasn't that the way it worked,
men sold themselves to redeem their lives?
If there was an answer I didn't get it.
Korea broke, I took off for anywhere
living where I could, one perfect season
in your mountains. The years passed,
suddenly I was old and full of new needs.
When I went back to find you I found
instead no one in the old neighborhood
who knew who I was asking for, the Sure Shot
had become a porno shop; the plating plant
on Trumbull had moved to Mexico
or heaven. In its space someone planted
oiled grass, stripped-down cars, milkweeds
shuddering in the traffic. The river was here,
still riding low and wrinkled toward a world
we never guessed was there, but still the same,
like you, faithful to the end. If your sister,
widowed now, should call today and ask
one more time, "Where is he at? I need him,
he needs me," what should I tell her?
He's in the wind, he's under someone's
boot-soles, he's in the spring grass, he lives
in us as long as we live. She won't buy it,
neither would you. You'd light a cigarette,
settle your great right hand behind my neck,
bow down forehead to forehead, your black hair
fallen across your eyes, and mutter something
consequential, "bullshit" or "god a-mighty"
or "the worst is still to come." You came north
to Detroit in winter. What were you thinking?

131

The Death of Mayakovsky

PHILIP LEVINE

Philadelphia, the historic downtown,
April 14, 1930.
My father sits down at the little desk
in his hotel room overlooking an airshaft
to begin a letter home: "Dear Essie,"
he pens, but the phone rings before he can
unburden his heart. The driver from Precision Inc.
has arrived. Alone in the backseat, hatless,
coatless on this perfect spring day,
my father goes off to inspect aircraft bearings
that vanished from an army proving ground
in Maryland, bearings he will bargain for
and purchase in ignorance, or so he will tell Essie,
my mother, this after he takes a plea
in the federal courthouse in downtown Detroit.
I knew all this before it happened. Earlier that
morning storm clouds scuttled in across Ontario
to release their darkness into our gray river.
Hundreds of miles east my father rolls down
the car window; the air scented with leaves
just budding out along Route 76
caresses his face and tangles his dark hair.
He lets the world come to him, even this world
of small machine shops, car barns, warehouses
beside the Schuylkill. The child I would become
saw it all, yet years passed before the scene slipped,
frozen, into the book of origins to become
who I am. I'd been distracted
in the breathless dawn by a single shot—
the Russian poet's suicidal gesture—
that would crown our narratives, yours and mine.

Library Days

PHILIP LEVINE

I would sit for hours with the sunlight
streaming in the high windows and know
the delivery van was safe, locked in the yard
with the brewery trucks, and my job secure.
I chose first a virgin copy of *The Idiot*
by Dostoyevsky, every page of which confirmed
life was irrational. The librarian, a woman
gone gray though young, sat by the phone
that never rang, assembling the frown
reserved exclusively for me when I entered
at 10 a.m. to stay until the light dwindled
into afternoon. No doubt her job was to guard
these treasures, for Melville was here, Balzac,
Walt Whitman, my old hero, in multiple copies
each with the aura of used tea bags. In late August
of 1951 a suited gentleman reader creaked
across the polished oaken floor to request
the newest copy of *Jane's Book of Fighting Ships*
only to be told, "This, sir, is literature!"
in a voice of pure malice. I looked up
from the text swimming before me in hopes
of exchanging a first smile; she'd gone back
to her patient vigil over the dead black phone.
Outside I could almost hear the world, trucks
maneuvering the loading docks or clogging
the avenues and grassy boulevards of Detroit.
Other men, my former schoolmates, were off
on a distant continent in full retreat, their commands
and groans barely a whisper across the vastness
of an ocean and a mountain range. In the garden
I'd planted years before behind the old house
I'd long ago deserted, the long winter was over;

the roses exploded into smog, the African vine
stolen from the zoo strangled the tiny violets
I'd nursed each spring, the mock orange snowed
down and bore nothing, its heavy odor sham.
"Not for heaven or earth would I trade my soul,
rather would I lie down to sleep among the dead,"
Prince Myshkin mumbled on page 437,
a pure broth of madness, perhaps my part,
the sole oracular part in the final act
of the worst play ever written. I knew then
that soon I would rise up and leave the book
to go back to the great black van waiting
patiently for its load of beer kegs, sea trunks
and leather suitcases bound for the voyages
I'd never take, but first there was *War and Peace,*
there were Cossacks riding their ponies
toward a horizon of pure blood, there was Anna,
her loves and her deaths, there was Turgenev
with his impossible, histrionic squabbles,
Chekhov coughing into his final tales. The trunks—
with their childish stickers—could wait, the beer
could sit for ages in the boiling van slowly
morphing into shampoo. In the offices and shops,
out on the streets, men and women could curse
the vicious air, they could buy and sell
each other, they could beg for a cup of soup,
a sandwich and tea, some few could face life
with or without beer, they could embrace or die,
it mattered not at all to me, I had work to do.

On the Scrap

M. L. LIEBLER

"Come take a little trip with me in a 1913
To Calumet, Michigan, in the Copper Country." —Woody Guthrie

In a small, big town 1913
    At the northern most reaches
    Of America—sticking out
    Into the cold, deep waters
    Of Lake Superior—beautiful
    Body of lake and fresh earth
    Packed heavy with White Fish and copper
    Land, veins mined by immigrants:
Croatia, Hungry, Finland, England and beyond.

This was American multiculturalism
    Long before the academy labeled people
    Through longitudinal studies and statistics.
    It was here in Michigan where the working class
    Once again defined the country's future by building
    A firm foundation: Kewanaw County—just another place
    Where labor awakened to confront business
    Owners who were, as they've always been, determined
To keep workers enslaved, endangered and under

Control. When the first cry of "union" sprung
    From the workers' wintry lips from the frozen cold streets,
    The mine owners' mantra was loud and clear
    To the ears of the working poor. The managers' chant of
    "We'll let the grass grow on your streets
    Before we concede to the uncivilized.
    Working class," was an offense to the few who
Understood English. Those words were met with
    A reckoning response from labor everywhere.

Fortunately, for the mining men of Calumet
There was, once again as always, a strong willed
Woman who refused to let injustice trample
Her community down to ash in the name of
"Business as usual!" She was intolerable to the company's
Ideas that animals and equipment were more valuable

Than human life. So, just at history's darkest moment,
During the Great Mining Strike of 1913, Big Annie
Clemec of Calumet stood up to be counted and
To take on the mine owners by challenging them
To "Kill me! Run your bayonets and sabers
Through this flag and kill me! For I will not
Be moved. If this American flag will not
Protect me, then I will die holding it"

Sweet Annie Clemec, Eastern European angel of the mines, tall,
Beautiful Upper Peninsula woman of integrity
Who marched daily through
The copper-rich streets of Calumet with her American
Flag raised, stars, red, blue and white,
High above her flowing brown northern hair
Encouraging other men, women and children to stand
Together united for union and for their fair share.

Big Annie—Lady of Calumet—marched
Head on into the Federal Militia who watched her
From horsebacks with their silver sabers drawn
And ready to knock her flag of freedom from her
Steady hand, but Annie marched forward, always,
Spitting on the yellow-bellied soldiers who dared
To cowardly take the working man's birthright of fair
Pay for an honest day away from the many

To benefit the few who lined their pockets
With the blood money from the multitude of dead
And injured miners. The miners wanted to work
A little less and spend a little more time
With their families—good families values to be sure.

The miners wanted to be safer in the dark dungeon
Mines webbed with the evil sound of the widow-maker
Drill; to be paid a fair wage, and to have their union
Recognized. These are reasonable requests for people who live
    In the Land of the Free, but to the capitalists who own
    The stores and the towns, they saw a different country
    Where the many served the few and so on and so on.
    In the end, the company won the Strike of 1913
    In Copper County, Michigan. They broke the back
    Of labor in their typical, hurtful, murdering way
When they planted a scab-snitch in the old Italian

Hall on Main Street Calumet on December 24th at
    Big Annie's Christmas party for the penniless children
    And the families of the striking men. As gifts of oranges,
    Handmade dolls, cloths and such were passed to the children
    From Santa on the stage, a loud cry of "Fire-Fire!" rose
    Up over the heads of the children and the frantic strikers.
    A cloud of panic hung like a noose hung over the people who scrambled
Towards the one and only front door. A human stampede

Where body after body piled up on the stairway out.
    Few made it out that day. When calm was restored,
    74 people, mostly children, lay buried in a twisted heap
    Of bones, blood, skin and hair. Dead forever. A working
    Class nightmare in the Home of the Brave. All brought
    On by another nameless company snitch who yelled "fire,"
    From his stool pigeon perch. and was never seen again
In Calumet City. Big Annie picked up her flag one more time

To bury the dead children in the frozen, gray land—
    December 28, 1913. She led the funeral procession
    To the snow-covered, graveyard earth in the north.
    The Calumet newspapers reported that miners won
    Nothing of significance during the Great Strike.
    They went back to work as usual without
    Their babies, without a raise, without
Better working conditions and no recognition
For their union. All of that was buried in the cold

Michigan earth. By the time 1914 rolled around,
The same problems and troubles of before
Faced working people, but they drew some hope
And inspiration through their friend Big Annie whose
courageous Spirit drifted skyward past
a lone child's picket that read
"My papa is striking for us!"

Making It Right

M. L. LIEBLER

*—Lines composed after being asked to lecture on labor in Detroit during the depres-
sion at the Amerika Haus Lecture Series in Munich, Germany 2004*

*"You know what work is—if you're
old enough to read this you know what
work is, although you may not do it.
Forget you." —Philip Levine*

I bring no poetry today
From the oil and grease
Soul of my Detroit.

This history I am is
Only, and nothing more,
Than the son of an auto worker.

Just another Detroit man beaten
Down by the tortured years
Of Depression, World Wars

And the awful angst of unemployment.
This is my story without balance
Weighing heavier on the side

Of heartache and less on the side
Of the sacred and glorious.
This is my story of what no work is

And what it can do to the
Working class in the darkness
Of our desperation.

I wish, now, I did have some
Kind of a poem to say aloud,
Right here—to make you

All understand what is inside
The blackened heart and under
The whittled bones of the people

Who have been left behind
In the ashes of the plant. I guess

I could read you a poem about how labor
Takes a boy and makes him a worker
Before he is allowed to become a man.

How the factory humiliates
And intimidates all people
With endless assembly and useless work.

How the line takes one ounce
Of every soul lived for every
Minute it is sped up to completion.

How Henry Ford's great innovation
Doomed generations to continuous
Monotony in the name of "making a living."

But, I am afraid that I can only bring
The small news of what becomes of people
Who work hard with greasy hands.

About people who learn that their reality is
Having their names spelled out in factory
Smoke long before they were born. A birthright

For workers to endure through
The long loneliness of industry
And unemployment lines where

We are wait and wait for our
Bread and roses to fall from the sky
Like beads of perspiration upon our graves.

We dream that, maybe, prosperity
Is really just around the corner. So we
get up every morning with hope, and

We return each night to the broken houses
Of our lives, seldom realizing that it is our
Labor that keeps this whole world together.

I guess, in the end, we do not know
What work is, but still we continue to
Do it over and over making it right.

Riding into California

SHIRLEY GEOK-LIN LIM

If you come to a land with no ancestors
to bless you, you have to be your own
ancestor. The veterans in the mobile home
park don't want to be there. It isn't easy.
Oil rigs litter the land like giant frozen birds.
Ghosts welcome us to a new life, and
an immigrant without home ghosts
cannot believe the land is real. So you're
grateful for familiarity, and Bruce Lee
becomes your hero. Coming into Fullerton,
everyone waiting at the station is white.
The good thing about being Chinese on Amtrak
is no one sits next to you. The bad thing is
you sit alone all the way to Irvine.

The Builders

HENRY WADSWORTH LONGFELLOW

All are architects of Fate,
    Working in these walls of Time;
Some with massive deeds and great,
    Some with ornaments of rhyme.

Nothing useless is, or low;
    Each thing in its place is best;
And what seems but idle show
    Strengthens and supports the rest.

For the structure that we raise,
    Time is with materials filled;
Our todays and yesterdays
    Are the blocks with which we build.

Truly shape and fashion these;
    Leave no yawning gaps between;
Think not, because no man sees,
    Such things will remain unseen.

In the elder days of Art,
    Builders wrought with greatest care
Each minute and unseen part;
    For the gods see everywhere.

Let us do our work as well,
    Both the unseen and the seen;
Make the house where Gods may dwell,
    Beautiful, entire, and clean.

Else our lives are incomplete,
    Standing in these walls of Time,

Broken stairways, where the feet
  Stumble as they seek to climb.

Build today, then, strong and sure,
  With a firm and ample base;
And ascending and secure
  Shall tomorrow find its place.

Thus alone can we attain
  To those turrets, where the eye
Sees the world as one vast plain,
  And one boundless reach of sky.

The Deadhouse at the Workhouse

THOMAS LUX

You get sent to the workhouse because you worked
and worked
yourself so deep in debt
you took a loan to pay the debt,
then another to pay the interest on the loan
(all the while working: day labor,
night labor, and thumping
a bowl of porridge on the table each noon
for the kids and wife) and then
you make a deal with the local loanshark
who's happy to help you out
but breaks your knees the following week
when the bank won't remortgage your house
so you can pay his vig. Times
are hard. So like I said, you get sent to the workhouse
where you don't work (no jobs
there and everybody else ditto
out of work) and your only visitors
are creditors demanding
that you pay them. Then you die
and they put your body in the deadhouse
at the workhouse—which is like stabbing
a stab wound—until your wife or son
comes in with some money
to buy a box and buy you out of the deadhouse
through the workhouse
and hauls you home
and next goes out to borrow some money
to buy some dirt
into which they sink your box.

What I See When I Drive to Work

THOMAS LUX

(Boston to New York)

On clear days it's fast black dead west sixty miles,
New England blazing or granite-brown
on both sides of the slide. Then a dip southwest—the sun on my left cheek now flat
on my chest, and I'm warm,
with the other citizens, driving
to work. About lunchtime

I hit Hartford (each week a honk
for Wallace Stevens)—half a day done
for the insurance clerks and I'm halfway
to work. Twenty or so miles later,
on the arc of a long dropping curve, the sun
takes a quarry's gouged-out bowl.
I like the big machines, drills

and dozers, that eat
the rock and break it down to sand—at least
more than I like the insurance industry;
and then a town's announced
by a giant Jesus' coat rack
on a rubbled hill. It overlooks
a happy, placid burg known for brass

where I never stop
for gas or sandwich. I'm driving
to work—talk radio/gun control, Squantz
Pond, lunch pail, Ruby Road, never-cross-
a-picket-line, on my way
to earn a wage: Massachusetts, Connecticut,
and now nudging into New York.

just over which border
I follow for a few miles a river
that opens to a lake
that each day this fall
is open to more and more ducks,
which makes me happy, at this point,
driving to work with the rest of America,

who mostly get there before I do.
The last leg's most scenic, woodsy,
and takes me past a publishing complex,
Reader's Digest, Inc., massive buildings
on a hill, where a man someday
might reduce this poem to haiku.
I'm nearing now and exit by the exit

by the blind school—two more miles,
if I take the shortcut past some mansions,
to my office, which is
199.4 mi.
from my home. It's a lengthy motoring,
but the work is honest
and the customers human.

The Houseplant

CAROLINE MAUN

It was a tour, like any one may take
when visiting the home of an old friend.
We stepped into the side yard to see
a sight so arresting it required explanation.
The plant wasn't doing well inside, she said,
So I brought it out here and forgot about it.
Perhaps a single tendril of root
had slipped to the soil of the ancient Florida hammock.
Now, roots the size of biceps had broken the pot;
released from its cylinder of soil, the plant
wound around the pine like a killing anaconda.
The leaves, which previously spanned a human hand at best,
now like the painted faces of ancient warriors,
savoring the sun in the moment before victory.

The Abdication of the Bees

CAROLINE MAUN

Long in toil
half-domesticated
some trucked on site to manage the load
between Maine, Florida, California:
today blueberries, tomorrow oranges.
Maybe they grew angry
from the displacement,
the field never ending
the hive never where it was.
They started to remove themselves
after four centuries
unrepresented,
their queens artificially inseminated.
Maybe, maroon, they left
in search of independent flowers.

Beginning with a Line by di Prima

MICHAEL MCCLURE

"The only war that matters is the war against the imagination!"
The only love that shatters
is the love of despondence and horror.
The only honor that shines
is the one that smashes
the
lust
for duty.

ANY

CRIME

THAT

DIMINISHES

THE

SOUL

is not credible

—such as:
the foulness of stuffing one's gut with the junk of greasy meat
and consumerist propaganda, of filling one's nose
and veins with drugs, of cutting the beaks from chickens & then
loading them with poisons and light and madness and eating
their eggs and spirits. BODY AND SPIRIT

ARE

ALL

ONE THING. IT IS JUST ONE WAR

AND THE BIG BOMB HAS ALREADY EXPLODED

THERE'S TIME TO LOOK YOUR LOVE
IN THE EYES AND SAY

no

more

shit!!!!!

In my insides I am a man or woman
I am heart and lung and meat and vein and breath
going back through a deep
phylogeny. I AM A DEEP OLD HISTORY MADE NEW
FOR THE FIRST TIME IN THE SMILING GUISE
of the universe that whispers with my breathed air
and my soft toes. WHY THEN AM I HANDED
THIS
GARBAGE

THESE LIES, that are told

over and over
that grow tighter and tighter
and prey on my health? Why am I diminished
and portrayed as a fool?
AND TOLD TO BUY AND CONSUME TILL
I AM ONLY A FOOL??

How come I am a tool of this explosion

a tool of tools in the midst of this
SLOW MOTION BLOW UP!!!

STAND
UP
!!!

STAND
UP
!!!

Get off your back and turn off the box
with the moving pictures.

Go for a walk in the woods or on the plains.
Speak to a cliff!

The only war that matters is the war
against the imagination.
The only honor that shines
is the one that smashes
the
LUST
for duty.
It is your duty to absorb the social propaganda
and become crazed with the need for overpopulation
and to stimulate the greed to devour what has been
out there for a billion years
and to burn petroleum in endless
and countless flames in the ceremonial vehicles
and the machines that change the climate.
It is duty to torment the innocent
and the less privileged

AND

TO

FINGER

&

TORTURE

&

TEASE

right out of their homes and lives, a million
species of brother and sister beings.

It is duty to dissolve any signs of an inner life
that is different in any way from the outer lies
of consumerist propaganda.
IT IS DUTY TO BE OF ONLY
One Dimension,
so that the inside soul is no different
from the commercial for tennis shoes.

The Finances
of
ROCK AND ROLL
sings anthems of cheap beer
straight into your ears
as you shove your green paper over the counter

to trade for burgers that are fried in the tallow
of cows grazed where there were once forests in the Amazon!

The only war that matters is the war against the imagination!!!

Grandfather's Breath

RAY MCNIECE

You work. You work, Buddy. You work.
Word of immigrant get-ahead grind I hear
huffing through me, Grandfather's breath,
when he'd come in from Saturday's keep-busy chores,
fending up a calloused hand to stop
me from helping him, haggard cheeks puffing
out like T-shirts hung between tenements,
doubled-over under thirty-five years a machine
repairman at the ball-bearing factory, ball-bearings
making everything run smoother—
especially torpedoes. He busted butt
for the war effort, for profiteers, for overtime pay
down-payment on a little box of his own,
himself a refugee from the European economy,
washed ashore after *The War to End All Wars.*
Cheap labor for the winners.

I hear his youth plodding through the hayfields
above Srednevas, and the train that wheezed
and lumbered to the boat where he heave-hoed
consumptive sister, one-two-overboard.
I hear him scuffling along factory smoke choked streets
of Cleveland, coughing out chunks of broken
English just to make it to Saturday morning balinca—
how he grunted off a week's worth of grit
hurling wooden balls down the pressed dirt court,
sweaty wisp of gray hair wagging from his forehead,
This is how the world turns. You work hard. You practice.
And I hear his claim as we climbed the steps
of Municipal Stadium, higher, into the cheap seats,
slapping the flat of his hand against a girder,
I built this, Buddy. I built this.

But mostly I hear how he'd catch
what was left of his breath after those Saturday chores,
pouring out that one, long, tall cold beer
that Grandma allowed, holding it aloft,
bubbles golden as hayfields above Srednavas,
before savoring it down and taking up
the last task of his day off—cleaning the cage,
letting *Snowball,* canary like the ones once used
to test coal mines for poison air, flap clumsily free
around the living room, crapping
on the plastic covered davenport and easy-chair
they only sat in twice a year.

And I'm still breathing, Grandfather, that day
you took me down the basement to the cool floor
to find out what was wrong. *Come on, Snowball,*
fly. Fly! The bird splayed out on the same linoleum
where they found you, next to your iron lung,
where Grandma mopped for weeks after,
pointing with arthritic fingers, *See. There.*
There's where he fell and bumped his head
See the specks of blood? She can't work out.
And now I sing "One fine morning when my work is done
I'm gonna fly away home, fly away home."

Come on, Snowball, fly. Fly . . .

Lazy Russ

TONY MEDINA

I've walked
through
many rooms
on my journey
from the womb
to the tomb

I've lived in
tin can shacks
where my mother
held a pan
beneath melting icicles
for water to drink
and for bathing

We ate breakfast
out of glove compartments
that didn't have
enough room
for feet

I've rolled over in
alleys hugged
up to a heap
of dung
to keep from
freezing

I've slept
on park benches
and laid out
in subway stenches

I even slept
in open heart surgery
shelters

Where sometimes you
check in
but you don't
check out

And I've
also checked
out in search
of no-income housing
in the sky
Only to be
brought back
by paramedics
in the back
of ambulances

Dropped off
outside of
emergency rooms
Onto the streets
wandering off
to alleys
and ashcans
and lobbies

Or to lay out
onto the warm
open wound
of street graters

Grandfather: Frailty Is Not the Story

D. H. MELHEM

—for Dana and Gregory

Remember your grandfather tall and straight
Remember him swimming in deep water
Remember his stories of exile and travel
  and immigrant dreams
Remember his ship models designed from memory
Remember him netting shiners with you in Gardiner's Bay
  or digging for clams
  or cleaning a fish
  or driving us fast
  to catch the sunset at Maidstone

I remember him climbing the stairs
  after all the stairs he had climbed
  with his satchel of fabrics
I remember him on stepladders in the Depression
  or holding my hand on the way to school
  me proud of him in his overalls
I remember watching for him at six o'clock
  he would lift me at the door
and then we would sit over roast lamb shanks or chicken
while my mother related the family news.
Afterwards he rose to "stretch his legs,"
  read the paper, and doze.
And I remember discussions, the arguments over politics
  how he taught me to reason, to wield logic
  as he had done when captain of the debating team
  in Tripoli Boys' School, Lebanon
  and the photos of him there, where he was becoming
  the tallest and handsomest man in the town.

I remember the pipes arrayed like sentinels on a cabinet
the talk of building or buying a boat
explanations of algebra (which I learned to enjoy)
and the excursions—
    walking over Brooklyn Bridge into Chinatown
    walking down Ocean Parkway to Sheepshead Bay
or later in a Ford, the three of us, singing
    of the San Fernando Valley
    where we would settle down
    and never more roam.

Remember your grandfather
in his vigor
and that a loving life
takes imagination.

Anonymous Donation

GARY METRAS

It got to twenty-seven below that winter,
which is harsh for Massachusetts,
even as far west as the hills near Pittsfield.

I mixed stucco that week, by hand.
The mixing bed was splashed with ice.
We set it on the cement floor of a large box.

The box became a luxury condominium.
With every third pull of the hoe, I rested,
to let the lungs thaw, to exhale a cloud

and waste a moment watching my crystal breath.
Such scenery would never be framed
and hung on these walls when finished.

So I mixed it into the stucco.
And quit the job.

Telephone Repairman

JOSEPH MILLAR

All morning in the February light
he has been mending cable,
splicing the pairs of wires together
according to their colors,
white-blue to white-blue
violet-slate to violet-slate,
in the warehouse attic by the river.

When he is finished
the messages will flow along the line:
thank you for the gift,
please come to the baptism,
the bill is now past due:
voices that flicker and gleam back and forth
across the tracer-colored wires.

We live so much of our lives
without telling anyone.
He thinks of the many signals
flying in the air around him,
the syllables fluttering,
saying *please love me,*
from continent to continent
over the curve of the earth.

Ed's Auto Repair

JOSEPH MILLAR

When I bring the car in for brakes
everybody's out front eating donuts,
one of the children jumping
from the stack of tires by the door,
wearing a hat that says Fast Orange.

Edward's out back in the shop
welding the exhaust on a blue Chevelle
and mumbling to himself. I thread my way
past a Pontiac engine block balanced
on the black tines of a forklift,
a gold Cutlass with the driveshaft
hanging down in front,
to watch his torch flame splash
its lizard shapes onto the dark steel.

I'm not often permitted entry to this dim cool mine
smelling of gas and iron
where the air hoses hiss in the corners,
sparks spray onto the floor,
and everything seems combustible
as though the fire in the Cadillac manifold
leaning against the wall
still glowed under the rust.

Edward's smooth Hawaiian face, greasemarked
under one eye when he peels off the goggles,
wears a half-smile, his hair matted down
with ashes and dirt,
the big vein on his right hand
shining with sweat. What's up,
he says, turning toward me,

while Vulcan, his grandfather,
misshapen god of the forge,
slides through the shadows under the muffler, the new
metal ticking
as he breathes on the weld.

from $00 / Line / Steel / Train

MARK NOWAK

1.

The basic form is the frame; the photograph of the factory predicts how every one (of the materials) will get used. **and I can remember Mark & I talking about the possibility of Lackawanna becoming a ghost town** Past (participle) past (participant) past (articulating) an incessant scraping (away). **and what would we do. You know—it wasn't just losing a job in the steel industry, but your entire life, the place that you grew up in was going to be gone.** As I scraped (grease, meat, omelettes), the (former) railroad workers and steel workers (still) bullshitting in the restaurant where for eight years I short-order cooked.

*

Who knew

the crisis

from the conditions—

presumably

the Capital [Who]

92.

Doors torn away in Detroit, 1974. A picture in a frame is (still) the object here. [The ex-steelworkers] will use excuses, like prejudice against mill hunks, and only make a marginal effort to salve their conscience or get the wife off their backs. Case worker mimics gendered speech while cutting class (early). We try to strip them bare (steel/workers), and then show all the ways to look for a job—"The 'hot' economy created three million jobs in 1996, about half of them paying minimum wages (and half of those temporary or part time)." how they can even use the obituaries to find work.

*

When coming to

a stop   stopping

stopping Them [when]

from continuing—
    from coming to

222.

When we were kids we thought the steel mill was it. The (scrape) wage of labor (scraping by). We'd seen the men comin' out, all dirty, black. The only thing white was the goggles over their eyes. "[S]till more important is the idea that the pleasures of whiteness could function as a 'wage' for white workers." We thought they were it, strong men. (The missing word is white.) We just couldn't wait to get in there. When we finally did get in, we were sorry. (Chuckles.) It wasn't what it was cut out to be.

*

America
[history's
          signs]   :   "No

Parking
          Anytime"

257.

Because the (brake) past is used because the tearing (past) of the (brick) form is used is used because the fence (in) of the (goddamn) frame is used is used is utterly used against us and by us and upon us and for us is used is used in the present (past) future (form) we are used yet users yet used.

Every day you put your life on the line when you went into that iron house. Every day you sucked up dirt and took a chance on breaking your legs or breaking your back. And anyone who's worked in there knows what I'm talking about.

*

             -roads]
    Closing

                  words   :

[Rail

Cameron

MATTHEW OLZMANN

The entire crew has vanished and for all I know they are probably dead. Cameron and I are the only survivors and I'm not sure how much longer we can hold on. Lost at sea on a sinking ship. Miles from anything other than water; a 45 ft. wave crashes over the starboard rail threatening to break this boat in two. I spit out saltwater and choke on the wind. My skin is raw from weeks on this ocean. I might never make it home.

Another wave hits the boat, and then come the sharks. We are surrounded. Cameron takes out one with the harpoon gun and another with the sword. I toss grenades blindly into the blue and watch the meat explode into the sky. I turn around and one of the bastards finally gets to me. It is tearing off my arm. I think things can't possibly get any worse, but Cameron finds a way to hit me with even more bad news:

"I can't find my driver's license!" he yells.

"What?"

"I can't find my driver's license and I can't find my keys!"

"Well, where are they?"

"I think they're in the truck!"

"Well, why don't you go get them?"

Cameron runs across the water to the truck. It is a '99 Dodge Dakota and a woman who looks vaguely familiar hands him his license and his keys. He is screaming,

"We gotta get this stuff to the bank!"

"What about the sharks?" I yell back.

"No! We gotta get this stuff to the bank. We will outrun them!"

Now, there's something you should know.

Cameron is three years old. He lives in East Detroit. He's my girlfriend's son, and we are on a boat being chased by sharks, on our way to the bank because, he says, "WE ARE ON A BOAT BEING CHASED BY SHARKS ON OUR WAY TO THE BANK!"

So that's the way it is.

I understand this because I remember when I was his age. Imagination was not a concept, it was a way of life. If I wanted to see the ocean, I *saw* the ocean.

Not my backyard. Not the scent of lawn clippings. Not my mother calling me in for dinner. I could smell the salt water, hear the cries of seagulls, feel the rush of waves racing by. Every single day, I built castles on the sun, won the grand prix on my big wheel, and defended the moon against the aliens. I discovered America and drank Kool-Aid with Jesus. Y'all got me to thank for being alive today 'cause I saved this human race every afternoon. I fought the Decepticons. Joker & Penguin? I kicked their asses.

But now, it is Tuesday night and the sun is setting.

Cameron is waving his arms in these big wild circles, turning the sharks into dolphins, swimming backstroke through tall blades of grass, and what am I doing? All I ever do is work, hit the bar when I'm done, watch the news when I can find the time, and I wonder when I lost it. When did I finally sell my soul to this reality?

I'm checking for my keys and my driver's license again.

Getting ready for work.

They've got me on the midnight shift tonight.

Ode to Dirt in an Old Farmer's Lungs

ANNE-MARIE OOMEN

To tell it simply as it happened,
after the surgery on his colon
took out two tumors, the one they
knew about, the other a mushroomed surprise,
and how they found the blockage in his lungs,
down at the bottom they said, and how
they also said it might be simple to fix,
not even another surgery, but instead,
an apparatus with a mist of expectorant,
and that it began to clear after only three days—
is to go at the story all wrong.

What granules from dry clay—
what molecules of soil rising from the drought
he plowed through in eighty-two—
what constellations of mud dripping
into his panting mouth from the eight-inch rain—
what dark clots spitting from furrows,
kicked into his face from the wheels
of a muck-covered John Deere—
what manic wind winding across a two-forty plot
where he spread manure for fifty years—
what building of loam—what leaning into it, tasting it,
breathing it into his cells—
oh, earthen aeola
where emptiness had been—what
chemistry of dust!

When the mucus spilled up,
they tested it, said it was
just dirt.
He asked if there was enough to grow

anything, if they could check the PH.
(A small joke in light of all the tests.)
After that he stared out the hospital window
at a flat roof that would grow nothing;
folded the pillars of his arms, looking
like Samson after they cut his hair,
like a man from whom something
had been taken.

Carolina Summer

RICHARD PEABODY

There is hope in the garage.
Hope in the oily puddles,
the work bench littered
with toys, with bottles,
rags, nails, screwdrivers.
I plan to explore the rusting cans,
the wasp's nest hanging in the rafters.
In one corner is a pile of potatoes.
I could sit on that pile and read all afternoon.
Gourds are floating on thin brown stalks
by the windows, tomatoes scattered on the sill.
My grandfather's hoe is resting by the door.
The old vintage radio is there too,
the one that scared Aunt Hazel so badly
when Orson Welles conquered the world.
Uncle John's MG takes up most of the place
in sleepy green magnificence. He plans
to fix it up someday. Both his daughters
want it for their own. I guess everybody
has a dream.

And still the garage is filled
with hope. I can smell it.
I smell turpentine, paint, and oil.
I can remember collecting lightning bugs
in my grandmother's old mason jars.
I see the lawnmower and the plow.
Remember my grandfather working in the garden
at sunset, his straw hat pulled down
over his eyes, the sun gleaming scarlet
off his glasses. I used to climb peach trees
in the backyard, their branches now as twisted

as the wrinkles on an old man's face.
There were apple trees and grapevines too.
Rotten fruit on the ground covered
with yellow jackets.

I long to kneel before the broken window
like a child again and imagine my
grandfather asleep in his garden.

The Forgiveness Device

RICHARD PEABODY

"Hold that flashlight still."

But I can't. It's impossible.
I'm only a child and I watch
As he puffs up bigger and bigger
—like a barrage balloon—
pushing back his glasses
that are smeared with grease
as he winds the clicking
ratchet again and again
changing sparkplugs in the dark.

The garage light won't reach outside
to where we stand around the
burgundy Chrysler. I'm scared.
Snot dripping down my face. Tears.
The fender is too big for me
to lean over, but I try
and my arm is so numb
it tingles. The drop light
flickers against the hood.
My father is stripping skin
off his knuckles as the ratchet
slips and dings off the manifold.
He's talking to himself.
Saying he can't see and
beginning to cuss.

I realize now—
that he's angry at himself,
at his failure to fix
something so elementary

and his anger
is misdirected at me.
But back then I was just
a bookish little kid
afraid of failing.
I didn't know yet that
it's okay to fail.
That my father was
just trying to save a buck
and afraid of aging.
The price was high.

Why can't you wait till morning?
I wanted to say, but didn't dare.
He drinks another Ballantine,
crumples the can and drops
it on the driveway.

If I could
I'd materialize at that exact moment
the aluminum still rattling
against the concrete.
Tell him, "It's not that important Dad.
It's just a couple of sparkplugs.
Don't get so stressed."
I'd rub my red bandanna
across his forehead
and soothe his brow.
Tell him, "Relax."
And watch his features soften.
Hear that laughter again.

And I'd forgive him.
I really would.

Factory Horn Exodus

JEFF PONIEWAZ

After broiling all day
in the hellhole factory
I'm buried in a busload
of armpits remembering
the glowing letter the Company sent
accepting me for summer employment
and welcoming me to the Free
Enterprise system.
Suddenly the bus, which has already
been moving like a choked turd
grunts to a dead stop.
I look out the window to see
a bridge going up.
Some nitwit in an admiral's outfit
and with a mast just high enough
to stop traffic, hoists what looks like
a glass of ice-cubed booze
and his wife throws kisses at cars
which bleat like frantic ovens.

Well Paid Slaves

JEFF PONIEWAZ

Just because some
slaves are well paid
doesn't mean they
aren't slaves,
doesn't mean
they're free.
Just because some
concentration camps
pay a higher minimum wage
and have a few more
"creature comforts"
than Dachau
doesn't mean they aren't
concentration camps.
Almost the whole human race
is slaves
to the world
they've imposed
(super imposed)
over the real world
and all the eons of Creation—
bricking up our natural souls
in Gothic walls of Civilization.
All the skeletons
in all the dark closets of History!

Poetry brings light,
visions bring sight—
human race getting ready for
a giant step of the Mind
that dwarfs the baby step to the Moon.
A Giant Step,

a gentle giant step
more daring than stealing fire
or a goose that lays golden eggs.
A far step, a vast step,
a step in the right direction—
an evolutionary sport
more thrilling than the Olympics.
A daring step out of the Dark Ages
into the Ages of Light!

Day Off

MINNIE BRUCE PRATT

Walking toward the clutch of drunks sitting in the sunshine
is like hearing a radio station come clear. The grumbling,
the accusations, *He stole from me!* The singing, one man
in a pure doo-wop solo, *One day, one day, one day.* Homeless, their only work on Sunday is to remind us of shame.
The way earlier a man coming toward me crowded the fence,
averted his eyes while his hand wrung his mouth, the gesture
of one who is about to fail, the eyes down, remembering.
While tomorrow, on our workday, there will be the one who
holds out a paper cup at the subway, names the next train
so we don't have to run. After the door chimes shut, there will be
the man selling newspapers with his preacher's fear-god voice.
There will be the woman, singing, who steps the aisle between us,
past our averted eyes, shaking her collection cup like a tambourine.

Ancestors

DUDLEY RANDALL

Why are our ancestors
always kings and princes
and never the common people?

Was the Old Country a democracy
where every man was a king?
Or did the slave-catchers
steal only the aristocrats
and leave the fieldhands
laborers
street cleaners
garbage collectors
dishwashers
cooks
and maids
behind?

My own ancestor
(research reveals)
was a swineherd
who tended the pigs
in the Royal Pigstye
and slept in the mud
among the hogs.

Yet I'm as proud of him
as of any king or prince
dreamed up in fantasies
of bygone glory.

George

DUDLEY RANDALL

When I was a boy desiring the title of man
And toiling to earn it
In the inferno of the foundry knockout,
I watched and admired you working by my side,
As, goggled, with mask on your mouth and shoulders bright with sweat,
You mastered the monstrous, lumpish cylinder blocks,
And when they clotted the line and plunged to the floor
With force enough to tear your foot in two,
You calmly stepped aside.

One day when the line broke down and the blocks reared up
Groaning, grinding, and mounted like an ocean wave
And then rushed thundering down like an avalanche,
And we frantically dodged, then braced our heads together
To form an arch to lift and stack them,
You gave me your highest accolade:
You said: "You not afraid of sweat. You strong as a mule."

Now, here, in the hospital,
In a ward where old men wait to die,
You sit, and watch time go by.
You cannot read the books I bring, not even
Those that are only picture books,
As you sit among the senile wrecks,
The psychopaths, the incontinent.
One day when you fell from your chair and stared at the air
With the look of fright which sight of death inspires,
I lifted you like a cylinder block, and said,
"Don't be afraid
Of a little fall, for you'll be here
A long time yet, because you're strong as a mule."

Old Witherington

DUDLEY RANDALL

Old Witherington had drunk too much again.
The children changed their play and packed around him
To jeer his latest brawl. Their parents followed.

Prune-black, with bloodshot eyes and one white tooth,
He tottered in the night with legs spread wide
Waving a hatchet. "Come on, come on," he piped,
"And I'll baptize these bricks with bloody kindling.
I may be old and drunk, but not afraid
To die. I've died before. A million times
I've died and gone to hell. I live in hell.
If I die now I die, and put an end
To all this loneliness. Nobody cares
Enough to even fight me now, except
This crazy bastard here."

                    And with these words
He cursed the little children, cursed his neighbors,
Cursed his father, mother, and his wife,
Himself, and God, and all the rest of the world,
All but his grinning adversary, who, crouched,
Danced tenderly around him with a jag-toothed bottle,
As if the world compressed to one old man
Who was the sun, and he sole faithful planet.

Groundskeeper Busted Reading in the Custodial Water Closet

KEVIN RASHID

Waterboy!
I come all this way just to see you
and look what kind of disappointment I got waiting.
Let me figure—should I nibble at your ear, or bite your
whole damn head off?
You tell me, Waterboy,
is the work too hard, or is it
just too much like work?
Or are you just way ahead of your time?

Come all this way—

'Cause it really pains me—
    pains me to talk like I was your daddy—
You got a daddy, don't you Waterboy?
    or d'you just pop out the backside a some possum
    what coughed too hard?
We pay you to pick trash, pull churches, mow, and get the
    dog stuff off the sidewalks
    so the patrons won't complain and here you are
    putting their tax dollars to work for you!
Just to see you, I come.

What's that you reading, Waterboy?
    Ten Days that Shook the University . . . political
    Whatever.
Reminds me of a little girl used to be on the crew.
'Course she'd read on break—
she was a worker
She'd come to work
    and I'd come out to watch her,

talk: to her,
    watch that old red gallon can-o-gas
    bounce off her left thigh . . .
"Ho a rabbit just sit
Ho a fox just look just look
Ho a rabbit just dreamin'
Ho a fox just schemin'
A rabbit screamin'
and a fox like a demon
It's a hold-on-tight
It's a feel wrong/right
It's a way-off sound
Lowdy, turn around
It's the way of the world
It's a boy, it's a girl."
'Course she had to ruin every damn thing
    filing that complaint on me.
Would a lost my job too, if my boys hadn't
    hushed it and got her a job in the trades . . .
Just to see you, I come . . .

Anyway, yesterday, I was anglin' my wife
    for some biscuits and red-eyed gravy
And she said she wasn't up to it
    and I got nasty and got to cussin' her out
    and I realized I was in a mood 'cause I know'd
    you wasn't doin' your job.
So I deemed it to deal with my labor problems at work—
'Course I could fire you now
    but I got the feeling you'd thank me for it,
Got the feeling, if you had the excuse,
    you'd go your own way.
I see you, sleeping and reading and collecting that
    government check
    and that doesn't sit well.
Naw, instead, let's dock you, plus five days off
    without pay.

I see you.

Naw, Waterboy,
I got to keep you around here
I want to will you to your next kind a boss,
One of these numbers-crunching, stop-watching, time-checking
    neckties.
Ten days, hell, you'd have ten minutes to cut & trim that
    lawn out back!

Yeah, Waterboy, I got to keep you here
    as my little legacy to the world of work.

Tools

JOHN R. REED

—for Steve Tudor

Some men breed deep attachments to their tools,
knowing the special purpose each instrument serves,
how the square-bar and Phillips screwdriver, for example,
have peculiar vocations, as do the ratchet,
Stillson, and monkey wrench. So the plumber
lays out his pipe-cutter and copper tube
the way a priest selects his vestments, set
to say a mass, and the carpenter holsters
his level, his hammer and nails, his retractable rule,
like the gunslinger you see in films. And often
these men are ex-G.I.s, who learned how certain
inattentions to detail can mean disaster,
or sailors who know the specific intent of every
rope and cleat and understand why
ribbon, wind, and sail agree or not.
And poets, too, can sense the appropriate time
to nail two lines together with a rhyme.

What We Do to Live

JUDITH ROCHE

When they ask you what you do for a living
Tell them what you do to live.
—Mia Johnson

Are you now or have you ever been
a witch against them?
> Yes. I've made my spells
> so daughters could escape.
> I've refused to feed them my sister.
> I've hid my son from their wars.

Are you now or have you ever laughed
in their exhausted assemblies?
> Yes. I've pealed like crystal bells
> crunching under their feet,
> shattered glass sound staying in their ears
> like ghosts to haunt their airways.

Do you now or have you ever
danced their dance or sang their songs?
> Yes, but with a skipped beat
> to transform the rhythm,
> a great vowel shift along the consonants
> to embrace inherent contradictions.

Are you now or have you ever been
naked for them?
> Yes, but I didn't wear their hat
> with the company name on it,
> inhaled deeply
> and only did it for joy,
> weeping openly
> for the lost children in them.

We tie ourselves to great wheels
    and turn toward the wind.
We shift what we carry from arms
    to balance against a hip,
    later to shoulder,
    straining each muscle group
    until it's bloodless before we shift again.
We slit the throat of sleep
    and let our stories soak into sands.
We are forced to lick corruption like salt
    from the palms of their open hands.
Starved,
    we grow thin enough
    to slip through cracks,
    their locked
    file drawers,
    walk down dusty roads,
    bathe in the colors of light refracted tears.
We grow taut and develop
    tensile strength,
    which we use like lines
    to catch loaves and fish
We build bridges to break barriers,
    open prisons to find song.
We put back removed park benches
    to fill the sleepers with green
    dreams of great trees.
We grow flowers
    cut them to braid
    as the long hair of graves.

We practice stubborn refusal in the backseat
We dance together, each to each.

Summer

JUDITH ROCHE

Those wetly heavy summer nights of long twilight,
dishes over, the adults safely on the front step, and
one by one the kids would gather
to play kick-the-can or hide-and-go seek,
a single telephone pole on the corner,
our safe stop, home free.
We ran so fast we hardly knew we were free,
or what it was that later might light
our way down future corridors to each corner
along the way. We just took each step
as the next logical one in front of us to seek
the place where children chase and gather.

Shouting taunts and chants our voices gather
a high pitch of *free! free! free! free!*
we'd tackle each other and roll to seek
the most delirious moments just before streetlights
came on when we'd be stuck on our own front step,
leaving the liberated zone on the corner

deserted at the precise point twilight turned its corner
to indigo night, the sky a seamless gathered
hem to finish day. Grudgingly, we'd step
away from the prescribed space we were free
and into houses lit with thin blue light
of TV, stupid even then. We'd seek
what we needed with each other. Seek
our animal bodies tumbling and turning corners
into the unknown. In those days our own mysterious light
would shine with strong song and gather
all innocent cruelty and joy to our stories set free, flowing
a river of milky stars to step

into before we found the lock-step
of what overtook us. And still we'd seek
our ways in every outlawed action to be free. I'd
dream of horses wheeling and turning corners, of
tall green grass, crossroads gatherings
and rich black starry light.

Since then I've found each step to be a corner
and each seeking a seed to gather
what freedom I could find in purple light.

Work Work Work

TRINIDAD SANCHEZ, JR.

—for Ron Allen

You can work to live or live to work.
If you live to work—you work, work, work.
If you work to live you enjoy life.
You can get it on and you get it off.
You're a person of leisure.
Your life is more than your work,
your work is more than a job,
is a line from a song.
JOBS NOT JAILS!
is a bumper sticker.

Trabajo, illavoro, travail, arbeit, trabrahe—
work is the same in any language.

You can work for free,
work for a fee or your work can be
a labor of love!
Depends on the perspective.
If you see it from the right
you believe in the right to work!
If you view it from the left
you believe in "worker's rights"—right on!
Eight hours of work is a work day—
9 to 5, 4 to 12, 11 to 7.
40 hours of work is a work week
more than this, you are being exploited!

Work, work, work, not easy to define
 but easy to delineate
by those standing in line

to punch a clock
to buy a sandwich off the truck
to catch a bus / to catch a bus
to cash a check . . .
easy to delineate
by those standing in long lines of unemployed, underemployed and food
stamp lines.

Lack of work, over work, under worked
are the conditions of life!
You can become a workaholic
or an alcoholic who works—
a famous side effect of work.

Every mother is a working woman
not all working women are mothers
some workers, you wonder if they had a mother.
Men work three and four jobs
and are labeled dead beat
but it's because they don't want to be
dead broke. Being a mother and father
is not a job but is a lot of work.

Research indicates
Monday is the day most people choose to die
because they don't want to return to work.

So why is it, when rich people work, they become richer,
when poor people work, they become poorer and
when Ron Allen works, he gets tired?

Webster became rich working at defining workable words like:
Work bag   work box   work horse
Work basket   work shop   workmanlike
Work bench   work house   workmanship
Work book   work table   work out . . .
experience has taught us that when you 'break out in a sweat'
you are probably busting your ass at work.

Studs Terkel wrote a best seller on WORKING—
People talking about work and how they feel
about what they do; most felt
"work needed to be redefined"
don't tell Webster!
One worker said: "Work makes a person noble!"

Remember: NAFTA and Fair Trade
are not about making your work place
a better place to work.

Finally and in conclusion
It is all up to you . . .
You can work for the f—— but
"Don't screw up the work"—
that's what the boss said.

Excuse me while I go for a coffee break!

Arise, O Wobblies!

EDWARD SANDERS

On July 7, 1905
    200+ socialists and trade union workers
        met in Chicago
            to overthrow capitalism

They called themselves the Industrial Workers of the World
&, for a reason lost in the chrono-mists
    came to be known as the Wobblies.

They organized unskilled, exploited nonwhites, immigrants
women, migrant workers
    those who were not allowed in the skilled-worker craft unions
    of the American Federation of Labor

        Arise arise on the shores of America
          Wobblies Wobblies

The Wobblies were known for
          the fierce tactics of direct action
    and for their wildly dynamic leaders.
They wanted OBU! One Big Union
to enable the workers
    to own production & distribution

        thus
        Society
        would be
        TRANSFORMED

through on-the-job acts
which, in the elegant words of historian Joyce Kornbluh,
"would wage effective war on the great combinations of capital."

The IWW had an impact
                        much greater than its numbers
(just like the ruling class)

Dues were kept extremely low
                        so as not to exclude
so at its height had 100,000 dues-payers

Arise arise on the shores of America
    Wobblies Wobblies

The Preamble to the IWW Constitution
became famous for
                its clear, revolutionary prose:

"The working class and the employing class
have nothing in common.

There can be no peace so long as hunger and want
are found among millions of working people and the few,
who make up the employing class,
have all the good things of life.

Between these two classes a struggle must go on
until all the toilers come together
        on the political as well as on the industrial field,
and take and hold that which they produce by their labor,
through an economic organization
                of the working class
                without affiliations with any political party . . ."

The money-maddened brokers of power
wanted to laugh at it
        especially ignore it
but they couldn't

Arise arise on the shores of America
    Wobblies Wobblies

From 1905 to say around 1920
            they had their heyday run
They owned what Americans call "guts"—
They REALLY
            did want a rev.

Much of it was done through education:
Billions of words! Galactic fire-squalls of ink!
& they attracted some of the best graphic artists & cartoonists

There were thousands of meetings in ethnic halls
National newspapers (printed in fifteen languages)
Union halls with well-stocked libraries
and a school in Minnesota
            The Work Peoples College

There were summer camps for "junior Wobblies"
& the very very popular *Little Red Songbook*

Joe Hill was a famous iww songwriter
Other Wobbly poets & tune-creators
were Richard Brazzier, Ralph Chaplin, Covington Hall,
Laura Payne Emerson, and T-Bone Slim.

iww songs filled America's air
            on picket lines, in hobo jungles, and from the dais
                        at thousands of meetings
& Chaplin's "Solidarity Forever"
            had a destiny as America's premier labor tune
For a while
            it looked as if the Wobblies
                        were rowing the Boat of Betterment

Seize Power & Sing
on the shores of America
O Wobblies!

The Great Wobbly Free Speech Struggles

EDWARD SANDERS

From their founding in '05 to wwı
   the Wobblies were
        a ceaseless vector
           against the capitalist class

The right wing arrayed itself against them:
police, company mobs, the army, courts, establishment newspapers.

When towns, counties and cities passed laws preventing their free
   speech
      the Wobblies defied the laws

For instance, in Spokane '09
a law banned street meetings

& an ıww organizer was arrested—
A Wob-flood
   marched to Spokane's main drag
      and began to speak
         one by one

till 600 Wobblies were arrested
The jails were horrible, and two Wobblies died there
but finally
   the ıww won
      & could speak in downtown Spokane.

   In Fresno in 'ıı

   another protest for the right of free speech
   again the jails were packed

and Wobblies were singing and giving speeches
　　to supporters and the curious
　　　　gathered outside the jail

Fire trucks were brought
and hosed the prisoners
　　with icy water
　　　　to stop their singing

The Wobblies propped up mattresses to ward off the water
and kept on singing
　　till the water was knee high in their
　　　　　　　　entrapments.

When it was obvious that
more and more Wobblies were coming to Fresno
　　　　to commit civil disobedience

the power structure relented
　　and rescinded the ban on speaking in the streets

There were other Free Speech struggles
　　　　　　　　in many other cities.

How many of our cherished freedoms
to march & speak in the streets
are owed to th' Wobbly men and women
　　　　　　　of 1909?

The Shirtwaist Makers Strike of '09–'10

EDWARD SANDERS

Let us sing the Shirtwaist Makers Strike
     known as the "Uprising of 20,000"
from the genius of teenage immigrant women
November 22, there was at big rally at Cooper Union
        8th St. & 3rd Avenue
Clara Lemlich, one of the farbrente maydelekh
      the burning young women
         arose to speak in Yiddish:

  "I have listened to all the speakers,
  and I have no further patience for talk.
  I am one who feels and suffers from the things pictured.
  I move we go on strike."

15,000 walked out the next morn, growing to 20

  The NY Women's Trade Union League
      surged to glory
 & the male-dominated ILGWU
       was thrown off guard

There was a forgivable optimism
among Women radicals
    who came forward to
  teach the strikers the facts of socialism
  no doubt envisioning
     an American proletariat
        to force a new economy.

There were 20 halls where the strikers were headquartered
The WTUL coordinated the
    picket lines, raising money, bailing out strikers,

setting up parades, getting articles in sympathetic papers,
paying out benefits
                                    & signing up women for the union.

Cap-slime hates this sort of thing
but knows, if anything, how to co-opt

The Socialist women who came aboard
& the Women's Trade Union League both
     pledged support for the central issue:
     recognition of the union
          and the closed union shop.

     This cross-class strike
          was pocked with tergiversation
               and what we shall call here
                         soc-baiting
     (the baiting of Socialists)

This came about when the Women's Trade Union League
                         picked up the support of a few
                              wealthy fellow travelers
notably Alva Belmont, suffragist and rich,
and Anne Morgan, daughter of financier J. P. Morgan

Anne M wanted to ban Socialists in public meetings
to keep them from teaching "their fanatical doctrines."

WTUL refused to defend the Socialists in its midst
     so that some resigned and criticized the WTUL

     An activist named
     Theresa Malkiel was the chief target of Anne Morgan's sneers

     Malkiel wrote a fictionalized autobiography
                    Diary of a Shirtwaist Striker
          & had pointed at "mainstream activists"
                    including suffragists
                              as Class Enemies

The Strike ended in Feb. 1910 without a closed shop agreement
Socialist women blamed their former allies the WTUL

    The shirtmakers' strike
  showed in vividity
        the problems of cross-class efforts
                  to make a change in money.

from *America: A History in Verse*
Volume 1 1900–1939

EDWARD SANDERS

October 15, 1914
>   Congress passed the Clayton Anti-Trust Act, giving labor unions
>   bargaining power in negotiations with management
>   This somewhat strengthened the Sherman Antitrust Act,
>   around since 1890.

>   It exempted unions from the anti-trust law

>   Big biz had spurted in size for 20 years
>   with power blocks forming
>   and all types of industry
>   railroads, farm equip, public utilities,
>   tobacco, oil
>   controlled by single corporations

>   For instance, the baleful
>   monopolist, J. D. Rockefeller
>   hirer of goon-squads
>   had once owned
>   85 percent of domestic oil, and 90 of exports

October-November
>   The Germans came to
>   the little Belgian town
>   known as Ypres

>   for th' first battle of WWI (there were three such battles at Ypres)

By early November
>   Russia, France, Britain
>   bared their guns on Turkey
>   and the weak Ottoman empire
>   (which was supporting Germany).

Meanwhile on election night
    in New York's Lower East Side
        it was party time!
They danced through the cobbled streets till dawn
when Meyer London
    whose father had worked in an
        anarchist print shop
was elected a socialist to the
    u.s. Congress!

London said,
    "As a Socialist
    instead of denying the existence
        of the class struggle
    I seek to minimize its bitterness"

(London was trapped inside
    one of those ghastly sociologic sandwiches
    he wasn't left enough for the left
    nor right enough for the pro-war right

and the Zionists disliked him because
    he refused to endorse a home for Jews in Palestine.

Dems and Reps united behind a single "patriotic" candidate
        and axed London in 1918

though in '20 he rewon his seat
but then odious gerrymandering
    so much a tool of the Republicrats
        axed him again in 1922)

    Meanwhile, nothing can prevent
      the fine knowledge
        of the night-long party
          in the Lower East Side
    when the socialist Meyer London
        knew glory.

The Injustice against Debs

EDWARD SANDERS

The great Eugene Debs
    came to a jail in Canton, Ohio
                on June 16, 1918
    to visit three socialists who opposed the draft

    then across the street he spoke
        two hours to supporters

Among his many sentences:
". . . That is war in a nutshell.
The master class has always declared the wars,
the subject class has always fought the battles."

"The sun of capitalism is setting," said Debs
and the sun of Socialism is rising. . . .
    In due time
    there will come the hour to
    proclaim the emancipation
        of the working class
        and the brotherhood
        of all mankind."

        Go, Debs, Go!

He was arrested within days
for violating the Espionage Act
in that there were draft-age kids in the audience
    & his language tended to
        "obstruct the recruiting or enlistment service."

    Wilson kept him in jail
        the rest of his term

The Hard Way Was the Only Way You Knew

VIVIAN SHIPLEY

Daddy, now it is just your smell that is heavy,
musky as buttonweed with bare dark stems, thick
and knobby, that I helped you chop out of field corn

in Kentucky. Slip a hook around a woody branch,
thicker than a thumb, yank back hard and roots
would pull out, but a stem of five or six feet hung

on, vining stalks until the first heart-shaped leaf.
Not like you, I'd peter out, have enough sense
to quit after a few rows when sharp-edged leaves

of corn sliced my hands. Stiff with bristles
at their base, small white and pale purple flowers
were funnels like a megaphone for you, my father

the cheerleader, trying to get me back on the field.
Goading never worked: I was weak as smoke from
wet wood fire, lazy as a fattening hog, would not

work trying out mattresses, or in a candy store.
Preaching never failed: nothing worth knowing
slips from a straight trunk, is gotten without a pull.

Pink Slip

BETSY SHOLL

Twenty years I gripped your press,
yanked down as the belt rattled past.
You stamped my checks, the bank sent letters saying
what I owed on my house, my car,
my teeth. Now the expressway roars overhead, and
how can I argue back, when I can't

even get my car out of the tow lot?
Inside the gatekeeper's shed a TV surfs
out of control: soap commercial, canned laughter,
profile of Martin Luther King, skinny woman stepping
out of a fat woman's clothes
as I would like to step out of this night

onto the last day of earth and accuse you once
again, only now with smoke and lights, some kind
of music to back me up:
how my kids are the same age as yours, my kids,
with too many teeth in their heads, and one who
still can't pronounce "thr—."

All you did was to check your watch, all
you did was back me to the door,
where outside they were hauling my car,
a pirate company, so not even the cops could say
where it is. Is this America?
I've seen countries on TV where the natives

give funny looks to the fat men they serve drinks to
on patios. "Bastard," would be
my translation. Or whatever the deaf woman is
banging onto the locked windows of cars jammed at

the on-ramp trying to leave the city. You on your top
floor look down, waiting

for the crowd to thin, you with those women in
high heels printing out memos that shut
down a whole plant. You're calm now.
But if just one loony on the picket line decides to
fling a bucket of paint,
if a pack of kids with bats comes hooting out

of a bar, you wouldn't have a clue.
One more John Doe in fancy clothes, high-class
words foaming on your lips,
but just as helpless, you bastard,
at the end of the world, if there is an end,
if people like me get to rise up and speak.

Little Guy

MARC KELLY SMITH

I'm for the little guy.
I'm for the guy who lost the fight
That day on the school yard
When the bully stole the nerd's hat
And the nerd let him have it,
The hat, that is,
And it wasn't right.
Demanded fight.
So the little guy nobody
Stepped forward and said,
"Hey, You can't do things like that,"
And the bully laughed.
"Oh yeah. Watch this."
And pushed little guy nobody's face
Into the chain link fence,
Massaged it there
While the nerd looked on
Mewling. "It's only a hat.
It's only a hat."
Until the little guy nobody
Had had enough of being a hero.
Feeling the knots
Of the chain link fence
Cut into his cheeks.
And called it quits.
Yeah. I'm for that guy
Walkin' away feelin' like shit.
Feelin' as if he'd lost something
Losin' to a guy twice his size,
Because, in the movies, a real hero
Chops those bullies down.
Rights the situation.

But it never worked out that way for this kid,
Righteous though he was,
And in his lifetime he found out
That the bullies were always winnin'.
And the nerds were always helpless.

And caught between them,
Forever pathetically engaged,
Were guys like him
Trying to set things right,
Trying to undo the damage,
Trying to live in accordance with ancient ideals
That even in ancient times
Must have been just that,
Ideals.

But what the hell, I'm for him
Whoever he is.
Because, even today,
When it comes to a stolen hat,
A stolen chance, a stolen you name it,
He stands up
Right in the face of it,
Come what may, and says,
"Hey . . .
         . . . HEY!
You can't do things like that."

Day Worker

LAMONT B. STEPTOE

. . . and much of her life would be spent on her knees in white folks' kitchens
. . . or with her back to the sun with huge windows across her thighs, feet
dangling inside, hands full of damp, wet newspaper shining the thick glass
. . . but she would leave these "mansions" these "out to the houses" as she
called them, she would. leave them with shopping bags full of old clothes,
unwanted food . . . yes, she would leave with this and think how kind these
white people were . . . she would take these "gifts" back with her to her
"third floor home" and teach her sons how to be gentle, how to be gentle . . .

. . . momma . . . momma . . . after all those cold winters, after all those
hot summers, after all those years of your life you gave to those white people for our sake, how can it be that you could teach us how to be gentle? do
you know what that has cost me, momma? do you know how many city
streets i've walked? do you know how many times i've cried? do you know
the madness i've endured?

. . . and when buses weren't running because of snow or strike, she
would walk. she would bundle up in old clothes and new clothes . . . she
would wear the majority of her meager wardrobe to keep warm . . . she
would keep her son home from school so she could wear his boots, keep her
daughter from work, so she could wear her overcoat . . . but she would go,
she would walk . . . she would freeze but she'd go to do her floors, her dusting, her wall washing . . . she would go . . .

. . . she'd be one of many of this race of black women, who would walk
or limp or shuffle on frostbitten feet, feet full of corns because they never
wore shoes meant for them, feet swollen by dampness, cellar dampness, feet
wore-out-walked-out, used up feet, feet only kept going by hot salt baths at
night and corns trimmed by razor blades . . .

. . . these were the feet of this army of women who were "day workers"
to survive . . . the years would pass and the faces would sag, the breasts
become limp and rest on bellies, the feet more grotesque and misshapen, the
hands gnarled and rough, the hair grayer and grayer, the back more and more
painful, the teeth fewer and fewer . . . but still they would go . . . they would
go until they died of sunstroke on some hot summer afternoon with the

heavy windows across their thighs or their high blood pressure would kill them as they scrubbed some kitchen floor and they fell face first in the soap suds, or they would complain of headaches and backaches for a week or so and then one day go home and die . . . but they would go and do those same windows and same floors year after year . . . this was what they were caught in . . . this vicious trap . . . with every swipe of the mop, one more dream would be forgotten, one more hot-cold-rush-of-youth used up, dried out, dusted off, hung up, put away . . . forever, forever, forever . . .

Seamstress

LAMONT B. STEPTOE

—for Guadalupe Leon

she stitched for years on machines the whirr in her ears forever

the needle a blur a blinding blur she stitched and sewed sewed

and stitched the whirr in her ears in her blood in her bones the work

was necessary and numbing numbing and necessary she joined and

seamed seamed and joined stitching and stitching and stitching

stitching the father to the house the house to the father the son to the

world the job to the cross stitching forever stitching the whirr of the

machine in her bones in her dreams in the Puerto Rican dishes she

prepared the whirr of the machine there always there stitching her son to

school to railroads of light joining and seaming finally left to stitch her

husband to death even in retirement stitching her life to grandchildren

grandchildren to God stitching joining seaming Spanish to English

Carribbean beauty to Philadelphia barrio stitching joining seaming her

spirit to God her bones to her land her dust her sunrise her rhythmic

nights of Afro-Taino-Spanish blues

Poem for My Brother Timmy

QUINCY TROUPE

We walked streets
of river-rhythm town counting
cars that passed
for nothing else better to do
warm cold days now packed
away in straw

& when at home on Delmar
& Leonard streets, living over Joe's
Super Market, on weekends
would repeat from our window
the same ritual
all over again

this counting of passing cars
(you took the Fords
eye took the Chevrolets
but the Cadillacs would win.)

& from our window on saturday nights
we would watch the drunken fights
across the street
at Meyer's tavern
where people died with
ridiculous ease from street surgeons' knives

Summers brought picnics & barbecues
baseball games & hot funky parties
where we styled hard laid off
in bad summer rags

& on warm idle days
on concrete playground courts

eye would beat the hell out of you
playing basketball until it got dark

In winter, we would bundle up tight
in fast shrinking clothes
bought three years before
when daddy was making money playing baseball
in Batista's Cuba, or bought when
mother was working downtown being
a deskclerk at Sonnenfeld's

& on frozen winter nights
we would fight like two vicious alley cats
over who pulled the cover off of who
afterwards, we would sleep side by side
in the dark in our own spilt blood

& if someone was ever foolish enough
to mess with either one of us
they had to contend with the both
of us sho-nuff righteously stompin
eleven-thousand corns on their
                              sorry asses

But time has worn away those days
as water rubs smooth in time
                    a rough & jagged stone

You took the blues of those days
filled with sun dues & blood & turned them
into rhythms you played
superbly on your talking drums
before you heard the calling of your Lord sanctified

Eye took that beautiful song
you gave to me & turned into poetry
this poem eye give to you now

with a brother's deep love

This Is Not My Beautiful House: Five Uncanny Sites

CHRIS TYSH

And chance which has spared us
Choice, which has shielded us
As if a god. What is the name of that place
We have entered
—George Oppen

666 WILLIS

The Alpine would've been an innocuous building were it not for its devil's number and nightly filles de joie strategically deployed at the SE corner of Willis and Third, a sort of permanent 3D promo for the Willis Show Bar; high-ass and rouged to death. "Come on, honey, you know you want it!"

Inside we dance to our own nerve war, confusing transparency with lack as in Richard Pryor's inimitable words, "I have no place to ride my horsy." Whose mouth will break the pale green walls of these morals? There are lovers parked on a sofa, oblivious to the soft rain of gunshots, endless smoking, some-one else's huge dog left behind as a reminder it is not over between us. Under the neon martini glass, the night's at a loss for words. I grope for my key in the dark corridor. Here's the door to the communal bathroom, one per floor, slimy concrete and the din of fear. I press it open and all hell breaks loose: in the deafening alarm, wave after wave of scorn washes at my feet while the fleshy super barks, "Whatsa matter with ya, you simple or sumpthin? Off the boat," she adds more to herself. In my head a bomb goes off after the noise dies down. I forget what I say when I return to the crowded room.

87 PURITAN

A commune, it was not. Although with its six bedrooms and generous pro-portions, it would've made perfect sense for some underground politicos in search of a cause. I could just picture morning's assemblies in the high-ceilinged dining room, discussing the merits of shoplifting or eradicating the notion of the couple for being hopelessly bourgeois. But let's face it! The '60s were gone and only chance, dressed and disheveled like some street maniac, had thrown us together pell-mell into this foolish arrangement.

215

I distinctly remember names neatly penciled on various sundries in the refrigerator: Rachel's milk, Sharon's cheese, X's coffee, as if an entire summer camp was stashing its goodies in our kitchen. There was something particularly distasteful to these crude cries, "it's mine!" and decades later I can't help but laugh at those pathetic engravings in perishables and wish someone had switched labels, wreaked havoc, just to see the owners' discomfit. Toutes proportions gardées, like the Czechs did with the street-signs when the Russians invaded Prague in 1956.

39 MOSS

Finally, we are able to begin somewhere; a boy or a girl is on its way in the sweetly complicated transaction we call love. Curtainless windows disclose the news and sweep all corruptions away. Oh how I love this moment's light like a billboard painting of ordinary objects: big American cars glide on the avenue; "I heard it through the grapevine" swells my nipples, the women say it's like heaven when it happens. Down by the river, G. and G. haul mail onto the Westcott, the only boat in the whole world to have its own zip code: 48222. We have black τ-shirts printed, white letters stretching across our breasts as if we owned an island or record company.

It must be spring and the whole house mimics my fortune, open and flowing to the unfolding profusion of cells. Here's the clarity we yearn for. A rustle in the yard catches my breath: I spy a teenager holding a small gun, perfectly still, as if posing for a photograph or looking for a context to place his gesture.

11843 FLEMING

Stella was a bitch the way other people are concierges or hairdressers, that is, licensed and practicing. She lived in one of those closely packed wooden houses built for the Detroit working class around the '20s when Dodge Main became the daily bread of thousands pressing at its gates. You could stand on the porch and, looking either way, see a perfect vista down to the end of the block. It made you think of the scene in *The Odyssey* when the aged Ulysses disguised in rags takes up Penelope's challenge to shoot a single arrow clean through all twelve axes. Uniformity, solidarity of perspective were as much part of the design as two-by-fours, rail nails and elevation points. They leveled any frivolous notions of difference. These homes, these stamp-sized lawns were now your pastless legacies, your world of cramped contingencies.

Did I mention she was the landlady of the never-washed heels, blackened and crusty as a pumpernickel? Stella didn't approve of high heels nor of people who wrote you postcards in illegible script. She scowled, not even close to feeling guilty for reading folks' mail. "I didn't know you were pregnant! Are you gonna move now or what?" "You bet!" All the paczkis in the world couldn't keep me another day under your thumb, sad-eyed lady of distrust.

2371 PULASKI

In this "touch of Europe" neighborhood, Maruka and I are neighbors, both mothers with young children. From her, I learn to drink Turkish coffee in dainty demitasses as if I'd done nothing else for years. I don't push my zeal as far as grinding my own beans in a long brassy mill like Maruka uses. There are limits to my penchant for ethnic . . . engouement. I almost wrote the word ethnic purity and practically gagged at the thought, my mind traveling to barbed wire camp, mass grave and unspeakable suffering no well-intentioned Hague court will ever appease. I don't shave my boys' heads either like Tommy's mom "good for health," she points out while a ragtag gang of six-year-olds races their big wheels, cheeks chubby and angelic, their convict dos nonobstant. I don't get up either when males enter my purview to wait on them hand and foot, but where I come from, men are supposed to hold doors, coats and lighters until we deign to murmur a thank you.

One day I ask Maruka if she and the girls would like to go to the park with us, wanting to get her out of the house, something her vast clan never bothers with. She says she'll be right there. Give me a sec. Sure, no problem. My boys and I pace up and down wondering what's taking her so long, ready to just leave her behind if she doesn't step on it. And then there she is: 6' Albanian beauty, made up from head to toe, chiffon dress, high heel pumps, dark hose, hair freshly set, à la Charlie's Angels, shiny leather purse, smiling timidly like a young girl on a first date. My eyes fill with tears thinking of the ratty park we're headed for, not even a bench to frame such longing, not even a tree to rest her heart.

Lakeshore Drives

ANCA VLASOPOLOS

When first I came to Detroit they took me, well-wishers,
to show me the materialized American dream
what
if I persisted and worked very very hard
I still could never have

They drove me of course
past the mansions facing Lake Saint Clair
and said, loud and pointing, because they weren't sure
I knew enough English to understand,
"Look, look,"
while my eyes, I being still more than half child,
could not unglue themselves
from the immensity of pale-blue water

Over the years I too drove visitors by
studying the huge houses where children never played
on conspicuous lawns leaching slowly
lethal soup into the water table
guarded by hedges coiffed in razor-sharp style
that each spring tried in vain to grow into themselves

When I say there isn't one house that I like
it isn't the death of desire this time
merely an escalation of standards
or perhaps there is one that I like
but it's farther north, past the yacht club
where the big houses hog all the shore again
only I can't be sure
I can only catch a glimpse of it from the fast flow
on this street where every fifty feet
there's a sign

NO
Parking
No Standing
No Stopping
No Fishing
No Swimming
No Picnicking
No Loitering
Even No Biking Nor Walking
if you're wearing a skin a shade or two darker
than what Crayola used to call "flesh"
unless it's covered by a maid's or gardener's uniform
or it's a South American tan in midwinter
No Being an unruly woman who shouts
at the rude future Captains of Commerce and Industry
whizzing by on rollerblades at perilous speeds
"Assholes, little pricks, emphasis on little"
trust me I know

Today, dense February, the houses have vanished
there is no lake no shore
signs appear every few feet
intermittent negations
all else vaporized
NO . . . NO . . . NO . . .

Trees twisted by offshore winds
beyond any landscaper's cure
float
out of all context of earth and sky
rise
like specters from what this shore once was
reach
in this preternatural hush
as if to claim their due

Window Repair

MICK VRANICH

captured by your own body
forced to pay attention
to the fragile parts
sitting at this altar
called a window
watching the blue jay
pick up a peanut
off the sawhorse
on the back porch
up hill down hill
the level killing field
staring at a piece of blue
through the hole in the wall
morning must be here
the sun must be shining
burning up in the fury
the way it does so
constantly we think
is a steady stream of heat
and power getting closer
we got to go and fix some
broken windows in the apartment
house on second avenue
single room occupant
old folks home battleship
gray hallways army green trim
we can only look at the sky
we can't be in it
we are in it at ground level
the wind is gentle today
everything stays in place
for awhile.

The Butcher's Apron

DIANE WAKOSKI

When I was a child, we lived in the midst of orange groves on Russell Street in East Whittier, California, just up the road from the Nixon family grocery store, where I bought my popsicles from old Mr. and Mrs. Nixon, father and mother of the late president. When they expanded, adding a much bigger butcher's counter and a coffee shop, their son Don Nixon, later featured in real estate scandals, became the butcher.

—for Edward Allen

Red stains on the clean white bib,
the butcher's apron hanging like an abstract expressionist painting,
on the museum wall of my
childhood.

—the most we ever ordered—
a pound of hamburger
to be fried in the black iron skillet
till the edges formed an ugly crust
like a scab on a skinned knee/
The art of the grill
was not found in our manless house.

The beauty of the red on the butcher's
white canvas, which occasionally streaked like an etching
across the white butcher paper
in which he wrapped the chuck, never translated
to the food eaten: grey meats
like steel wool, canned vegetables
with the colors of hospital walls,
sliced white bread like old often-washed
sheets and pillowcases.

My shock one day in the school cafeteria
to see Carol Gregory
    whose mother sewed her
    dresses as elegant as those in
    Vogue magazine
unwrap a waxed paper packet of bright red
meat, in a puddle of something thin and dark/
to realize it was
Roast Beef,
the puddle
was beef blood! There in the Lowell School cafeteria
I saw my first still-life painting, beautiful and
different food among the thermoses
of milk, the wax wrapped peanut
butter or bologna sandwiches. Perhaps
I have added this detail:
    next to Carol's rare roast beef slices,
    another piece of waxed paper on which
    was spread
        several spears of bright green
        asparagus.
Food eaten by kids whose parents were rich
or had been to college
was different,
was like a painting?

My first-generation American mother grew up
in a house with a dirt floor, went to school
in a one-room schoolhouse. She drank German
coffee instead of milk
as a child. She lifted herself out
of North Dakota, became a bookkeeper
but never learned
about food, the telltale class
marking. In old age, she loves salty things like
Campbell's soups, frozen enchiladas in processed cheese sauce,
bacon white bread sandwiches, and hates the nursing hospital

where they don't salt the food at all.

Plath imagined blood red tulips in white hospitals
as I think of Georgia O'Keeffe's poppies.
My mother who voted for Nixon and hates foreigners
dreams of those red and white cans
which might hold Chicken Noodle or Tomato
soups. She's never heard of Andy Warhol who
mimicked such cans, just as a butcher I talked to in our Michigan
supermarket said that he had never eaten
shrimp, or knew what people did with oxtails. His apron
too had the same bright red stains, not yet faded into
rust. Crimson blood on canvas, the art
of childhood. Unhealed scars,
still capable of bleeding.

—*from* The Emerald City of Las Vegas

Tony's Dad

BARRY WALLENSTEIN

carried him across a river of blood.

The fat in the slaughterhouse,
in the stone room
adjacent to the killing rooms,
would clog in the drain
and the steers' blood puddled
high enough for a young Tony
to need either hip boots
or a lift onto father's difficult shoulders.

Tony loves to tell the story:
"As a small boy I hugged a white butcher's coat
blotted red. By the end of the day
slick and greasy, more red than white
already, during the ride, foul and smelly
and I was right in it, almost joyful
and afraid especially of the butchers' eyes
as they turned from the knives and hooks
to my position on the boss's back.

He was their boss
not mine exactly, but
blame him not now for my imagination
then about bosses and papas and
different kinds of muscle than my own.
And what did I own really,
other than the lift and carry?

They bled the cattle
but clubbed the calves—
all to do with the taste of the meat
and young as I was, I studied it."

1943

MARY ANN WEHLER

We lived on the border. I never knew why I walked over a mile to Guyton Elementary when Keating was so close. I never questioned why I was allowed to ride my bike on Grosse Pointe streets, never towards Conner Avenue and the old Hudson plant. One black family, the father a doctor, lived in a big house on Marlborough Boulevard. The only street I knew paved with bricks. Riding my bike, I'd pretend I was on the Road to Oz. Even the porch was brick, not wood like ours. Two wooden rocking chairs with ruffled cushions, a rug spread beneath; no one ever sat there. The doctor's son was the only black child at Guyton. Most folks were renters.

When my father started on the day shift, eating supper with us, words like *nigger, polack, kike,* and *spick* were served with the meal. He mouthed J. Edgar Hoover's FBI alleging Mrs. Roosevelt had Negro blood.If I snuck a ride in the wrong direction most faces on the porch were brown or black. 1943, year of the Belle Isle riot, four miles from my house, WWII, I never got that far. No one on my street had a car. The fathers took buses or streetcars to the auto plants, built tanks or airplanes. Mothers walked to the grocery store daily, holding ration stamps in their handbags. The *Detroit News* said, "Eleanor Roosevelt urges Detroit to allow Blacks in the Sojourner Truth Housing Project." Next in pecking order, the Polish community, didn't know Sojourner was an African Heroine, but objected. 200 Negro families were moved into the project; the riots began. Weren't there whispers, talk on my block? Was it kept from me?

June, 1943, our street, Piper, the border, between rich and blue collar, a street of flats. No rockers on the porches; people sat on the steps. Twenty-five years later, driving from the airport to their Florida condo, Father baited me. *Niggers live on the other side of Federal Highway,* watching for my reaction in the rearview mirror, he couldn't wait to start a fight. That night Flip Wilson clowned on "The Ed Sullivan Show." *Makes you believe in evolution.* Having a daughter who knew he'd been scared all his life stuck in his craw. He's buried in a vault in Boca, safe from his hates.

Ode to Elizabeth

JOE E. WEIL

"Grimy Elizabeth," *Time* magazine intones.
This city escaped the race riots
Never quite sank and, consequently, never rose.
It's not a town for poets.
You live here, you work the factory or a trade.
Down the burg, in Peterstown,
Italian bricklayers sit
on stoops, boxes, chairs, playing poker
into one a.m.
Drive up Elizabeth Avenue
and you'll hear the salsa music blast from every window.
Even the potted geraniums dance.
In La Palmita, old Cuban guys sip coffee
from little plastic cups.
They talk politics, prizefights, Castro,
soccer, soccer, soccer.

Our Mayor looks like a lesser Mayor Daley:
smokes cigars, wears loud plaid suits,
the penultimate used-car salesman.
He's been in since '64, a Mick with a machine.
He's re-elected because he's a consistent evil
and, here in Elizabeth, we appreciate consistency.

Half the law of life is hanging out, hanging on
to frame houses, pensions.
Every Sunday, ethnic radio: Irish hour, Polish hour,
Lithuanian hour. My father sits in the kitchen
listening to Kevin Barry.
He wishes he could still sing.
Two years ago, they cut his voice box out:
Cigarettes, factory, thirty years' worth of

double shifts. My father's as grimy as Elizabeth,
as sentimental, crude.
He boxed in the Navy, bantamweight.
As a kid I'd beg him to pop a muscle
And show off his tattoo.

We are not the salt of the earth.
I've got no John Steinbeck illusions.
I know the people I love have bad taste
In furniture. They are likely to buy
Crushed-velvet portraits of Elvis Presley
And hang them next to the Pope.
They fill their lives with consumer goods,
Leave the plastic covering on sofas
And watch *Let's Make a Deal.*
They are always dreaming the lottery number
That almost wins.
They are staunch Democrats who voted for Reagan.
They are working class, laid off when
Singer's closed, stuck between chemical dumps and oil
refineries in a city where Alexander Hamilton
once went to school.
In the graveyard by the courthouse,
lie Caldwells, Ogdens, Boudinots.
Milton is quoted on their graves.
Winos sleep there on summer afternoons
under hundred-year-old elms.
They sleep on the slabs of our Founding Fathers
and snore for History.
I have no illusions.

The Irish of Kerry Head have vanished,
but up in Elmora, you still can see
the Jewish families walking home from synagogue.
They are devout, they are well-dressed,
They read the Talmud.
Twelve years ago, I used to go to the Elmora Theater
with twenty other kids.
It was a run-down movie house that never

got the features till they'd been out a year.
Because the Elmora was poor, it showed
foreign films; art films we didn't know were art:
Fellini, Wertmuller, Bergman. It cost a dollar to get in.

We'd sit there, factory workers' kids, half hoods,
watching *Amarcord*.
When the grandfather climbed the tree
in *Amarcord* and screamed, "I want a woman!,"
we all agreed.
For weeks, Anthony Bravo went around school
screaming, "I want a woman!" every chance he got.
I copped my first feel there,
saw *Hester Street, The Seduction of Mimi*.
Once they had a double feature:
Bruce Lee's *Fists of Fury* with Ingmar Bergman's
The Seventh Seal.
I remember two hundred kids exploding
when Jack Nicholson choked the nurse in *Cuckoo's Nest*.
Sal Rotolo stood up, tears streaming down his face,
screaming, "Kill the bitch! Kill that fuckin' nurse!"
and when they took Jack's soul away,
we all sat there silent.
It lingered with us all the way home,
empty-eyed and sad.
Here in Elizabeth, the tasteless city,
where *Amarcord* was allowed to be just another flick,
where no one looked for symbols,
or sat politely through the credits.
If Art moved us at all, it was with real amazement;
we had no frame of reference.

And so I still live here,
because I need a place where poets are not expected.
I would go nuts in a town where everyone read Pound,
where old ladies never swept their stoops
or poured hot water on the ants.
I am happiest in a motley scene,
stuck between Exxon and the Arthur Kill . . .

I don't think Manhattan needs another poet.
I don't think Maine could use me.
I'm short, I'm ugly, I prefer Mrs. Paul's Fish Sticks
to blackened redfish.
I don't like to travel because I've noticed
no matter where you go, you take yourself with you,
and that's the only thing I care to leave behind.
So I stay here.
At night, I can still hear mothers yelling,
"Michael, supper! Get your ass in gear!"
Where nothing is sacred, everything is sacred;
where no one writes, the air seems strangely
charged with metaphor.
In short, I like a grimy city.
I suspect "Culture" because it has been given over
to grants, credentials, and people with cute haircuts.
I suspect Poetry because it talks to itself
too much, tells an inside joke.
It has forgotten how to pray.
It has forgotten how to praise.
Tonight, I write no poem. I write to praise.
I praise the motley city of my birth.
I write to be a citizen of Elizabeth, New Jersey.
like a goddamned ancient Greek, I stand for this smallest
bit of ground, my turf, this squalid city.
Here, in the armpit of the beast.
Tonight, the ghosts of Ogdens, Caldwells, Boudinots
walk among the winos.
They exist in the salsa music blaring on Elizabeth Avenue.
They rise up and kiss the gargoyles of Cherry Street.
They are like King David dancing naked
unashamed before the covenant.
even the stones can praise.
The Irish dead of Kerry Head are singing in their sleep,
and I swear, the next time someone makes a face,
gives me that bite the lemon look, as if to say,
"My Gawd . . . How can you be a poet and live
In that stinking town?" My answer will be swift:
I'll kick him in the balls.

Father Hunger and Son

ROGER WEINGARTEN

A pedestal ashtray next to the son who hadn't seen
or spoken to his father for years of blame, and another
man wrapped in a coat, both hands pressed
into a fist between his thighs, the cleanshaven
pendulum of his chin muttering under a petrified
tear that magnified the bloodshot corner. Jealous
of his thirty years side-by-side with my father
working the phones for sales, I assumed his grief
was for the tenuous life at the far end
of the corridor suspended between
a bag of blood and a monitors
vigilance. I touched his shoulder like a stranger
interrupting another on an empty bus. He'll be okay.
Who? he answered, as he grabbed
the ashtray and pulled it to him, whispering
through something stuck in his throat
that he'd found an unmailed
letter from his wife to another man
sticking out from under
the car seat as he'd reached to turn the key
that morning in the garage. I want him to masturbate
to death, he said. You can see
your father now, the nurse told me.
After I passed my stepsister and Aunt Delilah, her eyebrows
raised into dollar signs beneath a pale
beehive, my stepmother pulled me aside and said,
Why are you here? You're not welcome. You'll kill him
if you step foot in that room. I pushed
my sad cuckold into a cab that dropped us
in the industrial flats under cranes looming
by the revolving bridge of my childhood
over the river that burned once. While we tried

to light it again with matchbooks and wads
of old receipts from his pockets, scraps
of smoke drifting nowhere, he wanted to know
what I thought he should say to his wife. I asked him
if my father loved me. He hunkered down
and stared at his wingtips. When your mother
left him for that other guy, something
died inside of him. I'm not saying he didn't laugh
or give a shit about anyone. But if
your name came up—which was almost
never—you could see something
sidestep in his face, like he was dodging
a sucker punch. What do I know after thirty years
of lunches and hustle? I worked for the bastard.
He signed the checks like clockwork every week.
As I started to cry, he said, C'mere, child,
crying too and pulling me
to his sandpaper cheek. I don't know my wife
any better than your old man. Or anyone else
for that matter. I don't know.

The Big Three Killed My Baby

JACK WHITE

The Big Three killed my baby
no money in my hand again
the Big Three killed my baby
nobody's coming home again

Their ideas made me want to spit
a hundred dollars goes down the pit
30,000 wheels are rollin'
and my stick shift hands are swollen
everything involved is shady
the Big Three killed my baby

The Big Three killed my baby
no money in my hand again
the Big Three killed my baby
nobody's coming home again

Why don't you take the day off and try to repair
a billion others don't seem to care
better ideas are stuck in the mud
the motors runnin' on Tucker's blood
don't let them tell you the future's electric
cause gasoline's not measured in metric
30,000 wheels are spinnin'
and oil company faces are grinnin'
now my hands are turnin' red
and I found out my baby is dead

The Big Three killed my baby
no money in my hand again
the Big Three killed my baby
nobody's coming home again

Well I've said it now, nothing's changed
people are burnin' for pocket change
and creative minds are lazy
and the Big Three killed my baby

And my baby's my common sense
so don't feed me planned obsolescence
yeah my baby's my common sense
so don't feed me planned obsolescence
I'm about to have another blow-up
I'm about to have another blow-up

I Hear America Singing

WALT WHITMAN

I hear America singing, the varied carols I hear,
Those of mechanics, each one singing his as it should be blithe and strong,
The carpenter singing his as he measures his plank or beam,
The mason singing as he makes ready for work, or leaves off work,
The boatman singing what belongs to him in his boat, the deckhand singing
    on the steamboat deck,
The shoemaker singing as he sits on his bench, the hatter singing as he stands,
The wood-cutter's song, the ploughboy's on his way in the morning, or at
    noon intermission or at sundown,
The delicious singing of the mother, or of the young wife at work, or of the
    girl sewing or washing,
Each singing what belongs to him or her and to none else,
The day what belongs to the day—at night the party of young fellows, robust,
    friendly,
Singing with open mouths their strong melodious songs.

2

SHORT FICTION

Turn the Radio to a Gospel Station

JEANNE BRYNER

Every night here at Riverbend General it's the same stuff over and over. Babies grab their mamas' hot curling irons from the dresser or root around grandmas' purses. They swaller pain pills like baby shower mints or suck down blood pressure tablets which can stop a heart. Young girls, who haven't got their period for three months, find out they're in the family way, then act surprised. Pretty women from Preston County show up with black eyes, from falling down. Men squirm and wiggle and sweat with chest pain.

Maybe you don't know it but there are tubes for every hole in the body. And if the doctor takes a notion, he cuts another hole, makes a new place for a tube. Laws, I never seen so much trouble in one spot as this here 'mergency room. The supervisor put me here to clean since Thelma had her back surgery. I surely hope Thelma's coming along. This is no place for a God-fearing woman to work. No sir.

Merle, one of the dayturn girls, told me our lobby has bulletproof glass around the girls who register the sick ones. "Why we need that kind of glass in a hospital?" I asked her. She said, "Wait a week or two, you'll see how folks get when their babies are puking and their legs are broke and they call the whole family in for a death. They're mad but they don't know who to hit. They're hurting, not just on the red blistered and burned skin or the bleeding places but deep, deep inside. Sometimes, they march over to the dead one, grab her face, and yell *Why? Why? Why?* 'Course the dead ain't got no answer. They just lay there getting bluer and stiffer and colder in those thin cotton gowns. Sometimes, a preacher comes, and sometimes, that helps. Sometimes, can't nothing help. Take that grandma who had those little boys in her car. She left them for not more than two minutes to fetch her mail. One of those little fellers got the car in gear and drove it straight into her pond. Firemen came with axes and chains. They broke windows and winched the station wagon back to the yard's dry place. Firemen said them little fellers was pounding with their fists and yelling until the pond water swallered them like minnies. The grandma, she was right there screaming in her orange polyester pants, telling the firemen to hurry up and save her daughter's babies. Our nurses and doctor worked and worked on those soggy towhead boys, but the Lord done took them angels home. Their daddy and mama came then. Behind the curtain, I saw Twila and Gail, crying over them angels when they was pulling out needles and tubes. Twila and Gail 'bout the youngest nurses on second shift. I saw they was gentle when they washed and combed and wrapped those sweet babies in blankets and finally, handed them to their mama. They sent me to Labor and Delivery to fetch a rocking chair. It was maple, and though it did not seem heavy, I was plum out of breath after hurrying and pushing it from the elevators. Their mama rocked and cried and rocked and sang them a lullaby. Her arms holding death like that, just singing soft and low. Their daddy was all leaned over them, stroking their faces and saying their names, *Timmy and Tommy.* Me, I was on the other side of the curtain, kept shoving gloves into a box and pulled trash in the next room. My nose ran just like a faucet while I heared them twin names being wrote in the holy book. When the doctor told her those little boys was dead, the grandma done fainted and cut her head. She had to get herself sewed up. Her heart was blew apart like an old tire. I saw it in her eyes.

"Sorrow makes 'em crazy," Merle went on, "and with all the cutbacks, they took away our security guard. I liked curly Burl. He was good with the drunks and crazies. Something about seeing a uniform and a shiny badge I figure."

Merle showed me this job. She spins a good story and wrings a mean mop. She's been here ten years longer than me. She knows dirt about the big shots' wives and the maintenance men. Once, on midnights, she caught a doctor with two women in the laundry (a girl from the kitchen and one from the lab). Naked. All of them. Sickness. A body just got to keep her head down and squeeze dirty water from the mop night after night.

Most of our nurses are good girls: clean shoes, shiny hair, pressed uniforms. But there's a couple who won't give patients a call light. I hear them snickering 'bout it by the station. I seen an old lady press her buzzer, then wait and wait for the nurse to come. Finally, the old lady pooped in her hand. When the nurse walked around the curtain, the old lady gave it a sling. 'Course the old lady, she wasn't right in her head, but the nurse she was surprised about poop hitting her just like that and madder than a mule with a burr in his ear. After they washed her and changed her sheets, the nurses tied the old lady up, strapped her down, and gave her a shot. Then, the old lady laid there moaning about Mamie Eisenhower making corncob jelly. I don't figure she even knows she's in Brier County. No. I don't 'spose she knows she's on this planet. No sir. I don't believe half the folks here even know they're walking straight up.

In the broom closet, there's a list of my What To Dos on a yellow paper. Everyday, I know what to clean, stock, dust, and when to strip and wax floors. Dusting is everyday. Mopping is dayturn's job and night's if we get time. I do it here like I do at home. I mop whenever mud and slop gets tracked. Blood is everybody's business. Not one drop is to stay on the floor. Not one. Dirty needles are 'sposed to go in red containers with lids. Thelma's daughter got the jaundice from a needle when she was pulling trash. Somebody messed up. Then her daughter got real sick, turned yellow as a buttercup. Now, she has heart trouble. Thelma's daughter is twenty-eight. Her body is more like seventy. Thelma moved her and the grandkids in. That's how Thelma hurt her back. Too much lifting. See, that's how things happen. This job don't pay much, and Thelma's daughter was part time. No benefits. No insurance. She has bills and two kids and an ex-husband who don't care spit about holding a job or paying support. Thelma is not a young woman, but it's her daughter. Blood is a big deal.

Nurses and orderlies get in a hurry, get sloppy, and some people are just plain lazy. They wouldn't let nasty Band-Aids or sticky tissues stay on their kitchen floors, but they make no never mind to missing the trash cans, and hardly ever bend down to pick up a missed throw. They aren't children and I'm not their mama. Still, I'd like to twist their ears and tell them what for, but it's none of my put.

Nobody tells me much. One Tuesday, I went to clean a room and found a woman in a white coat cutting eyes out of a dead man's head. I dropped to my knees, all weak and sweaty, the whole room twirlin'. Nobody tells me nothing. I'm just going from room to room trying to get my work done before the Sup walks around with her clipboard, and the next thing I know, nurses have smelling salts to my nose because I saw an eyeball cut loose from a body like a red radish pulled from the garden. Lordy, it makes a body plum afraid to pull the curtains back.

Another night, I started into the dirty utility room to dump my mop water and saw a little baby floating in a green-lid jar. Little feller wasn't much longer than a pencil, tiniest fingers and toes I ever did see. In a cereal bowl, I could have bathed him. I could have. There was a label on the jar, and an orderly snatched him from the counter and stuffed him inside a lunch sack just like he was a hunk of cornbread. After I saw that little baby, who was not a pickle, but a person in a jar, labeled and all, I had a notion to dump my bucket over and watch the water rush every which way, make everybody just stand still for a minute, maybe turn the radio to a gospel station.

The nurses rushed his mama to surgery bleeding like a river. 'Course she didn't see her baby boy like I did. I saw him clean down to his baby toes. I saw he was a boy and that he had a boy's heart to hurry up and run too soon into this crazy world. I wasn't nosing around. Tending to my work is all. Getting me some clean water and more solution. 'Course it stops a body to see something precious. So, I straightened my glasses and looked him over good. I did not pick him up. I am not allowed to do such things.

Once, when I worked Labor and Delivery and it was a full moon, the nurses were short handed, they let me help with feeding. They said to wash-up real good, put on gloves and a yellow gown and come into the nursery. When you hold a new baby, the way they smell, better than fresh-baked bread, all lotiony and powdery, a body can't help but feel close to God, 'cause maybe He is right there in your arms. Labor and Delivery is a good floor to work. All the girls want that floor.

In this here 'mergency room, no telling what a body'll find. Liable to be somebody's brain or arm floating in a room one day. It wouldn't surprise me. Nurses wrap fingers and thumbs in wet gauze like they're sausage links and put them on ice before men are shipped out to big city hospitals. Not one hand surgeon in Brier County. My friend's husband, Cole, lost a thumb once, and they fastened it back. A team of surgeons used microscopes. They say it's finer stitching than tatting lace or quilting. The surgeons' eyes get real, real tired.

In Brier County, we know what we can fix on a man and what we cannot. That's why we voted for a tax and made a landing pad for helicopters. There is something quieting about seeing a pilot and his starched white shirt. Helicopter noise makes us pay attention to another person's bad luck. When the helicopter lands and takes off, everybody in the waiting room gawks out the window. The blades' wind bends our trees in the parking lot and stirs up a heap of dust for me near the big doors. Folks track it in. No way to stop that. I just mop again.

When a table saw steals part of a man, he gets gray and soaking wet with sweat. Women, they always do better with pain. Ask any nurse. I reckon we're just used to it. I've been in this hospital over fifteen years. Never saw a woman faint from a shot. No sir.

My supervisor wanted an old war-horse for 'mergency when Thelma hurt her back. So, I was bumped to nights. There's no union. Eight months I've been working here, and only two nurses know my name, Cora and June, the midnight girls. The other nurses look straight through me when they carry their shots and enemas and thermometers. Like I said, they couldn't hit a bathtub with a soup can, so they never worry about hitting a trash can with IV bags or dirty Kleenex or bloody bandages. They care less about the stuff that falls on this floor. They like coffee and sweet rolls and potato chips in the side room. They like joking with the doctors and medics.

Doctors all look the same to me: white lab coats, starched shirts, and silky ties which look like slippery tongues. Before they come on duty, it's like somebody pulls a string on their backs. They ask the same questions the same way and half the time, don't even lay a hand on the sick ones. By the gallons every night, lab girls take blood. After second shift, stray needles are everywhere. I find them stuck in mattresses, under pillows, and on the floor. I report it to the charge nurse. I'm 'sposed to do that. She takes up for her nurses. *They're busy. It was a bad patient, a bad shift, a hard IV start. You didn't get stuck, well, then what's the big deal?* I would like to drive her to Wagon Run Road, take her to Thelma's house. She could meet Thelma's daughter, feel that swelled belly under the gown, hear her coughing and spitting into Kleenex, and touch her ankles puffed up like water balloons.

• • •

The tan x-ray machine is more like a robot than anything I've ever seen. The techs roll it from one bed to another and take pictures. They yell *x-ray* and step way back like something's gonna fly off and hit them. Lord, I hope that x-ray stuff don't harm this old body of mine. Half the time, I never hear them yell, but I see nurses and doctors run plenty of times. Must mean something bad. I asked my supervisor. She said, "Just do your work Lucy. Mind that your beds are shiny and the floors are clean. Tend to your business. They'll tell you if anything needs telling."

What's she care about me? She's up there in her office sitting in a twirly chair, calling out girls to cover report offs, and reading dirty books. We've seen them in her drawers with the Bon-Bons. She has blood pressure trouble and sugar. What's she care about me and the stuff that x-ray machine shoots at this old body? Shoot, she don't care one bit. No sir. Tonight, I'm gonna ask Cora and June 'bout that x-ray stuff. They gave me a piece of pizza last week and sent a get well card to Thelma. They'll tell me what's what with the x-ray machine. They done told me why the bulletproof glass. Said some crazy man came into a hospital in Preston County and shot the nurse, a registry girl, and two patients in the waiting room. Shot 'em dead, then turned the gun on himself.

• • •

More than fifteen years here, no wonder I got me a little heart troubles. When I get to hurting and pop a Nitro, Cora and June let me take a rest in the family room. I put my feet up and sit a spell. Cora and June don't wear makeup, and they won't take a cussin', not from patients or doctors. They don't make a fuss about Ellie Lance sitting in the lobby after Saturday bingo to wait for the late, late movie. Ellie brings her own popcorn and soda. Her TV hasn't worked since Earl died in '87. When Sonny Crawford shows up half crocked in his army fatigues shivering snow and needing a place to sleep, Cora and June give him coffee, three blankets, and put him in a corner chair.

Once, when I was mopping my side of the station, a doctor stopped his writing and asked me, "Do you like your job?"

Mind you, it's three in the morning, my feet and back are on fire with aching. Somebody plugged the lobby toilet with a bloody Kotex. We have sixteen patients, an ambulance on the way, and Cora's waiting to discharge a squalling baby. She needs to give his mama what the doctor's writing. I look over my shoulder, nothing but the blanket warmer and the clock, so I know for sure he is talking to me. I straightened myself, pushed a gray hair from my face, and said, "I like my job fine." Cora winked at me, then, I marched my cart into the lobby where spilled cocoa messed up a stack of *Life* magazines and a dirty diaper's stuck under a chair and the toilet's full of trouble, fixing to flood my floors.

Selling Manure

BONNIE JO CAMPBELL

Mid-May of last year, after school was out, I found myself staring six weeks of unemployment in the face. My mother Susanna, a former horse trader who has no patience for idleness, soon let me know I would not be spending my time reading novels in the tree house. She lined up myriad farm chores to occupy me, including mucking out her big horse barn. The manure was so deep in places that the horses were scraping their heads on the ceilings.

"How are we going to get rid of this stuff?" I asked.

"You're going to load it in the back of the truck," said Mom, who was conveniently under doctor's orders to refrain from activities such as scooping, lifting, and flinging. "And then we're going to sell it."

She placed ads in the *Kalamazoo Gazette* and the *Kalamazoo Shopper*, offering manure for 35 dollars a truckload. My portion for doing the physical work was a generous 20 bucks; Mom got 15 for providing the truck and the product. Right away we got calls. A surprising number of people wanted the stuff we were so anxious to get rid of.

I spent much of that unseasonably hot May and June sweating inside the barn, moving layer after layer of manure and urine-soaked straw. Periodically, Mom brought me quart jars of iced tea to keep up my spirits and electrolytes—I could tell she was even feeling a little guilty about my working so hard. I didn't tell her that, far from feeling wretched as I loaded the truck, I was feeling revived. For one thing, I was in good company. The horses and donkeys wandered through and sniffed at me; the dogs lay in holes they'd dug outside the barn door and chewed on chunks of manure; a little garter snake who lived in a hole in the dirt floor slithered in and out of the barn under the wall. And I was enjoying letting my thoughts wander. After months of sitting in class, focusing on the drone of professors and poring over books and notes, I finally had rejoined the world of the living.

Delivering the manure was a little embarrassing at first. The body of my mother's pick-up truck was rusting away and the two sides of the bed were held together with shock cords. Most of our deliveries were to westside neighborhoods, and it was problematic that construction crews had narrowed

West Main to one lane in each direction. Stuck in a traffic jam, in ninety-five degree heat with a half a ton of manure in the back, we made quite a sensation. In the beginning, I put my hand over my face and hoped that I wouldn't see anyone I knew.

Within about a week, however, I began to see the absurdity of our situation as liberating. As we rattled through well-kept neighborhoods in a pickup full of stinking manure, I loosened the safety belt and hung my leg out the passenger side window, and I felt like master of all I surveyed. Perhaps this was how a prostitute felt toward a wealthy, respectable client; I might be dirty, but I have something you need.

Mom and I provided an excellent quality product at a fair price to decent folks. The people who bought our product were nice—after all, only very earthy people would order manure from the farm rather than buying it deodorized and sterilized in bags from the store. Customers often tried to help me shovel, but after I rebuffed their advances they stood back and smiled at the cascading dung. Hands on hips, eyes sparkling, they might have been fantasizing about late-summer gardens brimming with tomatoes and acorn squash.

One man who lived just off Stadium Drive was planting a full acre of garden on land he'd rented from the utility company. After I unloaded the truck under the power lines, he took Mom and me to admire a mound across the way. "Do you know what that is?" he asked. "That's llama manure. And this pile over here, that's pig manure. And that's chicken." The pig pile was so fragrant that I figured he'd soon have trouble with his neighbors in the nearby apartment complex, but his enthusiasm was touching. I felt proud that our manure was out in the world, mingling with other manures, making things grow.

There is no vocation more honest than selling manure. Consider what most people do for a living. They go to work where they build crap, or sell crap, or move crap, or spin a line of bull over the telephone, all the while trying to convince the customer that their product is something other than crap. When I deliver a load of manure to someone's garden, the customer and I are both upfront about what we are dealing with. All I have to ask is, "Where do you want this shit?"

This experience has made me reflect on the idea of work in general. Any job is an important job, whether it is selling manure or selling insurance. People should take pride in what they do, and not assume that a low-paying job or a dirty job makes them second-class citizens. And even the smelliest job has its rewards.

My darling Christopher works second shift at a paper converting plant in Parchment. "What are you doing today?" he asked me, as I walked him out to his truck. I told him I was going to spend the afternoon shoveling manure.

"Aren't we all," he said, nodding. "Aren't we all."

King Cole's American Salvage

BONNIE JO CAMPBELL

On a windy evening in February, William Slocum Jr., eleven months out of prison, pulled into King Cole's driveway in a Jeep he'd stolen from an apartment complex near his girlfriend's house. He'd cut through the Jeep's canvas top with a utility knife, popped the ignition with a screwdriver, and hot-wired the engine, a trick William Slocum Sr. had taught him not long before passing out drunk on the railroad tracks.

Slocum's car had broken down two days ago, and King Cole, of King Cole's American Salvage, had given him seventy dollars for it, minimum scrap price. That old Mitsubishi Montero hadn't been registered or insured, so if he'd left it broken down on the road, the city of Kalamazoo would have impounded it, but still Slocum felt Cole had ripped him off, had not given him what the car was worth. Slocum and his girlfriend Wanda were now without any car, since hers had been repossessed two months ago. She also hadn't managed to pay her mortgage or get enough methamphetamine to keep herself going since she lost her job, and Slocum hadn't been getting any work either, so things were tight. He'd tried to make love with Wanda last night, but without the meth, it wasn't working, and he knew tonight he needed to hit a lick. If he didn't, Wanda was bound to lose faith in him.

Slocum got out of the Jeep, carrying with him a length of galvanized pipe he'd swiped from Parker's Auto Repair, where he bought meth sometimes and where he'd met Johnny Cole, King Cole's nephew. They'd known each other less than two weeks, but right off, Slocum knew Johnny was a solid guy. Although he was five years younger than Slocum and still pocked with acne, Johnny was generous with the homegrown and seemed like the kind of person you could trust—a rare quality. Slocum had liked the way the kid had asked his advice, had seemed to look up to him.

Slocum knocked hard on King Cole's ornate wood and wrought-iron front door, and in about a minute, King swung open an upstairs casement window and turned on the security light, which lit up the crusted snow. Slocum could see by the tire tracks that the tow truck was the only vehicle that had been there recently. According to Johnny, the man's wife had died years ago, and according to the sticker on the window, Cole had an alarm system.

"What do you want?" King said through the screen. The small man stood with one hand on his potbelly. His long beard and shoulder-length hair were black—Johnny had told him the old man dyed it because he thought it made him attractive to the ladies.

"I need a jump start. Or maybe a tow," Slocum said.

"I don't work at night. Call somebody else." Cole started to close the window.

"I'm a friend of Johnny's," Slocum said quickly and backed up so King could see him better. "Your nephew Johnny. You scrapped my old car the other day, the blue Mitsubishi."

Cole opened the window again. "That Jap crap isn't worth a shit."

"That's what you said."

Slocum had stayed up late smoking and drinking beer with Johnny a few nights ago, and when Johnny was stoned, he told Slocum what a cheap bastard King Cole was, how Johnny worked his ass off for his uncle, but the man wouldn't lend Johnny enough money to buy some old diesel truck. King Cole didn't like banks, Johnny had said, and he carried a shitload of money on him, thousands of dollars in hidden pockets in his jacket. "I should go out to his house late some night and negotiate my own loan," Johnny had said, and they'd both laughed.

"Your car went to the shredder," King said. "What do you want?"

"Johnny's down at the gravel pit. He told me to see if you'd come help him."

"He's got his Nova? Or that damned vw diesel piece of shit he's been driving around this week?"

"Yeah, it's Johnny's Nova needs a jump."

"I suppose if I don't go out and jump him he won't show up for work in the morning," King mumbled. He took a phone out of his pocket. "Kid acts like he's stoned half the time."

Slocum kicked at the ice and rust behind the back wheel of the Jeep, which was idling in the drive. The jump-starting method his daddy had taught him only worked on Jeeps made before 1982, so he'd lucked out finding this old one, and with a half a tank of gas. If King Cole reached Johnny on the phone, Slocum would jump in the Jeep, shift into reverse, and back out of the driveway.

"That numb-nuts forgets to charge his phone," King said. He closed the window and disappeared inside. A few minutes later he came out the front door wearing an insulated leather bomber jacket with "K C's American Salvage" sewn into the back. He wore no hat, so his black hair was blowing around his skull in long dark strands. Looking at him, Slocum realized that King Cole was an old man. Slocum wasn't sure he could do this—he hoped the guy would piss him off and make it easier.

"I think we need a jump," Slocum said. "That'll probably do it."

"Why can't you jump him off what you're driving?" King Cole asked.

"We tried, but it didn't work. Battery's weak. Got alternator trouble. That's why I'm leaving it running now."

"Sounds all right to me." Cole opened the door to his tow truck. Before he stepped up, he leaned out and said, "So you giving up driving Jap cars?"

Slocum moved in. He swung the pipe and hit Cole above the ear, resulting in a dull cracking sound. Cole had a delayed reaction to the news about his skull, and he turned slowly and looked at Slocum. Slocum thought the old man was gathering up some crazy zombie strength to come after him, and he closed his eyes and hit Cole again. The impact made a duller and wetter sound this time, and it knocked Cole down onto the truck's running board. It wasn't anything Slocum had done before, hitting a guy with a pipe, but he kept focused on how he and Wanda needed the money and how the bastard had ripped him off.

"Stay down. Just stay down and give me your money and I won't hit you again." Slocum wiped his hands on his jeans, one at a time, still holding the pipe.

"Where's Johnny?" King Cole whispered, as he pulled himself up to a kneeling position and clung to the truck seat. He got his arm hooked in the removable cloth seat cover.

"Just stay down," Slocum said, but the old man grabbed for the bottom of the steering wheel. Slocum thought about Wanda's green eyes and her milky skin and the way her arms and legs wrapped around him, how she always had something smart and funny to say, and he hit King Cole a third time, a fourth time, and a fifth time. King fell into the snow and lay still. Blood covered his face, soaked into his beard and into the snow around him. Slocum had never killed a man, and he hadn't wanted to kill this man, so he thought about buying carts full of groceries for Wanda's kids and getting them medicine for their ear infections.

Slocum unzipped Cole's jacket, found stacks of twenties, fifties, hundreds. He didn't bother with the envelope full of checks. He reached into Cole's pants' pockets, took a wad of bills from each side. The money didn't all fit in the pockets of Slocum's jacket and jeans, so he pulled off a hunk of ones and let them fly in the wind, let them slap against the naked-lady statue and catch in the bare bushes.

He left the man in the snow beside the tow truck and backed down the gravel driveway lined with pines, felt relief when the Jeep's tires hit asphalt. An hour later, he entered Wanda's house by the kitchen door, quietly so as not to wake the kids. She was lying on the couch holding a book on her chest. When she sat up, he tossed the cash and a bag of meth he'd bought onto the velvety cushion beside her. She put the book down.

"There's your house payment, babe."

"Look at you," she said, but she was looking at the money. With two fingers she lifted a fifty-dollar bill from the stack and held it away from herself. "Willie, this money's covered with blood."

"Sorry about that." Slocum looked at his hands, which were also covered with blood.

"We can wash it in the sink," Wanda said.

"How are the kids?"

"They're not here. My sister took them for the night because some bitch from Social Services came by. I want to know who the fuck reported me."

"I can't imagine who would do that, honey."

"Well, somebody did. I told the bitch if she didn't have a warrant she'd better get the hell off my property."

"You don't got to worry about nothing anymore. I'm going to take care of you."

"Yeah, right, Willie. You're a regular knight in shining fucking armor."

When Wanda noticed the plastic bag, she raised her eyebrows, slid out the tinfoil package, and unfolded it.

"Something's shining here," she said cheerfully and patted the couch, inviting Slocum to sit beside her. "Shall we smoke it, my dear? Or shall we shoot it?"

Some people said Wanda was mean, but Slocum loved his woman, loved that he could enter her house without knocking, loved the smart, funny things she said. He would do anything for her.

• • •

Johnny Cole stopped answering the salvage yard phone the next morning, because he was tired of trekking into the pole building to say King hadn't shown up yet. It wasn't any warmer inside, because King wasn't there to start the fire in the wood stove. At ten o'clock, Johnny began stripping an Oldsmobile: catalytic converter for its platinum, starter to sell to the rebuild guy, aluminum radiator good enough to resell rather than scrap, tires too worn to bother with. On other cars he might save hood ornaments or yank carburetors if they were Holley or Edelbrock. Even stainless steel brake lines sometimes, when the scrap price was high, although the brake fluid would chew up your flesh. Johnny liked that piles of what looked like junk to most people could be worth real money.

King refused to let Johnny part out foreign cars. Johnny complained about this policy every time somebody came in asking for Honda hubcaps or vw wheels, but King stuck to it. If he towed those cars at all, he took them directly to the shredder, although it meant less money. Johnny didn't see the difference nowadays, American or Japanese or German. The old diesel vw truck he was fixing up had been made in Pennsylvania, according to the door sticker, and Toyota had recently opened a plant in Kentucky. Slocum had said to Johnny that they should go down there and get jobs, except that Wanda couldn't legally take her kids out of state.

At eleven o'clock, King still hadn't shown up and wasn't answering his phone—never had that happened in the years Johnny had worked for him— so Johnny closed and locked the yard's stockade gate and drove out to King's. There, he found the tow truck with its door hanging open, the bushes decorated with dollar bills, and King Cole lying beside the driveway like a bundle of frozen, bloody rags. Johnny fell to his knees in the snow.

• • •

After three brain surgeries, the doctors determined that Johnny's uncle was most likely going to live. Johnny's ma, who was King's sister, came and went, said there was no sense in just sitting there, but Johnny stayed in the hospital waiting room, drinking coffee and sharing news of King's condition with everyone who stopped by—mostly women King flirted with and salvage yard regulars. Johnny had never been part of a medical trauma, and he thought somebody should stay alert so that the doctors and nurses would stay alert, too. Early evening on the fourth day, King's daughter arrived from Virginia, and so Johnny headed to Parker's garage to get himself something stronger than coffee. When he pulled in the driveway, one bay door was open despite the cold, and Slocum was walking out toward a Ford Bronco. Johnny parked and stumbled in his hurry to reach him.

"I'm glad to see you," Johnny said. "I really need to talk to somebody."

"Hi, Johnny." Slocum's eyes were bloodshot. "You look all dragged out, man."

"I've been at the hospital for four days, haven't even taken a shower. Did you hear what happened to my uncle? He got robbed and beat up bad, man, real bad. He's in a coma."

"Yeah, I heard about it. Keep your voice down, Johnny."

"There was so much fucking blood, man, and his face—" Johnny choked, but managed to hold back tears. "His brain was coming out through a hole in his head. They're saying that even if he lives he might be a vegetable for the rest of his life."

"It was bound to happen, Johnny, a guy going around with all that cash. You'd have taken the money yourself if you'd had the balls."

Johnny had hardly eaten in days, and he felt so dizzy suddenly that he had to reach out and support himself on the Bronco. He said, "You didn't do it, Slocum. Did you?"

Because Johnny was small, guys often treated him like a kid, but Johnny had felt a real kinship with Slocum. They'd shared dope and forty-ouncers and stories about missing fathers, about cops and bosses. Johnny had told Slocum how he felt beat down. Slocum had said Johnny had to stick to his principles no matter what. When Johnny had said he didn't know what his principles were, Slocum had laughed, and Johnny had joined in laughing.

"People do what they have to do, Johnny," Slocum said and opened the driver's-side door of the Bronco. "You can understand that."

"Slocum, man, we were just talking that night, you and me, saying crazy shit. I never wanted King to get hurt."

"Listen, Johnny, you told me your uncle was screwing you over. Then the very next day he ripped me off on my car."

"But the cops are saying this was attempted murder. A person could go to jail for life." Johnny didn't feel afraid, despite what Slocum might be capable of doing, despite Slocum's weighing twice as much as he did. Johnny wanted to keep talking until they figured this out, until Johnny could know Slocum was not the monster guilty of this crime. If they talked long enough, they would find the misunderstanding. And King might wake up any minute now and be o.k.

"Listen, Johnny, don't you think about turning me in. You turn me in, you're going down, too. If I did it, then you were in on it from the start."

"What are you talking about? I didn't do anything."

"I thought you were solid, Johnny. If I think you turned me in, I won't take it lying down. If I'm taking the stand, you're going to be the pimple-faced son of a bitch I point out to everybody as my accomplice. Don't you doubt it for a minute."

"But I was just talking that night. We were stoned, Slocum, just saying whatever came into our heads."

"I meant everything I said," Slocum said, "and I wouldn't have said it if I didn't think you knew what it meant to be a friend. Listen, Johnny, I've got to get back to Wanda now. Social Services is trying to take her kids away, and she's losing it."

Johnny didn't go into the garage. He watched Slocum peel out of the driveway, and he got into his Nova. On the way back to the hospital, he pulled into a gas station. He could barely see the numbers on the pay phone when he punched 911. He told the operator Slocum might have beaten up King, and then he hung up. In the hospital parking lot, he imagined Slocum's hands on his neck. He leaned out of the driver's side door and puked.

• • •

"It's a miracle Mr. Cole's alive," a doctor testified at Slocum's trial ten months later. He said King Cole survived because he'd been lying on his side in densely packed snow, so that the cold and the pressure had minimized the bleeding. The doctor said that Cole didn't freeze to death because he'd managed to pull the seat cover over his body and he'd held his hands against his belly. The doctor explained to the jury that Cole would never fully regain his lost verbal and cognitive abilities or his sense of smell or taste. On cross-examination, the doctor said he was indeed surprised to learn that King Cole had resumed driving his tow truck.

Johnny was sitting beside King. He took off his vw cap, wished for King's sake he had worn his Chevy Like a Rock hat. He put his cap back on, tried to stop his foot from tapping. King sat motionless beside Johnny, and although the courtroom was plenty warm, he wore a new insulated leather American Salvage jacket like the one he had been wearing when he was beaten up, but Johnny carried the cash now, deposited it in the bank each night. Scars the color of power-steering fluid stood out along King's hairline on the left side, from Slocum's pipe and the surgeons' tools. His hair and beard were coming in gray, and Johnny needed to remind him to go to the barber to get his black touched up—King seemed to feel better when he at least looked the same as before. For King Cole it had been ten months of learning again how to dress himself, how to shop for food, and how to force his mouth and tongue around words that used to come easy.

For Johnny it had been ten months of working by himself in the salvage yard, scrapping out metal, cleaning up and organizing the place. It had been ten months of sick anticipation, waiting for the cops to pick him up, but they never did, and Johnny never heard a word from Slocum, who was no doubt saving everything for the courtroom. Johnny's acne kept getting worse, and he'd weighed only a hundred and twenty pounds last time he stepped onto the scrap scale.

King took the stand on the first day. Under questioning, in his slurred speech, he said, "I guess my brain's messed up. I don't talk right anymore."

"How are you doing with your alphabet?" the prosecutor asked.

"I got a, b, c, but not what comes next," King said, stroking his long beard and then shaking his head in frustration. "I know it, but can't spit it out."

"What about writing? Can you write?"

"My nephew Johnny has to write shit down for me."

When the prosecutor asked King how his life had changed as a result of the beating, King said, "The ladies don't act the same with me. They don't want nothing to do with me except to feel sorry for me."

Johnny knew that several women had offered to help King, even to stay with him when he first came home from the hospital, but he told them he needed no help. Now that King's daughter had gone back to her husband and kids in Virginia and Johnny's ma had moved to Ohio with Johnny's little sister, King would accept help only from Johnny, and then only if Johnny made it seem like no big deal. First thing Johnny did every day, since they had reopened the salvage yard three months ago, was call King and tell him to wake up and eat some breakfast. When King got to the yard, Johnny checked that his buttons were buttoned right and his paperwork was in order for the shredder, where he hauled the cars after Johnny stripped them.

The defense lawyer looked like a drinker, Johnny thought, like someone who would come home with his ma from the bar and slip out before morning. He asked King, "What do you remember about the afternoon and night of the assault?"

"I don't remember nothing after lunch," King said. Johnny could see he was making an effort to pronounce each word.

"So you don't remember seeing Mr. Slocum at all that day. Is that right?"

King always claimed to remember nothing, but Johnny wondered if someday a brain cell would reignite, the way a fire you thought was out sometimes left a spark that could rekindle and burn a house to the ground. When Johnny had finally charged up his phone a week after the assault, he'd gotten the message from King, saying, "Johnny, some big dumb friend of yours is outside here saying you need a jump. Why the hell don't you keep your phone charged?" He plugged in his phone every night now, had not missed a single night since King was home from the hospital. He kept saving the message from King, month after month. At first he'd intended to share the message with the police, but cops scared Johnny, and he never could bring himself to tell them about it.

Johnny slipped his hat off when he went up to take the stand and wished he'd combed his hair once more. He had bought new jeans for the occasion, but he still felt as though he were stained with grease and oil.

"King was curled up in the snow," Johnny said under oath and choked on his voice. He felt Slocum's eyes on him, but he was afraid to look back, afraid of what monster he might see there. "He was beat so bad I didn't recognize him. Head swollen big as a basketball, his hair and beard was soaked with blood and his face was mashed." Johnny's heart pounded as he spoke. "I begged him to be alive. I turned him over and there was gray stuff coming out the hole in his head, and I could smell the blood. Then I saw he was breathing." Johnny had thought the blood and brains smelled like metal and chemicals, something from the salvage yard.

Johnny wiped at his face and felt Slocum still staring at him, probably enjoying dragging all this out. As far as Johnny could figure, until a year ago, nothing he had ever done or said had made any difference in this life. But what he'd said to Slocum that night at Parker's about his uncle's money being in his jacket meant everything, and what he said in this courtroom today meant everything else. Johnny testified that King was different since the assault, that he hardly joked, that he got frustrated and sometimes got lost. Johnny said, "King can't say ten no more. He says two fives. He can't say radiator. He says that thing in the car you put water in."

The prosecutor asked, "Did you know the defendant, William Slocum Jr.?"

Johnny meant to say yes, he knew Slocum, and then he would say, yes, he'd told Slocum about the money, but that was all. Johnny would explain how he would never have hurt his uncle. He tried to form the word yes.

"No," Johnny said. "I mean, I know who he is, but I don't really know him."

Slocum crossed his arms over his chest. In his creased green dress shirt, Slocum was the biggest person in the courtroom, bigger even than the cop sitting next to the prosecutor.

The case against Slocum hit its stride on the second day, when the prosecutor introduced into evidence the galvanized pipe. On the third day, Wanda Jones took the stand. Her cola-colored hair curled neatly onto her neck, her little shoulders pressed out against a soft-looking white sweater, and her make-up was perfect. She had a degree in accounting and had worked at a finance company, she said, before she lost her job and took up with William Slocum Jr.

"Yes, he brought me the money that night. He tossed the bloody money down on my couch. I had to wash the cushion afterwards."

Wanda chewed on the inside of her cheeks as she answered the questions. She pointed out Slocum when asked to do so.

"What happened to your children, Ms. Jones?"

"Social Services took them away."

"Why?"

"Because of the meth."

"Do you still use methamphetamine?"

"No, I've stopped. I'm trying to get my kids back." Wanda's hand trembled when she pushed her hair over her ear. She would not look at Slocum. She kept her eyes downcast in a way that Johnny thought made her look pretty, and she hardly opened her mouth when she talked. Slocum stared at her as though she were a life raft out of his reach and drifting farther and farther from him in the water.

Her testimony went long, because the prosecutor had her read aloud from a letter Slocum had sent from jail suggesting that he might try to escape during the trial. "Have your car parked on a main road. Please be ready to help me, Wanda. Please don't betray me," the letter said. "Burn this letter. I love you more than my own life."

"Do you love Mr. Slocum?" the prosecutor asked.

"No. He's a pig."

"Why were you with him?"

"For the meth."

"Did you encourage Mr. Slocum to rob Mr. Cole to make your house payment?"

"No. I told him to get a job."

On cross-examination, Wanda Jones admitted that she hoped testifying would help her get her kids back. When asked again if she had encouraged Slocum to steal money for her, she said, "I never told him to steal it. He got the idea from the junk man's nephew." She pointed at Johnny. "Hatchet face over there."

The prosecutor and the big police officer glanced over at Johnny.

Johnny shook his head no. Wanda crossed her arms and her lips peeled back to reveal gray-brown teeth to the courtroom. She said, "Oh, you think you're so good and holy, taking care of your uncle. You're just as bad as Slocum."

The judge, a slim, gray-haired man about King Cole's age, said, "Please just respond to the questions, Ms. Jones."

People in the room looked at Johnny. Everybody except King looked at Johnny. King kept staring at Wanda, as though fascinated by her doll-like

255

figure. The judge announced that Slocum, the final witness, would testify after lunch recess. Johnny considered getting into his Nova and driving south to Ohio or Kentucky. Instead he drank a bottle of pop and smoked cigarettes with a courthouse custodian. When it was time, he slogged back into the courtroom and sat beside King.

· · ·

Slocum felt like a bull for slaughter swaying above his shackled ankles as he shuffled to the witness stand. His dress shirt and khakis were wrinkled. He had demanded a jury trial on principle, had refused a plea bargain, but now the evidence against him was overwhelming. They'd found the pipe with fingerprints and bloody hair where he'd dropped it through the ice on the Kalamazoo River—who could have known there were two layers of river ice with an air space between them?

"How do you feel about Wanda Jones?" his lawyer asked him.

"I loved that woman. I gave her everything, all the money I had," Slocum said. Wanda was no longer in the courtroom, but he tried to conjure her, to get one more look at her. "I never loved a woman the way I loved her. Everything I did was for her or the kids. Them kids aren't mine, but I took care of them like they were mine."

Between his words, Slocum could hear himself moaning like an old woman or an animal, as though something wretched in him, something like regret or sorrow, was trying to get out through his voice.

"Did she ask you to rob Mr. Cole to pay her mortgage?"

"I was her one-man army," Slocum said. He didn't know how much longer he could keep going without breaking down. His ache felt so big inside him that no amount of meth or pot would soothe him ever again. "I was her knight in shining fucking armor. She needed money so she wouldn't lose her house. I had to get it for her."

The judge interrupted. "Please just answer the question, Mr. Slocum."

"No, she didn't ask me to rob him." He should have seen this coming—Wanda hadn't written to or visited him in jail for months—but somehow he hadn't seen it coming. Her betrayal was like punches to the head and the kidneys and the gut, and he couldn't punch back.

"Were you trying to kill Mr. Cole?" his lawyer asked.

"No, man. I wasn't. If he just would've stayed down when I told him to I would have stopped hitting him," Slocum said. He needed to be alone right now. He regretted testifying—his lawyer had advised against it, but he'd insisted. "The old guy just wouldn't stay down." Slocum looked around the courtroom, hoping, but not expecting, to find someone there who would understand. He saw Johnny staring at him. Slocum met Johnny's gaze, asked him wordlessly, begged him with his eyes: "You understand, don't you? You if nobody else."

Slocum saw Johnny nod, just barely. He saw concern in Johnny's face. It was the first time anyone had looked at Slocum in this courtroom with anything other than scorn. Slocum wanted to shout that he wasn't a hateful person, that he'd loved someone with all his heart, but all he could do was look at Johnny. The acne on the kid's face made Slocum feel sorry for him, for that mean crack Wanda had made, hatchet face.

• • •

Johnny nodded to Slocum, not in agreement with anything he was saying, but because he realized that the man was indeed a monster and that he was also a regular guy like Johnny, the same guy Johnny had talked to until four in the morning. Slocum was a screwup, the way Johnny was a screwup, only much worse. Slocum should go to prison for life, but that didn't mean he was all that different from Johnny or anybody else.

When Slocum's lawyer asked whether he'd had an accomplice, Slocum finally looked away from Johnny. He did not hesitate before answering. He said, "No."

"Why would Ms. Jones say Johnny Cole was involved?"

He said, "Maybe she wants to hurt the guy for some reason. I don't know."

Johnny squeezed his eyes shut. When he opened them again, he couldn't believe he was still sitting upright on the long wooden pew, and nobody was looking at him.

Johnny noticed that King, sitting beside him, was abnormally fixated on Slocum. King's eyes widened and his left hand began to shake. His right hand clutched the seat beneath him. King must have finally realized in his gut that he was facing his attacker. Johnny slid closer to King. He elbowed him gently and offered him a breath mint. King declined, but Johnny saw it was enough to break the spell. It didn't take much, really, to keep King on an even keel, but the concern he felt for his uncle gave Johnny a tired feeling, like he was growing old fast.

Closing arguments were over before noon—Slocum's lawyer asked the jury to find his client guilty of aggravated assault rather than attempted murder—and Johnny went back to work and started scrapping out a Lincoln Town Car. King was watching him, and it made Johnny conscious of his own breath forming a cloud that hung around him, a cloud that kept him down here on the oily, hard-packed dirt of the salvage yard, down here wearing his greasy clothes, picking through the piles of engines and axles with his filthy hands, down in this neighborhood of ramshackle houses with dogs barking in the torn up yards.

Johnny jacked up the back end of the Lincoln, pried off the passenger-side hubcap and spun off the lug nuts. The wheel did not come right off, so Johnny swung the sledgehammer. The wheel flew six feet and landed in the slush right next to King.

"Sorry, man," Johnny said, but he thought he couldn't take King's silence. At least Slocum would have guys to talk to in prison, probably some bored cellmate who'd be awake at four in the morning. Johnny said, "I don't know if I can stay here, King. Every day there's guys coming through that gate who'd kill me for the money in my pockets. And it ain't even my money."

King's phone rang, interrupting Johnny, and Johnny was glad. He hadn't known what was going to come out of his own mouth next. King listened blankly to the first ring, stroked his beard on the second ring, picked the phone out of his pocket on the third, and answered on the fourth. All the while he stared at the sledgehammer in Johnny's hands.

"Okay, half hour," Cole said into the phone. He became alert in matters of towing, often sounding like his old self. "Hold on, let my nephew write down the address."

He held the phone out to Johnny, more hesitantly than usual. Johnny left the sledgehammer standing up by itself and wiped his hands on his jeans. He spoke to the woman on the other end for a while and wrote down directions. He told her, "If King don't show up in an hour, you call the shop."

He handed the phone back to his uncle and said, "King, that woman has a Honda with a blown engine. Why don't you bring it here instead of taking it to the shredder?"

King was forming a response, but Johnny didn't wait as he usually would have.

"Please King, just tow the damned Jap scrap back to me. Guys are coming in here all the time asking for parts we don't got. Something's got to change around here."

After a long pause, King said, almost without slurring, "Sure. No big deal."

King did not get right into his truck. He stood watching while Johnny hoisted up the Lincoln's front end and hacked away at the pipe on both ends of the catalytic converter, practically brand new. Johnny twisted it free and tossed it across the yard. Both he and King watched the cylinder arc ten feet in the air and momentarily capture the cold sunlight. It landed with a resounding clang on the pile of catalytic converters—mostly they were dirty and rusted from the slush and mud and road salt, but each of their bodies contained a core of platinum.

Paul's Case

WILLA CATHER

A Study in Temperament

It was Paul's afternoon to appear before the faculty of the Pittsburgh High School to account for his various misdemeanors. He had been suspended a week ago, and his father had called at the Principal's office and confessed his perplexity about his son. Paul entered the faculty room suave and smiling. His clothes were a trifle outgrown, and the tan velvet on the collar of his open overcoat was frayed and worn, but for all that there was something of the dandy about him, and he wore an opal pin in his neatly knotted black four-in-hand, and a red carnation in his buttonhole. This latter adornment the faculty somehow felt was not properly significant of the contrite spirit befitting a boy under the ban of suspension.

Paul was tall for his age and very thin, with high, cramped shoulders and a narrow chest. His eyes were remarkable for a certain hysterical brilliancy, and he continually used them in a conscious, theatrical sort of way, peculiarly offensive in a boy. The pupils were abnormally large, as though he were addicted to belladonna, but there was a glassy glitter about them which that drug does not produce.

When questioned by the Principal as to why he was there Paul stated, politely enough, that he wanted to come back to school. This was a lie, but Paul was quite accustomed to lying; found it, indeed, indispensable for overcoming friction. His teachers were asked to state their respective charges against him, which they did with such a rancor and aggrievedness as evinced that this was not a usual case. Disorder and impertinence were among the offences named, yet each of his instructors felt that it was scarcely possible to put into words the real cause of the trouble, which lay in a sort of hysterically defiant manner of the boy's; in the contempt which they all knew he felt for them, and which he seemingly made not the least effort to conceal. Once, when he had been making a synopsis of a paragraph at the blackboard, his English teacher had stepped to his side and attempted to guide his hand. Paul had started back with a shudder and thrust his hands violently behind him. The astonished woman could scarcely have been more hurt and embarrassed had he struck at her. The insult was so involuntary and definitely personal as to be unforgettable. In one way and another he had made all his teachers, men and women alike, conscious of the same feeling of physical aversion. In one class he habitually sat with his hand shading his eyes; in another he always looked out of the window during the recitation; in another he made a running commentary on the lecture, with humorous intention.

His teachers felt this afternoon that his whole attitude was symbolized by his shrug and his flippantly red carnation flower, and they fell upon him without mercy, his English teacher leading the pack. He stood through it smiling, his pale lips parted over his white teeth. (His lips were continually twitching, and he had a habit of raising his eyebrows that was contemptuous and irritating to the last degree.) Older boys than Paul had broken down and shed tears under that baptism of fire, but his set smile did not once desert him, and his only sign of discomfort was the nervous trembling of the fingers that toyed with the buttons of his overcoat, and an occasional jerking of the other hand that held his hat. Paul was always smiling, always glancing about him, seeming to feel that people might be watching him and trying to detect something. This conscious expression, since it was as far as possible from boyish mirthfulness, was usually attributed to insolence or "smartness."

As the inquisition proceeded one of his instructors repeated an impertinent remark of the boy's, and the Principal asked him whether he thought that a courteous speech to have made a woman. Paul shrugged his shoulders slightly and his eyebrows twitched.

"I don't know," he replied. "I didn't mean to be polite or impolite, either. I guess it's a sort of way I have of saying things regardless."

The Principal, who was a sympathetic man, asked him whether he didn't think that a way it would be well to get rid of. Paul grinned and said he guessed so. When he was told that he could go he bowed gracefully and went out. His bow was but a repetition of the scandalous red carnation.

His teachers were in despair, and his drawing master voiced the feeling of them all when he declared there was something about the boy which none of them understood. He added: "I don't really believe that smile of his comes altogether from insolence; there's something sort of haunted about it. The boy is not strong, for one thing. I happen to know that he was born in Colorado, only a few months before his mother died out there of a long illness. There is something wrong about the fellow."

The drawing master had come to realize that, in looking at Paul, one saw only his white teeth and the forced animation of his eyes. One warm afternoon the boy had gone to sleep at his drawing board, and his master had noted with amazement what a white, blue-veined face it was; drawn and wrinkled like an old man's about the eyes, the lips twitching even in his sleep, and stiff with a nervous tension that drew them back from his teeth.

His teachers left the building dissatisfied and unhappy; humiliated to have felt so vindictive toward a mere boy, to have uttered this feeling in cutting terms, and to have set each other on, as it were, in the gruesome game of intemperate reproach. Some of them remembered having seen a miserable street cat set at bay by a ring of tormentors.

As for Paul, he ran down the hill whistling the Soldiers' Chorus from *Faust* looking wildly behind him now and then to see whether some of his teachers were not there to writhe under his lightheartedness. As it was now late in the afternoon and Paul was on duty that evening as usher at Carnegie Hall, he decided that he would not go home to supper. When he reached the concert hall the doors were not yet open and, as it was chilly outside, he decided to go up into the picture gallery—always deserted at this hour—where there were some of Raffelli's gay studies of Paris streets and an airy blue Venetian scene or two that always exhilarated him. He was delighted to find no one in the gallery but the old guard, who sat in one corner, a newspaper on his knee, a black patch over one eye and the other closed. Paul possessed himself of the place and walked confidently up and down, whistling under his breath. After a while he sat down before a blue Rico and lost himself. When he bethought him to look at his watch, it was after seven o'clock, and he rose with a start and ran downstairs, making a face at Augustus, peering out from the cast room, and an evil gesture at the Venus de Milo as he passed her on the stairway.

When Paul reached the ushers' dressing room half a dozen boys were there already, and he began excitedly to tumble into his uniform. It was one of the few that at all approached fitting, and Paul thought it very becoming—though he knew that the tight, straight coat accentuated his narrow chest, about which he was exceedingly sensitive. He was always considerably excited while he dressed, twanging all over to the tuning of the strings and the preliminary flourishes of the horns in the music room; but tonight he seemed quite beside himself, and he teased and plagued the boys until, telling him that he was crazy, they put him down on the floor and sat on him.

Somewhat calmed by his suppression, Paul dashed out to the front of the house to seat the early comers. He was a model usher; gracious and smiling he ran up and down the aisles; nothing was too much trouble for him; he carried messages and brought programs as though it were his greatest pleasure in life, and all the people in his section thought him a charming boy, feeling that he remembered and admired them. As the house filled, he grew more and more vivacious and animated, and the color came to his cheeks and lips. It was very much as though this were a great reception and Paul were the host. Just as the musicians came out to take their places, his English teacher arrived with checks for the seats which a prominent manufacturer had taken for the season. She betrayed some embarrassment when she handed Paul the tickets, and a hauteur which subsequently made her feel very foolish. Paul was startled for a moment, and had the feeling of wanting to put her out; what business had she here among all these fine people and gay colors? He looked her over and decided that she was not appropriately dressed and must be a tool to sit downstairs in such togs. The tickets had probably been sent her out of kindness, he reflected as he put down a seat for her, and she had about as much right to sit there as he had.

When the symphony began Paul sank into one of the rear seats with a long sigh of relief, and lost himself, as he had done before the Rico. It was not that symphonies, as such, meant anything in particular to Paul, but the first sigh of the instruments seemed to free some hilarious and potent spirit within him; something that struggled there like the genie in the bottle found by the Arab fisherman. He felt a sudden zest of life; the lights danced before his eyes and the concert hall blazed into unimaginable splendor. When the soprano soloist came on Paul forgot even the nastiness of his teacher's being there and gave himself up to the peculiar stimulus such personages always had for him. The soloist chanced to be a German woman, by no means in her first youth, and the mother of many children; but she wore an elaborate gown and tiara, and above all she had that indefinable air of achievement, that worldshine upon her, which, in Paul's eyes, made her a veritable queen of Romance.

• • •

After a concert was over Paul was always irritable and wretched until he got to sleep, and tonight he was even more than usually restless. He had the feeling of not being able to let down, of its being impossible to give up this delicious excitement which was the only thing that could be called living at all. During the last number he withdrew and, after hastily changing his clothes in the dressing room, slipped out to the side door where the soprano's carriage stood. Here he began pacing rapidly up and down the walk, waiting to see her come out.

Over yonder, the Schenley, in its vacant stretch, loomed big and square through the fine rain, the windows of its twelve stories glowing like those of a lighted cardboard house under a Christmas tree. All the actors and singers of the better class stayed there when they were in the city, and a number of the big manufacturers of the place lived there in the winter. Paul had often hung about the hotel, watching the people go in and out, longing to enter and leave schoolmasters and dull care behind him forever.

At last the singer came out, accompanied by the conductor, who helped her into her carriage and closed the door with a cordial auf wiedersehen which set Paul to wondering whether she were not an old sweetheart of his. Paul followed the carriage over to the hotel, walking so rapidly as not to be far from the entrance when the singer alighted, and disappeared behind the swinging glass doors that were opened by a Negro in a tall hat and a long coat. In the moment that the door was ajar it seemed to Paul that he, too, entered. He seemed to feel himself go after her up the steps, into the warm, lighted building, into an exotic, tropical world of shiny, glistening surfaces and basking ease. He reflected upon the mysterious dishes that were brought into the dining room, the green bottles in buckets of ice, as he had seen them in the supper party pictures of the *Sunday World* supplement. A quick gust of wind brought the rain down with sudden vehemence, and Paul was startled to find that he was still outside in the slush of the gravel driveway; that his boots were letting in the water and his scanty overcoat was clinging wet about him; that the lights in front of the concert hall were out and that the rain was driving in sheets between him and the orange glow of the windows above him. There it was, what he wanted—tangibly before him, like the fairy world of a Christmas pantomime—but mocking spirits stood guard at the doors, and, as the rain beat in his face, Paul wondered whether he were destined always to shiver in the black night outside, looking up at it.

He turned and walked reluctantly toward the car tracks. The end had to come sometime; his father in his nightclothes at the top of the stairs, explanations that did not explain, hastily improvised fictions that were forever tripping him up, his upstairs room and its horrible yellow wallpaper, the creaking bureau with the greasy plush collarbox, and over his painted wooden bed the pictures of George Washington and John Calvin, and the framed motto, "Feed my Lambs," which had been worked in red worsted by his mother.

Half an hour later Paul alighted from his car and went slowly down one of the side streets off the main thoroughfare. It was a highly respectable street, where all the houses were exactly alike, and where businessmen of moderate means begot and reared large families of children, all of whom went to Sabbath school and learned the shorter catechism, and were interested in arithmetic; all of whom were as exactly alike as their homes, and of a piece with the monotony in which they lived. Paul never went up Cordelia Street without a shudder of loathing. His home was next to the house of the Cumberland minister. He approached it tonight with the nerveless sense of defeat, the hopeless feeling of sinking back forever into ugliness and commonness that he had always had when he came home. The moment he turned into Cordelia Street he felt the waters close above his head. After each of these orgies of living he experienced all the physical depression which follows a debauch; the loathing of respectable beds, of common food, of a house penetrated by kitchen odors; a shuddering repulsion for the flavorless, colorless mass of everyday existence; a morbid desire for cool things and soft lights and fresh flowers.

The nearer he approached the house, the more absolutely unequal Paul felt to the sight of it all: his ugly sleeping chamber; the cold bathroom with the grimy zinc tub, the cracked mirror, the dripping spigots; his father, at the top of the stairs, his hairy legs sticking out from his nightshirt, his feet thrust into carpet slippers. He was so much later than usual that there would certainly be inquiries and reproaches. Paul stopped short before the door. He felt that he could not be accosted by his father tonight; that he could not toss again on that miserable bed. He would not go in. He would tell his father that he had no carfare and it was raining so hard he had gone home with one of the boys and stayed all night.

Meanwhile, he was wet and cold. He went around to the back of the house and tried one of the basement windows, found it open, raised it cautiously, and scrambled down the cellar wall to the floor. There he stood, holding his breath, terrified by the noise he had made, but the floor above him was silent, and there was no creak on the stairs. He found a soapbox, and carried it over to the soft ring of light that streamed from the furnace door, and sat down. He was horribly afraid of rats, so he did not try to sleep, but sat looking distrustfully at the dark, still terrified lest he might have awakened his father. In such reactions, after one of the experiences which made days and nights out of the dreary blanks of the calendar, when his senses were deadened, Paul's head was always singularly clear. Suppose his father had heard him getting in at the window and had come down and shot him for a burglar? Then, again, suppose his father had come down, pistol in hand, and he had cried out in time to save himself, and his father had been horrified to think how nearly he had killed him? Then, again, suppose a day should come when his father would remember that night, and wish there had been no warning cry to stay his hand? With this last supposition Paul entertained himself until daybreak.

The following Sunday was fine; the sodden November chill was broken by the last flash of autumnal summer. In the morning Paul had to go to church and Sabbath school, as always. On seasonable Sunday afternoons the burghers of Cordelia Street always sat out on their front stoops and talked to their neighbors on the next stoop, or called to those across the street in neighborly fashion. The men usually sat on gay cushions placed upon the steps that led down to the sidewalk, while the women, in their Sunday "waists," sat in rockers on the cramped porches, pretending to be greatly at their ease. The children played in the streets; there were so many of them that the place resembled the recreation grounds of a kindergarten. The men on the steps— all in their shirt sleeves, their vests unbuttoned—sat with their legs well apart, their stomachs comfortably protruding, and talked of the prices of things, or told anecdotes of the sagacity of their various chiefs and overlords. They occasionally looked over the multitude of squabbling children, listened affectionately to their high-pitched, nasal voices, smiling to see their own proclivities reproduced in their offspring, and interspersed their legends of the iron kings with remarks about their sons' progress at school, their grades in arithmetic, and the amounts they had saved in their toy banks.

On this last Sunday of November Paul sat all the afternoon on the lowest step of his stoop, staring into the street, while his sisters, in their rockers, were talking to the minister's daughters next door about how many shirtwaists they had made in the last week, and how many waffles someone had eaten at the last church supper. When the weather was warm, and his father was in a particularly jovial frame of mind, the girls made lemonade, which was always brought out in a red-glass pitcher ornamented with forget-me-nots in blue enamel. This the girls thought very fine, and the neighbors always joked about the suspicious color of the pitcher.

Today Paul's father sat on the top step, talking to a young man who shifted a restless baby from knee to knee. He happened to be the young man who was daily held up to Paul as a model, and after whom it was his father's dearest hope that he would pattern. This young man was of a ruddy complexion, with a compressed, red mouth, and faded, nearsighted eyes, over which he wore thick spectacles, with gold bows that curved about his ears. He was clerk to one of the magnates of a great steel corporation, and was looked upon in Cordelia Street as a young man with a future. There was a story that, some five years ago—he was now barely twenty-six—he had been a trifle dissipated, but in order to curb his appetites and save the loss of time and strength that a sowing of wild oats might have entailed, he had taken his chief's advice, oft reiterated to his employees, and at twenty-one had married the first woman whom he could persuade to share his fortunes. She happened to be an angular schoolmistress, much older than he, who also wore thick glasses, and who had now borne him four children, all near-sighted, like herself.

The young man was relating how his chief, now cruising in the Mediterranean, kept in touch with all the details of the business, arranging his office hours on his yacht just as though he were at home, and "knocking off work enough to keep two stenographers busy." His father told, in turn, the plan his corporation was considering, of putting in an electric railway plant in Cairo. Paul snapped his teeth; he had an awful apprehension that they might spoil it all before he got there. Yet he rather liked to hear these legends of the iron kings that were told and retold on Sundays and holidays; these stories of palaces in Venice yachts on the Mediterranean, and high play at Monte Carlo appealed to his fancy, and he was interested in the triumphs of these cash boys who had become famous, though he had no mind for the cash-boy stage.

After supper was over and he had helped to dry the dishes, Paul nervously asked his father whether he could go to George's to get some help in his geometry, and still more nervously asked for carfare. This latter request he had to repeat, as his father, on principle, did not like to hear requests for money, whether much or little. He asked Paul whether he could not go to some boy who lived nearer, and told him that he ought not to leave his school-work until Sunday; but he gave him the dime. He was not a poor man, but he had a worthy ambition to come up in the world. His only reason for allowing Paul to usher was that he thought a boy ought to be earning a little.

Paul bounded upstairs, scrubbed the greasy odor of the dishwater from his hands with the ill-smelling soap he hated, and then shook over his fingers a few drops of violet water from the bottle he kept hidden in his drawer. He left the house with his geometry conspicuously under his arm, and the moment he got out of Cordelia Street and boarded a downtown car, he shook off the lethargy of two deadening days and began to live again.

The leading juvenile of the permanent stock company which played at one of the downtown theaters was an acquaintance of Paul's, and the boy had been invited to drop in at the Sunday-night rehearsals whenever he could. For more than a year Paul had spent every available moment loitering about Charley Edwards's dressing room. He had won a place among Edwards's following not only because the young actor, who could not afford to employ a dresser, often found him useful, but because he recognized in Paul something akin to what churchmen term "vocation."

It was at the theater and at Carnegie Hall that Paul really lived; the rest was but a sleep and a forgetting. This was Paul's fairy tale, and it had for him all the allurement of a secret love. The moment he inhaled the gassy, painty, dusty odor behind the scenes, he breathed like a prisoner set free, and felt within him the possibility of doing or saying splendid, brilliant, poetic things. The moment the cracked orchestra beat out the overture from *Martha*, or jerked at the serenade from *Rigoletto*, all stupid and ugly things slid from him, and his senses were deliciously, yet delicately fired.

Perhaps it was because, in Paul's world, the natural nearly always wore the guise of ugliness, that a certain element of artificiality seemed to him necessary in beauty. Perhaps it was because his experience of life elsewhere was so full of Sabbath-school picnics, petty economies, wholesome advice as to how to succeed in life, and the inescapable odors of cooking, that he found this existence so alluring, these smartly clad men and women so attractive, that he was so moved by these starry apple orchards that bloomed perennially under the limelight.

It would be difficult to put it strongly enough how convincingly the stage entrance of that theater was for Paul the actual portal of Romance. Certainly none of the company ever suspected it, least of all Charley Edwards. It was very like the old stories that used to float about London of fabulously rich Jews, who had subterranean halls there, with palms, and fountains, and soft lamps and richly appareled women who never saw the disenchanting light of London day. So, in the midst of that smoke-palled city, enamored of figures and grimy toil, Paul had his secret temple, his wishing carpet, his bit of blue-and-white Mediterranean shore bathed in perpetual sunshine.

Several of Paul's teachers had a theory that his imagination had been perverted by garish fiction but the truth was that he scarcely ever read at all. The books at home were not such as would either tempt or corrupt a youthful mind, and as for reading the novels that some of his friends urged upon him—well, he got what he wanted much more quickly from music; any sort of music, from an orchestra to a barrel organ. He needed only the spark, the indescribable thrill that made his imagination master of his senses, and he could make plots and pictures enough of his own. It was equally true that he was not stagestruck—not, at any rate, in the usual acceptation of that expression. He had no desire to become an actor, any more than he had to become a musician. He felt no necessity to do any of these things; what he wanted was to see, to be in the atmosphere, float on the wave of it, to be carried out, blue league after blue league, away from everything.

After a night behind the scenes Paul found the schoolroom more than ever repulsive; the bare floors and naked walls; the prosy men who never wore frock coats, or violets in their buttonholes; the women with their dull gowns, shrill voices, and pitiful seriousness about prepositions that govern the dative. He could not bear to have the other pupils think, for a moment, that he took these people seriously; he must convey to them that he considered it all trivial, and was there only by way of a jest, anyway. He had autographed pictures of all the members of the stock company which he showed his classmates, telling them the most incredible stories of his familiarity with these people, of his acquaintance with the soloists who came to Carnegie Hall, his suppers with them and the flowers he sent them. When these stories lost their effect, and his audience grew listless, he became desperate and would bid all the boys good-bye, announcing that he was going to travel for a while; going to Naples, to Venice, to Egypt. Then, next Monday, he would slip back, conscious and nervously smiling; his sister was ill, and he should have to defer his voyage until spring.

Matters went steadily worse with Paul at school. In the itch to let his instructors know how heartily he despised them and their homilies, and how thoroughly he was appreciated elsewhere, he mentioned once or twice that he had no time to fool with theorems; adding—with a twitch of the eyebrows and a touch of that nervous bravado which so perplexed them—that he was helping the people down at the stock company; they were old friends of his.

The upshot of the matter was that the Principal went to Paul's father, and Paul was taken out of school and put to work. The manager at Carnegie Hall was told to get another usher in his stead; the doorkeeper at the theater was warned not to admit him to the house; and Charley Edwards remorsefully promised the boy's father not to see him again.

The members of the stock company were vastly amused when some of Paul's stories reached them—especially the women. They were hard-working women, most of them supporting indigent husbands or brothers, and they laughed rather bitterly at having stirred the boy to such fervid and florid inventions. They agreed with the faculty and with his father that Paul's was a bad case.

The eastbound train was plowing through a January snowstorm; the dull dawn was beginning to show gray when the engine whistled a mile out of Newark. Paul started up from the seat where he had lain curled in uneasy slumber, rubbed the breath-misted window glass with his hand, and peered out. The snow was whirling in curling eddies above the white bottom lands, and the drifts lay already deep in the fields and along the fences, while here and there the long dead grass and dried weed stalks protruded black above it. Lights shone from the scattered houses, and a gang of laborers who stood beside the track waved their lanterns.

Paul had slept very little, and he felt grimy and uncomfortable. He had made the all-night journey in a day coach, partly because he was ashamed, dressed as he was, to go into a Pullman, and partly because he was afraid of being seen there by some Pittsburgh businessman, who might have noticed him in Denny & Carson's office. When the whistle awoke him, he clutched quickly at his breast pocket, glancing about him with an uncertain smile. But the little, clay-bespattered Italians were still sleeping, the slatternly women across the aisle were in open-mouthed oblivion, and even the crumby, crying babies were for the nonce stilled. Paul settled back to struggle with his impatience as best he could.

When he arrived at the Jersey City station he hurried through his breakfast, manifestly ill at ease and keeping a sharp eye about him. After he reached the Twenty-third Street station, he consulted a cabman and had himself driven to a men's-furnishings establishment that was just opening for the day. He spent upward of two hours, buying with endless reconsidering and great care. His new street suit he put on in the fitting room; the frock coat and dress clothes he had bundled into the cab with his linen. Then he drove to a hatter's and a shoe house. His next errand was at Tiffany's, where he selected his silver and a new scarf pin. He would not wait to have his silver marked, he said. Lastly, he stopped at a trunk shop on Broadway and had his purchases packed into various traveling bags.

It was a little after one o'clock when he drove up to the Waldorf, and after settling with the cabman, went into the office. He registered from Washington; said his mother and father had been abroad, and that he had come down to await the arrival of their steamer. He told his story plausibly and had no trouble, since he volunteered to pay for them in advance, in engaging his rooms; a sleeping room, sitting room, and bath.

Not once, but a hundred times, Paul had planned this entry into New York. He had gone over every detail of it with Charley Edwards, and in his scrapbook at home there were pages of description about New York hotels, cut from the Sunday papers. When he was shown to his sitting room on the eighth floor he saw at a glance that everything was as it should be; there was but one detail in his mental picture that the place did not realize, so he rang for the bellboy and sent him down for flowers. He moved about nervously until the boy returned, putting away his new linen and fingering it delightedly as he did so. When the flowers came he put them hastily into water, and then tumbled into a hot bath. Presently he came out of his white bathroom, resplendent in his new silk underwear, and playing with the tassels of his red robe. The snow was whirling so fiercely outside his windows that he could scarcely see across the street, but within the air was deliciously soft and fragrant. He put the violets and jonquils on the taboret beside the couch, and threw himself down, with a long sigh, covering himself with a Roman blanket. He was thoroughly tired; he had been in such haste, he had stood up to such a strain, covered so much ground in the last twenty-four hours, that he wanted to think how it had all come about. Lulled by the sound of the wind, the warm air, and the cool fragrance of the flowers, he sank into deep, drowsy retrospection.

It had been wonderfully simple; when they had shut him out of the theater and concert hall, when they had taken away his bone, the whole thing was virtually determined. The rest was a mere matter of opportunity. The only thing that at all surprised him was his own courage—for he realized well enough that he had always been tormented by fear, a sort of apprehensive dread that, of late years, as the meshes of the lies he had told closed about him, had been pulling the muscles of his body tighter and tighter. Until now he could not remember the time when he had not been dreading something. Even when he was a little boy it was always there—behind him, or before, or on either side. There had always been the shadowed corner, the dark place into which he dared not look, but from which something seemed always to be watching him—and Paul had done things that were not pretty to watch, he knew.

But now he had a curious sense of relief, as though he had at last thrown down the gauntlet to the thing in the corner.

Yet it was but a day since he had been sulking in the traces; but yesterday afternoon that he had been sent to the bank with Denny & Carson's deposit, as usual—but this time he was instructed to leave the book to be balanced. There was above two thousand dollars in checks, and nearly a thousand in the bank notes which he had taken from the book and quietly transferred to his pocket. At the bank he had made out a new deposit slip. His nerves had been steady enough to permit of his returning to the office, where he had finished his work and asked for a full day's holiday tomorrow, Saturday, giving a perfectly reasonable pretext. The bankbook, he knew, would not be returned before Monday or Tuesday, and his father would be out of town for the next week. From the time he slipped the bank notes into his pocket until he boarded the night train for New York, he had not known a moment's hesitation. It was not the first time Paul had steered through treacherous waters.

How astonishingly easy it had all been; here he was, the thing done; and this time there would be no awakening, no figure at the top of the stairs. He watched the snowflakes whirling by his window until he fell asleep.

When he awoke, it was three o'clock in the afternoon. He bounded up with a start; half of one of his precious days gone already! He spent more than an hour in dressing, watching every stage of his toilet carefully in the mirror. Everything was quite perfect; he was exactly the kind of boy he had always wanted to be.

When he went downstairs Paul took a carriage and drove up Fifth Avenue toward the Park. The snow had somewhat abated; carriages and tradesmen's wagons were hurrying soundlessly to and fro in the winter twilight; boys in woolen mufflers were shoveling off the doorsteps; the avenue stages made fine spots of color against the white street. Here and there on the corners were stands, with whole flower gardens blooming under glass cases, against the sides of which the snowflakes stuck and melted; violets, roses, carnations, lilies of the valley—somehow vastly more lovely and alluring that they blossomed thus unnaturally in the snow. The Park itself was a wonderful stage winterpiece.

When he returned, the pause of the twilight had ceased and the tune of the streets had changed. The snow was falling faster, lights streamed from the hotels that reared their dozen stories fearlessly up into the storm, defying the raging Atlantic winds. A long, black stream of carriages poured down the avenue, intersected here and there by other streams, tending horizontally. There were a score of cabs about the entrance of this hotel, and his driver had to wait. Boys in livery were running in and out of the awning stretched across the sidewalk, up and down the red velvet carpet laid from the door to the street. Above, about, within it all was the rumble and roar, the hurry and toss of thousands of human beings as hot for pleasure as himself, and on every side of him towered the glaring affirmation of the omnipotence of wealth.

The boy set his teeth and drew his shoulders together in a spasm of realization; the plot of all dramas, the text of all romances, the nerve-stuff of all sensations was whirling about him like the snowflakes. He burnt like a faggot in a tempest.

When Paul went down to dinner the music of the orchestra came floating up the elevator shaft to greet him. His head whirled as he stepped into the thronged corridor, and he sank back into one of the chairs against the wall to get his breath. The lights, the chatter, the perfumes, the bewildering medley of color—he had, for a moment, the feeling of not being able to stand it. But only for a moment; these were his own people, he told himself. He went slowly about the corridors, through the writing rooms, smoking rooms, reception rooms, as though he were exploring the chambers of an enchanted palace, built and peopled for him alone.

When he reached the dining room he sat down at a table near a window. The flowers, the white linen, the many-colored wineglasses, the gay toilettes of the women, the low popping of corks, the undulating repetitions of the Blue Danube from the orchestra, all flooded Paul's dream with bewildering radiance. When the roseate tinge of his champagne was added—that cold, precious, bubbling stuff that creamed and foamed in his glass—Paul wondered that there were honest men in the world at all. This was what all the world was fighting for, he reflected; this was what all the struggle was about. He doubted the reality of his past. Had he ever known a place called Cordelia Street, a place where fagged-looking businessmen got on the early car; mere rivets in a machine they seemed to Paul—sickening men, with combings of children's hair always hanging to their coats, and the smell of cooking in their clothes. Cordelia Street—Ah, that belonged to another time and country; had he not always been thus, had he not sat here night after night, from as far back as he could remember, looking pensively over just such shimmering textures and slowly twirling the stem of a glass like this one between his thumb and middle finger? He rather thought he had.

He was not the least abashed or lonely. He had no especial desire to meet or to know any of these people; all he demanded was the right to look on and conjecture, to watch the pageant. The mere stage properties were all he contended for. Nor was he lonely later in the evening, in his lodge at the Metropolitan. He was now entirely rid of his nervous misgivings, of his forced aggressiveness, of the imperative desire to show himself different from his surroundings. He felt now that his surroundings explained him. Nobody questioned the purple, he had only to wear it passively. He had only to glance down at his attire to reassure himself that here it would be impossible for anyone to humiliate him.

He found it hard to leave his beautiful sitting room to go to bed that night, and sat long watching the raging storm from his turret window. When he went to sleep it was with the lights turned on in his bedroom; partly because of his old timidity, and partly so that, if he should wake in the night, there would be no wretched moment of doubt, no horrible suspicion of yellow wallpaper, or of Washington and Calvin above his bed.

Sunday morning the city was practically snowbound. Paul breakfasted late, and in the afternoon he fell in with a wild San Francisco boy, a freshman at Yale, who said he had run down for a "little flyer" over Sunday. The young man offered to show Paul the night side of the town, and the two boys went out together after dinner, not returning to the hotel until seven o'clock the next morning. They had started out in the confiding warmth of a champagne friendship, but their parting in the elevator was singularly cool. The freshman pulled himself together to make his train, and Paul went to bed. He awoke at two o'clock in the afternoon, very thirsty and dizzy, and rang for icewater, coffee, and the Pittsburgh papers.

On the part of the hotel management, Paul excited no suspicion. There was this to be said for him, that he wore his spoils with dignity and in no way made himself conspicuous. Even under the glow of his wine he was never boisterous; though he found the stuff like a magician's wand for wonder-building. His chief greediness lay in his ears and eyes, and his excesses were not offensive ones. His dearest pleasures were the gray winter twilights in his sitting room; his quiet enjoyment of his flowers, his clothes, his wide divan, his cigarette, and his sense of power. He could not remember a time when he had felt so at peace with himself. The mere release from the necessity of petty lying, lying every day and every day, restored his self-respect. He had never lied for pleasure, even at school; but to be noticed and admired, to assert his difference from other Cordelia Street boys; and he felt a good deal more manly, more honest, even, now that he had no need for boastful pretensions, now that he could, as his actor friends used to say, "dress the part." It was characteristic that remorse did not occur to him. His golden days went by without a shadow, and he made each as perfect as he could.

On the eighth day after his arrival in New York he found the whole affair exploited in the Pittsburgh papers, exploited with a wealth of detail which indicated that local news of a sensational nature was at a low ebb. The firm of Denny & Carson announced that the boy's father had refunded the full amount of the theft and that they had no intention of prosecuting. The Cumberland minister had been interviewed, and expressed his hope of yet reclaiming the motherless lad, and his Sabbath-school teacher declared that she would spare no effort to that end. The rumor had reached Pittsburgh that the boy had been seen in a New York hotel, and his father had gone East to find him and bring him home.

Paul had just come in to dress for dinner; he sank into a chair, weak to the knees, and clasped his head in his hands. It was to be worse than jail, even; the tepid waters of Cordelia Street were to close over him finally and forever. The gray monotony stretched before him in hopeless, unrelieved years; Sabbath school, Young People's Meeting, the yellow-papered room, the damp dish-towels; it all rushed back upon him with a sickening vividness. He had the old feeling that the orchestra had suddenly stopped, the sinking sensation that the play was over. The sweat broke out on his face, and he sprang to his feet, looked about him with his white, conscious smile, and winked at himself in the mirror. With something of the old childish belief in miracles with which he had so often gone to class, all his lessons unlearned, Paul dressed and dashed whistling down the corridor to the elevator. He had no sooner entered the dining room and caught the measure of the music than his remembrance was lightened by his old elastic power of claiming the moment, mounting with it, and finding it all sufficient. The glare and glitter about him, the mere scenic accessories had again, and for the last time, their old potency. He would show himself that he was game, he would finish the thing splendidly. He doubted, more than ever, the existence of Cordelia Street, and for the first time he drank his wine recklessly. Was he not, after all, one of those fortunate beings born to the purple, was he not still himself and in his own place? He drummed a nervous accompaniment to the Pagliacci music and looked about him, telling himself over and over that it had paid.

He reflected drowsily, to the swell of the music and the chill sweetness of his wine, that he might have done it more wisely. He might have caught an outbound steamer and been well out of their clutches before now. But the other side of the world had seemed too far away and too uncertain then; he could not have waited for it; his need had been too sharp. If he had to choose over again, he would do the same thing tomorrow. He looked affectionately about the dining room, now gilded with a soft mist. Ah, it had paid indeed!

Paul was awakened next morning by a painful throbbing in his head and feet. He had thrown himself across the bed without undressing, and had slept with his shoes on. His limbs and hands were lead heavy, and his tongue and throat were parched and burnt. There came upon him one of those fateful attacks of clearheadedness that never occurred except when he was physically exhausted and his nerves hung loose. He lay still, closed his eyes, and let the tide of things wash over him.

His father was in New York; "stopping at some joint or other," he told himself. The memory of successive summers on the front stoop fell upon him like a weight of black water. He had not a hundred dollars left; and he knew now, more than ever, that money was everything, the wall that stood between all he loathed and all he wanted. The thing was winding itself up; he had thought of that on his first glorious day in New York, and had even provided a way to snap the thread. It lay on his dressing table now; he had got it out last night when he came blindly up from dinner, but the shiny metal hurt his eyes, and he disliked the looks of it.

He rose and moved about with a painful effort, succumbing now and again to attacks of nausea. It was the old depression exaggerated; all the world had become Cordelia Street. Yet somehow he was not afraid of anything, was absolutely calm; perhaps because he had looked into the dark corner at last and knew. It was bad enough, what he saw there but somehow not so bad as his long fear of it had been. He saw everything clearly now. He had a feeling that he had made the best of it, that he had lived the sort of life he was meant to live and for half an hour he sat staring at the revolver. But he told himself that wasn't the way so he went downstairs and took a cab to the ferry.

When Paul arrived in Newark he got off the train and took another cab, directing the driver to follow the Pennsylvania tracks out of the town. The snow lay heavy on the roadways and had drifted deep in the open fields. Only here and there the dead grass or dried weed stalks projected, singularly black, above it. Once well into the country, Paul dismissed the carriage and walked, floundering along the tracks, his mind a medley of irrelevant things. He seemed to hold in his brain an actual picture of everything he had seen that morning. He remembered every feature of both his drivers, of the tooth-less old woman from whom he had bought the red flowers in his coat, the agent from whom he had got his ticket, and all of his fellow passengers on the ferry. His mind, unable to cope with vital matters near at hand, worked feverishly and deftly at sorting and grouping these images. They made for him a part of the ugliness of the world, of the ache in his head, and the bitter burning on his tongue. He stooped and put a handful of snow into his mouth as he walked, but that, too, seemed hot. When he reached a little hillside, where the tracks ran through a cut some twenty feet below him, he stopped and sat down.

The carnations in his coat were drooping with the cold, he noticed their red glory all over. It occurred to him that all the flowers he had seen in the glass cases that first night must have gone the same way long before this. It was only one splendid breath they had, in spite of their brave mockery at the winter outside the glass; and it was a losing game in the end, it seemed, this revolt against the homilies by which the world is run. Paul took one of the blossoms carefully from his coat and scooped a little hole in the snow, where he covered it up. Then he dozed awhile, from his weak condition, seemingly insensible to the cold.

The sound of an approaching train awoke him, and he started to his feet, remembering only his resolution, and afraid lest he should be too late. He stood watching the approaching locomotive, his teeth chattering, his lips drawn away from them in a frightened smile, once or twice he glanced nervously sidewise, as though he were being watched. When the right moment came, he jumped. As he fell, the folly of his haste occurred to him with merciless clearness, the vastness of what he had left undone. There flashed through his brain, clearer than ever before, the blue of Adriatic water, the yellow of Algerian sands.

He felt something strike his chest, and that his body was being thrown swiftly through the air, on and on, immeasurably far and fast, while his limbs were gently relaxed. Then, because the picture-making mechanism was crushed, the disturbing visions flashed into black, and Paul dropped back into the immense design of things.

The Friday Night Shift at the Taco House Blues (Wah-Wah)

WANDA COLEMAN

It is 1973 and "we" are low on everything.

Down at the Taco House is where we work, Shurli and me. Shurli's an old-timer and was managing the night shift when I first came on the gig. The night shift starts at six in the evening. That's five-forty night people's time. We night folks go by bar time, which in Los Angeles means the clock is always twenty minutes fast. When 2 a.m. rolls around (booze curfew) that's about how long it takes for the customers to finish their drinks, for us to coax the hypes out of the john or jane and sober up the drunks with hot coffee and send them all out into the night and presumably home. Since most waitresses have been barmaids at one time or another, the process is essentially the same. Our night lives—shaped by complete boredom one minute and mayhem and murder (not to mention robbery) the next.

So like, Shurli's been working the Taco House off and on for ten years. Actually, Shurli daylights as a welfare mother supporting six kids, their three fathers (two kids per father, a pretty good ratio), a three-hundred-dollar-a-month car note on her customized Cadillac Coupe de Ville and her one-hundred-and-fifty-a-month note on that raggedy-ass crib she calls a house located in the neighborhood about twelve blocks away. Me—I'm just passing through, I hope, on my way to bigger and better things.

I got my eye on a government job—trying to get on as a reception-ist/secretary as they say in the want ads. I struggled awake yesterday morning about ten o'clock. Just in time to keep my eleven o'clock appointment for the typing, math, memory and the rest of the aptitude tests they give you. Me—I live alone, having no kids. That's one mistake I refuse to make. Not me. I've got to make my fortune first. The Taco House stays open twenty-four hours in order to catch the night trade. Some are decent folks who work nights. Some are professional hoods, gamblers, pimps, hypes, prosties and shit like that—and of course, the cops, narks and plainclothesmen who are after their asses, and inevitably, the customers they've hooked on one trick or another. So like, Shurli gets in right at five-forty when Redd completes her run. Redd is a bright-skinned woman who runs the day shift. She's called "red" like most niggahs what got that kind of orangy skin tone and rust colored hair that usually comes from certain black/white combines. She's a good person, everybody likes her, but I don't really know her, with her working the day shift. Shurli bounces over to the register and takes over as we other girls come in. I say bounce, because Shurli is five feet four and weighs about three hundred pounds. She's got the meatiest forearms—a lot of that just plain muscle. She works the register the way she drives that Caddy, smooth and with profound grace. As me and the girls come in, Jesus hands us our aprons. There are four of us. Me, Kathy, Li'l Bit and Sharita. Sharita is a tall slender chick whose old man rides with Scarlet Fever, a raunchy all black lightweight version of the Hell's Angels. She thinks she has clout. We don't like each other and I'm waiting for the day when I have to get off into that bitch's ass.

So we check in while Chuck (that's the owner) runs through the one hundred and fifty dollar bank with Shurli. You see, the register always gets a bank. That way the boss knows if you're stealing or not and can gauge his profit and loss margin against the tape. Actually, the money never stays in the register long. Periodically, Shurli removes part of the take, locks it and moves most of the tens, twenties and fifties (we don't change ben franks) to the back where there's a safe built into the floor which is usually hidden under a mat. All the girls work the register.

So like, anyhow, we come in, and Jesus hands us our aprons, and we go in the back, hang up coats and sweaters and then duck our purses under the counter so we can keep our eyes on what few pennies we do have. The set-up here is the usual. Black girls on the counter, Mexicans do the cooking and the owner (who's either white or Jewish as the case may be) rakes in the bread.

Chuck, who speaks Spanish fluently, puts one girl (in this case, Shurli) in charge of the girls, cause he knows that won't no niggah bitch take orders from no Mexican cook. Jesus has two assistants, Don and Herman. They look like Castilians. Don speaks faulty English, and when he does, he talks like us blacks. Herman grins a lot and can only get through the basic hello and goodbye. Jesus speaks both and although his English is usually very simple, I often get the feeling that where he's from in Mexico, he's big shit and can rattle off the King's English as well as any Harvard grad. Of course, just as most of the waitresses (with the exception of myself and Sharita) are welfare mothers, the Latinos are all illegal aliens. But nobody ever says anything and it's cool.
Chuck, the boss man, has a rep for messing around with the girls. Chuck usually hangs around for an hour or so after changeover, then goes home. Shurli tells me that he's slept with everybody except me and Li'l Bit. About

herself she don't say. I grunt and shrug. The turkey has pulled at my bra strap a-couple of times, but that's as far as it got. He's a family man with one of those pale sickly blonde wives—a classic. And his children are dark haired, slenderer images of himself. I've never seen his son, but his daughter runs through occasionally. Rumor is she's a campus activist and that she and her old man don't get along too well when it comes to politics, but she keeps the books and records and runs that end of the business for him. Shurli says that she's heard 'em arguing a lot about her shacking with some dude he thinks is a shiftless creep. As far as I'm concerned it's their business. I'm just looking forward to the day when I can clear out.

At the changeover, when we hit the counter, business is fairly heavy with the dinner trade. At the Taco House, people have the choice of fast food service in or out. The counter is long and on a curve. The first and the longest arm of the curve is where all the food preparation takes place. The customer can clearly see the de-wormed tomatoes (diced well for color), the week-old onions, the bleached lettuce, pickle, relish, mayonnaise, refried beans, ketchup, hot sauce and chili as we apply it in varying degrees per order. They can even watch as Jesus and the boys fry a barrage of hot dogs, corn tortilla shells (soft, semi crisp and crunchy), steam buns and flour tortillas, fry hamburger patties, taco meat patties (mainly pork and cereal), toast hot dog buns and boil wieners.

People come and go in a steady stream and then the tide breaks about eight o'clock. Usually things are sporadic during the weekdays. Work is on a six-day schedule with alternating days off. All the girls work on Sunday. Days off usually fall on Mondays and Tuesdays. You work half a day on Christmas. On weekends the traffic is killing. The people never stop and periodically Chuck will take on a new girl for the summer just to keep the stream of cash flowing smoothly. But normally, things pick up again about ten o'clock, get spotty, and then around twelve get heavy again for about a half hour. Then from twelve-thirty to two-thirty it's nightmare time. People come and go so fast, time becomes a blur. From two-thirty until five o'clock time comes to a complete halt. It's usually during this period when we girls start to get bitchy with one another. But about five things pick up again, with people coming in for eggs, coffee, donuts and shit. I was surprised to see the number of people who like to eat tacos and stuff for breakfast. The days of ham and eggs are numbered.

I start in filling the orders. We mark abbreviations for each order on each bag, figure the prices and totals in our heads, mark the price on the bag and circle it. We hand the bags to Shurli or whoever's on the register at the moment. She rings it up, takes the cash, makes change and hands the bag to the customer.

So like, this night I'm preparing orders, my hands stinging from continual dippings into the tomatoes. It's cold and the middle of November. Outside, it's crisp and clear and the lights from the bar across the street shine brightly. The juke is blasting rhythm and blues. Shurli is leaning across the counter talking to one of the local dope dealers, trying to score some white folks (bennies) for her and her old man. Li'l Bit and Kathy are feeding their faces on their break, jaw-ing over two plates heaped with burger meat and frijoles (none of the girls will touch the taco meat including me) and gulping down coffee. Sharita has slipped out to turn a trick with a don who stuck twenty dollars in her paw.

I reach for a towel to wipe my hands when a lone customer walks in. He's a tall, lanky guy in his mid-twenties. He's brown-skinned, just a shade lighter than me, and has his grayish brown hair cut to a crew cut, a style that spells jerk on the black side of town. He looks like he's safe enough, orders a tostada and a cup of coffee. I glance at the girls, know I'm elected, and wait as Jesus tosses a tortilla into the fat vat. K.P. comes in and it's on me to take his order for two chili burgers heavy on the onion. K.P. is one of the regulars. He practically lives here and will come in two or three times a night. Shurli has jammed me that he and a couple of other old cronies are Chuck's paid spies. They give Chuck clandestine reports on the conduct of the girls. And it must be true, because Chuck always knows everything that goes down. The Latinos report on the girls, the girls report on the girls and the spies report on everybody. Another dude comes in. He's dark-skinned, youngish, looks like a thug. He knows the lighter guy and yells, "Hey! Ray, mah man!" They slap hands between placement of his order. After Shurli rings them up, they take their plates and sit at the counter. By now K.P. has joined them and everybody is on the two extreme ends of the counter. I look and decide to join Shurli and the fine piece of meat she's now talking to, K.P. and the two dudes on their end. Everybody's listening to the dude called Ray tell what's apparently an interesting story. I come up and lean against the soda fountain.

"Yeah," Ray is continuing. "She was dead—just like that. I mean, I can't get over it. I went out and went down to Jack's to shoot some pool, hustle up a couple of bucks. She wanted a fifth and neither one of us didn't have no money, man. She hadn't got her check—you know how it is . . ."

He talks like he's high on reds (seconal) slurring his words, stretching each syllable. But I know what that is. That is that high you get—the one I call Pain. Yeah, that's it all reel.

"She had come home and washed her hair. You know, she hadn't been feeling good lately and had been complaining a lot but you know how womens are. Theys always complainin' about one thing or another." The men nod in agreement. Shurli grunts.

"And she was older than me, you know! I don't know how old she was, I guess about forty-five. And I'm only twenty-four, but to me that didn't make no difference. I loved the broad. You know what I mean?"

"Amen," snorts K.P. His crony shakes his head in agreement. I shift my weight to my left leg. Shurli grunts.

"She was good lookin' for her age too, you know how it is with us—we don't age like white peoples do. She had on her favorite wig, a brown one all done up in curls—kind of like yours only shorter." He's speaking to me and everybody turns to look at the wig I'm wearing. A sort of controlled afro.

"I really loved that woman. I mean—I had other girls, you understand me?" Everybody nods. "But she was my wo-man. She was my heart."

"Hey—bring yo' ass over here, Carol."

A shout from Li'l Bit interrupts the bemoaning. I look around to see that fifteen people have suddenly appeared from nowhere, Jesus and his boys are popping at the griddle and Li'l Bit and Kathy are tossing plates, tacos and beans as fast as they can move. I speed to the counter, pencil and bag in hand. "Next, please place your order." Shurli bustles over and helps out. The dude, Ray, and his partner take their plates from the counter and move to a table against the wall in the back. K.P. sips his coffee and picks at his plate, keeping a watch on us and the register.

I work, having trouble keeping the orders in my head as they come rapid-fire. I kind of have my eye on the dude Shurli was talking to. He is real clean cut, wearing a camel hair mack coat and brim to match, clean beige threads underneath. He's built smooth-skinned and muscular on a wiry frame, has even white, pearly teeth and heavy-lidded, sexy brown eyes. I jam Shurli between a chili tamale order and an enchilada plate.

"Who's that—he sho 'nuff fine."

"Oh, Tommy? He's like a baby brother to me. Him and his other brothers are in here all the time."

"Do they all look as good as him?"

She laughs. "Pretty good. I'll introduce you to 'em sometimes. They're nice too—and they all work for a livin'."

I look up suddenly and catch his eyes. He smiles slowly, slightly. He knows I'm asking about him. The smile goes through me and straight to my tenderloin. Whoowhee, baby!

"Get that order," Kathy barks and I'm back into the grind.

"Where in the fuck is Sharita?" Li'l Bit pipes.

Kathy sniggers, "That bitch puts a high premium on her pussy."

As if having heard the summons, Sharita shows up through the glass window, footing up the pavement. She pushes the door and enters, throwing off her coat and rushing behind the counter. She glances at K.P. for a second (all of us know Chuck's paid spies) and then slips into the grind.

We're on our feet three hours solid. Seems like a few people did get their county checks and it's Friday night anyhow. Fridays are always busy. By one o'clock a hundred people have come and gone and we're cranky for another break. Sharita is eyeing my stud who briefly introduced himself to me when I maneuvered service at one of the tables which is strictly Shurli's domain (the tables leave better tips than the counter—sometimes a girl can add ten to fifteen dollars a night to her salary). I catch Sharita eyeing him as he talks to some old man who's taken the stool beside him. Sharita looks dead to me. I stare daggers. She shrugs and backs off.

At one, Tod comes in. Everybody calls Tod crazy.

"Here comes that crazy Tod," Chuck always said whenever he was around and spotted Tod coming in. Tod is a regular. Tale was that he worked for Chuck between jobs and good women. He is supposed to be the best fry cook Chuck has ever had. Everyone is fond of him and regrets the fact that Tod is a Viet Nam veteran.

"He was a fine boy, all right before he went into the Army, I tell you. I don't know what they did to him over there, Viet Nam. Ever since he's been out, he's been crazy like that. He's a good person, but nutty as a fruit cake." Tod won't eat the taco meat either.

Tod's wardrobe is limited (a sign of immense and extreme poverty among blacks) to denim overalls, the remains of his military uniforms replete with ribbons from numerous deeds of heroism and sharp shooting, karate, etc. and a raggedy trench-type overcoat he sports like a private eye. I had seen Tod several times before. He was in at least two or three nights a week on my shift. He knew I was a new girl, and made it a point to get to know me. I kept picking up the vibe that he lusted after me. But I'm ambitious and he doesn't suit my qualifications. The first of which is to have a car and every time I saw him, he was walking, which is a sin in Car City, Los Angeles.

Tod orders his usual, twenty tacos with hamburger meat and fifteen hamburgers. Jesus groans as he always does when Tod places his order. We only charge him half price as is the policy for Chuck's favorites (twenty percent off for the cops from the local precinct and any other officer of the law). Tod is always boozed up, high if not stumbling drunk. His habit is to come in, size up the joint, go out, come back minutes later, order something for himself, eat, go out, come back an hour later, place his big order, which it always takes Jesus an hour to prepare between other orders we take, while Tod cuts the bull with anyone he can find to cut it with, and sometimes comes back just before the shift change for a cup of coffee to sober up and go down to the unemployment office.

I jam Shurli about his order. "He comes in like that all the time. Who's all that stuff for?"

"Oh—that's his mother. She's got twelve kids, girl—still at home. Two girls are married. Tod makes fifteen. Tod's the oldest."

"How old is he?"

"Must be twenty-six by now. All the rest of 'em is still at home. It's pitiful child, pitiful. I ain't never seen folks so poor."

As the lull comes on, I immediately forget about Tod. My eyes go back to Tommy and I can tell he's warming more and more to the idea of waiting out the night and seeing me home after my shift is over. He keeps giving me approving looks as I move back and forth behind the counter. It's rough, trying to be a waitress and look sexy, but most of the girls manage it, me included. It's rough in them white uniforms and white brogans Chuck insists we wear, plus the heavy cloth aprons.

I'm built, no brag. Brothers keep telling me how I've got plenty of butter. A compliment to any black woman—cause our men, for the most part, like their women on the fleshy side. Skinny legs usually get a black gal laughed at although, as Shurli always says, "It ain't the beauty—it's the booty."

The place clears out about a quarter after two and we all settle in for the long haul. The guy whose old lady had died moves back to the counter and perches on a stool one down from my jazzy potential lay. Tod is still sitting on the service end of the room with Sharita and Kathy, cutting the bull and they accommodate him with their laughter. Li'l Bit is jawing with a youngster closer to her own age, which I figure to really be sixteen, although, she swears by nineteen and one six-month-old son. Li'l Bit is a green-eyed sandy-haired, sweet-looking yellow-skinned girl with very small features, except for her eyes. Li'l Bit is married and her old man grumpily picks her up in their 1954 Chevy struggle buggy when shift is over. She doesn't like marriage and wants to leave her child to its grandparents (either set will do) and her old man to the dogs. I notice Li'l Bit is copping something from her friend. Must be some bush (marijuana) or white folks, I figure. But my attention is on my foxy gentleman catch who's listening to Ray talk again, continuing his story which he's managed to tell anyone he can collar.

We check out his loneliness. He just doesn't want to be by himself and we can appreciate his feelings. Tommy, Shurli and me, listening. It gets quieter and quieter, and pretty soon even Crazy Tod, Sharita and Kathy can hear him talking. Jesus has put down the ladle and is leaning against the griddle, listening. His two compañeros have gone around back. Li'l Bit is in the jane.

"She bought me a Christmas present, you know? She showed it to me. We had had an argument that morning. She wanted to know what I was gonna get her—her having spent all that bread for me a present. She'll never know how doggish she made me feel. I been trying. I really been tryin'. But like you know how it is with the slump and alls goin' on." Shurli sighs deeply.

"I wanted to get her something. I planned to. I just hadn't figured on what, yet. And there she was, screaming at me and tossing my present around. She had got me a leather coat. It's really beautiful—all lined inside with red fur and got fur on the collar and cuffs. Real natty, you know? She liked to get her shoppin' done early—to avoid the rush. I wasn't even thinkin' 'bout it."

A beat down pause.

"I just can't get over her dying like that. So sudden. So quick. One minute and then—the next."

"Ah mannn, why don't you shut up all that sad talk! Ain't you got nothin' better to do than complain?" It was Tod. We bristle. I get up from the counter as a customer appears.

"Shut up Tod and let the man finish talkin'," Shurli chastises gently.

"Finish talkin'? He been talkin' all night and sayin' the same thing over and over again."

"Ah—go on," Shurli comes back. But the guy, Ray, had fallen into silence and is staring down into the coffee he was sipping. He pours sugar into it, takes a spoon and stirs slowly, his head bent. It aggravates all of us. Tommy stares a question at Tod.

A few people are coming in, a group of stragglers from the bar across the street. It is two o'clock. It's enough to keep everyone busy, with me and my man making eyes between orders. Tod catches us, then holds my glance for a second. I was giving the looks he wanted to someone else. He bristles, takes a sharp breath. I signal my intentions and for him to back off. Tod ignores me. He looks at Tommy, then Ray.

Crazy Tod starts pacing, loud talking. "Yeah man, hush up all that whining. Be a man. Shows you a man. I'm a man! One hundred percent man! I don't do no whining, no complaining and no crying." He is pacing the length of the Taco House, going around to Tommy and tapping him on the shoulder at intervals. "Ain't that right, man?" He taps Tommy who smiles, puzzled, but friendly, and nods.

"Can't argue that, brother."

"Shit—a man has got to stand up, show no pain—ain't that right bruh?" He talks to Ray who is shriveled up on his stool.

"I proved I'm a man. See these here ribbons? I got this one for sharp shootin'. I can kill a niggah so dead so quick, quicker than the eye can see! You name it and I can fire it with deadly accuracy. If a man can't defend himself, he ain't a man. And I can always defend myself. I can do that if'n I can't never do nothin' else."

As he talks, Tod paces. His pace gets quicker. He waves his hands and his talk gets louder and louder. He keeps coming over to Tommy and tapping him. We can all see that Tommy don't like what is happening. It's getting on his nerves. He realizes that Tod is a taste unhinged.

"Come on, sit down and have some coffee." Shurli reaches out and grabs Tod by his overcoat, pulling him to her. He about-faces and slams into her huge torso.

"Emmm—Shurli, I loves yah!" Everybody laughs.

"Gimme a cup of coffee, Carol," Shurli orders.

I move to the coffee pot and pour a hot steaming cup, then slide the cup past Tommy and into Shurli's chunky outstretched hand. "Here, Tod, drink this and come to your senses."

Tod reaches awkwardly for the cup, knocking it out of her hand and into Tommy's lap. "Goddamn!" Tommy yells, jumping up, scalded, hastily brushing coffee from the lap of his fresh beige jumpsuit. "Shit, man—what's wrong with you?" He yells at Tod.

Tod, having gotten the desired response, spins, grabs up a handful of napkins and starts "helping" Tommy clean up.

"Oh, oh, sorry brother. I didn't mean to make a mess!"

Li'l Bit comes out of the jane and walks past the two. "Tod, what you done gone and did now?"

"Hey, man, I can help myself! You've done enough for one night!" Tommy snaps.

"I'm just trying to help." Tod's words are slippery.

"Back off brother. You helped enough." We can see Tommy is short tempered and deeply pissed about his clothes. "If you was a man, as you claim you are, you'd offer to pay for my clothes. But that's all right, brother, I understands."

"Hey, now—well, wait a minute bruh! I'm just bein' nice."

"Niggah, you can take your being nice 'n shove it!"

Tommy's super pissed and moves to the door to leave. My heart does a slow painful sink. I'm getting pissed at Tod also.

Tod moves and halts Tommy at the door, hooking him at the elbow. "Don't run away, bruh! Don't run away from me like that!"

Tommy looks at Tod's hand on his elbow. "Man—is you crazy? What kind of fool is you? Let go of my elbow!"

Tod takes his hand away slowly, stepping back cautiously. "You think you man enough to take me?" Everybody groans. "Huh? You think you *man* enough?" Tod goes into a karate stance. "I gots my piece, man, and, like I say—I gots a deadly aim."

"Oh? You want to duel? I gots my piece too. It's out in the car. I'll be just a minute." He takes off his coat and goes through the door. Shurli turns to me, panic in her eyes.

"Girl, he always carries a .38 in his car. He'll kill Tod. I best go try and stop him." Shurli runs out into the night after Tommy.

Kathy takes her tall dark lithe healthy self and goes up to Tod. "Why don't you behave yourself, crazy, and quit actin' like everybody's a gook? Sit down and drink some coffee, take your order and go home!"

Tod turns to the counter. I hand him another cup of coffee. Shurli and Tommy come back in. She's mollified him, reasoned him down to a simmer.

She seats Tommy at the counter where he's left his coat. "I'll fix you a plate and you eat, O.K.?" He nods and turns up, spotting me, smiling, remembering our "date." I smile, then turn as another customer straggles through. "I'll get it," Li'l Bit slurs. Humph, I think—red devils.

Tod winds his drunken way over to Tommy, coffee in hand. "Like I said, man—I'm sorry." He stumbles and spills the coffee again. This time on Tommy's shoulder.

"Son-of-a-bitch!" Tommy jumps up screaming. "Sorry! You goddamned right you sorry. Now what you want to do sucker? Let's do it now!" Tommy tears off his hat, tossing it into one of the booths, revealing long matted brown hair. "Now do somethin', sucker, do somethin' now!"

"Aw niggah—I'm a black belt in karate. I'll kill your ass, sucker."

"Well, man, you better kill it then!" Tommy raises up his arms in a boxing stance, frustration in his eyes. I can see the thought traveling through his mind—images of being flipped through the plate glass window as he sizes up Tod. They are both about the same height, 6' 1", and frame. Tommy is worried about what his first move might be. He moves to hit Tod. Tod ducks.

Tommy reverses, moves and swings again. Tommy misses. Tod grabs his extended arm, raises him up and flings him into the table next to the john. Everybody is out of the kitchen area now, watching. Not a sound but that of the two men fighting.

Tommy struggles up from the floor, beneath the confident Tod. "Get up niggah, get up and come and get me!" Tommy is feeling his way, blinded and dizzy from the impact of his head against the solid edge of the table which is bolted to the floor and the west wall. Tod turns away, mocking him, announcing to us: "That's how a man fights!"

Doggedly, Tommy is halfway to his feet, leaning against the table for support, trying to get his focus. His hand brushes against the glass sugar canister. He secures it and pushes forward, stumbling after Tod, catching him by the flapping tail of his overcoat. "Okay, sucker, let's see you karate this!"

Wham, into Tod's skull. The scrunch of glass and blood spurting. Tod spins. Sugar everywhere. He reels under the impact. That is all Tommy needs. He rains blows down on Tod's neck and face. The sound of flesh pounding flesh. Jesus stands, awed. "Hey, man! Somebody call the cops. He's killing that man!" No one moves. Jesus hastily disappears around back to the pay phone.

"You's a man—huh? You's a man—huh?" Tommy screams like a chant. He's on top of Tod, slamming Tod's head into the floor with both of his hands. We all stand, frozen. Shurli finally runs from behind the counter, the unfinished plate still in her grasp. "Jesus is calling the cops. You best get outta here, quick!" She manages to pull him off of Tod with her free hand. Tommy stands, staggering—his eyes glazed, wild. He looks at me, through me, grabs the coat and hat Shurli hastily shoves at him, then stumbles through the door.

Silent, we all turn and look at Tod. He's struggling against the counter, trying to get to his feet. Blood everywhere, mixed with sugar and glass. Blood runs down from the gash in his head, in both directions, down his neck and down the front of his face. One eye seems to be partially out of its socket. His face torn, lumpy and jagged. I look away. Shurli barks, "Carol—go get some cold wet towels and help me clean him up."

The ambulance and the cops arrive an hour later and Tod is taken away mumbling incoherently on the stretcher. The police sergeant lingers to take testimony, but nobody is talking, not even Jesus. No, we can't identify the assailant. No, we never seen him before. No one got his name.

It's five-thirty and the new shift is coming on in about ten more minutes. Chuck'll probably come in too, if I know K.P. He was sitting at one of the booths on the south wall and saw it all. Shurli and I are sitting at the counter along with Sharita, listening to Ray talk about his wife. He has that look in his eyes, it's fresh strong and sparkles. The one I mentioned at the jump, pain.

"That coat. I got it at the pad. All new and shiny. I just can't bear to go back to that empty room. All her stuff is still there. She'll be buried Sunday. Her sister is takin' over everything. She gave me a week to split."

I nod, trying to keep awake. The ten minutes crawl by. "She tried to tell me, you know? We were arguing and she threw the coat at me, and then clutched her heart sudden like. I asked her what was the matter and she said she was having a heart attack. I thought she was pretending."

Shurli and I look at each other.

It's sunup and Redd hits the door letting in the chilly morning. I reach down under the counter for my purse, go out back and get my jacket.

Outside, Ray is waiting for me. "Say, what's your name?"

"Carol."

"You know, I just can't stand being alone. How about coming over to my place. We'll have a drink, huh?"

I look at him and into Pain. "Thanks—but no thanks." I turn away and shudder into the moist dawn. My struggle buggy, a tore down '69 Buick is de-icing behind the Taco House.

"Carol, wait up!"

It's Shurli. "I needs a lift, gal. My old man came and took the Cadillac. He has the duplicate keys. Just wait till I get my hands on that son-of-a-gun!" We get into the car and I crank up. Shurli is grinning like a coon and plowing through that tremendous brown vinyl purse she always carries.

"Looka here what I gots," Shurli chuckles and shows me. It's about three pounds of hamburger meat. "I'm gonna feed my kids!" she announces.

We break into laughter. I neglect to mention the fifty-dollar bill in my bra. I wonder what Chuck'll say when he totals up the take this morning.

from *Maggie: A Girl of the Streets*

STEPHEN CRANE

Eventually they entered a dark region where, from a careening building, a dozen gruesome doorways gave uploads of babies to the street and the gutter. A wind of early autumn raised yellow dust from cobbles and swirled it against a hundred windows. Long streamers of garments fluttered from fire escapes. In all unhandy places there were buckets, brooms, rags and bottles. In the street infants played or fought with other infants or sat stupidly in the way of vehicles. Formidable women, with uncombed hair and disordered dress, gossiped while leaning on railings, or screamed in frantic quarrels. Withered persons, in curious postures of submission to something, sat smoking pipes in obscure corners. A thousand odors of cooking food came forth to the street. The building quivered and creaked from the weight of humanity stamping about in its bowels.

A small ragged girl dragged a red, bawling infant along the crowded ways. He was hanging back, baby-like, bracing his wrinkled, bare legs.

The little girl cried out: "Ah, Tommie, come ahn. Dere's Jimmie and fader. Don't be a-pullin' me back."

She jerked the baby's arm impatiently. He fell on his face, roaring. With a second jerk she pulled him to his feet, and they went on. With the obstinacy of his order, he protested against being dragged in a chosen direction. He made heroic endeavors to keep on his legs, denounced his sister, and consumed a bit of orange peeling which he chewed between the times of his infantile orations.

As the sullen-eyed man, followed by the blood-covered boy, drew near, the little girl burst into reproachful cries. "Ah, Jimmie, youse bin fightin' agin."

The urchin swelled disdainfully.

"Ah, what d'hell, Mag. See?"

The little girl upbraided him. "You'se allus fightin', Jimmie, an' yeh knows it puts mudder out when yehs come home half dead, an' it's like we'll all get a poundin'."

She began to weep. The babe threw back his head and roared at his prospects.

"Ah," cried Jimmie, "shut up er I'll smack yer mou'. See?"

As his sister continued her lamentations, he suddenly struck her. The little girl reeled, and, recovering herself, burst into tears and quaveringly cursed him. As she slowly retreated, her brother advanced, dealing her cuffs. The father heard, and turned about.

"Stop that, Jim, d'yeh hear? Leave yer sister alone on the street. It's like I can never beat any sense into yer wooden head."

The urchin raised his voice in defiance to his parent, and continued his attacks. The babe bawled tremendously, protesting with great violence. During his sister's hasty maneuvers he was dragged by the arm.

Finally the procession plunged into one of the gruesome doorways. They crawled up dark stairways and along cold, gloomy halls. At last the father pushed open a door, and they entered a lighted room in which a large woman was rampant.

She stopped in a career from a seething stove to a pan-covered table. As the father and children filed in she peered at them.

"Eh, what? Been fightin' agin!" She threw herself upon Jimmie. The urchin tried to dart behind the others, and in the scuffle the babe, Tommie, was knocked down. He protested with his usual vehemence because they had bruised his tender shins against a table leg.

The mother's massive shoulders heaved with anger. Grasping the urchin by the neck and shoulder she shook him until he rattled. She dragged him to an unholy sink, and, soaking a rag in water, began to scrub his lacerated face with it. Jimmie screamed in pain, and tried to twist his shoulders out of the clasp of the huge arms.

The babe sat on the floor watching the scene, his face in contortions like that of a woman at a tragedy. The father, with a newly ladened pipe in his mouth, sat in a backless chair near the stove. Jimmie's cries annoyed him. He turned about and bellowed at his wife:

"Let the kid alone for a minute, will yeh, Mary? Yer allus poundin' 'im. When I come nights I can't get no rest 'cause yer allus poundin' a kid. Let up, d'yeh hear? Don't be allus poundin' a kid."

The woman's operations on the urchin instantly increased in violence. At last she tossed him to a corner, where he limply lay weeping.

The wife put her immense hands on her hips, and with a chieftain-like stride approached her husband.

"Ho!" she said, with a great grunt of contempt. "An' what in the devil are you stickin' your nose for?"

The babe crawled under the table, and, turning, peered out cautiously. The ragged girl retreated, and the urchin in the corner drew his legs carefully beneath him.

The man puffed his pipe calmly and put his great muddied boots on the back part of the stove.

"Go t'hell," he said tranquilly.

The woman screamed, and shook her fists before her husband's eyes. The rough yellow of her face and neck flared suddenly crimson. She began to howl.

He puffed imperturbably at his pipe for a time, but finally arose and went to look out of the window into the darkening chaos of backyards.

"You've been drinkin', Mary," he said. "You'd better let up on the bot', ol' woman, or you'll git done."

"You're a liar. I ain't had a drop," she roared in reply. They had a lurid altercation.

The babe was staring out from under the table, his small face working in his excitement. The ragged girl went stealthily over to the corner where the urchin lay.

"Are yehs hurted much, Jimmie?" she whispered timidly.

"Not a little bit. See?" growled the little boy.

"Will I wash d' blood?"

"Naw!"

"Will I—"

"When I catch dat Riley kid I'll break 'is face! Dat's right! See?"

He turned his face to the wall as if resolved grimly to bide his time.

In the quarrel between husband and wife the woman was victor. The man seized his hat and rushed from the room, apparently determined upon a vengeful drink. She followed to the door and thundered at him as he made his way downstairs.

She returned and stirred up the room until her children were bobbing about like bubbles.

"Git outa d' way," she bawled persistently, waving feet with their disheveled shoes near the heads of her children. She shrouded herself, puffing and snorting, in a cloud of steam at the stove, and eventually extracted a fry-ing-pan full of potatoes that hissed.

She flourished it. "Come t' yer suppers, now," she cried with sudden exasperation. "Hurry up, now, er I'll help yeh!"

The children scrambled hastily. With prodigious clatter they arranged themselves at table. The babe sat with his feet dangling high from a precari-ous infant's chair and gorged his small stomach. Jimmie forced, with feverish rapidity, the grease-enveloped pieces between his wounded lips. Maggie, with side glances of fear of interruption, ate like a small pursued tigress.

The mother sat blinking at them. She delivered reproaches, swallowed potatoes, and drank from a yellow-brown bottle. After a time her mood changed, and she wept as she carried little Tommie into another room and laid him to sleep, with his fists doubled, in an old quilt of faded red and green grandeur. Then she came and moaned by the stove. She rocked to and fro upon a chair, shedding tears and crooning miserably to the two children about their "poor mother" and "yer fader, damn 'is soul."

The little girl plodded between the table and the chair with a dish pan on it. She tottered on her small legs beneath burdens of dishes.

Jimmie sat nursing his various wounds. He cast furtive glances at his mother. His practiced eye perceived her gradually emerge from a mist of muddled sentiment until her brain burned in drunken heat. He sat breathless.

Maggie broke a plate.

The mother started to her feet as if propelled.

"Good Gawd!" she howled. Her glittering eyes fastened on her child with sudden hatred. The fervent red of her face turned almost to purple. The little boy ran to the halls, shrieking like a monk in an earthquake.

He floundered about in darkness until he found the stairs. He stumbled, panic-stricken, to the next floor. An old woman opened a door. A light behind her threw a flare on the urchin's face.

"Eh, child, what is it dis time? Is yer fader beatin' yer mudder, or yer mudder beatin' yer fader?"

• • •

The babe, Tommie, died. He went away in an insignificant coffin, his small waxen hand clutching a flower that the girl, Maggie, had stolen from an Italian.

She and Jimmie lived.

The inexperienced fibers of the boy's eyes were hardened at an early age. He became a young man of leather. He lived some red years without laboring. During that time his sneer became chronic. He studied human nature in the gutter, and found it no worse than he thought he had reason to believe it. He never conceived a respect from the world, because he had begun with no idols that it had smashed.

He clad his soul in armor by means of happening hilariously in at a mission church where a man composed his sermons of "yous." Once a philosopher asked this man why he did not say "we" instead of "you." The man replied, "What?"

While they got warm at the stove he told hearers just where he calculated they stood with the Lord. Many of the sinners were impatient over the pictured depths of their degradation. They were waiting for soup tickets.

A reader of the words of wind demons might have been able to see the portions of a dialogue pass to and fro between the exhorter and his hearers.

"You are damned," said the preacher. And the reader of sounds might have seen the reply go forth from the ragged people: "Where's our soup?"

Jimmie and a companion sat in a rear seat and commented upon the things that didn't concern them, with all the freedom of English tourists. When they grew thirsty and went out, their minds confused the speaker with Christ.

Momentarily, Jimmie was sullen with thoughts of a hopeless altitude where grew fruit. His companion said that if he should ever go to heaven he would ask for a million dollars and a bottle of beer.

Jimmie's occupation for a long time was to stand at street corners and watch the world go by, dreaming blood-red dreams at the passing of pretty women. He menaced mankind at the intersections of streets.

At the corners he was in life and of life. The world was going on and he was there to perceive it.

He maintained a belligerent attitude towards all well-dressed men. To him fine raiment was allied to weakness, and all good coats covered faint hearts. He and his orders were kings, to a certain extent, over the men of untarnished clothes, because these latter dreaded, perhaps, to be either killed or laughed at.

Above all things he despised obvious Christians and ciphers with the chrysanthemums of aristocracy in their buttonholes. He considered himself above both of these classes. He was afraid of nothing.

When he had a dollar in his pocket his satisfaction with existence was the greatest thing in the world. So, eventually, he felt obliged to work. His father died and his mother's years were divided up into periods of thirty days.

He became a truck driver. There was given him the charge of a painstaking pair of horses and a large rattling truck. He invaded the turmoil and tumble of the downtown streets, and learned to breathe maledictory defiance at the police, who occasionally used to climb up, drag him from his perch, and punch him.

In the lower part of the city he daily involved himself in hideous tangles. If he and his team chanced to be in the rear he preserved a demeanor of serenity, crossing his legs and bursting forth into yells when foot passengers took dangerous dives beneath the noses of the champing horses. He smoked his pipe calmly, for he knew that his pay was marching on.

If his charge was in the front, and it became the key-truck of chaos, he entered terrifically into the quarrel that was raging to and fro among the drivers on their high seats, and sometimes roared oaths and violently got himself arrested.

After a time his sneer grew so that it turned its glare upon all things. He became so sharp that he believed in nothing. To him the police were always actuated by malignant impulses, and the rest of the world was composed, for the most part, of despicable creatures who were all trying to take advantage of him, and with whom, in defence, he was obliged to quarrel on all possible occasions. He himself occupied a down-trodden position, which had a private but distinct element of grandeur in its isolation.

The greatest cases of aggravated idiocy were, to his mind, rampant upon the front platforms of all the street cars. At first his tongue strove with these beings, but he eventually became superior. In him grew a majestic contempt for those strings of street cars that followed him like intent bugs.

He fell into the habit, when starting on a long journey, of fixing his eye on a high and distant object, commanding his horses to start and then going into a trance of observation. Multitudes of drivers might howl in his rear, and passengers might load him with opprobrium, but he would not awaken until some blue policemen turned red and began frenziedly to seize bridles and beat the soft noses of the responsible horses.

When he paused to contemplate the attitude of the police towards himself and his fellows, he believed that they were the only men in the city who had no rights. When driving about, he felt that he was held liable by the police for anything that might occur in the streets, and that he was the common prey of all energetic officials. In revenge, he resolved never to move out of the way of anything, until formidable circumstances or a much larger man than himself forced him to it.

Foot passengers were mere pestering flies with an insane disregard for their legs and his convenience. He could not comprehend their desire to cross the streets. Their madness smote him with eternal amazement. He was continually storming at them from his throne.

He sat aloft and denounced their frantic leaps, plunges, dives, and straddles.

When they would thrust at, or parry, the noses of his champing horses, making them swing their heads and move their feet, and thus disturbing a solid, dreamy repose, he swore at the men as fools, for he himself could perceive that Providence had caused it clearly to be written that he and his team had the unalienable right to stand in the proper path of the sun chariot, and if they so minded, to obstruct its mission or take a wheel off.

And if the god-driver had had a desire to step down, put up his flame-colored fists, and manfully dispute the right of way, he would have probably been immediately opposed by a scowling mortal with two sets of hard knuckles.

It is possible, perhaps, that this young man would have derided in an axle-wide alley, the approach of a flying ferry boat. Yet he achieved a respect for a fire-engine. As one charged towards his truck, he would drive fearfully upon a side-walk, threatening untold people with annihilation. When an engine struck a mass of blocked trucks, splitting it into fragments, as a blow annihilates a cake of ice, Jimmie's team could usually be observed high and safe, with whole wheels on the sidewalk. The fearful coming of the engine could break up the most intricate muddle of heavy vehicles at which the police had been storming for half an hour.

A fire-engine was enshrined in his heart as an appalling thing that he loved with a distant, doglike devotion. It had been known to overturn a street car. Those leaping horses, striking sparks from the cobbles in their forward lunge, were creatures to be ineffably admired. The clang of the gong pierced his breast like a noise of remembered war.

When Jimmie was a little boy he began to be arrested. Before he reached a great age, he had a fair record.

He developed too great a tendency to climb down from his truck and fight with other drivers. He had been in quite a number of miscellaneous fights, and in some general bar-room rows that had become known to the police. Once he had been arrested for assaulting a Chinaman. Two women in different parts of the city, and entirely unknown to each other, caused him considerable annoyance by breaking forth, simultaneously, at fateful intervals, into wailings about marriage and support and infants.

Nevertheless, he had, on a certain star-lit evening, said wonderingly and quite reverently, "Deh moon looks like hell, don't it?"

· · ·

The girl, Maggie, blossomed in a mud puddle. She grew to be a most rare and wonderful production of a tenement district, a pretty girl.

None of the dirt of Rum Alley seemed to be in her veins. The philosophers, upstairs, downstairs, and on the same floor, puzzled over it.

When a child, playing and fighting with gamins in the street, dirt disgusted her. Attired in tatters and grime, she went unseen.

There came a time, however, when the young men of the vicinity said, "Dat Johnson goil is a puty goodlooker." About this period her brother remarked to her: "Mag, I'll tell yeh dis! See? Yeh've edder got t' go on d' toif er go t' work!" Whereupon she went to work, having the feminine aversion to the alternative.

By a chance, she got a position in an establishment where they made collars and cuffs. She received a stool and a machine in a room where sat twenty girls of various shades of yellow discontent. She perched on the stool and treadled at her machine all day, turning out collars with a name which might have been noted for its irrelevancy to anything connected with collars. At night she returned home to her mother.

Jimmie grew large enough to take the vague position of head of the family. As incumbent of that office, he stumbled upstairs late at night, as his father had done before him. He reeled about the room, swearing at his relations, or went to sleep on the floor.

The mother had gradually arisen to such a degree of fame that she could bandy words with her acquaintances among the police justices. Court officials called her by her first name. When she appeared they pursued a course which had been theirs for months. They invariably grinned, and cried out, "Hello, Mary, you here again?" Her grey head wagged in many courts. She always besieged the bench with voluble excuses, explanations, apologies, and prayers. Her flaming face and rolling eyes were a familiar sight on the island. She measured time by means of sprees, and was eternally swollen and disheveled.

One day the young man Pete, who as a lad had smitten the Devil's Row urchin in the back of the head and put to flight the antagonists of his friend Jimmie, strutted upon the scene. He met Jimmie one day on the street, promised to take him to a boxing match in Williamsburg, and called for him in the evening.

Maggie observed Pete.

He sat on a table in the Johnson home, and dangled his checked legs with an enticing nonchalance. His hair was curled down over his forehead in an oiled bang. His pugged nose seemed to revolt from contact with a bristling moustache of short, wire-like hairs. His blue, double-breasted coat, edged with black braid, was buttoned close to a red puff tie, and his patent leather shoes looked like weapons.

His mannerisms stamped him as a man who had a correct sense of his personal superiority. There was valor and contempt for circumstances in the glance of his eye. He waved his hands like a man of the world who dismisses religion and philosophy, and says "Rats!" He had certainly seen everything, and with each curl of his lip he declared that it amounted to nothing. Maggie thought he must be a very "elegant" bartender.

He was telling tales to Jimmie.

297

Maggie watched him furtively, with half-closed eyes, lit with a vague interest.

"Hully gee! Dey makes me tired," he said. "Mos' e'ry day some farmer comes in an' tries t' run d' shop. See? But d' gits t'rowed right out. I jolt dem right out in d' street before dey knows where dey is. See?"

"Sure," said Jimmie.

"Dere was a mug come in d' place d'oder day wid an idear he wus goin' t' own d' place. Hully gee! he wus goin' t' own d' place. I see he had a still on, an' I didn' wanna gi' im no stuff, so I says, 'Git outa here an' don' make no trouble,' I says like dat. See? 'Git outa here an' don' make no trouble,' like dat. 'Git outa here,' I says. See?"

Jimmie nodded understandingly. Over his features played an eager desire to state the amount of his valor in a similar crisis, but the narrator proceeded.

"Well, deh blokie he says: 'T' blazed wid it! I ain' lookin' for no scrap,' he says—see? 'but,' he says, 'I'm 'spectable cit'zen an' I wanna drink, an' quick, too.' See? 'Aw, goahn!' I says, like dat. 'Aw, goahn,' I says. See? 'Don' make no trouble,' I says, like dat. 'Don' make no trouble.' See? Den d' mug he squared off an' said he was fine as silk wid his dukes—see? an' he waned a drink—quick. Dat's what he said. See?"

"Sure," repeated Jimmie.

Pete continued. "Say, I jes' jumped d' bar, an' d' way I plunked dat blokie was outa sight. See? Dat's right! In d' jaw! See? Hully gee! He t'rowed a spit-toon true d' front windee. Say, I taut I'd drop dead. But d' boss, he comes in after, an' he says: 'Pete, yehs done jes' right! Yeh've gota keep order, an' it's all right.' See? 'It's all right,' he says. Dat's what he said."

The two held a technical discussion.

"Dat bloke was a dandy," said Pete, in conclusion, "but he hadn' oughta made no trouble. Dat's what I says t' dem: 'Don' come in here an' make no trouble,' I says, like dat. 'Don' make no trouble.' See?"

As Jimmie and his friend exchanged tales descriptive of their prowess, Maggie leaned back in the shadow. Her eyes dwelt wonderingly and rather wistfully upon Pete's face. The broken furniture, grimy walls, and general disorder and dirt of her home of a sudden appeared before her and began to take a potential aspect. Pete's aristocratic person looked as if it might soil. She looked keenly at him, occasionally wondering if he was feeling contempt. But Pete seemed to be enveloped in reminiscence.

"Hully gee!" said he, "does mugs can't phase me. Dey knows I kin wipe up d' street wid any tree of dem."

When he said, 'Ah, what d' hell!' his voice was burdened with disdain for the inevitable and contempt for anything that fate might compel him to endure.

Maggie perceived that here was the ideal man. Her dim thoughts were often searching for faraway lands where the little hills sing together in the morning. Under the trees of her dream gardens there had always walked a lover.

• • •

As thoughts of Pete came to Maggie's mind, she began to have an intense dislike for all of her dresses.

"What ails yeh? What makes ye be allus fixin' and fussin'?" her mother would frequently roar at her.

She began to note with more interest the well-dressed women she met on the avenues. She envied elegance and soft palms. She craved those adornments of person which she saw every day on the street, conceiving them to be allies of vast importance to women.

Studying faces, she thought many of the women and girls she chanced to meet smiled with serenity as though forever cherished and watched over by those they loved.

The air in the collar-and-cuff establishment strangled her. She knew she was gradually and surely shriveling in the hot, stuffy room. The begrimed window rattled incessantly from the passing of elevated trains. The place was filled with a whirl of noises and odors.

She became lost in thought as she looked at some of the grizzled women in the room, mere mechanical contrivances sewing seams and grinding out, with heads bent over their work, tales of imagined or real girlhood happiness, or of past drunks, or the baby at home, and unpaid wages. She wondered how long her youth would endure. She began to see the bloom upon her cheeks as something of value.

She imagined herself, in an exasperating future, as a scrawny woman with an eternal grievance. She thought Pete to be a very fastidious person concerning the appearance of women.

She felt that she should love to see somebody entangle their fingers in the oil beard of the fat foreigner who owned the establishment. He was a detestable creature. He wore white socks with low shoes. He sat all day delivering orations in the depths of a cushioned chair. His pocket-book deprived them of the power of retort.

"What do you sink I pie fife dolla a week for? Play? No, py damn!"

Maggie was anxious for a friend to whom she could talk about Pete. She would have like to discuss his admirable mannerisms with a reliable mutual friend. At home, she found her mother often drunk and raving. It seemed that the world had treated this woman very badly, and she took a deep revenge upon such portions of it as came within her reach. She broke furniture as if she were at last getting her rights. She swelled with virtuous indignation as she carried the lighter articles of household use, one by one, under the shadows of the three gilt balls, where Hebrews chained them with chains of interest.

Jimmie came when he was obliged by circumstances over which he had no control. His well-trained legs brought him staggering home and put him to bed some nights when he would have rather gone elsewhere.

Swaggering Pete loomed like a golden sun to Maggie. He took her to a dime museum, where rows of meek freaks astonished her. He contemplated their deformities with awe, and thought them a sort of chosen tribe.

Pete, racking his brains for amusement, discovered the Central Park Menagerie and the Museum of Arts. Sunday afternoons would sometimes find them at these places. Pete did not appear to be particularly interested in what he saw. He stood around looking heavy, while Maggie giggled in glee.

Once at the menagerie he went into a trance of admiration before the spectacle of a very small monkey threatening to thrash a cageful because one of them had pulled his tail and he had not wheeled about quickly enough to discover who did it. Ever after Pete knew that monkey by sight, and winked at him, trying to induce him to fight with other and larger monkeys.

At the museum, Maggie said, "Dis is outa sight!"

"Aw, rats!" said Pete; "wait till next summer an' I'll take yehs to a picnic."

While the girl wandered in the vaulted rooms, Pete occupied himself in returning stony stare for stony stare, the appalling scrutiny of the watchdog of the treasures. Occasionally he would remark in loud tones, "Dat jay has got glass eyes," and sentences of the sort. When he tired of this amusement he would go to the mummies and moralize over them.

Usually he submitted with silent dignity to all that he had to go through, but at times he was goaded into comment.

"Aw!" he demanded once. "Look at all dese little jugs! Hundred jugs in a row! Ten rows in a case, an' 'bout a t'ousand cases! What d' blazes use is dem?"

In the evenings of weekdays he often took her to see plays in which the dazzling heroine was rescued from the palatial home of her treacherous guardian by the hero with the beautiful sentiments. The latter spent most of his time out at soak in pale-green snow-storms, busy with a nickel-plated revolver rescuing aged strangers from villains.

Maggie lost herself in sympathy with the wanderers swooning in snow-storms beneath happy-hued church windows, while a choir within sang "Joy to the World." To Maggie and the rest of the audience this was transcendental realism. Joy always within, and they, like the actor, inevitably without. Viewing it, they hugged themselves in ecstatic pity of their imagined or real condition.

The girl thought the arrogance and granite-heartedness of the magnate of the play were very accurately drawn. She echoed the maledictions that the occupants of the gallery showered on this individual when his lines compelled him to expose his extreme selfishness.

Shady persons in the audience revolted from the pictured villainy of the drama. With untiring zeal they hissed vice and applauded virtue. Unmistakably bad men evinced an apparently sincere admiration for virtue. The loud gallery was overwhelmingly with the unfortunate and the oppressed. They encouraged the struggling hero with cries, and jeered the villain, hooting and calling attention to his whiskers. When anybody died in the pale-green snow-storms, the gallery mourned. They sought out the painted misery and hugged it as akin.

In the hero's erratic march from poverty in the first act, to wealth and triumph in the final one, in which he forgives all the enemies that he has left, he was assisted by the gallery, which applauded his generous and noble sentiments and confounded the speeches of his opponents by making irrelevant but very sharp remarks. Those actors who were cursed with the parts of villains were confronted at every turn by the gallery. If one of them rendered lines containing the most subtle distinctions between right and wrong, the gallery was immediately aware that the actor meant wickedness, and denounced him accordingly.

The last act was a triumph for the hero, poor and of the masses, the representative of the audience, over the villain and the rich man, his pockets stuffed with bonds, his heart packed with tyrannical purposes, imperturbable amid suffering.

Maggie always departed with raised spirits from these melodramas. She rejoiced at the way in which the poor and virtuous eventually overcame the wealthy and wicked. The theatre made her think. She wondered if the culture and refinement she had seen imitated, perhaps grotesquely, by the heroine on the stage, could be acquired by a girl who lived in a tenement house and worked in a shirt factory.

No Pets

JIM RAY DANIELS

I gunned the engine, and my old Mustang II kicked up some gravel, shooting out of the Ritz's parking lot and onto Mound, a long, straight road full of factories and bars. The Ritz was a square, brick dive that filled a gap between two small tool-and-die shops across the street from my Ford plant. Drunk again. I swerved back and forth, trying to miss the potholes. At Eight Mile Road, a car full of high school kids turned right from two lanes over and cut me off. I slammed on the brakes and rolled down the window to yell, flip them the bird, but they squealed down a side street, radio blasting. I spent a lot of high school nights in cars like that. I cranked up my own radio.

Back home, I parked the car in the street and headed toward the yard. I could already hear Bud howling, pulling against his chain. I hissed at him to shut up. He wiggled his butt and jumped in the air while I sat in the damp grass and unchained him. How could he still like me after the way I treated him? He ran in circles fast enough to make me dizzy. Bud was a pretty dog— white with black spots, sleek and alert to the world. His tail was cropped, and his whole butt wagged when he was happy, as if he was making up for what wasn't there. When he jumped in the air, it seemed as if he hung suspended for a moment or two, like a star basketball player. I was only twenty-nine, but he seemed to have a kind of energy I'd never get back. "Whoa boy. Come here." He almost knocked me down. "I have to get rid of you. Bud. Find you a good home." He licked my face. I gave a factory howl and fell back in the grass.

"Hey, quiet down out there! And teach your dog to be quiet too!"

It was Turner, the owner of the house who lived on the first floor.

"What are you gonna do about it," I shouted back, "call the cops?"

"I just might." A window slammed shut. I turned back to Bud. "We ought to kick his ass, eh boy? One day I'm gonna."

Turner always complained about Bud's barking, about dog crap in the yard, paw prints in his garden. He said the dog was a nuisance, and maybe he was right. I knew I didn't give Bud enough time or attention. I didn't blame him for barking, for destroying things, for any of it. Turner had given me a week to get rid of him.

I usually had a few at the Ritz at the end of my shift, then drove home and slept, and in the morning I was tired or hungover, or both. I'd hoped getting Bud might help me break that routine, but even with him there, I couldn't stand being alone in that tiny apartment.

Turner was a young lawyer close to my age, but he seemed more like fifty. He was always dressed up, even on weekends, and talked like he was reading the news on TV. He drove a foreign car. His wife Lorraine was a nurse. They lived on the first floor and rented out the second to me while their "dream house" was being built out in Rochester Hills. People like Turner are always building dream houses—people who can afford to have dreams and fuck the rest of us over in the process. I'd lived in the house for three years. Turner had inherited it from his father, who'd never bothered me about the dog. He'd moved in three months ago after he kicked out the tenant on the first floor, an old retired guy from GM who had helped take care of Bud while I was at work. Though the first floor was bigger and nicer, I think Turner eventually figured out he got rid of the wrong guy.

I wanted to hit him, to bloody that perfect face of his, but I knew better than to hit a lawyer. Turner always got me mad—on the one hand, his superior attitude made me feel like dirt, and on the other, he was so slimy and phony, I felt like I should wash my hands after talking to him. And he always wanted to shake my hand. My father told me never trust a stranger who wants to shake your hand. That might sound unfriendly, but that's the kind of advice my father gave, and he was usually right.

I didn't want to talk to the cops, so I called Bud, and we went into the house together and up the stairs to bed.

• • •

I got up around noon and let Bud out, then sat on the porch drinking coffee while he ran free. I was thinking about Connie, a woman I'd met at my friend Boomer's wedding two weeks earlier. She gave me her phone number after we danced awhile, shared a few drinks. We kissed in my car afterwards. She must've been the only single woman there, and me the only single guy. "Fate," I told her all night, till she had enough drinks to start believing me. She was a phone operator and worked strange shifts too. She was sarcastic and sexy, and she made fun of herself in a way I wish I could do. I wanted to see her again.

I saw Lorraine Turner striding up the street toward the house, and I jumped up looking for the dog: "Bud, Bud, come here boy!" But he was already running down the street toward her. "Oh shit!" Bud jumped up against her thighs, and she pushed him away, patted his head.

"Hi, boy!" She glanced up at me on the porch—she looked like an angel smiling there in the sun in her white uniform, her blonde hair shining. But not the kind of angel that ever had anything to do with my life. "He likes me," she said. "I give him some attention once in a while."

It was like her to start in on me, even while seeming friendly. I slouched back against the bricks and looked at her through the hair hanging in my eyes. I looked like shit, and now I felt like shit—I didn't know how the Turners did this to me. She stepped up on the porch. "Do you mind if I sit down?"

"Hey, it's your porch." I moved aside the morning paper, and she sat down, tucking her short skirt underneath her tight little ass. She was sharp, no doubt about it. I sucked in my gut.

"Listen, I wanted to talk to you about the dog and everything. My husband and I don't want a feud." She lit a cigarette, then caught me staring at her. "Smoke?"

"Yeah, thanks." I squinted against the sun. The street was quiet. Bud sat at our feet—like a good dog, for once. "Sorry about last night. I was a little drunk. It's just that Bud . . ."

"My husband is sorry too. It's not easy being tactful at three in the morning."

I nodded my head. "You can say that again. What I want to know is if you're all hot for me to get rid of the dog, how come it seems like you like him?" I held Bud by the collar and patted his head. I knew she must have thought I was a real loser. I felt like I was waiting in some doctor's office and she was taking my medical history, a history I wasn't proud of.

"It's not that we don't like the dog. It's not his fault. Well, I don't mean to blame you. It's not anybody's fault, I guess. The main thing is he barks at night when you're not here."

"I know. I wish I could get on days—it'd be better if I was on days. Been working a lot of overtime, too. This boy needs to run a little more. While I'm going crazy at work, he's going crazy here." We sat smoking in silence, then she ground hers out hard into the cement, smashing it into shreds. I patted Bud on the belly, and he grunted.

"Yeah, I go out drinking now and then, too. Sometimes I get home pretty late."

"I know," she laughed. "I hear you stumbling up the steps some nights." She looked at her watch. "Listen, we just want you to know this is nothing personal. We hope you don't hold it against us. Maybe it's best for everyone, including the dog. I'll ask around," she gave me a teethy smile, "and see if I can find someone who'll take him."

304

Her voice rankled me some. I know when I'm being talked down to. "So, it's settled then, is it?"

She squinted at me. "What do you mean?"

"Well, it doesn't seem like I have much of a say in all this."

"Remember, we asked you to do something before."

"Yeah, yeah," I scratched Bud's chin. I wanted to say something clever, something that might put us back on the same level. I could smell her perfume and knew she could smell my sweat.

She touched my shoulder lightly. Like she was giving me a blessing. "I know it's hard. I had a dog once too." I shrugged off her hand—I almost wished I was talking to Turner instead. "And who are you, the Virgin Mary?"

She shook her head and laughed. "Not hardly. Come on, you'll find a place for him. Cheer up." She stuck out her hand.

I took it and held it for a second. "Okay, no hard feelings."

"Good. Fred will be happy. You know, despite the arguments, I think he does like you." She said that as if I should be honored. "I think you've got us—me—pegged wrong."

"We'll just be one big happy family," I mumbled as she turned away and started down the steps and onto the sidewalk. I stood up and looked down the street, saw Bud running toward her. It was too late—he jumped on her from behind, bouncing off the back of her legs. "Eddie!" she shouted, as if I was the dog. I called once, twice, three times, before Bud turned and ran to me. She shook her head, "Keep him on a leash—before he bites somebody." I grabbed Bud, led him in the house.

• • •

Before I went to work, I called the *Free Press* and placed an ad: "young springer spaniel, friendly, needs good home. Call 463-3495 btw. 11-2." My mother called to say she'd put an ad in the church paper too. I'm the oldest of five children, the only one not married, the only one who didn't leave town when the factory layoffs started and everything got tight around here. She reminded me my father's birthday was coming up. "At least get a card," she said. My father'd been a lifer too, at the same plant. He's retired now, and not much interested in what happens at work. I don't blame him. "You're not supposed to like your job, that's why they pay you," he told me when I came to him after my first week, ready to quit.

Maybe if I'd gotten an older dog who was already trained. But Bud was a six-week-old puppy when I picked him up last January at my uncle's farm out near Brighton. The last of the litter—part spaniel, part something else. I walked the last quarter mile because of drifts across the road. On the way home, holding him in my lap, I thought it would all work out. I was sure of it. He was the softest thing I'd ever touched. A year-and-a-half later, Bud still had too much puppy in him, too much energy to spend his days alone, chained in the yard.

When I started in at the plant right out of high school, I thought I'd only be there a few years, until I got enough money together to figure out what I really wanted to do. Eleven years later, I was still there. Maybe it was the new car that got me hooked, the payments I locked myself into during the years I might have been tempted to break away. I realized now how ugly it was compared to the original Mustangs. That's why I always have to say "Mustang II"—so people don't get disappointed when they see the car. Most people give a little laugh and shake their heads when they see it for the first time. What I wouldn't give to have one of the originals. Around Detroit, the rust gets everything in a few years. My brother Joe out in California tells me there are lots of old Mustangs still on the road out there. I can't imagine a place where cars don't rust.

I washed my car every week, waxed it once a month for the first couple of years. Now, small pieces of rust fall off my driver's side door whenever I slam it. Though I could afford to go into debt again, I'm happy with my junker. Cars just don't have the attraction they did for me when I got that new one, though when I'm on the road sometimes I still find myself naming make, model and year of the cars around me, especially the older ones. In high school, me and my friends spent our time drinking beers and crawling under cars. My brothers used to look up to me then—they were always hanging around listening to us cuss and argue about who had the fastest car, about which girls we'd like to get into our backseats. I taught them all how to drive.

I rarely spent money on anything besides rent and my bar tab. I knew I was saving for something, but I wasn't sure what. I didn't want to buy a house—I was afraid of taking on more empty space. Besides, I knew I could always get laid off again.

• • •

At work that night, on my nine o'clock break, I tried to call Connie. At a phone booth near the front gate where it was quiet, I squinted at the smudged scrap of paper in front of me. It had spent the night in the back pocket of my work pants, and now it was blurred with sweat. I tried one number, but it was wrong. Tried another and got no answer. I kicked the booth, then went back to our break table, which sat between two of the big presses. While I stared at the sheet of paper trying to figure out the number, I felt a punch in the shoulder. I turned around—it was BJ, my best friend in the plant. He pantomimed a smoking motion and nodded his head toward the factory yard. I shook my head. He shrugged and walked away.

I didn't know what it was, the thought of losing Bud or the talk with Lorraine Turner that afternoon, or fucking up the damn phone number, but I was really feeling desperate. Lorraine's smell and touch made me a little crazy. She was so beautiful and out of my league—I hated her. Kissing Connie in my car. Shit. Maybe she wasn't home. I could probably find her through Boomer's wife, but I wasn't sure I wanted to seem so hard-up to them. Boomer was one of my high school friends who'd done pretty well for himself. He went to school at Lawrence Tech and became an engineer. He worked for Ford too—at the other end of things, as he liked to say. Who knows, maybe she gave me the wrong number in the first place.

In high school, I did pretty well for myself too, but I'm not exactly a prize now. Going bald, for one thing. Work kept me in pretty good shape. Had some muscles, though all the beer tended to gather around the middle. I ran out of breath trying to keep up with Bud on walks. In high school, I played football—one of the grunts on the line, just like now. I had few interests or hobbies outside work and the bar. Bud was one of those interests, but he'd be gone soon. I wondered if I'd been working in the factory too long—the crude, loud factory talk was what I was used to. I liked taking girls to the movies because then I didn't have to talk so much. I wondered what it'd be like to have a date with someone like Lorraine. What would we talk about?

The day after Boomer's wedding, I was pretty excited, thinking about Connie's laugh, the way she danced, her kiss. I hadn't had a girlfriend, a real girlfriend, since Cindy. Nine years since she dumped me. After graduation, she went away to college, and I started in the plant. I paid her a surprise visit around Halloween her freshman year. Her roommate tried to cover for her, calling "a friend's room" to tell Cindy I was there. I knew the story— what the guys in the plant had kidded me about since September was true— she'd gotten herself a college boy. As I stood waiting with her roommate, I planned how I'd kick the guy's ass. But Cindy took a long time to get there, and she was alone, and it was just real sad. I turned around and drove home. At work on Monday, a couple guys razzed me after word got out, but most simply patted me on the back or left me alone. Someone even suggested getting a carload to drive up and kick some college-boy butt.

I get maybe half-a-dozen dates a year. I know it probably seems weird, but I keep count. Working afternoons was a problem, and when things picked up at work, I put in a lot of overtime. When I do get a date, I can't seem to read the signals. I probably come across as seeming pretty horny—but, hell, I am. I'm comfortable in a place like the Ritz, but that's not a place to meet women unless you want to pay to get your rocks off in a van in the parking lot.

• • •

I sat in front of my locker, taking off my work clothes, wishing I'd smoked that joint with BJ. I thought of trying the number I'd gotten no answer at earlier, but it was late, and I was beat to hell. I scrubbed my hands with the cleansing powder that reminded me of sawdust; whatever it was, it scrubbed off the day's grease. Even when my hands were clean, I rubbed that stuff on them. It relaxed me, circling the water over my hands, trying to wash away another day—though it usually took a few beers across the street at the Ritz to really get clean of that place.

Bobbie Joe came up and washed next to me. BJ was a good old boy who never seemed to be bothered by what happened at work. He was always ready for a good time afterwards. Years ago, he tried to make it on his own as a carpenter, but lost too much money trying to establish himself. He packed it in for the security of the plant, and it was a secure job then—the boom years, as they called them now, when there were jobs for just about everyone. Bobbie Joe and his wife Caroline had me over for dinner once in a while, and Caroline sometimes helped find me dates. She was BJ's high school sweetheart, and they seemed happy together. Sometimes she'd come down to the Ritz and meet us for beers after our shift. She worked at K-Mart's world headquarters out in Troy. They were like an older brother and sister to me—at least that's what I'd tell them some nights around closing time. He worked in a different department at an easier job now, because of his senior-ity, but when I was hired in, me and BJ tossed axle housings onto pallets in department 16 together, one of the worst jobs in the plant. It was a shared job that either started fights or friendships. He carried more than his share until I got used to the hard work.

"BJ, you want a dog?"

"Hey, I've got enough trouble handling my old lady," he joked.

"I gotta get rid of my puppy—landlord says he goes or we both go."

"You should tell that landlord to cram it up his ass."

"I don't know if I want to fight it. I'm no fucking good for that dog. Either he's inside shitting on the floor or outside barking 'cause he's lonely;

308

when I'm not working, I'm either at the bar or sleeping. I can't remember the last time I took him for a walk."

"I'm sorry, Eddie, we can't take your dog. Caroline and I decided a long time ago, no kids, no pets."

"I just can't take him to the pound. I've treated him shitty enough as it is. The least I can do is find him a good home."

"Okay, man, I'll spread the word. What about your folks?"

"My old man? With a dog? When we were kids, we had a dog that bit him on the ass. He took that dog straight to the pound. He said kill this motherfucking dog. It was the first time I heard my dad say motherfucker. I was ten, I think. I'd heard shit and asshole before, but never motherfucker."

"Oh yeah? Motherfucker was my old man's nickname for me. He'd come home from work and say, 'How's my little motherfucker?' I can't remember if it started before or after my momma left us."

"Well, you're a big motherfucker now, BJ." I smiled and laughed, punching him in the shoulder, but I was remembering hating my dad for taking our dog away. Two of my brothers were a year apart, and so were my youngest brother and sister. I was three years older than any of them, the mistake that prompted the marriage. It was a worthless dog, but it was mine by default. Maybe I hadn't taken very good care of that dog either.

"This motherfucker's gonna beat your ass at the pool table tonight," BJ said.

I hesitated. "Nah, BJ, I'm beat. Heading home tonight."

BJ's jaw dropped, and he jumped back. "I can't believe it. Are you sick or something?" He shouted down the row of lockers, "Hey guys, Buford's not going to the Ritz tonight."

"Must be love," somebody piped in.

"Nah, I think Buford's too ugly for anybody to love."

"Maybe Buford thinks he's too good for us."

"Shit," I said, "Fuck you guys."

They locked up their lockers and quickly joined the wave heading out the factory gate. I hung back for a minute. It'd been a long time since I missed a night at the bar, but this Bud thing had me all twisted up inside. I punched myself in the side of the head. The humid August heat was suffocating me. I slammed the car door shut, threw my lunch bucket and thermos on the backseat. I started to squeal out of the parking lot, but had to slam on the brakes and get in line behind the others at the red light on Mound.

At home, I dug out the leash and took Bud for a walk around the block. He yanked me along, scrambling from tree to tree. It was after midnight—a few lights on here and there, but the streets were quiet. The Turners' apartment was dark. I didn't hear a thing as I climbed the stairs. I heard her moaning sometimes when they were going at it, but not tonight, and I was glad of it.

• • •

A week later, I still had Bud. Turner threatened me with an eviction order. I got some phone calls asking if he "had his papers"—if he was purebred. They'd hang up on me when I said no. "That's what's wrong with this country," I told BJ down at the Ritz, "everybody wants purebreds—nobody wants a dog just because it's friendly. Friendly don't count for shit anymore."

"Never did, bro, never did," BJ said, "But I'll buy you another beer anyway." We both laughed. It bothered me though. I started hanging up first, as soon as they asked the question. I didn't know quite sure why I got Bud, but it wasn't for his bloodline.

"Rich people are like purebreds—they inherit everything—like the Fords."

"And the GMs," BJ joked. "How come you don't hear about the GM family?"

"What a boring name for a company: General Motors. Would you drink a beer from the General Beers Co.?"

"If it tasted good, I wouldn't care if it was the Monkey Fart Beer Co." He let out a big belch. "Don't worry, somebody'll take that mutt of yours."

Everybody liked BJ. Our table at the Ritz was always busy, BJ handing out advice on everything from home improvements to taxes to marriage. He was a company man and never caused trouble. Even the foremen liked him. The monotony of the work never bothered him. "It's just like watching TV, man," he told me. "I just tune out."

• • •

I could by rights take every third weekend off if I wanted, but I hadn't taken one in six—weekends off had been pretty depressing, and I'd come to almost like the numbness of going in every day, the weeks blurring together. It scared me to think that I was one of the "old guys" now, one of the lifers, that my life outside work had come down to beer, TV, and a visit to my parents' once in a while. I wondered if I'd ever be as content as BJ.

For a year, I'd shared a house with two other guys from work, and we had a lot of parties with not enough women and too much beer.

"The wrong crowd," my parents had said. "Where do I meet the right crowd?" I asked. One of the guys was married now, and the other moved to Texas. It didn't seem like much at the time, but I missed those guys—anything was better than the long quiet hours Bud couldn't quite fill.

At least a couple times a year, my mother asked me if I wanted to move back home, but I saw that as the final defeat. I knew my family and friends would snicker at that. I could imagine my brothers and sister coming home at Christmas and finding me back in my old room. Damn, that would kill me. And my mother already nagged me about my drinking as it was. And the old man, he'd have a field day. I had to do a lot of work breaking in my parents for the others. I spent too much time doing that and forgot to think about my own future. When my parents gave up and let me do what I wanted, I thought that meant drinking beer in the basement or staying out all night.

I never considered college. They placed me in the vocational training track in high school, and I stayed there like a good boy, trusting their judgment that I was dumb. I liked history, and I took a course once at the community college to make my mother happy. She believed they were wrong about me, about all her kids. They may have been wrong about a couple of us, but I don't know—maybe they were right about me.

My professor in the history course was a pale, skinny guy—bald, with a long beard. He told us he was a Marxist. I couldn't understand most of what he said. It seemed like he hardly ever talked about things that really happened in history, which is what I was interested in. Instead, it was all this theory and big words. I don't think anyone in our class knew what they meant. It was mostly housewives and a few guys like me who were still young enough to hope taking a few classes could change our lives. I got the prof out for a few beers after the last class and started arguing with the guy. He broke down and started crying right there in the bar, so I lied and told him he was a good teacher. It wasn't the Ritz—some fern place next to the school. I guess they don't make much teaching community college. We finally agreed it was all bullshit.

I had a fling with a married woman in the class, the wife of a salesman. When I think of that class, I think of her. She was bored and generous, and for a while it seemed like we loved each other.

It seems to me the more education people have, the harder it is for anyone to understand what they're saying. It was that way with Turner too—when he started in with his legal mumbo-jumbo, I just scratched my head. "Now tell me that in English," I said when Turner came to me last. Turner said, "It means 'get rid of your dog'. Now."

"See this fist," I told him. "Know what this means?"

I probably sounded like what he expected me to sound like—a dumb-ass factory rat. Maybe I was trying to show him that he didn't scare me with his money and his status and his beautiful wife. But he did scare me. Threatening to punch him was the dumbest thing I could do. But what would've been a smart thing?

I decided that when my lease was up in a few months, I was leaving Turner's, dog or no dog.

• • •

Saturday morning, I sat on the porch, tired and surly after a long Friday night at the Ritz. I knew it was a weekend-long hangover I was dealing with—I could have just worked it off making double-time. I had Bud chained up out front. I couldn't worry about chasing him down this morning, and besides, I wanted him close by.

Around noon, Lorraine stepped out onto the porch in a white pantsuit that was almost see-through. I tried not to stare, but I couldn't help noticing the white of her bra and panties, the dark shape of her flesh. I groaned and squinted up into her face.

"Working today?" I asked.

"Yeah. Aren't you?"

"Nah. Taking a break. A couple old folks coming over later to look at Bud here." They'd seen my ad in the paper and had woken me up with a phone call that morning. They'd asked how well-behaved Bud was. "He's a prince," I lied through my haze. "Very calm." I'd been worried ever since.

"That's great!" Lorraine said.

"Yeah, I knew you'd be pleased . . . Hey, where's the old man?"

"He's up north visiting his mother."

I perked up a bit. "He left you here all by yourself? You probably need a break from him anyway. I'm not even married to him, and I need a break from him."

"Eddie," she said, one hand on her hip, her head cocked. But she smiled as if I'd hit a little truth. "Hey, where'd you get that scar?" She crouched down beside me and traced a thin scar running down my arm.

I was surprised again by her touch. "Piece of metal cut me, couple years back."

"How many stitches?"

"Fifteen."

"Whoever sewed it up was a butcher."

"Plant doctor. He's a drunk. No one bitches too much because you can bribe him to send you home on medical—and he's been known to dish out some choice drugs." I paused a moment. She was a nurse—it was worth a try. "Lorraine, I know we're not the best of friends, but you wouldn't happen to have something in your medicine chest to calm Bud down a bit when these people come to look at him?"

"Eddie, you've got to be kidding."

"No, I just want to mellow him out some. They want a calm dog. If he's doped up some, they might take him."

"Then after it wears off?"

"Then they'll like him so much they'll—"

"They'll be stuck with him," Lorraine said.

"No—put up with him. Like I do. Besides, he'll growl at work." I didn't blame Bud—some nights driving home from work, I howled out the window myself. I watched him reach the end of the chain and get yanked back.

The old folks showed up around 3:30. I had cleaned up the crap in the yard and brushed Bud. I also shaved, showered, and combed my hair, put on clean jeans, and a sport shirt my mother gave me for my birthday.

"Hi," I said, smiling and sticking out my hand, wondering if I was being too cheerful, but they responded just as cheerfully. Bud was lying at my feet, stoned. He picked up his head and wagged his tail at them. They sat down, and Bud rubbed his head against the old man's leg. It was as if it'd been rehearsed. I gave them the dog's history and explained that a new landlord had bought the house who didn't allow pets. My hands shook as I tried to pet Bud. "Damn good dog," I said.

They bought it all, took Bud with them that afternoon, along with his chain, his bowl, leftover dog food—the works. I took a minute to say goodbye to him—hugged him hard, surprised myself by crying. I felt like Bud was the only thing worth holding onto in my life, and I was giving him away. Even as the tears came, I was angry with myself for getting sentimental. I closed my eyes, and the moment passed. I let go. As they got in the car, Bud climbed in behind them without hesitation.

Shocked by how quickly it had happened, I went out and bought a case of beer. I downed a couple quick ones, then fell asleep in the sun. When I woke up, it was almost dark. I called my mother and thanked her for her help. She was all sympathy and asked me to come over for dinner Sunday. I said yes, even though I knew after an hour, I'd feel claustrophobic there. It'd be a good first hour though, sitting in the old living room, staring at the TV, the old knickknacks and photos.

I tried the number in my pocket again—I couldn't remember which guess had gotten no answer before, but the number I tried this time was busy. "Fate," I said as I hung up the phone. I looked around: Bud's hair was everywhere. I tossed an empty beer against the wall, and it clunked to the rug near the door.

I boiled a couple of hot dogs for dinner while watching the end of a fight on TV. It was two heavyweights, and they hung on each other, hardly throwing any punches. I felt as exhausted and discouraged as they looked. I had to get out of the apartment, so I wolfed down the dogs and walked over to the closest bar—Angelo's pizza joint two blocks over. I never went to the Ritz on my days off—it reminded me too much of work, almost as if going to the bar was part of what I had to do to get paid. Besides, they'd only make fun of the way I was dressed. At Angelo's, I sat at a small table by myself and watched the families around me eat pizza and argue, the parents drinking pitchers of beer, and the kids drinking pitchers of Coke, everyone getting a little wired. I drank fast, drawing in the moist circles under my beer bottle on the checkered tablecloth. A banjo player came out and stood in front of the screen they used to show old movies on—and song lyrics. I'd forgotten about "Saturday Night Singalong." I paid the waitress, who reminded me what I was missing. "I'll sing along at home, O.K.?" She gave me a dirty look. Heading out the door, I heard the banjo player shout, "Everybody ready to sing?" As the door slammed shut, I heard muffled screams.

I wasn't sure I wanted to go home yet. I took the long way, through streets of barbecues and loud weekend voices. Like most neighborhoods around Detroit, mine was full of people who helped make cars. An old Mitch Ryder tune blasted from a passing car. It was like everyone felt they had to make as much noise as they could on their days off to convince themselves they were alive. Maybe that's why I'd worked so many weekends lately—I was tired of shouting.

• • •

Back home, I sat on the porch and opened another beer. I didn't want to climb the stairs again, so I walked into the yard and pissed under the tree. I missed the sound of Bud's jangling chain and started to get choked up again, standing there in the dark. I went back on the porch and caught my breath. Finally, I did go upstairs and sat at the kitchen table nursing the warm beer.

I heard the front door open, then Lorraine's voice shouting up the stairs. "Eddie? Eddie, are you up there?"

I walked out the door and leaned over the stairs. "They took him."

"Great!" she said. I closed my eyes and shook my head. "Or, not so great. Eddie, I didn't mean exactly . . ."

"I know."

"Listen—why don't we have a beer together? It's a nice night—we can sit on the porch."

"The neighbors might complain," I said sarcastically, but quickly added, "Sure." She was probably feeling sorry for me, or guilty. I didn't care—I was glad she asked.

"We'll whisper," she whispered.

I grabbed six long necks, sliding them between my fingers, and headed down the stairs.

"You don't mind if I'm a little sweaty, do you?" she asked.

"No problem. I drink with sweaty people all the time." I sat next to her on the stoop. It was a clear night. "Nice moon," I said.

She giggled. "Hey Eddie, you look pretty sharp tonight. You don't look half bad when you dress decent."

I tucked in my shirt. "Got dressed up for the visitors."

"How was Bud?"

"Fine. Cheers." I lifted my bottle. She clinked hers against mine and took a long swig. I watched her, then took a long swallow myself. She handled the bottle like she handled her cigarette—she knew what she was doing.

"Lorraine, I got a little something for you." I reached into my pocket and pulled out a handful of change and a couple of black capsules. I dropped the drugs onto her lap. I didn't know how she'd react, but drugs for drugs seemed like a fair exchange.

"Hey," she said, "what's this—speed? I don't do this stuff—anymore. I promised Fred."

I thought I'd screwed up again.

"But he's not here," she laughed and quickly popped one in her mouth. "Here." She gave me one back. "You take one too, and I'll tell you my life story."

"Cheers." I said again and tossed it in my mouth, took another swallow of beer. I was surprised as hell, almost a little giddy. We both put away two quick ones while she talked about herself. She went to Mercy College and was an RN, not a LPN—that distinction seemed important. She'd met Turner at a bar near the University of Detroit where he was in law school. His family was old money—Grosse Pointe money. Her family was from East Detroit, the working-class suburb that changed its name to eliminate the "Detroit" part because of its bad rep. It's called East Pointe now. She talked about her days in school like they were the best times in her life. I could relate to that.

"I can't tell you how good this tastes," she said, draining her bottle, setting it on the cement stoop. "I used to be pretty crazy, you know. In my younger days," she laughed. "Before I met Fred. When he finished school, he got a job with this big firm—his father's old firm. Ever since then, he seems so damn serious about everything. And he's always right, that's what kills me. He's really a nice man, though. He's been good to me. His family hates me."

"I used to be pretty crazy too."

"You're still pretty crazy, if you ask me. Sometimes when I hear you coming home drunk . . . I remember getting wasted, stoned, like in the old days. Listen—don't ever tell Fred this—I almost got married right after high school. To a guy something like you, a little rough around the edges—no offense." She looked down at the grass. I thought about the long, depressing nights at the Ritz and said nothing. I couldn't believe she was telling me this. I peeled the label off an empty bottle. I wanted to rest my hand on Bud's head to steady myself.

"We partied all the time," she said, "I guess I grew out of him once I started college. But sometimes I wish old Fred had a little more kick to him, if you know what I mean . . . Eddie, if you got out of the factory, I bet you could really go someplace. I almost didn't go to college. And I was thinking of quitting when I met Fred. He talked me into staying. I got a good job down at the hospital. Now look at me."

I looked. She talked on and on, about their dream house, the Jacuzzi and sauna, the swimming pool. She brought out pictures. It turned out the reason she didn't go with Fred was that his mother wasn't speaking to her. And that she was pissed off at Fred because he didn't want her to see her old friends anymore.

"We'll have to have you out to the new house," she said.

I just shook my head at that one. "You must be stoned."

"Hey, maybe we can all go out sometime, me, you, Fred. He doesn't drink much, especially since we've been married. He thinks being married means you can't have fun anymore. If we get a couple in him, maybe he'll loosen up some."

"Ha," I said.

• • •

We finished the beers I'd brought down. She looked up at the sky and rubbed her arms.

"Cold?" I asked.

"Yeah."

"Maybe it's the speed." My heart blasted away in my chest. What the hell, I thought, and moved closer and put my arm around her.

"Hey," she complained, but she was smiling. "No funny stuff. I'm a married woman, you know." She laughed. "Shit."

I laughed too. I didn't know she'd been busting to get out. "We've all got our chains, eh Lorraine?" I paused. "Why'd you marry him?"

"Oh, it was some stupid idea of growing up and being respectable. My parents love him. He's got money. But he's sucking up all my life," she blurted suddenly. "If he isn't, then something is."

"It sounds like you have your fun, judging from what I hear."

She shook her head, laughed, and swayed toward me. "You pervert."

"It's not like I try to hear or anything."

"Oh, Eddie," she said. She wrapped her arms around my neck and pulled me to her, kissing me awkwardly on the mouth, our teeth clicking. We wrapped our arms around each other and rolled off the steps and onto the grass. I ran my hands down her hips, over the tight uniform. "Wait. Eddie. Wait. Hold on." She froze, pushed me away. "We can't do this." I let go of her and sat back up on the stoop. She sat too. "Whew." She was breathing hard. "Eddie, you're a little wild. We can't get carried away here.

"Oh, shit, look what you did. I got grass stains on my uniform. How am I going to explain that to Fred? I'll have to get up early and wash these before he gets back. What time is it anyway?"

I held my head carefully between my hands, like it might break. It was throbbing. I couldn't believe the whole day. I was already trying to remember what Bud looked like, what her kiss was like. She got up and hurried past me into the house.

• • •

I knew it'd be awhile before the speed wore off. I started walking quickly, a speed walk—no sense of direction or purpose, just movement. I was pissed off at Lorraine and pissed off at myself. I wished Bud was there to pull me along, to give me some kind of focus.

I ended up along the edge of a city golf course, where I heard the sprinklers shooting off their timed spray. Floodlights lit the old clubhouse, a hangout for retired auto workers who played cards and golf for money. I jumped up and karate-kicked the air. I did it again, and again. I'd taken karate classes for a little while—when I was working midnights, I bought a lifetime membership in a club that folded within two years. I only went for about six months, then I got transferred back to afternoons, the deadly shift when all that was open after work was the bars. I was too tired after the factory to want to actually work out anyway. I thought it might be a way to meet or attract women. All it got me were some aches and pains. When I shifted to afternoons, I just couldn't make it there before going in to work. If only I'd get transferred to days. I kicked the air again.

The first green was partly lit by one of the floodlights. The flag stick was tilted, a beer can stuck on top. I stood waiting for one of the wings of spray to circle around to me. My skin tightened, but when the water hit, it only brought relief. Relief. The water gently slapped my face. I walked past and into the dark green of the fairways. I lingered at each sprinkler until, deep into the course, I was soaked skin through. I lay down on the soft grass of the eighteenth green and let the sprinklers circle their spray down over me. I wanted to take my clothes off, but I heard giggling nearby. A young man and woman were passing, holding hands. They laughed at me as if I was drunk or stoned. But I wasn't, not really. Here I was, both sober and not at work.

I'd saved a few bucks. My expenses were few. Maybe giving Bud away would actually free me up to change my life. My lease was up in a few months. Where would I go? What might I do? I knew there were no angels or saints, but sometimes I felt a certain magic in the world—I'd have a date with someone that would end with plans for another, I'd tell a story at work that everyone would laugh at, it'd feel good to visit my parents, and they wouldn't bug me. Maybe this would be the beginning of one of those times.

When I got back to the street, someone in a passing car yelled at me "Hey Vie," then something with "fuck" in it, then he held his thumb out in the air. I couldn't tell if it was a mean gesture or a friendly one, but I wasn't Vie, and that made me sad. I waved to the car in the distance.

On my way home, I passed an old man at a bus stop rocking back and forth on his heels, holding his lunch bucket in front of him like a pregnant belly. I passed a man staring at a mannequin in the window of a dress shop, mumbling a little prayer. I passed a punk kid in a dirty apron emptying garbage into a dumpster under the bright lights of a restaurant parking lot. I passed a crying woman in her robe sitting on the stoop of a house. My hands were shaking. I started walking faster. My clothes were already almost dry.

As I rounded a corner and headed back down my street, I noticed a dead squirrel in the road. Under the streetlight, I could see a little blood trickled from its open mouth. I know they tell you not to touch dead animals, but I pulled it to the side of the road. When I got back to the house, the first floor was dark. I stood for a moment in front of Turners' door. "What about my life story?" I shouted.

Spring Today

KATHLEEN GLYNN

When I sew in seams so long, a road rises up from my quilt and I see Mommy driving the car, big and blue, 1966. The tires bump over the asphalt that is aching from the winter, no way to restore itself for the springtime already flirting today. We drive by the carcasses of discount stores, huge and hulking, telephone poles joined by threads against the sky, grayness all around, sometimes a promise of grass, but not really.

The scabs like little stitches careful around her cuticle store information: bank balances, insufficient funds, overdue notices, and worry about Daddy's paycheck, brought home last night short from lack of overtime. Her teeth, not often laid bare for the dentist, for the hygienist, for a toothbrush, nibble now at a fingernail, pulling and tearing hard tissue away from soft, searing flesh and storing pain inside.

There is a welding shop by the railroad tracks. "Don't look there kids," our parents say when it's nighttime. "You'll be blinded." But we do look as we get older, the sparks light the paths of our future, from graduation line to employment office. Fireworks in our eyes, pride in our hearts, we will get the job, we will go every day. In the bright sun of this afternoon's ride, however, there is no shower of light tempting us to lose our sight. We stay on the road, straight ahead. We follow Mommy. We follow Daddy.

Left turn signal. Mommy's ring finger touching the knob on the handle, alone. The silver wedding band secures her, gives her a place. Her pocketbook, beside her, is the size of a shoebox, full of remedies and receipts. Heavy today with rolls of nickels, scraped across a poker table by Daddy last weekend, some small change made large. Slid in the side pocket is the check book that just skirts balance. She signs the checks in pretty handwriting for household expenses, "Mrs. William Benson" on the straight line where she should.

We pull into a lonely parking lot, only seven cars in two hundred places. "Can I wait in the car?" I ask. Petula Clark sings on the radio turned down low. Mommy stops and looks past me at the doughnut shop. "C'mon," she says, and turns off the ignition. I open the car door just enough to inch my body out sideways. I like the heavy metal pressing against my straight and stiff middle and the noise my corduroys make against the blue vinyl

319

upholstery. "Watch your fingers," Mommy says as I slam the door shut hard. I drag my feet along the worn yellow lines marked on the concrete and stop to look at a shopping cart turned upside down. "We don't have all day, there's still groceries to get," she yells. She waits while I turn and walk backward through the doorway. "Oh brother," she says.

Remember yesterday? After school, the baby cried. There is a sweet potato growing roots and sprouting on the kitchen windowsill, domestic botany. I brushed my face against the feathery leaves that hung low. They tickled my ear and all the way to the bottom of my back. It was Friday night, pizza night, Chef-Boy-R-Dee box torn open on the counter, tin can of sauce nearby. I climbed up on the countertop and turned the cold water faucet on and off. Mommy talked to her Aunt Goldie on the phone, and made a plan, "See you in the afternoon, I'll be by." She hung up and held the round pizza pans, burnt black, for a long time while she stared at me. "Don't," she said.

Inside the Goodwill, clothes hangers squeak as shoppers push them along the metal racks. Aunt Goldie holds two sacks, not new, kraft paper soft from wear, torn in little rips around the serrated top edge, forgiving. She is old to me and I am young to her, a novelty, but a smell she doesn't want in her nose. Her earrings clip on flat lobes, and I think they are like buttons fastened through buttonholes. Her dress is straight, narrow to her knees, with colors bright all over. Clasped at her neckline, her sweater is massed around her like a polyester cobweb. Her little red shoes are made of shiny crocodile plastic. They have wide white buckles, they are slippery on the bottom, they are brand new. She is not the boss, but the head of the sorting section at the Goodwill. She pulls squares of fabric out of the sack. Lifted high over my head, the colors tumble long to the floor. Some she stretches across her, arms spread wide. She sneaks a look around. Then she wraps yellow and white checks around me. "Go," she says to Mommy, "You don't have to pay. Just get quick before he sees."

Groceries in boxes and cans. They sit small in a corner of the cart. Mommy writes numbers on a little pad and puts back sugar cereal. I walk along with her, my fingers hooked in the cage of the cart reading a Golden Book I am too old for. Some cans of green beans are marked at two cents less than the others. Mommy says, "Get those." She counts her money twice and tells me to put back the Golden Book and then she puts Coca-Cola and potato chips in the cart for Saturday night.

In our neighborhood, the houses stand the same all down the block. The expression of doors and windows are a little different, but barely change from address to address. Daddy takes the groceries inside, they're heavy. Mommy takes the treasures from the Goodwill up the stairs of the porch. Daddy presses her against the screen door and the fabric spills from the sack. His mouth is on her neck for a very long time. Mommy says his name soft and quiet, like it's two words joined, "Bill-ill." I hear Daddy say "Mmmmm," into Mommy's ear. He shifts his weight and he steps now on the yellow checks, they are caught by the breeze, held by his foot, flapping like a flag in the springtime. Organza floats up and away from the porch like a cloud above my reach. Sturdy red corduroy tangles around my feet and brings me down, knees scraping bloody against the concrete. I cry. Mommy and Daddy lift me together, swinging me between their arms toward the sky. Again, I am too old for this. I am thrilled.

No school today. Mommy holds the thermometer above eye level then snaps it one, two, three times against her forearm. "102," she says and lays her hand against my forehead. It's like a message to my body, cool. Down on her knees she crouches over the fabric on the living room floor. She cuts with the scissors through tissue, beside pins, around the marked lines, through the yellow and white checks. "Oh, I'm not so young anymore," she says and rests back against Daddy's blue chair. Her forehead wrinkles into a center knot as she carefully reads the pattern instructions. "Huh," she says. I doze with fever on the scratchy sofa that used to be in Grandma's basement. Mommy says it is the wrong color, but it will do. I dream of the dark spaces in Grandma's house and the closets under the eaves that smell like lilac. When I wake, I hear the clunck clunck of the sewing machine needle, and the thump of the scissors dropped on the wooden cabinet. "Dammit," Mommy says when a pinprick of blood falls from her finger and onto the collar.

Easter morning comes. Go to church. There are new tennis shoes for me in a woven vinyl basket on top of the TV. A chocolate rabbit from Grandma. Eggs tinted pastel smashed in the carpeting. Bits of green plastic grass left in the bathtub, the toilet, in the hallway. Mommy's nylons have a run. It's brisk outside, a grown-up word. Daddy and the neighbor, today in suits, jump the car battery. The elastic on my Easter bonnet breaks because I pull on it. My cold and picky slip chafes against my skin and my white tights bag at my knees. I reach to tug them up and red Kool-Aid spills across my dress, finished by Mommy while I was at school and the baby had her nap. Yellow and white checks.

from Just Like in the Movies

BILL HARRIS

SATURDAY, APRIL 3
1. THE CUSTODIAN OF THE DREAM BOOK

"I still need me a good figure for today," Adair said.

Raz told him to ask Fastball.

Everybody looked at Eddie at the rear of the shop where he was working on a pair of pointed-toed black Stacy Adams oxfords with white stitches around the soles. Eddie's customers had to ascend the two, high gray marble steps in order to take a seat and place their shine-needy shoes on the ornate metal footrests. The stand was a three seater of darkening oak, chocolate brown leather, and brass-headed brads. The curved arms that separated the padded seats featured carved fauna of as an anonymous a phylum as the real life giants on the platform that ran the length of the front window. There the two, big, more brown than green, thick-stalked potted plants framed the storefront window with the arching sign in red letters shadowed in white:

RAZ'S TONSORIAL PARLOR.

"He just a boy," Adair said.

A boy getting a chance none of us didn't have, or didn't take advantage of, Raz said, talking about education. And he's doing something with it, Prentis added.

Prentis was the little barber who had the middle chair, on Raz's right. Raz had the first chair, the one nearest the entrance.

The barbershop was across the street from the New Villa Bar, Eddie's father's favorite, in the eleven thousand six hundred block of Oakland, between Englewood and Rosedale, the second block down on the way to school from Mrs. Beasley's.

"I've known plenty of educated fools," Adair said.

Raz and Prentis, the two regular-through-the-week barbers, had been arguing about whether Charles Laughton or Sydney Greenstreet played Captain Bligh in *Mutiny on the Bounty.*

They led most of the arguments because they would argue about any-thing and their opinions were almost assuredly as different as they were in appearance. Mutt and Jeff. Prentis could not have been much taller than five foot nothing soaking wet, as Raz said. He kept his chair cranked all the way down and stood on a wooden Pespi-Cola crate to cut hair.

Raz, on the other hand, as Prentis said, was well over six foot plenty some-thing. His chair was cranked up almost as high as it could go. Raz kept a cigar clamped in his teeth all during the day. He wouldn't light it until he had cut the last customer's hair and was stropping his razor in preparation for the next day's work.

Eddie was sometimes called on by Raz to be the arbiter in certain kinds of disputes. These were usually ones that involved what the barbershop reg-ulars called school learning—where a specific answer, such as a name or date or an amount—would clear up the point of contention. Eddie had settled the Charles Laughton versus Sydney Greenstreet question, reminding them of Laughton's appearances in *The Hunchback of Notre Dame* and *Captain Kidd,* and Greenstreet's *Maltese Falcon* and *Casablanca* roles.

Eddie was never called on to decide any matter than had to do with women or how things had been down home, things, they said, that couldn't be learned out of no books, and were therefore outside his experience.

Eddie liked Raz. He liked when Raz called him Little Professor some-times, Fastball or School Boy at other times. Others sometimes called him Little Jack. Jack was what they called his father; real name John. It all started when he and his father began rooming over the candy store with Mrs. Beasley, two blocks up Oakland, and came to the Raz's to get their haircuts. In those days, 6 or 7 years ago, when Eddie was 5 or 6, Raz had to place a board across the arms of the barber chair for Eddie to sit on for the extra height. Eddie remembered the day his father said to Raz that he was think-ing maybe the board wasn't needed anymore. Raz agreed.

"Besides," Adair continued, almost pouting, "he ain't the only one been to school."

Raz told Adair, Eddie was the only one *in here* been to school *up here,* where the school got more than one room, meet most the year 'round, and the teacher cared whether you learn something or not.

"What?" Mr. Jenkins said. He was a little hard of hearing and didn't like to miss anything.

Mr. Jenkins came in every morning about ten o'clock when his daughter, who had left her husband and moved back home, got out the bed and started stirring around. He leaned forward a little in his chair, lined with the others along the wall facing the barbers.

Behind Raz and Prentis was the big mirror where, when they'd finished cutting a customer's hair and had given him a chance to appraise the results with a hand mirror, they would spin him around (Prentis getting down off his box first) and let the customer face himself head-on in the looking glass lighted by the glow of a line of near-blue florescent tubes.

Scotch-taped to the mirror behind Raz's chair was the license certifying Willie Lee Simpkins qualified to provide tonsorial services in the State of Michigan. Taped next to it was the photograph. Eddie remembered it from the days when he still had to sit on the board. Even then the photo was curling at the corners and changing color like an eternal autumn leaf. Young Raz and the other members of the all-colored baseball team in their loose-fitting uniforms with BROWNS in bold letters sewn in an arch across each of their shirts.

His nickname Raz, short for razor, came not from his present profession, but from his pro baseball days. The name was given to him, he had explained, by the poor, unfortunate colored, and occasional white boys, who faced him when he was playing in the Negro Leagues, back before Jackie Robinson broke the barrier into the white professional big leagues in '47. His fastball had been so sharp the nickname naturally followed.

Windexing the mirror was one of the chores Eddie had been responsible for the last four months of Saturdays he had been Raz's Tonsorial Parlor's shoeshine boy. He also ran errands, kept track of the order in which the customers came in, brushed them off with a whisk broom after their haircut, and swept and mopped up at closing time.

Forrest, who had been dozing, mumbled into his chest, agreeing with Adair about educated fools. Prentis was giving him a razor line along his neck. As a preamble to a story Forrest was starting to say he remembered one time when, when Adair said a figure had to feel right before he would put his money on it. He said it quick and loud, trying to cut Forrest off.

Adair continued cursing himself for playing 263 the day before. It had come out straight. He'd known better than not to play it, but he hadn't been thinking. 263 fell every time he had a buzzing in his ear and his old lady's mama made meatloaf! The last time it'd come out was in February.

Mr. Jenkins nodded, verifying it, and agreed 263 was a good number. Lovecraft, who was getting his Stacy Adams shined, had caught it that time. Hadn't had but a dime on it. Should've sweetened it, but he hadn't, even though he'd seen it on a license plate yesterday morning as he was coming out of the Big Bear market up on Woodward. Lovecraft had lost his right hand in a stamping machine up the street in Highland Park Chrysler plant.

He was on a disability pension. He kept saying he was going to get a ticket and go back to Georgia, buy a farm and raise chickens and hogs.

"All right, Raz right," Adair said. He looked to Eddie. "Fastball, you got a good mind. Give a good number." His earlier attitude was forgotten. Nobody, no matter how loud the argument, seemed to stay angry for long.

Eddie did not remember when he had first realized how much the men in the barbershop respected education, even though, or maybe because, they generally had so little formal schooling themselves. That was, he thought, why they bothered with him. They had heard, through his father or Raz, how well he did in school, and some of them were proud of him, just as proud in their way as his father or Mrs. Beasley were in theirs, and they sought to encourage him.

The greatest proof of their pride was not in the tips they gave him for services rendered, followed by an admonishment to put it in the bank "or his education." Even greater than that was making him the custodian of the Dream Book.

> The New
> 1954 Edition
> The Original
> Lucky
> Three Wise Men
> Dream Book

The number's players Encyclopedia Britannica and Bible.

It was kept in the shoeshine stand drawer next to the ones where Eddie kept his polish, rags and brushes. "The Red Devil Almanac," the "Black Cat," or "Prof. Hitts' Rundown and Workout" among them. But the barbers and customers of Raz's preferred "The Three Wise Men."

"938," Eddie said.

Mr. Jenkins smiled.

"938," Adair said, nodding. "Yeah—938. That sound like one I can work with. I knew you had lots of sense. 938."

938—Hoping.

2. WORKING, MAN

"Hey, Eddie, man!"

"Hey, DeWitt, man!"

"What you doing here?"

"Working, man,"

"Shining shoes, huh?"

"Yeah, man."

"Yeah, man, cool. I come to get me a haircut."

"Yeah, man, cool."

Eddie introduced DeWitt as his new friend. Had just transferred into school from down south. Raz said he'd take good care of him.

No Puedo Bailar

LOLITA HERNANDEZ

—for Gerardo

Ahi está la pared
Que separa tu vida y la mía
Ahi está la pared
Que no deja que nos acerquemos
—from the song "La Pared" by Roberto Angleró

When Los Reyes hit the first chord of their signature bolero rítmico, "La Pared," Orquidia jumped to her feet from the rickety folding chair in the basement apartment of an old building on the main drag of southwest Detroit. It was her favorite tune on the CD because it could stand for many different walls of love, for example bitter sweet emotional walls might make lovers fear intimacy or their vulnerability in a love relationship. Or the song could stand for all of the misery she and her compañeros in the room with her right then had experienced just trying to come to the city from across many borders and over real walls. Or it could stand for all the love of familia—children, spouses, parents, cousins—left behind. Maybe that was the worse part, leaving lovers and loved ones, leaving all those parts of self behind. Or maybe the fear to immerse oneself in new love because of the walls that surround you as you move about the city to work or gather with new friends similarly situated.

The others tapped their feet and snapped their fingers to strengthen tempo, the men in the group waiting to see who was the brave one that evening with enough energy to take on Orquidia.

mía nada más
mía mía nada más

And then their voices joined those of Los Reyes.

¡ah zi!
esa maldita pared

As the song began its crescendo, Carlos lined up shots of tequila on a tall bench that served as a counter for drinks and Joaquin flipped open caps on bottles of Corona.

Orquidia was winding up her still soft and supple body, all the while recalling one live and magical performance of Los Reyes in the Plaza de Armas in San Luis Potosí, where she had traveled from Oaxaca to spend the summer with her uncle who was also her padrino. That was all so long ago, in another gentler period of time in her life on one special Sunday, in a special plaza on el Día de los Padres. Orquidia found herself transported to the plaza in San Luis Potosí on a hot night. Many in the city were drawn to Plaza de Armas just to hear Los Reyes, the live band for the evening. They provided music for the danzón performance where those in the crowd craned to see each elegant couple, a don y doña, gliding under the porticos of the town hall. After the danzón they performed their own music, boleros from her grandmother's era, music untainted by yanqui border influence.

Earlier, the plaza was electric with activity. Groups of men and young boys practiced drumming in a military style while buglers blew and marched around as if they, too, were military. Clowns cajoled the crowd into buying jewelry from the various Indian vendors from the mountains or elote mixed with peppers, mayonnaise, and cheese from the many carts that ringed the plaza. The air smelled of sun and corn. Later, hundreds and hundreds of people gathered for the danzón festival in honor of Father's Day. Some influential people in the city were honored guests. At least a dozen couples all dressed alike—the ladies in beige sequined tops with fringed bottoms and high heels, the men in black tuxedos—performed the formal Cuban-inspired danzón in front of the Government Palace. Orquidia and her cousins squeezed through the crowd to climb on a band shell where they could only see the crowd—the dancers were now mere specks—but could sway their bodies back and forth arms interlocked in time to the music. Then as now her mother's medallion gently shifted from one side of her chest to the other, also in time to the music. She wore the medallion always to keep close the spirit of the mother who died birthing her. Her uncle in San Luis Potosí was her mother's oldest brother and the one closest to Orquidia.

Eberardo gazed longingly at the glittering medallion, watched Orquidia's hips as she dipped and rose to the music as if climbing the wall referenced in the song. He smiled almost lasciviously, well not quite because he was too young for that, but he was rubbing his hands in anticipation of holding hers in dance. Almost every Friday evening anywhere from eight to twelve of them celebrated life with tequila, Corona and a variety of botanas in Radames' sparsely-furnished basement apartment. Always they dressed in their Sunday best. Usually the men outnumbered the women, but on this night they were even steven, five of each, not quite partners. Carlos and Joaquin were being faithful to their women back home. But at least two of the men, Eberardo and Radames, had eyes for Orquidia. For sure, Radames yearned for Orquidia's hot body next to his. At work the gringos called him Radman: *Hey Radman bring that box over here, and then take it over there! Radman, yeah, that's a good boy.* For her part Orquidia thought Radames had good possibility—plenty man as far as she could tell from the bulge between his legs. And, of course, Eberardo wanted her in the worst way. But as life would have it, Orquidia was most interested in the least attainable of the men there—César. He normally occupied a corner seat in the room, smiling always. He was the one most preoccupied with his former life in Chiapas and what was happening with his children there. Of all in the group he had come from the furthest away, and he was the one least tied to Detroit, in spite of the intense friendship of those who gathered on Fridays. True the brothers Carlos and Joaquin had wives back home, but at least they had each other and their mother's secret tamale recipe—always in the masa, she said, the masa. César had told Orquidia several gatherings ago when she invited him to dance that he could not. *No puedo bailar hasta que pueda ver otra vez a mis hijos.* He could not or would not dance until he could see his children again. Orquidia, who had no children, sympathized with him anyway, but thought that one little salsa wouldn't hurt the memory of his children and might even revitalize him for the long time ahead before he would be able to see. Still, although she did not take his rejection of the opportunity to dance with her personally, she accepted César as a personal challenge.

This is how it was every Friday. Carlos, who made and sold tamales as a business with his brother Joaquin, often cooked nopales y huevos at the gatherings to the delight of his compañeros. Joaquin, as usual, assisted. The brothers were from San Luis Potosí, the area where cactus grew as far as the eye could see. All came to wash down the sweat and dirt from their various occupations during the week, although almost all of them still would find themselves on Saturday or even Sunday scrubbing restaurant dishes, stamping out an automobile part or arranging fruits and vegetables in one of the large markets in the city. But Friday evenings were theirs in amistad and mirth. Time to forget everything: immigration problems, familia en la patria and utilities that may be cut off at any moment. If anyone should want to forget troubles, certainly Orquidia would top the list. She was the one who experienced the toughest crossing, a textbook horror journey north from Oaxaca to Arizona and then across to Detroit. Whoever wants to come to Detroit? Especially after nearly losing a foot in the dessert running from the local militia and the dogs. But Detroit was where she landed, full of tales about the cabrones in Arizona and laughter in awe that she had survived, so far.

An Arizona dog may have two of her left toes, but no mind; she still had enough of the left foot to assist the right in twirling and stomping her way through the CDS Radames contributed to the Friday gatherings. He had papers of a sort, at least enough documentation to provide him with cover for the odds and ends jobs he hustled reconstructing kitchens and bathrooms, as well as laying tile and other flooring. The papers also protected him for jobs in stamping plants that made parts for larger union-organized auto assembly factories. None of them in the room, no matter what work they did, were in any kind of union. They were their own informal self-help organization. Because of their papers, Joaquin and Carlos were able to get drivers licenses, a major boon because they were often called upon to drive others without any kind of documentation to various appointments. These runs occurred between tamale drop-offs during which their passengers often arrived to their destination filled with tasty tamales. Radames provided the same service, especially helpful for Orquidia because she didn't know how to drive anyway. ICE, the immigration authorities who prowled the streets of southwest Detroit looking for paperless people, would demand identification of Joaquin, Carlos, their friends and anyone else looking like them, whether walking or driving, or in their homes, for that matter. So having the ability to drive legally was a little bit helpful for necessary trips that people could not make by bus or taxi. That was the reality of the world out there every minute of every day, except Friday evenings when the crew gathered, each breathing a sigh of relief as their members entered, still free people, for at least that moment.

Esa maldita pared
yo la voy a romper algún día

At this, Orquidia stomped her cowboy-booted right foot to emphasize her intentions to break a wall one day, however it would present itself, wherever, alone if necessary. Another foot stomp and she pulled Eberardo up from the corner, he sheepishly grinning at the opportunity to dance with this woman of desire. He rose singing with her the chorus:

no puedo mirarte
no puedo abrazarte

no puedo besarte
ni sentir de mía

As he pulled her closer to him their lips nearly touched, the song ended and Eberardo held Orquidia a moment longer as the melody lingered in the air and in the hearts of those gathered. All eyes were on the couple, the only ones on the dance floor, established by moving a couch and a few folding chairs closer to the wall.

Carlos called out, vamos a cenar, indicating that his specialty was ready and that the assorted chips and salsas and frijoles were arranged buffet-style on the tiny counter in the kitchen. Eberardo rushed to fix a plate for Orquidia, indicating his intention by a look and the slightest touch on her elbow, not a direct connection to her bare skin, but just close enough to allow the electricity from his body to cross over to hers through an invisible channel moistened by anticipation and possibility. In this way he escorted her to a seat at the table to wait for her plate. Conchi, a woman who lived with a family in Birmingham during the week as the nanny for two little girls, eyed the exchange between Eberardo and Orquidia with glee. He was her cousin and best friend. She knew he suffered from having to leave his novia in Monterrey and who knows if they would ever be reunited. She linked her arm in his and kissed him gently on the cheek as the two entered the kitchen for food. Radames grunted at Eberardo before entering the kitchen.

By the time everyone had a plate of food in front of them, including César, who normally waited last, even after Carlos the chef, it was time for the first toast of the evening. Eberardo, as usual, jumped up with a wish for good health to all, especially to Orquidia, may she keep dancing to bring light and love to our lives. He was a bit of a poet. That initial guzzle of Tequila 1800, washed down by a few sips of Corona followed by the nopales y huevos, chips and so on, fueled the first round of discussion—always about work. These weren't typical whiners, complaining of too much work and too little pay. They, indeed, worked too much for way too little money in jobs that were unsafe. César was probably in the worst situation of all of them because he worked for an asbestos removal firm that provided the worst masks and protective equipment of all similar businesses in the area. If it weren't for a guy there, a worker like him, who spoke fluent English and Spanish and who fortunately would speak up for his undocumented compañeros de trabajo, César would never have received decent equipment nor would he have understood the cleansing procedure after each day of work. Even with those precautions, César wondered if he would return to his homeland, the lush but troubled state of Chiapas, with any lungs left with which to once again hurl laughter at his children and dance in celebration of his return.

Next on the list of topics was always a thorough and lively exploration of what they could do to improve their lot. Past discussions included door-to-door approaches to targeted areas in the barrio to discuss migra actions. This they eventually deemed too dangerous; their undocumented selves would be too exposed. For all they knew they could just as easily knock on the door of an immigration officer as that of a sympathizer. The discussion this evening in Radames's basement apartment took an unusual turn, perhaps because of a brand new portrait of la Virgen in the form of a banner Joaquin had been eyeing ever since he arrived. This is what he proposed: We must warn everyone about la migra, Joaquin proclaimed with only the leading edge of tipsy informing his discourse.

¿Como? asked everyone.

La Virgen, he replied, pointing to the banner hanging prominently in the room. This led Orquidia's fingers to caress her medallón of la Virgen de Guadalupe while others scratched their heads in confusion. Joaquin continued, explaining the overall intent of his plan for leaving messages from la Virgen to everyone in the barrio.

Radames, demanded to know, ¿Y como le vamos a hacer? How are we going to do this?

That discussion would call for at least two more shots of 1800 and another bottle of beer per discussant. Conchi could handle only one shot of tequila, but she was good for at least two beers. Orquidia varied her intake, depending on her engagement with the direction of the discussion. On this night tequila passed her lips almost without touching them, for Joaquin had proposed an adventure that the ten compañeros would debate back and forth with unbelievable passion.

I'll tell you how, said Joaquin, who was now feeling free enough to trot out the English he had to learn in order to sell tamales to the gringo tourists who crossed over from Canada on the Ambassador Bridge. We are going to make up signs in the form of dichos from la Virgen, avisos warning our people about certain things to do if confronted by la migra.

¿Por ejemplo? This was Eberardo's question.

For example, la Virgen dice no abra la puerta. Nunca. Don't open the door for la migra. Never. Joaquin fully showing off his English now. Orquidia and others nod. They understand.

Laritza, who worked in a Birmingham house next door to Conchi, piped up, A si, la Virgen dice no firme nada.

Conchi chimed in, No conteste ninguna pregunta. Tell them nothing. Everyone got the idea. Soon instructions from la Virgen even touched on health issues, such as don't smoke or have unprotected sex. Those were proposed by the two cousins, Adela and Adriana, often lovingly called the "A Team."

The rest of the discussion focused on logistics—how to create the signs, how to post them, both of which could possibly engage several Fridays.

• • •

The last of the nopalitos y huevos disappeared along with the first bottle of 1800. The Corona was holding strong on this particular night when emotions peaked at the possibility of a solution. Maybe not a solution, but something to do besides commune by themselves and hope alone. La Virgen could be their public show to others, and they would have her power behind them. Maybe they could unite and become something, some people in this land, this crazy city where people who think they are some-bodies have no real power anyway. That's what they wanted to say to the world they were in now. You're no better than us. Remember that. But they had each other and la Virgen and a fresh bottle of 1800, a few Coronas and lots of memory. Orquidia was still going strong. She had placed her medallón inside her shirt for some strange protectionist reason. She had a feeling they had reached a turning point, this grupo, her compañeros in misery and faith and hope, and she needed la Virgen of her mother to be closer to her than ever.

Los Reyes recycled on Radames's one extravagant purchase, a five-CD changer. The selection had now returned to "La Pared." Orquidia perked up immediately and decided that the smiling, silent César needed to get up from his seat and dance. Why not? You can only hold things in for so long. You must let go if only for a moment. Didn't he have a moment for her? Just a moment for her to feel fully herself, minus a few toes. He did-n't look like a man who cared about toes. The other two did. Maybe. But, of course, she hadn't tried any of them out. But tonight was the night. Maybe. She carried more scars besides her missing toes. César looked more genuine, more forgiving, as if she could take off her blouse and the scars wouldn't offend him. As if he might find a way into her interior past the wounds on the route up her vagina. She wasn't even sure if it could func-tion anymore. There were more than four-legged dogs after her on the trip through Arizona.

So, sure in the protection and wisdom of la Virgen, she got up again to dance. By this time she was full of 1800 and nopales probably originally from

San Luis Potosí. She was feeling the power and support of her tío and padrino and all of the familia over there. Los Reyes hit her favorite section of the song.

mía nada más
mía mía nada más

And Orquidia slapped her hip. The others laughed and clapped.

¡ah zi!
esa maldita pared

She plopped herself in front of César, folds of her long multicolored skirt draped in her right hand, her eyes intent on his. He looked up, startled in a way, but understanding that it was time for him to make some kind of move. You can't get from Chiapas to Vernor Avenue in Detroit, Michigan, in zero to five, no matter what they say. There has to be time for reflection, time to search out truth, time to figure out what is real. Now he was being called upon to place all of that in order and then dance?

Orquidia swayed to the bolero rítmico as she never had, harking memories beyond what she ever experienced personally. How would her mother have done this? That's what she was thinking. But she saw this intense hombre, Don César, the most guapo of them all, guapo in her eyes beholding him sitting there, and she knew she had eight-toed power to get the man up.

And he got up. No, he jumped up. Arms, covered as usual in a long-sleeved black shirt, wide like an eagle's wings, eyes closed and one huge smile spreading across his face. Orquidia, in truth, didn't know what César was about to do at that moment. No one in the room knew. The other women grouped close to each other. Radames and Eberardo furrowed their brows in amazement. The brothers shifted to the rear of the room, smiling. But they all watched his outstretched arms, his taut body, his apparent ecstasy, and waited for the performance.

¡ah zi!
esa maldita pared

The Old West

CHRISTOPHER T. LELAND

Since he could see Chuck through the screen door, he didn't even bother to knock; just came right in and slung the suitcase onto the kitchen table.

"Blue Ribbon?"

"On special this week. We got a shitload."

Chuck reached in his back pocket and pulled out a ratty five.

"Shove it." Tim tore back the cardboard and pulled out two cold ones. "This is Sid's treat."

Tim had been working at his brother's liquor store since the plant shut down.

"He know that?"

Tim smirked.

Chuck shrugged and popped the tab on the beer Tim set in front of him. He looked like he'd already had a couple shots of something. For a moment or two, they did not talk.

Tim looked across the table warily. "Sally still gone?"

"Yep."

"Becky told me. Lucy down at Smather's heard about it."

"Whatever."

Outside, amid the stands of weeds in the trailer park, the crickets thrummed through the vaguest breeze. Far to the west, there was heat lightening.

"They took my truck yesterday."

"Yeah?"

"Little faggot from GMAC. He was headed out of the park before I even seen him."

"How far behind were you?"

"Seven months. Figured they'd be after it, after all the notices. I was keeping a couple distributor cables pulled at night, so they'd have to bust the hoodlatches to get it going. But daytimes I had to use it. Didn't figure they'd snitch it right under my nose. Took the boy over to K-Mart for flip-flops and we wasn't back five minutes . . ."

Chuck's voice thinned and he took a slug of beer.

"That's hard." Tim shook his head. "You know, Billy Eckard's living in his old man's Winnebago. Kicked him out of that duplex on Third Street."

Things were bad in Olinda since the plant closed down. Things had never been very good, at least as far back as most people could remember. Almost anybody who had a job now worked over in Rhymers Creek or up in Mockdon. There'd been some flush times when the bridge was in the old-timers said, and bootlegging when the county was still dry. There'd been some other attempts to jumpstart the town. The fittings plant was only the latest promise to die on the vine.

Chuck shrugged. "Least he's got wheels."

Tim took two more cans out of the suitcase. "'Nother one?"

"Sure."

He passed him the beer. "That why you hit her?" he said casually.

"Huh?"

"The truck."

Chuck looked curious, as if it hadn't occurred to him. "Maybe. I guess. That what she says?"

"That's what Lucy told Becky."

"Oh." Chuck scratched his temple. "Never ran off about it before." There was a big hole of quiet. "Time before, she said she might. Said she was afraid I'd hit the boy."

"You would, wouldn't you?"

Chuck snorted. "Well, hell. Sure. I mean, if he deserved it?"

Tim wondered, in the silence, how many boozy nights they had spent like this, ever since they were kids in high school. It seemed strange to try and even tote them up now, sucking a brew on a muggy night with Chuck, whose wife was gone.

"Where you figure she went?"

"Don't know." Chuck rolled the can back and forth between his palms. "Her mother woulda sent her back. Lucy didn't say?"

"If she knows, she's not telling."

"Maybe she went to that shelter the lezzies set up in Lemon Grove." He huffed a laugh. "She won't last long there."

"Damn women's libbers," Tim belched. "The world sucks anymore."

"Yeah." Chuck looked at his beer. "Maybe it always did."

"Shit, man. We had good times. All those Saturdays down at the dry lake."

"I guess," Chuck said morosely, "but that was a long time ago."

They were quiet again for a moment or two. Chuck stood up. He wobbled a little when he got to his feet. He walked over to the door.

"You know, I started to think that even when we thought it was good, it wasn't. For me, anyhow. Like my whole life's screwed up like this whole country's screwed up like this whole town especially." He swung around to face Tim and leaned on the doorframe. "I was thinking before you got here that the only goddamn thing I ever had enough of was space. When I was a kid, that was the only thing worth a good goddamn, so I could run away when my old man went for his belt, or when Billy Thompson and Reggie Lesser cracked up on Blood Alley, or when Sally Wills ran off." He coughed. "Except that finally all you can do with space is be alone."

Tim shifted in his chair. He hated that kind of talk. He thought about Becky and was glad.

"You figure she'll come back?"

"Sure." Chuck shrugged, looking out into the night. "Where's she gonna go?"

They drank more beer and played seven-card stud for a while, then watched a detective show. They didn't talk about Sally. It got to be eleven, and the news came on.

"I should get on back," Tim said, his voice a little thick. "You o.k.?"

"I guess."

They walked out to the drive in front of the trailer, to Tim's pickup. Chuck looked it up and down. Wistfully.

Tim opened the door.

"Today," Chuck said suddenly, "when that fucker took my truck, when I saw it go 'round the corner, you know what I did? Do you know?" He let out a little hoot that might almost have been a laugh. "I started to cry. I did. Before I ever knew it." He grabbed Tim's shoulder, and his voice came out raspy with beer and a hurt beyond time. "That's something nobody should ever do. Make a man cry in front of his boy."

They stood there for a minute. Then Tim gently lifted Chuck's hand off his arm. He got into the truck and put the key in the ignition.

"Is that when you hit her?"

Chuck scuffed his boot in the gravel. "Yeah."

• • •

Becky was brushing her hair at the vanity they bought from the Penney's cat-alogue just before the plant went bust. Tim came back from the bathroom and flopped face-up on the bed.

"He all right?" she asked.

"No." He turned so he could watch her—seventy-four, seventy-five, seventy-six, seventy-seven. "He needs her back bad."

Becky stroked the brush rhythmically. "Then he shouldn't've hit her."

"I know." Tim nodded wearily. "But he's in bad shape. No Sid in his family to see him through the bad times." He paused. "They took his truck."

Eighty-nine. Ninety. Ninety-one. "So?"

He almost hesitated to tell her. "It made him cry. He couldn't help it." He let his breath out slowly. "His boy was there."

Ninety-five. Ninety-six.

"I mean. That's bad. A woman's got to understand."

One hundred.

Becky laid the brush down, and turned from the mirror to face him. She looked beautiful in that instant, proud and soft all at once. He felt a little shiver of desire.

But when her voice came out, it was cold like sleet.

"No she don't, Tim. Some things a woman don't have to understand at all."

Swallowing Camels

M. L. LIEBLER

The street smelled fresh. It really wasn't. But, you see, it seemed that way, at that time, in its own peculiar way. To us, I guess, it was the best odor and the best time to utilize it to our advantage. Other things didn't seem as important. I mean who really cared if Tommy's feet stunk or if Eddie's ears were puffed so full of wax that his mother lit him at night to see her way to bed? I don't know if that was so much the truth, but some of the guys spoke of it from time to time. But like I said, who cared? Smell was the greatest sense back then, and there wasn't one of us who didn't understand and enjoy it. The street did smell fresh, and I can't quite explain that, but I think it is important that you try to understand.

I'm thinking about the time my brother, Tommy, and I ran into a jazz bar smoking cigarettes and, at age ten, asked the bartender for two short beers. Well this guy was massive, or so he seemed to us. He swallowed two huge drags from his Camel and said, "I'll tell ya boys what I'm going to do for ya: two short beers, if ya dance over there by the Wurlitzer." We giggled and circled our heads around over our shoes and said, "Ya-ya, sure mister; you got a deal. Two beers? For one dance?" The bartender tossed a painted dime over to a drunk who had his stinky mouth and oily head pressed up against the jukebox. Then the bartender yelled, "Put Dizz on—The boys are gonna dance." The bum at the box pressed "Summertime," and I yelled that we couldn't dance to such a slow song. Everyone in the bar laughed and began chanting "Dance! Dance! Dance!" The bartender looked up and said, "Boys, ya peers have just passed sentence on ya!" I didn't want to dance next to my brother; I couldn't stand sleeping next to him as it was. Again the chant, "Dance! Dance! Dance!"

The faces of those guys were horrid, and they became more terrifying with each chant to dance. I was getting very nervous. My brother was bewildered. "Dance ya punks, before I calls the cops and tell em you come in here askin for beer," the bartender screamed. I began sweating like a pig. In the window of the Wurlitzer, I saw my parents and police images pounding to get out. In fear, I slowly began dancing with my brother. The drunks closed a tight circle around us and forced us cheek to cheek. Then, they started yelling for us to kiss. "Kiss!" I thought, "My GOD, what is this?" Even at age ten, I realized something was seriously wrong. I whispered in my brother's ear, "What are we going to do?" He said, "Kiss me, would ya, I'm crappin my pants!" I kissed him and just then, the music stopped. We both smiled at the bartender and asked about those two beers. And he said, "The beers? Oh ya, beers! Here ya go!" And with that he threw the beer in our faces and screamed, "Now get the hell outta my place you faggots, and don't come round again!" He picked us up and threw us both out in the street. As we walked home, my brother asked me if I would ever try to kiss him again. I looked at him and said, "Only if I'm thirsty and beer is all there is to drink." We laughed our guts out and went into the house for dinner.

Work

BRET LOTT

When we make love, I forget we live in a one-room apartment above a liquor store four blocks from the ocean, and that our bed folds up into the wall. I forget I work part-time at the liquor store, Linda at the Golden Sails Inn up on Pacific Coast Highway. She's a cocktail waitress and wears a short, tight dress cut low across her breasts, layers of ruffles beneath her skirt so that it sticks out like a tutu.

I forget that each workday, before she leaves and I go to work downstairs, I zip up her dress for her and say, "You're a fool, going to work in a getup like that."

She says, "Who's the fool? Me? Or you, working part-time in a liquor store?"

We always say those things before we go to work, but I am kidding. She makes most of our money. I also forget that she has stopped smiling when she says, "Me? Or you?"

• • •

I work. I do a lot of the odd jobs around the store. I sweep the sidewalks, sort returned bottles, wash all the windows whenever Dick, the manager, tells me to.

About a week ago I asked Dick if I could go full-time at the liquor store.

"Daryl," he said, "first thing is, is that we're not a 'liquor store.' 'Liquor store' makes it sound like all we do is sell Muscatel, Night Train, and T-Bird. We're a specialty store."

Dick calls it that because in the rear of the store, behind the coldboxes, is a section of dirty magazines, some greeting cards, a poster section and display rack. Still, he didn't answer my question. I didn't ask again.

• • •

A guy in a wheelchair came into the store tonight. He was about thirty-five, brown hair down to his shoulders. He wore an Army fatigue jacket, the name Jenkins stenciled above the right breast pocket. He seemed to have no problem opening the front door and wheeling in.

"Howdy," I said from behind the counter.

"How you doing tonight?" he answered.

I said, "Oh, all right, I guess."

I watched him wheel around the store, looking at booze, chips, magazines. He spent some time flipping through the poster display rack, and when he finally came to the register he had one of the posters and an Almond Joy.

"I wish you had a couple more of this one," he said. "I know some people'd like this one. Are those back there all you have?"

"Yes," I said, "but let me go back and check. What number is it?"

He handed me the rolled-up poster. I read the numbers out loud from off the yellow tape on the end of the roll, then went back to the display rack and checked all the cubbyholes for his number. There weren't any more.

Then I went through the display rack, just to see which one he'd picked. I wondered if it was the nude blonde running on the beach, or maybe the brunette with her hair covering only the least bit of her breasts. I knew those posters by heart.

Then I found it. The poster was an autumn scene of oak and maple trees lining a clear stream. In the distance a log-pole bridge crossed the stream, a bridge it would have been difficult to cross even for me.

I walked back to the register, shook my head without looking at him.

"Didn't think so," he said, and gave me the money.

He was at the door before I said anything to him. I called out, "Sure you don't need any help?" I started to move out from behind the counter.

"No, no," he said, waving me away. "If I don't make it a practice to move myself, I'll lose it." He opened the door. "So long," he said.

I said, "Thanks."

At midnight I closed the store. I usually go upstairs and watch TV until Linda comes home a little after one and undresses in front of me, not always because of me, but because of the one room. But tonight I decided to drive up PCH to the Golden Sails for a drink before she got off. I parked the car and went into the lounge, sat down at the bar and ordered a beer.

"Where's Linda?" I asked the bartender. He smiled and pointed to a table where five or six businessmen laughed and smoked, ties loosened, collars unbuttoned.

Linda was serving drinks all the way around. The men laughed as she set down cocktail napkins and then drinks. Linda leaned across the table and served a man who pulled the swizzle stick from his drink and put it down the top of her dress, wedging the stick between her breasts. The men laughed. So did Linda. She pulled the stick out and dropped it back into his drink while the man she stood next to placed his hand on her skirt, pressing down the ruffles until his hand contoured her buttocks. She served the man his drink last, then traced his lips with her fingertip.

She turned from the table, headed back to the bar, but stopped smiling when she saw me there. I heard her call my name once as I pushed the doors open and went for the car.

She came home a little after one and shook a fistful of cash in my face. She said, "See? This is it. This is it. You think I like this? I do it for the money. So we can live."

I yelled, and then she yelled some more. I unzipped her dress for her, and she undressed in front of me, peeling off the top of her dress and wriggling out of the ruffles. Then we made love.

I forgot about the night, about my job, about Linda. The only thing I remembered was that guy in the wheelchair at the door, pushing it open, wheeling out into the dark, and I knew I'd be a fool if I didn't take his advice and move myself away from here.

But then things came back: first Linda, then the darkened room, cars on the highway outside, and the world moved right back in. I started over again, the way I do each time.

Sister Detroit

COLLEEN MCELROY

When Buel Gatewood bought his Gran Turismo Hawk, folks around Troost Avenue and Prospect Boulevard hadn't learned how to talk about Vietnam vets. After all, Bubba Wentworth had just returned from Korea, and the v.a. had helped him get a job at Swift Packing House. Grace Moton was just recovering from having to bury her brother, who'd been shot in a border skirmish at the Berlin Wall. "Ain't much of a wall if it can't stop bullets," Grace had wept. And Andre Clayton had taken his sissy self off to some white school in the East just to test all that Supreme Court business about integration.

But Buel Gatewood had plunked down a goodly portion of several pay-checks in full certainty that with his deluxe edition $3,400 Hawk, he would own the best wheels on the block for some time to come. There was one thing for certain about that notion: he was going to have the biggest car pay-ments on the block for at least five years.

Still, there was no doubt that Buel's Hawk was tough enough. It was all grille and heavy chrome borders, black like a gangster's car, but road-ready for a sporty-otee like Buel. "Any car got the name of Hawk is bound to be good," Buel had said. "That's the name of that wind that blows off the lake in Chicago. Hawk! That wind says: Look out, I'm the Hawk and I'm com-ing to get you. Now I got me a Hawk, so look out!"

• • •

In that car Buel could outgun Dejohn Washington's '54 Coupe de Ville, and outshine the Mere Meteor his brother, Calvin, owned. And, despite its retractable hard top, he simply dismissed the Ford V8 Roger Payton had bought on the grounds that only somebody working in a gas station could afford a gas guzzler. "I don't go around talking 'bout other folks' mistakes," he'd said, but according to Buel, almost everything about Roger and the oth-ers was a mistake. Unlike Calvin, Buel had a high school diploma and didn't have to tend bar at Rooster's Tavern. And he didn't have to haul cow shit at Swift Packing, like Dejohn, or nickel-and-dime in a gas station alongside Roger. He had a good-paying job with Arbor Industrial Services, and once he bought his Hawk, he'd settled into outrunning the competition. That competition completely surrounded Buel and his Turismo Hawk.

That year the Detroit exhibition of cars featured Freedom, bumper to bumper on a disc-shaped turntable. It amazed the public to see all that shiny metal swirling past them. That crowd should have come to Buel's neighborhood, where cars dazzled owners and passersby alike. The traffic moving down Brush Creek Boulevard, Blue Parkway, or the Paseo alone would have been enough to put Detroit on the map, but with the added interstate traffic between Kansas and Missouri, between the city and the suburbs, between the haves and have-nots, the need to have bigger and better wheels kept folks buying cars: Mustangs, Barracudas, Cougars, Meres, Caddies, or Falcons, speed-ohs or rattletraps, FOB factory or custom-cut to the owner's specs.

Cars were a part of the neighborhood, the status symbol of having arrived into your own, with wheels. Cars were the black man's stock portfolio, his rolling real estate, his assets realized. What roads the city didn't provide by way of streets, it made convenient with expressways that cut through the length of the town, leaving a trail of cheap motels, used-car lots, and strip joints at one end, and Swift Packing House and the bridge to the Kansas side at the other end. Any of the roads from the center of town allowed easy access to a state highway, but the convenience was counted only by those who needed to flee the city or cross the state line.

Real estate developers in the select sections of the inner city that were being upgraded for white residents called those expressways "the River of Lights." Folks around Buel's neighborhood called them "the Track," and tried turning their backs on the whole business unless they were unlucky enough to have a reason to skip town.

Sometimes Buell and his friends had vague dreams of eating up roadway in a hot machine of their choice, but Andre had been the only one to find a fast exit east, and when he'd left the city, he'd just vanished as far as Buell and the rest of the Technical High School class of '62 were concerned. Andre might have vanished, but Brush Creek, Swope Parkway, and Pershing Road were always there. And when cars from the neighborhood around Troost and Prospect passed each other on the road, their owners would honk their horns in recognition.

If someone had taken a photo of Buell, Dejohn, Roger, and Calvin back in 1964, they could have spotted the contentment on those four faces. In those days everything they set out to do seemed easy, especially when they stayed within the boundaries of the world they knew, places they could reach on one tank of gas. They couldn't imagine, did not bother to imagine, anything pushing them farther than that point. That would come later. For now it was enough to wait for Sunday afternoon, when Buel or one of the others would say, "Let's show Nab some tail feathers and floorboard these hogs."

On a good day, when the heat and humidity were in agreement, when there was no snow blowing off the Kansas plains or winds whipping north toward Chicago, the men took to the roads, their cars spit-clean from the fish-eye taillights and split-wing trim to the sleek roofs and grillwork. Their only worry was the occasional cop on the Nab ready to grab them as they sped past a billboard or crossed the state line at rocket speed. When Miss Swift raised her skirts over the Intercity Viaduct and they smelled the rancid odors of dirty meat, they knew they were heading west. And when the messages on billboard after billboard along Highway 40 were shattered by blinking neon-like black lights on a disco floor, they were heading east.

But for the women, those cars were the excuses that helped their men stay as fickle as the tornadoes that occasionally passed through the heart of town, the winds that sometimes danced through living rooms and took everything a family had managed to scrape out of a pinch-penny job, and sometimes turned corners down the centers of streets as if they were following traffic patterns. For the women those cars were merely another way to haul them from the house to a day job—"the hook between Miss Ann and the killing floor," as Autherine Franklin would say—because, for the women, the cars were to be looked at and paid for, but never driven.

Anna Ruth Gatewood remembered the family gossip about her Aunt Charzell, who had driven a Packard to Oklahoma City in 1927 all by herself. "The only way she did it was she dressed like a man and she was so light she could pass for some old honkie anyway." But Anna Ruth's family had fallen on hard times, and there were no Packards available for the women when the men could barely hang on to a job long enough to support one car.

Even when some old fool, like Dennis Frasier, went on pension and bought a new car, keeping the old car for a runabout and the new one for churchgoing, women weren't likely to take the wheel. All of them had excuses for not being able to drive: Luann Frasier claimed she was too old, Nona Payton said her babies made her too nervous, and Autherine Franklin told everyone she was too tired to do anything after spending all day scrubbing Miss Ann's floors out in the suburbs.

When Buel bought his Hawk GT, Anna Ruth told everyone that Buel had never said "boo" to her about buying a car, and if he had, she would have taken driving lessons before he'd signed the papers.

"He just showed up with it," she said. "Drove up to the house, big as cuff, and walked up the path like he'd just hopped off the Prospect bus and come home from work, as usual."

According to Anna Ruth, Buel had sat down on the sofa, picked up the paper and folded it back to the sports page the way he always did. But about a quarter of an hour after he'd been in the house, Anna Ruth came to the window to see what the commotion on the street was all about.

What she saw was a jet-black Studebaker Hawk surrounded by half the neighbors on College Street.

At first Anna Ruth didn't connect the car with Buel. All she saw was the top of the car, a bright swatch of black metal, a glob of shiny color that looked like the smear of tar road crews poured in the ruts along Brush Creek Boulevard every spring. At first she couldn't even determine what kind of car it was.

"Looked like some kind of funeral car," she said later. "First word that come into my head when I seen that car was death. If I was gonna buy a car and spend all that money, I'd have bought me a pink one, something bright and pretty like them cotton candy cones they sell over at Swope Park in the summer. But that thing looked like somebody had been laid out and the undertaker had come calling."

"Girl, if he was my husband," Autherine Franklin said, "I'd make him give me the keys to that car. That's why I don't have no intention of marrying that no-good Dejohn Washington. Can't never depend on men for nothing."

Anna Ruth almost told Autherine that men were all she'd ever depended on, but she held her tongue. Everybody knew Autherine was fast and loose, and that was why she and Dejohn didn't get married. But if anyone said anything to Autherine about it, she'd be ready to go upside their heads, and since Autherine was her best friend, next to Nona Payton, Anna Ruth had better sense than to pick a fight over nothing.

"I was thinking about going over to the YWCA," Nona said. "Tell me they got driving lessons over there for anybody to take."

"Girl, Roger ain't gonna let you spend no money learning how to drive," Autherine and Anna Ruth said at the same time.

Then they both leaned back and laughed at the sharpness of their perceptions. It was comforting to see some part of the world clearly, and the three of them had been friends for so long they clearly saw each other's worlds, even if they could not see their own.

What was happening to change their own worlds did not make itself known until Buel had owned his car for nearly a year. But in that time, he and Anna Ruth more or less settled into a routine, an edgy kind of quarreling mixed with hard loving that told the world they were still newlyweds. Each morning Anna Ruth still took the Prospect bus to the Plaza and her stockroom job in Ladies' Apparel. And each morning Buel drove his Hawk one block north of Arbor Industrials, where he parked and walked the rest of the way for fear one of his bosses might see the car and think he was trying to be a big shot.

"I ain't got the patience to be teaching you to drive," Buel told Anna Ruth. "Ain't no reason for a woman to be driving. Women too nervous. Besides, you got me to do your driving for you." He laughed and stroked her ass to make her forget the idea of his car.

No matter how many times they argued the logic of her learning to drive, or how many times Anna Ruth offered to help with the weekly simonize, the only time she sat in that Studebaker was on Sundays. And even then she only got a ride to church. Getting home was her problem, because Sundays Buel and his buddies went to Rooster's to listen to whatever game was being broadcast on the radio. Anna Ruth knew the seasons by sports more than she did by weather: football in the fall, basketball in late winter, track in the spring, and baseball all summer. In a pinch the guys even listened to golf or tennis, anything to keep their standing arrangement of Rooster's after church, then onto the Interstate or Highway 40 and one of the bag-and-bottle clubs until late Sunday night. Except for an occasional family gathering at one of their parents' houses, little had interfered with the boys' routine in the two years since they'd left high school.

None of Anna Ruth's complaints could keep Buel away from Rooster's after church.

Buel said, "Anna Ruth, you ought to feel good when I drive up to the church and help you out of this baby right there in front of the preacher."

"I'd feel a lot better if I was driving this baby by my lonesome," she said.

And Nona said, "Ain't that just like a man? Thinking that just 'cause he can drive you to church, you got to feel happy 'bout him driving off and leaving you alone at night."

"How you think they kept all them slaves in line?" Autherine asked. "Told them God meant for them to be slaves, that's how. Fed them a whole bunch of crap about God and church. That's why I don't like going to nobody's church. When I really want to talk to God, I just get down on my knees and commence to speaking."

"Honey, when you get down on your knees, you talking to Ajax and Spic and Span," Nona laughed.

"Nona Pettigrew Payton, we been friends since the second grade," Autherine snapped, "but if you don't watch your mouth, I'm gone make you one dead friend."

"Just hush," Anna Ruth said, "You know you don't mean that. Now just hush, both of you. I swear, seems I spent half my life listening to you two snapping at each other."

Autherine was ready to take the argument one step further, but Nona paid attention to what Anna Ruth had said.

"Aw, girl, come on," Nona said to Autherine. "You know I didn't mean nothing. Let's walk over to Bishop's and get a fish sandwich we can turn red with some Louisiana hot sauce."

"Ohh, now you talking," Autherine shouted, and linked arms with both Anna Ruth and Nona.

Still dressed in their Sunday best, they left church and headed toward Bishop's.

At one point their path took them down a two-block stretch of Brush Creek Boulevard. The trees lining the four-lane street rustled with the wind and debris, caught in the backwash, swirled down the creek bed that separated the traffic patterns into two lanes on either side of a concrete abutment. The creek itself was concrete, paved over years ago by the Pendergast political machine, which owned the local concrete plant. Now it resembled a spillway for a dam site, except it was flat, like the rest of the landscape, with sections of sewer pipe cut in half and laid open along a winding mile stretch through the middle of the city. And it was either full or empty. In dry seasons a trickle of water oozed through the mud that crept up in the middle where the concrete sections didn't quite meet. But the creek offered the neighborhood sudden flash floods during the wet seasons. In those times crossing the boulevard could be perilous, and more than one person had suddenly been faced with the prospect of drowning while the rest of the city stayed high and dry.

Still, the creek had its advantages, meager as they may have been. It separated the rush of traffic up and down the busy boulevard, and the trees stirred the wind so that gas fumes did not linger the way they did along Blue Parkway, the Paseo, and other thoroughfares. And in the winter, when the snows froze into ice, neighborhood kids used the creek as a playground, while the hot summer air left the trees heavy with fragrance, and wildflowers bloomed in the cracks edging the creek.

It was rough walking those two blocks, but Anna Ruth and her friends knew what kind of jaunty flash they made, laughing and high-stepping their way to Bishop's. Some days they walked to a chorus of car horns honking their owners' approval at the sight of three foxy ladies. Autherine had more interest in pointing out who was behind the wheel of a passing Bonneville, or a two-toned Barracuda, or a fishtailed Plymouth. Anna Ruth was busy counting the number of women maneuvering their old man's Oldsmobile or Falcon or Fleetwing. Only Nona was interested in how much money had been wasted engineering the Brush Creek project.

But Nona had always been the curious one of the group. As a child, she'd been more interested in playing Monopoly than Pick-up-Sticks or jacks. And in high school she'd taken a course in drafting along with her Executive Secretary program. Even now she was enrolled in night school in an effort to upgrade her job with the most successful black dentist in the city from receptionist to bookkeeping. Nona liked to read better than she liked to dance, and Nona had a library card that she used at least once a month. So Nona had been labelled the brains of the group.

"You so stuck up, you got no business over here in Tech," Autherine had told her one spring day after typing class, "You ought to be at Richmond where you could be wearing them football sweaters and going to the prom."

But Richmond wouldn't take Roger Payton, and more than anything else in the world, Nona Pettigrew wanted to be with Roger Payton. It was probably Nona who had put the idea of marriage into Anna Ruth Simpson's head. Anna Ruth had liked Buel well enough, but she hadn't thought much beyond her next date with him. Nona had plans for Roger Payton, and when she consulted Autherine and Anna Ruth on the best way to make Roger aware of those plans, the fever of marriage struck Anna Ruth as well. The three of them had giggled and plotted, and three months after Roger and Buel graduated, there had been a double wedding with Autherine and Dejohn acting as witnesses for both couples.

Once they were married, Anna Ruth had settled into not thinking past any given day again, but Nona simply worked around Roger's Midwestern ideas of what a wife should be and enrolled in night school. By the summer of 1964 she was working her way to convincing herself that she needed a driver's education course as well as those bookkeeping courses she took while Roger was on duty nights at the gas station, and by spring she would have enrolled if the country hadn't been faced with Johnson's Tonkin Gulf Resolution.

Suddenly the United States was fighting in Vietnam and Roger Payton was one of the first men in the neighborhood to be drafted. Within six months all of them were in uniform, and in the six-square-mile area between Prospect and Troost, families were learning to pronounce the names of places that even President Johnson had trouble wrapping around his tongue: Phan Rang, Chu Yang Sin, Quang Ngai, Dong Hoi.

Like everyone else, the women had been totally unprepared for the impact of Vietnam, but of them all, Autherine seemed hardest hit by the news of her man called to war. She saw it as a plot against black folks, and even after she helped Dejohn pack his clothes and sell his car, she preached against his participation in some white man's war games.

"Going to church and going to war is all black folks is allowed," she shouted. "We ought to form our own state. Let them white folks fight it out amongst themselves."

And as she wept and ranted, refusing to go to church anymore, refusing to go to movies or even press her hair in her protest against white injustice, Anna Ruth and Nona saw the revolutionary she would become within the next three years. But by the beginning of 1965, Nona and Anna Ruth became more troubled over the decrease in letters they received from their husbands.

Now walking along Brush Creek was a problem, no matter what the season. They ignored the cars that honked at them and tried to imagine what kind of scenery the men could see in that place called Vietnam, a small speck on the map that Nona had helped them locate one day in the library. Now each of them found ways to occupy their time, especially the nights, and Nona, free to take any classes she wished without hiding them from Roger, finally enrolled in a driver's ed course.

"I aim to tell him," she said to Autherine. "I aim to tell Roger all about that driving course next time I hear from him, but I don't want to be throwing him no surprises until I'm sure he got the other letters I sent him. I ain't heard from him since last September, and here it is January."

"I got a letter from Buel in November. Said he was being transferred to Roger and Dejohn's company. But I ain't heard from him since,"

"Dejohn don't write much, but I should've been hearing from him 'bout now. Last thing I heard, they was moving them farther north."

"Well, if I know the boys, they got themselves some hootch and up there painting the town," Anna Ruth laughed.

The others laughed with her, but no one believed what she'd said. The news was filled with stories of war casualties; B. L. Jefferson's boy had been killed on a destroyer in the South China Sea, and the Andersons, over on Bales Street, had lost a son and two nephews. And everyone was beginning to have news of another name added to the list of those missing in action. In June the names Roger Payton, Buel Ray Gatewood, and Calvin Gatewood were added to that list. And in June Dejohn's mother told Autherine she'd received a letter from the War Department telling her that Dejohn had been fatally wounded.

"Those cocksuckers can't even say dead," she screamed. "Just some shit about casualties and missing. Like we gonna turn a corner and find them standing there grinning. This is some shit. I want you to know, this is some shit."

"I just can't believe Roger's dead," Nona said. "Roger wouldn't just go off and die on me."

"Honey, Roger didn't die on you," Autherine snarled. "He died on Uncle Sam. He died fighting for some white man. He died same as Dejohn and Buel and Calvin."

"I don't believe Buel is dead," Anna Ruth said in a flat voice. "I just don't believe it."

"And Roger can't be dead," Nona wept. "Look. He didn't even sell his car." She pointed to the Ford parked at the curb in front other house. "He left the car right there. I mean, you can't see him going off and leaving that car."

"I don't see nothing but that car," Autherine said. "I don't see nothing but that car out there rotting in the rain. Ain't nobody in it. Roger ain't in his car, and Buel ain't in his. They might as well have sold them. Might as well have done what Dejohn did and sold that shit. And if you got any sense, that's what you'll do."

"I'm not gonna sell that car until Roger comes home and tells me in person to sell it."

"Then that car's gonna be sitting there till hell freezes over," Autherine snapped.

But Nona finished her driving course, and on Sundays, when Autherine didn't have a Black Panthers meeting, Nona would take her for a ride, the two of them zipping along Blue Parkway, the Paseo, the Interstate Viaduct, and Highway 40 in Roger Payton's Ford Skyliner. Loneliness for Nona became those Sunday rides where she tried to duplicate the outings Roger had taken, Buel and the others trailing him. Only Nona had Autherine spouting Black Nationalist doctrines in the passenger's seat beside her. Anna Ruth refused to come with them.

Anna Ruth said her Sundays were too busy. She had to make sure Buel's Hawk received its weekly simonize, she told them. And she had to attend meetings at the church where she helped the auxiliary track down government addresses so the ladies could write to the War Department and ask them to send their men home.

On Sundays Nona and Autherine drove by Anna Ruth's house on College Street, but every Sunday Anna Ruth was too busy to join them.

Through that whole summer Anna Ruth seemed too busy to have any time for them at all. By fall, Nona and Autherine noticed how Anna Ruth didn't wait for the weekend to simonize Buel's car. Often they would see her washing the whitewalls, polishing the chrome, or waxing that car on Wednesdays or Fridays or Saturdays, only to do the whole job again on Sundays. And more and more Anna Ruth retreated into a kind of unquiet muteness that was more like a scream than a silence.

And in early December, four months after the Watts riots, when the winds blowing off the prairie seemed loaded with little crystals of ice, and the bare limbs of trees along Brush Creek Boulevard crackled in the thin air, Anna Ruth snapped and took the wheel of Buel Ray Gatewood's Gran Turismo Hawk.

It seemed so natural, sliding into the driver's seat. For months she'd brushed the upholstery and floor with a clothes brush to keep the dust from eating the fabric. For months she'd polished the steering wheel, the wraparound windshield and dash. And from time to time, on orders from Buel, she'd started the engine and let the car idle. But on that day she'd slipped it into drive, popped the brakes, and eased away from the curb.

She was on Brush Creek before Nab spotted her. At three o'clock, when the cop pulled her over, she'd put the car in neutral and waited patiently.

It surprised her a bit that she didn't feel frightened. It wasn't as if she knew what she was going to say, but she had felt that heart-pounding rush she remembered feeling the day she'd worked Buel around to asking her to marry him, or the first time, a few days later, when she'd slept with him. In her rearview mirror she watched the cop lock his cycle in park, and waited until he tapped on the glass before she cranked down the window.

"It's my husband's car. He's in the army in Nam," she told him when he asked for her driver's license. "He's missing in action so I'm taking care of his car till he gets back."

The cop never blinked an eye. "I'm gonna have to take your keys," he said. "Why don't you just park this heap close to the curb and let me have your keys."

"This ain't no heap," Anna Ruth snapped. "It's a Gran Turismo Hawk, and it belongs to my husband. He's in Nam. Missing in action . . ."

"We got two hundred thousand boys in Vietnam, and not a one of them took his car. You got no driver's permit for this thing, so you park it. This car is impounded."

The cop walked to the rear of the car to take down the license number, and Anna Ruth leaned over to start the engine. She gunned it, giving the 255 horsepower full rein.

"Easy there, girl," the cop said. "Don't get fancy on me. Just slide her into that curb."

Anna Ruth slipped it out of neutral into drive, then while she was still inhaling, into reverse. The engine responded as if it had been starving for attention. In one fluid, sudden movement Anna Ruth took out the cop's motorcycle, and if that Nab hadn't stepped back, she'd have nailed him, too. Then she slammed it into gear and raced down Brush Creek. She was four blocks away before the cop stopped slapping his hat against his knee and yelling, "Goddammit! Goddammit!"

Passersby gawked, and some, heading toward Bishop's or Maxine's Bar-b-que, called to friends to see the sight. "Nab got creamed!" they shouted, and the news spread up and down the street like brushfire. Unfortunately, Anna Ruth had left the cop's radio intact.

But that was not her concern at the moment. When the cop finally realized he could call for help, Anna Ruth was careening off parked cars along the boulevard. Her foot seemed frozen on the accelerator, and when she entered the Paseo, she skidded into a spin at the icy intersection, circling twice before she headed north, leaving five crippled cars stuck in the middle of the street behind her. The police call reached patrol cars at 3:18 p.m. By 3:20 she was spotted on the Paseo, and two cars gave chase.

Somewhere along that thoroughfare, Anna Ruth came into her own, and the occasional clatter of metal when she sideswiped a parked car or grazed a driver too slow to move out of her path no longer made her gasp. When she saw Nab behind her, she left the Paseo at Plymouth and returned to it later off Linwood. The snowplows had been working in her favor. In fact, the weather was in her favor. It was a gloomy day, but cold and clear, so cold that no one was out that Sunday unless they had to be. So cold that slush hadn't formed on the roadway and the ashes left by the plow crews were still on top of the ice. Despite the damage she'd caused, for the most part, the path ahead of her was clear. But behind her there was a stream of police cars.

She had decided to head for the Interstate Viaduct and the Kansas side, but Nab began to descend in all directions, and she had to crisscross her own path across the Paseo and back. Once, when she was parallel to the Paseo on Troost, she saw two cop cars coming toward her. The units behind her knew they had her cornered, but Anna Ruth jerked the wheel and in one wild open circle of a swing, headed in the opposite direction, weaving between and around the cars that had been trailing her. Three cars ran into each other to avoid a head-on with Anna Ruth's Hawk.

As the cop driving the second car pulled himself from the wreck, he looked at Anna Ruth's retreating taillights and shook his head in begrudging admiration. "Goddamn, that bitch can drive," he said.

But whatever luck Anna Ruth had found in encountering very little traffic on newly plowed streets was about to run out. By all accounts, the police had brought in twelve units by the time she reached the last lap of her odyssey. By all accounts, Anna Ruth had travelled the length of the Paseo from Brush Creek to the Viaduct intersection and back by the time Nab had cut off her escape route. And just as she reentered the neighborhood, just before a line of squad cars flanked the street and forced her onto the lawn of the Technical High School, she'd left behind her a trail of more than twenty damaged cars.

But in those last two miles Anna Ruth had gathered a cheering section. Folks in the area between Troost and Prospect lined the street, yelling directions that would place her out of Nab's path. And sometimes folks blocked Nab's path by shoving junk cars that had been abandoned in the neighborhood in front of the cops. Young boys threw rocks, practicing for the riots that were soon to come to the city. And old men, rising from their Sunday afternoon slumber, marked the day as a turning point.

Nona caught up with Autherine just as Anna Ruth swerved off Brush Creek onto Euclid. Autherine had been helping make posters for a Panthers meeting in the basement of the school, and when Nona banged on the door and called to her, she was just warming up to an argument with a fellow Panther about the causes of revolution. The news of Anna Ruth's rebellion erased her need to convince the man.

The two women were running down the front stairs of the school when Anna Ruth turned onto the block. At the opposite end the police had parked several paddy wagons. Behind her, a phalanx of patrol cars, sirens blasting and lights flashing, raced toward her.

Perhaps she would have made it if Old Man Frasier had not been backing out of his driveway at that moment. Frasier had heard all the noise, and his neighbor, Charleston Davis, told him some crazy woman was tearing up Brush Creek. That was a sight the old man felt determined not to miss. He could not have known Anna Ruth had detoured off Brush Creek and was aiming for a new route north along Blue Parkway. He eased the big Pontiac out of his driveway and directly into Anna Ruth's path.

Even from the stairs, Nona and Autherine could see Anna Ruth didn't have much of a choice between Old Man Frasier or the school's snow-impacted lawn.

"Damn! I 'bout made Kansas, Nona," Anna Ruth whispered after the police had pulled her out of the wrecked Studebaker. "Halfway there and driving by myself."

Nona shushed her and, cradling her head, rocked her until the ambulance attendants got the stretcher ready.

"Buel's gonna be mad at me," Anna Ruth said, "Buel's gonna come home and find out I wrecked his car, and he's gonna have my ass."

"Don't worry about it, baby," Nona told her. "By the time Buel gets here, we gonna have everything fixed."

Autherine watched the cops trying to handcuff Anna Ruth even as the medics were placing her on the stretcher. "This is some shit!" Autherine shouted. "Some shit!"

Folks who lived around Troost and Prospect could do nothing but agree with her.

"I Can't Sleep"

CLIFFORD ODETS

Standing on a street corner, a beggar with the face of a dead man. Hungry, miserable, unkempt, an American spectre. He now holds out his hand in an asking gesture as a man walks by. The man stops, looks at the beggar, says:

MAN: (Angrily) I don't believe in it, charity! Maybe you think I'm a Rockefeller! (He walks away briskly; the beggar lowers his hand and shivers. The man now returns and silently offers him some coins. The beggar refuses by putting his hands in pockets.)

Take it . . . don't be ashamed. I had a fight in the shop . . . I was feeling sore. Take the money . . . You're afraid? No, I'm giving it to you (Waits.) I mean it. Take it. (Suddenly shouts.) Say, maybe you think I'll lay down on the ground and die before you'll take it! Look, he's looking at me! All right, I made a mistake, I yelled on you, too! Don't act like a fool . . . if a person gives you money, take it. I know. I made a mistake in the beginning. Now I'm sorry I yelled on you.

Listen, don't be so smart. When a man offers you money, take it! For two cents I'll call a cop in a minute. You'll get arrested for panhandling on the streets. You know this expression, "panhandling"? You can't talk? Who says you have to insult me? I got a good mind to walk away. Listen, what do you want from me? Maybe I look to you like a rich man. Poverty is whistling from every corner in the country. So an honest man gets insulted because he offers a plain bum money. Live and learn!

Look, he's looking at me. Maybe you think I'm not honest. Listen, in my shop the only worker the boss gives a little respect is Sam Blitzstein. Who's Blitzstein? Me! Don't think I'm impressed because he's a boss. I just said it to give proof. Everything, "he's tickled to death," a favorite expression by Mr. Kaplan. . . . Like all bosses: the end of the summer he gives away dead flies! Yes. Yes. . . .

Take the money . . . you'll buy yourself a hot meal. I'll take out a nickel from the BMT. I keep for myself five dollars a week and the rest goes in the house. In the old days I used to play a little cards, but in the last few years with such bad conditions I quit playing altogether. You can't talk? *(Laughs bitterly and shakes his head.)* Even my wife don't talk to me. For seven years she didn't speak to me one word. "Come eat," she says. Did you ever hear such an insult? After supper I go in my room and lock the door. Sometime ago I bought for myself a little radio for seven-fifty. I'm playing it in my little room. She tells the girls not to speak to me . . . my three daughters. All my life I was a broken-hearted person, so this had to happen. I shouldn't get a little respect from my own children! Can you beat it?

I'll tell you the truth: I don't sleep. The doctors says to me it's imagination. Three dollars I paid him he should tell me it's imagination! I don't sleep at night and he tells me it's imagination! Can't you die? I eat healthful food. For a while I was eating vegetarian in the Golden Rule Cafeteria. It didn't agree with me. Vegetarian, shmegetarian, they'll have a good time anyway, the worms. Headaches, backaches—these things I don't mention—it ain't important.

I like to talk to people, but I don't like political arguments. They think I'm crazy in the shop. I tell them right to their face, "Leave me alone! Talk politics, but let me live!" I don't hide my opinions from nobody. They should know what I know. Believe me, I'm smarter than I look! What I forget about Marx they don't know. *(Changes the subject.)* Friday night regular as clockwork I go on the corner and take a shave for twenty cents. After supper I walk in Prospect Park for two hours. I like trees and then I go home. By this time the youngest girls is sleeping but my oldest girl stays up late to do home-work. A very smart girl in school. Every month A-A-A. She leaves the report card on the sideboard and I sign it. This will give you an idea she likes me. Correct! Last week I tried to talk to her, a sensible girl, fourteen years old. She ran in the kitchen to my wife. Believe me, my friend, in a worker's house the children live a broken-hearted life. My wife tells her lies about me.

Look, he's looking. What did I do to my wife? I suddenly got an idea the youngest girl wasn't my girl. Never mind, it happened before in history. A certain man lived in our neighborhood a few months. He boarded downstairs with the Bergers, next to the candy store, a man like a sawed-off shotgun. I seen in my young girl a certain resemblance. Suddenly he moved away. On the same day I caught her crying, my wife. Two and two is four! I remember like yesterday I took a pineapple soda in the store. For three weeks I walked up and down. Could I work? Could I eat? In the middle of the night I asked her. She insulted me! She insulted my whole family! Her brother came from Brighton Beach the next day—a cheap race horse specialist without a nickel. A fourteen-carat bum! A person an animal wouldn't talk to him! He opened up his mouth to me . . . I threw him down the stairs!

But one thing—I never laid a finger on the girls in my whole life. My wife—it shows you what a brain she's got—she gives my oldest girl a name: Sydelle! S-Y-D-E-L-L-E! Sarah she can't call her or maybe Shirley. Sydelle! So you can imagine what's happening in our house!

Oh, I don't sleep. At night my heart cries blood. A fish swims all night in the black ocean—and this is how I am—all night with one eye open. A mixed up man like me crawls away to die alone. No woman should hold his head. In the whole city no one speaks to me. A very peculiar proposition. Maybe I would like to say to a man, "Brother." But what happens? They bring in a verdict—crazy! It's a civilized world today in America? Columbus should live so long. Yes, I love people, but nobody speaks to me. When I walk in the street I can't stand I should see on every block some beggars. My heart cries blood for the poor man who didn't eat for a few days. At night I can't sleep. This is an unusual combination of worries. I say to myself, "It's your fault, Blitzstein? Let them die in the street like flies." But I look in the mirror and it don't feel good inside. I spit on myself!

I spoke last week to a red in the shop. Why should I mix in with politics? With all my other troubles I need yet a broken head? I can't make up my mind—what should I do? I spoke to a Socialist on the street. A Communist talked in my ears for two hours. Join up, join up. But for what? For trouble?

Don't look at me. I'll say it straight out—I forgot my mother. Also a dead brother for thirty years dead. Listen, you think I never read a book? "Critique of the Gotha Programme," Bukharin, Lenin— "Iskra"—this was in our day a Bolshevik paper. I read enough. I'm speaking three languages, Russian, German and English. Also Yiddish. Four. I had killed in the 1905 revolution a brother. You didn't know that. My mother worked like a horse. No, even a horse takes off a day. My mother loved him like a bird, my dead brother. She gave us to drink vinegar we should get sick and not fight in the Czar's army. Maybe you think I didn't understand this.

Yes, my blood is crying out for revenge a whole lifetime! You hear me talking to you these words? Is it plain to you my significance? I don't sleep. Don't look at me. I forgot my working-class mother. Like a dog I live. You hear the truth. Don't look at me! You hear me, do you?!

Last week I watched the May Day. Don't look! I hid in the crowd. I watched how the comrades marched with red flags and music. You see where I bit my hand? I went down in the subway I shouldn't hear the music. Listen, I looked in your face before. I saw the truth. I talk to myself. The blood of the mother and brother is breaking open my head. I hear them cry, "You forgot, you forgot!" They don't let me sleep. All night I hear the music of the comrades. Hungry men I hear. All night the broken-hearted children. Look at me—no place to hide, no place to run away. Look in my face, comrade. Look at me, look, look, look!!!

The 7–10 Split

JOHN SAYLES

f you don't have your own shoes they rent you a pair for fifty cents. None of us are any big athletes, we meet at the lanes once a week, Thursday night. But some of us have our own shoes. Bobbi for instance, she got a pair cause the rented shoes have their size on the heel in a red leather number and Bobbi doesn't want everybody seeing how big her feet are. She's real conscious of things like that, real conscious of her appearance, like you'd expect a hairdresser to be.

We play two teams, four girls each, and take up a pair of lanes. It's Bobbi and Janey and Blanche and me against Rose Teta, Pat and Vi, and Evelyn Chambers. We've worked it out over the years so the sides are pretty even. A lot of the time the result comes down to whether I been on days at the Home or if Blanche is having problems with her corns. She's on her feet all day at the State Office Building cafeteria and sometimes the corns act up. I figure that I roll around 175 if I'm on graveyard but drop down to 140 if I already done my shift in the morning. Janey works with me at the Home and doesn't seem to mind either which way, but she's the youngest of us.

"Mae," she always says to me, "it's all in your head. If you let yourself *think* you're tired, you'll *be* tired. All in your head."

That might be so for her, but you get my age and a lot of what used to be in your head goes directly to your legs.

And Janey is just one of those people born with a lot of *pep*. Night shift at the Home, in between bed checks when all the aides and nurses are sitting around the station moaning about how little sleep they got during the day, Janey is always working like crazy on her macramé plant-hangers. She sells them to some hippie store downtown for the extra income. She's a regular little Christmas elf, Janey, her hands never stop moving. It's a wonder to me how she keeps her looks, what with the lack of rest and the load she's been saddled with, the hand she's been dealt in life. She's both mother and father to her little retarded boy, Scooter, and still she keeps her sweet disposition. We always send her up to the desk when the pinspotter jams, cause Al, who runs the lanes and is real slow to fix things, is sweet on her. You can tell because he takes his earplugs out when she talks to him. Al won't do that for just anybody. Of course he's married and kind of greasy-looking, but you take your compliments where you can.

It's a real good bunch though, and we have a lot of fun. Rose Teta and Vi work together at the Woolworth's and are like sisters, always borrowing each other's clothes and kidding around. They ought to be on TV, those two. The other night, the last time we played, they started in on Bobbi before we even got on the boards. Bobbi owns a real heavy ball, a sixteen-pounder. It's this milky-blue marbled thing, real feminine-looking like everything Bobbi has. Only last week it's at the shop having the finger holes redrilled, so she has to find one off the rack at the lanes. At Al's the lighter ones, for women and children, are red, and the heavier ones the men use are black. Bobbie is over checking on the black ones when Rose and Vi start up about there she goes handling the men's balls again, and when she blushes and pretends she doesn't hear they go on about her having her holes drilled. Bobbi hates anything vulgar, or at least she makes like she does, so she always keeps Pat in between her and the Woolworth's girls when we sit on the bench. Pat is a real serious Catholic, and though she laughs at Rose and Vi she never does it out loud. Pat's gonna pop a seam some day, laughing so hard with her hand clapped over her mouth.

It was just after the men's-balls business with Bobbi that Evelyn walked in and give us the news. We could tell right off something was wrong—she wasn't carrying her ball bag and she looked real tired, didn't have any makeup on. She walks in and says, "I'm sorry I didn't call you, girls, but I just now come to my decision. I won't be playing Thursdays anymore, I'm joining the Seniors' League."

You could of heard a pin drop. Evelyn is the oldest of us, true, and her hair has mostly gone gray, but she's one of the liveliest women I know. She and Janey always used to make fun of the Seniors' League, all the little kids' games they do and how they give out a trophy every time you turn around. Use to say the Seniors' was for people who had given up, that they set the handicaps so high all you had to do to average 200 was to write your name on the scorecard.

Well, we all wanted to know her reasons and tried to talk her out of it. Since she retired from the State last year, bowling was the only time any of us got to see Evelyn and we didn't want to lose her. She's one of those women makes you feel all right about getting older, at least till this Seniors' business come up. We tried every argument we could think of but she'd made up her mind. She nodded down the alley at the AMF machine clacking the pins into place and she says, "I'm the only one here remembers when they used to be a boy behind there, setting them up by hand. You give him a tip at the end of the night, like a golf caddy. I remember when Al had all his teeth, when the hot dogs here had beef in them. I'm the only one here remembers a lot of things and it's time I quit kidding myself and act my age. You girls can get on without me."

Then she said her good-byes to each of us and walked out, tired-looking and smaller than I'd remembered her. Wasn't a dry eye in the house.

But, like they say, life must go on. We evened the sides up by having either me or Blanche sit out every other game and keep score. While we were putting on our shoes we tried to figure out who we could get to replace Evelyn and even up the teams again. June Hundley's name was mentioned, and Edie McIntyre and Loraine DeFillippo. Of course Bobbi had some objection to each of them, but that's just how she is so we didn't listen. Janey didn't say a word all the while, she seemed real depressed.

Janey and Evelyn were really tight. In one way it's hard to figure since there's so much age difference between them, but then again it makes sense. They've both had a real hard row to hoe, Evelyn's husband dying and Janey's running off. And they both had a child with mental problems. Evelyn had her Buddy, who was Mongoloid and lived till he was twenty-seven. She kept him at home the whole while, even when he got big and hard to manage, and loved him like she would a normal child. Never gave up on him. To his dying day Evelyn was trying to teach Buddy to read, used to sit with him for hours with travel brochures. Buddy liked all the color pictures.

And Janey always puts me in the mind of that poor Terry on *General Hospital*, or any of the nice ones on the daytime stories who are always going blind or having their men stolen or losing their memories. Just one thing after another—as if having Scooter wasn't enough trouble in one lifetime. Janey has to bring Scooter on Thursdays cause there isn't a babysitter who could handle him. Al allows it cause like I said, he's sweet on her. There's no keeping Scooter still, he's ten years old, real stocky and wild-eyed, like a little animal out of control. At the Home they'd keep him full of Valium and he'd be in a fog all day, but Janey won't let the school use drugs on him. Says he's at least entitled to his own sensations, and from what I seen from my patients I agree with her. Scooter is all over the lanes, dancing down the gutters, picking the balls up, drawing on score sheets, playing all the pinball and safari-shoot games in the back when there's no coin in them. Scooter moves faster than those flippers and bumpers ever could, even pinball must seem like a slow game to him. The only thing he does that Al won't stand for is when he goes to the popcorn machine and laps his tongue on the chute where it comes out. He likes the salt and doesn't understand how he might be putting people off their appetite.

Anyhow, you could just look at Janey and tell she was feeling low. She's usually got a lot of color in her cheeks, it glows when she smiles and sets off nice against her hair. Natural blond, not bottled like Bobbi's is. Well, after Evelyn left she was all pale, no color to her at all, and when we started bowling she didn't have the little bounce in her approach like she usually does. One of the things that's fun is watching the different styles the girls bowl. Like I said, Janey usually comes up to the line really bouncy, up on her toes and lays the ball down so smooth it's almost silent. You're surprised when you hear the pins crash. Rose and Vi both muscle it down the alley, they're as hard on the boards as they are on the pins, and when they miss a spare clean the ball cracks against the back wall so hard it makes you wince. But when they're in the pocket you should see those pins fly, like an explosion. Bobbi uses that heavy ball and can let it go a lot slower—she always freezes in a picture pose on her follow-through, her arm pointing at the headpin, her back leg up in the air, and her head cocked to the side. She looks like a bowling trophy—sometime we'll have her bronzed while she's waiting for her ball to connect. Pat plays by those little arrows on the boards behind the foul line, she doesn't even look at the pins. She's like a machine—same starting spot, same four-and-a-half steps, same little kneeling dip as she lets go, like she's genuflecting. Blanche has this awful hook to her ball, some kind of funny hitch she does with her elbow on her backswing. She has to stand way over to the right to have a shot at the pocket and sometimes when she's tired she'll lay one right in the gutter on her first ball. She gets a lot of action when she connects with that spin, though she leaves the 10-pin over on the right corner a lot and it's hard for her to pick up.

I'm a lefty, so the lanes are grooved in my favor, but I don't know what I look like. The girls say I charge the line too fast and foul sometimes but I'm not really aware of it.

The other thing with Janey's style is the 7-10 split. It's the hardest to pick up, the two pins standing on opposite sides of the lane, and because Janey throws a real straight ball she sees it a lot. Most people settle for an open frame, hit one or the other of the pins solid and forget about trying to convert, but Janey always tries to pick it up. You have to shade the outside of one of the pins perfectly so it either slides directly over to take out the other or bangs off the back wall and nails it on the rebound. Even the pros don't make it very often and there's always a good chance you'll throw a gutter ball and end up missing both pins. But Janey always goes for it, even if we're in a tight game and that one sure pin could make the difference. That's just how she plays it. It drives Bobbi nuts, whenever Janey leaves a 7-10 Bobbi moans and rolls her eyes.

Of course Bobbi is a little competitive with Janey, they're the closest in age and both still on the market. Bobbi is always saying in that high breathy voice of hers that's so surprising coming from such a—well, such a *big* woman—she's always saying, "I just can't under*stand* why Janey doesn't have a man after her. What with all her nice qualities." Like it's some faculty of Janey's—like working split shifts at a nursing home and taking care of a kid who makes motorcycle sounds and bounces off the walls all day leaves you much time to go looking for a husband.

Not that Janey doesn't try. She gets herself out to functions at the PNA and the Sons of Italy Hall and Ladies' Nite at Barney's when they let you in free to dance. The trouble is, she's got standards, Janey. Nothing unreasonable, but considering what's available in the way of unattached men, having any standards at all seems crazy. Janey won't have any truck with the married ones or the drinkers, which cuts the field in half to start with. And what's left isn't nothing to set your heart going pitter-pat. When I think of what Janey's up against it makes me appreciate my Earl and the boys, though they're no bargain most of the time. Janey's not getting any younger, of course, and any man interested in her has got to buy Scooter in the same package and that's a lot to ask. But Janey hasn't given up. "There's always an outside chance, Mae," she says. "And even if nothing works out, look at Evelyn. All that she's been through, and she hasn't let it beat her. Nope, you got to keep trying, there's always an outside chance." Like with her 7-10 splits, always trying to pick them up.

But she never made a one of them. All the times she's tried, she's never hit it just right, never got the 7-10 spare. Not a one.

Anyhow, last Thursday after Evelyn left we got into our first string and Janey started out awful. Honey, it was just pitiful to see. None of the girls were really up to form, but Janey was the worst, no bounce in her approach, just walked up flat-footed and dropped the ball with a big thud onto the boards, turned away from the pins almost before she seen what the ball left, with this pinched look on her face that showed up all the wrinkles she's starting to get. Leaving three, four pins in a cluster on her first ball, then missing the spares. The teams were all out of balance without Evelyn, *we* were all out of balance. Blanche's hook was even worse than usual and Pat couldn't seem to find the right arrows on the boards and I couldn't for the life of me keep behind that foul line. Everyone was real quiet, Rose and Vi weren't joking like always, and the noise of the lanes took over.

Usually I like it, the girls all talking and laughing, that strange bright light all around you, the rumbling and crashing. It reminds me of the Rip Van Winkle story they told in school when I was a girl, how the dwarfs bowling on the green were the cause of thunder and lightning. It's exciting, kind of. But that night with Evelyn gone and the girls so quiet it scared me. The pins sounded real hollow when they were hit, the sound of the bowling balls on the wood was hollow too, sounded like we were the only people left in the lanes. It gave me the creeps and I tried to concentrate on keeping score.

Scooter was drawing all over the score sheet like he always does, making his motorcycle revving noise, but we've gotten used to reading through his scribble and I didn't pay it no mind. All of a sudden Janey reaches over and smacks his hand, real hard. It was like a gunshot, Pat near jumped out of her seat. Usually Janey is the most patient person in the world, she'll explain to Scooter for the millionth time why he shouldn't lick the popcorn chute while she steers him away from it real gentle. I remember how upset she got when she first come to the Home and saw how some of the girls would slap a patient who was mean or just difficult. She always offered to take those patients off their hands, and found some calmer way to deal with them.

But here she'd just smacked Scooter like she really meant it and for once his engine stalled, and he just stood and stared at her like the rest of us did. Then Bobbi's ball finally reached the pocket and broke the spell, Scooter zoomed away and we all found something else to look at.

It put me in the mind of when Evelyn's husband Boyd had his stroke and come to the Home for his last days. It was right when they'd moved Janey to the men's ward to help me with the heavy lifting cause the orderlies were so useless. Evelyn would come every night after work and sit by Boyd, and in between checks Janey would go in to keep her company. Boyd was awake a lot of the time but wasn't much company, as he'd had the kind where your motor control goes and all he could say was "ob-bob-bob-bob" or something like that. What impressed Janey most was how Evelyn kept planning this trip to Florida they'd set up before the stroke, as if the rehabilitation was going to make a miracle and Boyd would ever get to leave the Home. She'd ask him questions about what they'd bring or where they'd visit and he'd answer by nodding. Kept him alive for a good six months, planning that trip. "How bout this Parrot Jungle, Boyd," I'd hear when I'd walk by the room to answer a bell, "would you like to stop there?" Then she'd wait for a nod. Janey would come out of that room with a light in her eyes, it was something to see. And honey, three weeks after Boyd went out, didn't Evelyn go and take her Buddy down to Florida all by herself, stopped in every place they'd planned together and sent us all postcards.

Anyhow, the night went on. Sometimes it can get to be work, the bowling, and by the fourth string everybody was looking half dead. Dropping the ball instead of rolling it, bumping it against their legs on the backswing, waving their thumb blisters over the little air vent on the return rack—a real bunch of stiffs. Almost no one was talking and Bobbi had taken out her little mirror and was playing with her hair, a sure sign that she's in a very nasty mood. We'd had a few lucky strikes but no one had hit for a double or a turkey and there were open frames all over the place. Everybody was down twenty to forty points from their average and we'd only ordered one round of Cokes and beers. Usually we keep Al hopping cause talking and yelling gets us so thirsty. When I felt how heavy my legs were I remembered I still had to pull my eleven-to-seven shift, had to get urine samples from all the diabetics on the ward and help with old Sipperly's tube-feeding, I started feeling very old, like *I* should be joining the Seniors', not Evelyn.

Then in the eighth frame, Janey laid one right on the nose of the headpin, first time she hit the pocket square all night, and there it stood. The 7-10 split. Sort of taunting, like a gap-toothed grin staring at her. It was real quiet in the lanes then, the way it goes sometimes, like a break in the storm. Janey stood looking at it with her hands on her hips while her ball came back in slow motion. She picked it up and got her feet set and then held still for the longest time, concentrating. She was going for it, we could tell she was going to try to make it and we all held our breaths.

Janey stepped to the line with a little bounce and rolled the ball smooth and light, rolled it on the very edge of the right-hand gutter with just the slightest bit of reverse English on it and it teetered on the edge all the way down, then faded at the end just barely nipping the 10, sliding it across to tip the 7-pin as it went down, tilting that 7 on its edge and if we'd had the breath we'd of blown it over but then the bastard righted itself, *righted* and began to wobble, wobbled a little Charlie Chaplin walk across the wood and plopped flat on its back into the gutter.

Well, we all set up a whoop and Janey turned to us with this little hopeful smile on her face, cheeks all glowing again like a little girl who just done her First Communion coming back down the aisle looking to her folks for approval and even Bobbi, who was up next, even Bobbi give her a big hug while little Scooter drew Xs all over the score sheet.

The Problem with Mrs. P

MICHAEL SHAY

First problem: nobody was home to help. Not her two daughters, off to school. Not her husband Robbie, who hadn't been home for weeks, probably right this minute at that whore Gloria's house.

Second problem: she was seven months pregnant and bleeding like crazy. She pressed a cream-colored towel against her crotch; it bloomed with a red chrysanthemum of her own blood. She stood in the bathroom doorway, eyes sparking, knees shaking.

Third problem: her damn husband had the car. Not that she was in any shape to make the seven-mile drive into town, ten if you factored in the hospital which was way on the south side.

Fourth problem: the telephone was dead, thanks to Robbie not paying the bills like he was supposed to. She had her own cell phone with a few minutes still left on it. But it was downstairs on the kitchen table. Just the thought of negotiating the stairs brought a throbbing to her abdomen.

Fifth problem, or maybe it was the first: she and her baby boy might be dying.

She tried to bite back the tears, but they came anyway, raining down on her nightie, the blood-soaked towel, the tiled bathroom floor. It was all so ridiculous. Why had this happened? She should have known better than to let him back into her life, even if it had only been two weeks. He came back to her, all humble and lovey-dovey. She took him back into her bed and then he was gone again and there she was, pregnant again, standing in the doorway, bleeding to death.

Her main problem was getting down the stairs to the phone. Clinging to the wall, she made her way out of the bathroom and down the carpeted hallway. To the left was her daughter Kelly's room. She grabbed the doorknob of the hall closet as she slowly passed. There were only twelve stairs but it looked like a million. Maybe if she just sat on the top step, and bumped her way down . . . She sat, a good thing since a swoon was coming on. She waited for her head to clear, then carefully slipped down the carpet onto the second step, then the third one.

On the next one, her left foot caught the hem of her wool nightgown. She fell back, then felt herself slipping down the stairway; her feet, her butt,

368

her shoulders bumping with each step; wincing in pain as the vibrations traveled to her belly.

When she came to a stop, she noticed the quiet of the house. There was some sort of noise coming from outside the front door. She didn't know what it was but she stood and, after letting her head clear momentarily, stepped slowly through the sparsely furnished living room toward the door.

Which led to the morning's sixth problem: she passed out, sliding to the floor like a wet sack.

• • •

"Mrs. P! Mrs. P!"

She opened her eyes. A big hairy head swam in front of her. Maybe she was dreaming. "Mrs. P! Mrs. P!"

It was the big head's voice. For a minute she thought it was Robbie but her husband was thin and had a buzz cut in keeping with his role as musician on the make. Who was it? And where was she? For a minute, she hoped she was safe in bed. But then she felt the rough carpet under her, the stickiness between her legs. There was a big hand on her shoulder, shaking gently.

"Mrs. P!"

The hairy head's voice again. She wanted to say: "My name is Liz, short for Elizabeth and not Mrs. P, short for Politazzaro," Robbie's last name which he had hung on her, presumably forever, and which everyone seemed to want to use in the abbreviated form, making her seem old before her time. She could see the man now. It was Big Ed, her landlord's goofy son. "The Retard," Robbie called him, as if he had a right to call anybody that. Big Ed was a lumbering overgrown kid, slow, who probably had a birth defect or something. But, last summer, he had been dedicated to mowing the weeds that passed for their lawn. That winter, he had pursued the snow with a vengeance. He unclogged toilets and hauled the trash.

The girls had been afraid of him at first. Six-foot-five if he was an inch, and built like one of those no-neck linemen you see on NFL football. And that hair, a mass of wavy red curls that framed that moon face of his. But one summer afternoon he came over driving the tractor with the haywagon attached. He asked the girls if they wanted a ride and they said yes and they tooled around the property as she watched from the kitchen window. A few hours later the girls came in screaming, waving something that looked like a rope above their heads. "Snake! Snake!" they yelled, then told her how Big Ed had whacked the head off a rattler with a hoe and skinned it right there on the spot. He gave the girls the skin and the rattles. "This is one big freakin' snake, Mommy," said Lily, the youngest, sounding just like her father, New York accent and all.

"Mrs. P?"

"What are you doing here Ed?"

"Heard you yellin' while I was shoveling the walk."

"Was I yelling?"

He looked puzzled. "Somebody was."

"Call the hospital, Big Ed," she said weakly. "I'm bleeding to death."

"Hospital," Big Ed muttered. It was strange voice that blended a kid's cadence with the huskiness of a man. She felt his arms slide under her and, next thing she knew, she was being transported through the living room out into the cold bright winter day.

"You're light," he said, pressing her in his arms.

"Get my towel, Ed," she said. "And I need the phone."

"Don't have a phone," he replied. "Big Jim took it away. Said it was costin' him an arm and a leg."

Big Jim was his father, their landlord, a big fat guy who seemed eternally pissed off at his slow son.

"Get my cell," she said, motioning back to the house. "It's on the kitchen table. And the towel. For the blood."

"I know where the hospital is," he said. "I drove Big Jim there. Remember that time the tractor rolled over on him?"

She didn't remember and it didn't matter anyway. Big Ed had plans and there was nothing she could do. Die on the bathroom floor. Die on the way to the hospital. She opened her eyes and saw ice crystals glinting in a blue-drenched sky. She heard the crunch of Big Ed's boots in the snow. The wind slapped her bare, bloody legs. "I'm cold, Ed."

"Get you in the van and warm it up," he said.

They stopped. Ed's right arm shifted and she heard a door being pulled open.

"Crud," he said. "Gotta move some things around."

She could feel his indecision. This might be too much for him. "We can still call 9-1-1 on my phone."

"No need," he said briskly.

She felt a tug, then Ed was arranging something on the ground. He laid her down, then placed a covering over her.

"Sleeping bag," he said. "My camping stuff. I keep it in the van."

Camping? Well, she was warm on the snowy ground. She could see Big Ed shove his body in the van's side door. His shoulders moved like a machine. She had seen this van dozens of times. Usually she heard it first as it came down the county road and into the dusty drive, its rackety Volkswagen clatter floating in the window across the open Wyoming prairie. She had often wondered why he had this old hippie van and not a huge mud-spattered pick-up like his dad.

"Ed, I can sit up front," she said. "We do need to get to the hospital."

"Take a minute," he said. "Got a mattress in here and everything."

She wanted to laugh. She didn't need another mattress. They had always been trouble for her, even back in high school, when Tom Banner had pinned her to his bed under all those Bon Jovi posters and caused her to bleed for the first time.

There was a racket of shifting and moving. Then she was up again, fitting neatly through the van's open door. She was on the mattress, which was comfortable and didn't smell, which surprised her. She looked up and saw Big Ed smile as he covered her with the sleeping bag. "Hurry, Ed," she said. "Please."

A look of concern flashed across his face as he slammed the door shut.

Another door opened, and she felt the van shift to the driver's side. Big Ed was on the bus, taking her to the hospital. They would be there soon and all would be well. She wouldn't die and the baby would be born and she would call him anything except for Robbie and maybe she would get a divorce and go back to work at a grocery store where she used to make pretty good money.

"Crud." That was Big Ed.

"What's the matter?"

"Van won't start. Don't worry. I know what's wrong."

So she was going to die?

"Don't worry, Mrs. P. This happens all the time."

She heard him fumbling around in the front, obviously looking for something. Then he said "Ah-ha" and she looked up to see him brandishing a foot-long screwdriver. The sun glinted off its metal shaft, giving it the look of a knife. Go ahead, she thought, plunge it right into my heart and get it over with.

The van leaped up as it lightened its load. She heard his boots crunch the snow, then a couple of grunts. The van shifted slightly, and she figured he was underneath, groping for some gizmo or another. Then came the dreaded word again—"Crud"—and after a few grunts and groans, he was back with his head shoved into the driver's side.

"Got a problem," he said. "Need you to turn the key as I do this."

"Do what?"

"Bridge the solenoid."

"What the hell, Ed," she said. "I'm bleeding to death here."

"Hospital," he said. "Gotta get the van started."

She breathed deeply. She had a tom cat for a husband. Her father abandoned her decades ago. Now her life depended on this dimwit? Men were such worthless creatures. And she was going to give birth to another one? It didn't make any sense but she would be damned and damned again if she would stay here and die without doing something. She pushed herself off the mattress. Fireflies danced in front of her eyes. Her big bloated body felt as if it belonged to someone else, or something else, like an African elephant or one of those strange-looking sea lions she had seen at the Bronx Zoo when she was a kid. But she moved, slowly, inching her way out of the van and onto her bare feet in the snow.

"Where you goin'?" Big Ed asked.

"Inside to call the ambulance. Or walk to town. Anything but this."

"You can't."

"I can."

She still was bleeding, that was a fact, but she knew from experience that she wasn't in labor, which was good, because the last thing she wanted to do was deliver this baby two months early in the snowy yard with only Big Ed for assistance. Although she hadn't felt any of the baby's trademark kicks this morning, intuition told her that he still was alive. The house was a hundred feet away and if she could just reach the door and get inside, she could get to her cell phone, call the ambulance, and then take her chances. But those chances were better than the ones she had now.

She walked five steps—she was counting each one—before a whole flock of fireflies filled her vision and the house kicked up at a strange angle, flying off into space, leaving her on her side in the snow.

• • •

She was nineteen—that wasn't even ten years ago—and home from college for Christmas break when she had met Robbie. He was bass guitarist for the group that was playing at the local bar on New Year's Eve. She was with her high school girlfriends. They all thought the band guys were hot so they hung around after midnight and bought the band some drinks and at 5 a.m. they found themselves at some dumpy house in Jericho, she and her girlfriends making out with the band guys. Robbie was a good kisser. He wanted more, of course, but she wasn't that looped and she liked him when he didn't press her. He even gave her a ride home in the band's van, startling her mother when she sashayed into the kitchen, carrying her shoes in her hand. "I'm in love," she said, which surprised her and made Mom cry. The tear ducts really opened once she learned that Robbie was a rocker with pierced lip and nose. She shared that last part with her mother, just to see if the response would measure up to her expectations. It did.

She was two months pregnant when they got married that June. Nobody knew yet, except her mom and maybe one or two of her closest friends. Robbie's band, the Spectral Losers, played at the reception. The honeymoon was short. Robbie was awake all night banging away at her, even when she was dozing off from the champagne. She shouldn't have been drinking. Her mom told her to cool it a couple times. She promised that she would quit right after the reception, which she did, except for a couple little sips of wine now and again. The morning after she puked her guts out with morning sickness while Robbie snored away in the motel's vibrating queen-sized bed.

Not a terrific start to their marriage. She and Robbie were split up when Katie was born. She was living with her parents and her mom took care of Katie when she went back to work a few weeks later. She was just getting back on her feet when Robbie came back into her life and she turned up pregnant again. That's when her mother kicked her out. She and Robbie found an apartment closer to the city, so Robbie could go in nights and play at the clubs and not come home until dawn. She could not believe they were in that apartment for three years. Robbie brought home most of his pay. She was working, although a good chunk of it went to day care for Katie and Kelly. Still, they were making it. Taking the pill helped put a damper on any more baby-making.

Then Robbie came home one day and announced they were moving to Wyoming. She about hit the ceiling. One of Robbie's friends owned a music store in Cheyenne. He liked the idea of going West. So they had moved cross-country and here she was, bleeding in the snow like some pioneer woman from the olden days.

But she wasn't in the snow anymore. She was moving along on some vehicle that wasn't the van. She shifted her body and felt the crunch and crackle of something underneath. She opened her eyes to the bright sunlight.

"Hey!" It was Ed's voice.

She pushed up on her elbow. She was stuffed in a sleeping bag, surrounded by a tangle of hay stalks. Weathered gray boards marked the wagon's periphery. She craned her neck to the front to see the massive frame of big Ed bouncing on the seat of a green tractor. The tractor's engine had a throaty roar that actually sounded good to her. At least they were moving.

"Got your cell phone," he yelled.

"What?"

"Phone." Big Ed jerked a thumb over his right shoulder. She looked down and saw the cheapo black cell phone resting on the dark-green sleeping bag. Her mother had sent her a gift certificate and she had used it to buy this pre-paid cell phone which she kept hidden from Robbie, especially after the regular phone service was cut off. She picked it up.

The plastic phone was cold in her hand. She dialed 9-1-1. It rang twice before a mechanical voice said from somewhere very far away: "Your Celluphone pre-paid calling service has expired."

"Shit," she said. Had there been more minutes on her phone? Or had she just imagined it?

"What?" yelled Big Ed.

The computerized female voice said: "Dial one if you want to add minutes to your service with your credit card."

"Fat chance," she muttered.

"Dial two if you wish to talk to a customer service representative." She punched two. A few clicks followed. Then she heard a new voice: "All our customer service representatives are busy. Please hold on and one will be with you shortly." Canned music came on the line.

She felt like heaving the phone into the prairie. She imagined it sailing over the barbed wire fence and falling into a patch of snow-whipped weeds, right at the feet on those blank-eyed black cows she always saw wandering the open fields.

But not today. She liked the little phone. It was her only link to the outside world, which was very remote. She suddenly realized why Robbie had moved them so far away from town. She and the girls were isolated, dependent on him. He had the car 90 percent of the time. "Got a gig, babe," he would say, then be gone for a week. They would be down to their last crust of bread when he would magically arrive laden with grocery sacks. Junk food, mostly, heavy on donuts and ice cream and chips. His idea of dinner was warming up some macaroni and cheese, maybe cutting up some hot dogs, mixing them in. She got queasy just thinking about it. Dinner would be over and Robbie would be off again to a gig or recording session or God knows where or, maybe, she did know where.

"You O.K.?" shouted Big Ed.

"Just fine," she said. "Just dandy," using one of the westernisms she'd learned since coming to Wyoming. She was not going to cry, no matter what. "I am not going to cry," she said out loud. "I am not going to cry."

"What?" called Big Ed.

"Nothing, Ed."

"What?"

They moved slowly down the road, but she felt each bump in the rural road. The clouds were traveling faster than they were. Any increase in velocity and she might go flying from the haywagon.

A man's voice finally came on the other end of the phone. "Thanks for calling Celluphone," he said cheerily. "How may I assist you today?"

She almost laughed at that. Assist? Hah! Get me off this wagon and into the nearest hospital.

"Hello," said the voice.

"Hi," she said weakly. "I'm here."

"I see that I am talking to a Mrs. Politazzaro of Cheyenne, Wyoming."

"Yes," she said.

"Nice Irish name," he said.

"Listen. . . ."

"Call me Mark," he said.

"Listen, Mark, I'm in a bit of a fix here . . ."

"We have a variety of payment plans to fit your needs."

A wind gust rocked the wagon. "Mark, are you reading that?"

"They give us a script, if that's what you mean."

"Where are you Mark?"

"Denver," he said, "in a little airless, windowless room in the basement of a gray building."

"Guess where I am, Mark?"

"In a cozy kitchen baking cookies?"

"Don't hang up," she said. "Please. I got a real problem here and I'm asking for your help."

There was another pause. "This is real, isn't it?" His voice had changed, serious now.

"It's real." She gave him a condensed version of the morning's events.

"A haywagon?" he said. "Riding to the hospital in a haywagon?"

"Down a nice country road," she said. "Nice winter day."

"Can you go faster?"

"It's an old tractor, Mark."

"Are you passing any houses? You could stop at one and get some help."

"Nice suggestion, but Big Ed won't stop. He's determined to get me to the hospital."

"He's a little slow in the head, you mean?"

"That's right."

"You're not going to make it."

"That's right," she said, trying to imagine, for the first time, what Mark might look like.

"o.k.," said Mark, suddenly businesslike. "Give me your position and I'll call it in."

"Promise?"

"Promise. Now, where are you?"

"On a country road north out of town."

"Which one?"

"What do you mean, which one?"

"Listen, uh, what's your name anyway?"

"Mrs. Pol. . . . ."

"Your first name."

"Liz."

"Listen, Liz, there's got to be more than one road north of town. What's its number?" She raised her head and looked for a sign along the side of the road. Nothing but fence poles.

"Hey Ed!" she yelled, taking the phone away from her ear.

"What?" he said, turning to her. His shaggy red hair billowed like a wind-whipped fire.

"What road is this?" She could not see Ed's face, but she imagined it scrunched up in some sort of thoughtful look. But this thought was taking its time and she was running out of it. "Ed!" she barked.

"Some call it the Old Chugwater Road."

"The Old Chugwater Road," she repeated into the phone.

"What about a number?"

She cursed under her breath. "Does it have a number Ed?"

"Don't know a number."

"No number," she told Mark.

She heard chatter on the other end. "Look," said Mark, coming back on the line. "I've got another csr on the phone to the Sheriff's Department and the dispatcher says there are two Old Chugwater Roads."

"Two?"

"Yeah, one still goes to Chugwater and the other doesn't. Which one are you on?"

"It's north of town," she said brusquely. "It's where you go out north on Yellowstone Road and it turns into a two-lane and you come to a stop sign and you keep going out that rural road another five miles or so. Our little farmhouse is just before you come to that big curve . . ."

"Hold on, Liz," Mark said. More chatter on the other end. "County Road 237?"

"If you say so."

"We should tell the ambulance to look for a tractor pulling a haywagon, right?"

"Can't miss us," she said. "Green tractor, with Big Ed driving. Me bleeding to death in the haywagon in the back."

He laughed.

"Not so funny, Mark."

"Right. I'm sorry." More chatter on the far end on the line in Denver. "The ambulance is on its way," Mark said, almost breathlessly.

"No joke?"

"No joke."

"Stay on the line and talk to me."

"o.k., sure, I'll talk to you." Then he was so quiet she thought the line had gone dead.

"Say something," she said weakly.

"Think we'll get our names in the paper?"

"Ha ha," she said. "Names in the paper." She removed the phone from her ear. "Ed!"

"What!" Big Ed answered.

"Ambulance on its way."

"What?"

At least that's what she thought he said. The wind shredded his words on their way from his mouth to her ears. "Waaa," it sounded like. Then "wawa," just like the word the girls used for water when they were toddlers. "We want wawa Mommy," and she would get them water in those little paper cups she kept by the kitchen sink. The girls would spill it and there would be wawa everywhere.

"Wawa," she said to the wind, the sky, the wagon. She was so thirsty. Her head ached. The cold crept through the folds of the sleeping bag. She heard a voice and didn't know if it was Ed's or Mark's or the lowing of a cow or something she had never heard before.

"Waaaaa!" she heard, wondering if it was just in her head or maybe, just maybe, was the distant wail of an ambulance.

Outside the Millgate

LARRY SMITH

Walking home from school, I stop at the corner by the gym. Band practice is long over, and again I am the last student to go home. And so I look down the long hill into the deep throat of the steel mill which is always bellowing its shower of noise onto the life of this town. Mingo Junction for the Indians and the railroads, and we all know Ohio means "beautiful river." Beyond the millgate I look back in and watch the long swing of the crane feeding fresh red ore into the rust-colored blast furnaces which resemble most the leftover bombs from World War II. A lorry car glides north, while two blue engines haul steaming hot ladles of slag south to the piles. Always the motion, always the hard sound of making.

My grandfather rigged those cranes and dumper cars; my uncles works the blast furnace floor; my father is brakeman on those trains. And me—I walk across this street.

Climbing the steps to the back porch, I look down through the trees to the stadium stretched out before the smokestacks in the millyard. My father's wind chimes, made from aluminum pipe, are playing, and even the air says there is a game here tonight.

As I open the back door I am swept back by the sickening odor of "permanents" and Mom's corny music. Mom is seated on the kitchen stool in the middle of the room while my aunt buzzes around her with rubber gloves, and her own hair is wrapped in a scarf, like some "haji baba." Mom keeps her head down but manages to say, "Hi, Honey, there's some sugar donuts on the counter by the sink."

I grimace, "Ah—no thanks, ladies. I'd rather breathe than eat," and I make tracks through the mess, my fingers perched like a bird pecking off my nose and Aunt Mae chasing me, "Okay, wise guy," she laughs. "You're next!" And I race out, shouting, "If it's a 'permanent,' how come you have to keep doing it every month?" I leave the sounds of women laughing as I run up the stairs.

Walking down the dark hallway, I think how silence must rise with the heat in a house. My kid sister Jan is in the kitchen playing with her lipstick, her hair in ribbons and curlers, leaning into the mirror.

"Cute!" is all I yell.

"Go away!" she screams, then slams and locks the bathroom door about a second after I close my own. I remember I once locked myself in that bathroom while I snorkeled in the bathtub. I was going for an underwater record when Mom came knocking at the door. When I didn't answer, she went nuts and got Uncle Ray to come over and take the door off the hinges. He pulled me up by the hair, and we all just stared at each other for about a minute, till Mom started to laugh.

In the easy comfort of my room I do not turn on the lights. On the bed are two big envelopes from two colleges which I know we can't afford, wanting me to apply. All I did was fill out this card when I took my SAT's, and I've become a high school fish to which they all throw out their bait. Truth is, I'd be glad to go to any of them if we could afford it. But we can't—though Dad insists we can. There is a whole packet from the U.S. Air Force with a blue jet screaming across the envelope. I glide it gently into the wastebasket. I'd rather work in the mill.

Still with only the dusk for light, I sit on the bed and flip open my cornet case, click-click. It always has that cool metal heft to it as I lift it, bring the mouthpiece home to my lips, and press myself through. My fingers tap lightly, checking the precision of the valves, as my eyes close I stream a favorite phrase from "Sweet Lorain," like sugar icing squeezed onto a cake.

On my chair is the new sheet music I bought at Lombardy Brothers: "Deep Purple." Uncle Satch keeps telling me, "Now, that's a pretty tune—one from my era, you know!" And it really is a nice piece, so I decide to play it in the dark. I slide onto the chair before the open window, prop the music on the wooden stand which Dad made out of a old rocker, and I play . . . right out the window into the cool mill air.

The music phrases itself so sweetly that after one time through I can almost close my eyes and let go on it. I know I'm somehow singing to life as I play the ending twice with real vibrato. When I open my eyes, there's the millfield spread out like a ledge of scrap iron before the big river and the green West Virginia hills. I know the mill isn't all scrap iron and smoke, I know my family has earned a "good living" there for generations. Believe me, I know all this, and still my eyes and ears don't lie, and my heart does reach for more.

On some rusty fall days I walk out the tracks beside the creek and I stand there casting one stone at a time into the water below. First the splash, then the ripples, then the sinking into the brown water until it can't be seen. And I stand there thinking, I'll be next.

This time I play "my song" with eyes open wide upon the town I know, with its rows of old wooden houses, its barking dogs in alleys, its brick chimneys in the Ohio hills. It is just notes and phrases without words, but I play it pure and clear the way a horn can. The cornet is sweeter than the trumpet, but not everyone can hear it. You have to be able to listen and to care. The mouthpiece kisses back.

"Dinner, Sonny," Mom calls, and it's probably the second or third time, because I am just waking up. Dave's radio clock says 5:05, and I have to be at the band room by 5:45, so I go down with sleep still hanging from my eyes.

Somehow Mom has chased the cold odor of the Toni Home Permanent with the warm aroma of cabbage rolls. They're what's left of the batch she made on Monday, but with fresh mashed potatoes, warm bread, and coffee they're choice. Dad is on the second shift, and it's just Mom, Janis, and me, so we all sit at one end of the table. It's funny sitting in Dad's seat, the Captain's chair. I can feel him in the wood of the seat, see where his hands have worn smooth the arms. My older brother Dave is off studying to become a minister in some Presbyterian college in Tennessee. He got a scholarship to Maryville and works cleaning the cafeteria at night—old Mr. Responsible—and I miss him.

"That was a nice song you play, Sonny. I like it when you play a song," Mom says this while she is buttering her bread. She always breaks her bread before she butters it and says we should too.

"Which one, Mom?" I ask to prolong the praise, "That new 'Deep Purple' song?"

"Yes, that one too. But what's the name of that last one you played?"

Now taking a real compliment has never been easy for me. I get this scary, full feeling, like I'm walking across a railroad bridge at night.

"That's just some song he made up," Janis laughs. "Gee whiz, he plays that thing night and day!"

"I call it 'Daybreak.'" Then leaning towards Janis, "And some little people in this house have awfully big ears and mouths," and I twitch her buns till she slaps my hand away.

"Sonny, your father says he'll try to work it so his crew is hauling back ladles around the time of the halftime show," and Mom passes more potatoes while I nod, "He says the trouble is the other men want to see the game," and she looks away at her plate.

"I guess I know that," I say, like it means something, and we eat together in kitchen light.

Our band marches down the hill from school as though we are going to disappear into the mill or the river, but actually we march along Commercial Street under the railroad overpass and along the Bottoms into the stadium parking lot. At the gate, Mr. Morton calls for a roll-off—a long, then short whistle, four sharp drum taps, and we launch into our fight song. I am playing automatically, but still I get a chill.

I march in the first row, right guard, and right behind Marcia Lane, the majorette who moved here from Pittsburgh last year. My God, her dark red hair ignites me even more than her white, gleaming legs. She could lead me and my row right into the river and I'd follow. I am thinking all this when the band stops quickly and I keep marching right into Marcia. Stumbling, I grab her around the waist to keep her from falling, yet she turns her smallness against me and I feel myself falling, like a waterfall inside my heart.

"Sonny!" she laughs inside of herself, then faces me as I stumble still for my footing.

"Let's get a hold of ourselves, shall we?" Morton says to us, and we turn to see the whole band in a silent laughing fit.

"I'm sorry," I blurt out, a half lie.

When we line up across the field at halftime, the other band is already doing its show. The stands are a blur of stadium light in the shadows of the mill. Then, as if on cue, the fluorescent glow of the Bessemer furnace lines the buildings like a silhouette painting in the night. Marcia is standing beside me and I say, "Millflower."

"What did you say?" she smiles toward my face.

"I said, it's like a millflower, that orange-pink light around the dark buildings and us here inside." And she smiles again like she can feel it growing too.

"My father left my mother," she tells me softly. "That's why I'm living with my mom at my grandmother's." I am touching her sleeve. "I don't know," she sighs, "I hardly know anyone here, and sometimes I just want to cry all day, you know."

I hardly get out a "Yes, I do." I love hearing her speak so much. Then, the other band begins "The Stars and Stripes Forever," and the order goes out to "Line up!" I find myself touching the music of her hair. "Marcia," I hear myself speak, "Can I walk you home after the game?"

In a breath, "Sure, Sonny," and she runs off, "I'll meet you by the steps." Her hair and skirt bounce together in the light around my heart.

I blow air through my cornet to warm it up and press valves randomly to loosen them. Standing there on the far forty-yard line I turn from the stands to the fence and the millyard in the dark. For the first time I hear the mill siren whining. One learns not to hear things in a milltown. There is no train though, only the distant clank of gondolas jolting against each other. I look back into the stadium lights and suddenly feel empty and full all at once.

Four taps and we are into "When the Saints . . ." already halfway across the field . . . "Go Marching In."

At the band room, Morton motions me over. I am trying not too obviously to hurry so I don't miss Marcia, who has slipped into the girls' locker-room. I snap my case closed, circle behind the clarinets, and head towards the door.

Morton has this serious face on, like he's just had a drink of Clorox of something, so I follow him into one of the practice rooms.

"Sonny, I'm afraid I've got some bad news," and his hand is on my shoulder, guiding me down to a chair. He sits beside me like in a practice lesson, "I just talked to your uncle on the phone." I can feel my world melting into the darkness outside. "There's been a accident in the mill, and, well, your father's been hurt." My whole body goes limp, so I hardly hear him say, "Your uncle will be by to pick you up in a few minutes."

Something inside me forces a breath out—a senseless puff to keep my insides from imploding, "O.K.," I say, and wait out the silence.

"Just sit a while," says Mr. Morton, pressing my shoulder; then he goes outside to get the others out of the building. We've got ten minutes to get out.

I get up and walk numbly to the window. In the cold glass I see my father's face, his deep brown eyes and rugged cheeks, his mouth about to speak . . . and then it is Marcia's face. I turn to see her standing at the door, gazing at me.

I open the door. "Let's wait outside," I say, then hear myself, "My dad's been hurt in the mill."

"I know," she whispers and wraps her arm around mine as we walk outside.

Soon it is she who is crying as she leans against my shoulder, her soft hair a pillow for my cheek. I can feel her body shake against mine, and I want to live and die at once.

I just hold her.

At my father's funeral we all stand around the flowered rooms and try to talk. All these people—family and neighbors, people from church, my school friends—I know they are good to come, but I've told the story of the broken ladle and the hot iron spill so many times I can't do it again. None of it makes sense, anyway. It wasn't supposed to happen and it did. Nothing else to say.

Mom is holding up really well, although she seems tired inside, and we're all just numb with details. Dave is home and helping us bear up. He wants to say the words at the service tomorrow, and I want him to. Aunt Mae is taking charge of the food the neighbors send. Janis stays up at the house, mostly, but she's been to see Dad twice with the family. "That ain't Daddy," she whispered to me yesterday, and I didn't know what to say. Right now I feel like Dad's drifting around somewhere near, and I begin to see him more in all of us.

Uncle Satch comes out to stand with me on the front porch. He looks towards the mill and says, "Railroaders are a superstitious bunch, you know. You won't see many of them here, or at the funeral for that matter. They're spooked." I look into Uncle Satch's face and wish he would cry a little for me, for us all. This grief seems like such a long road right now.

Last night Marcia and her mom showed up. They were both really nice. She had her hair down long and wore a black suit with lace around her neck. I fell right into her eyes, and we held each other for five minutes out back. Her touch was like music in the dark, and we both cried while the mill roared.

On the front porch of the funeral home I discover that I can look across the street, over the tracks, to the stadium and the steel mill. Inside the house is what's left of a good man and the gentle sound of people trying to comfort each other. When I look around the side of the funeral home I can see our house two yards back, and I can hear Dad's wind chimes and see the window of my room. I want to go there and play my cornet into the night.

Dad was born in Grandma's house two doors over, lived for two years in West Virginia, then back to our house. He and Mom lived their lives in this town, never more than a block from each other. Now the mills are laying off, only working part of the year. The old-timers are being retired early and sit around on benches, mumbling, "It ain't the same." And it isn't, but who is to blame?

I'm glad Dad won't have to watch the mills die. He'd have fought to save them; this valley was his life. I don't know, really; it just seems that for anything to get born in this life, another thing has got to die.

As for me—I'm right here, right now, walking across this street.

Layoff

JEFF VANDE ZANDE

The rumor around town was that this layoff was going to last a long time. Old men talked about it in the supermarket, the sporting goods store, the liquor stores. Although it was spring, men talked about the iron ore mines and the layoff as though it were winter. Paul Wolfe waited behind them in lines at fast food restaurants, and their words suggested a blizzard coming down out of Canada, crossing Lake Superior, and shutting down the whole town. He remembered one layoff from his childhood, his father talking about how friends and relatives were moving below the bridge to find work in Grand Rapids or Saginaw. Some had gone as far as Detroit, others out-of-state altogether. That layoff had lasted three years. This one they said was going to be longer.

Paul was still surprised when his supervisor called him into the office and told him he had to send him home.

"How long before I get called back?" he asked.

"Wouldn't hurt to look for other work while you're riding out the wait."

"You think I'll be back within the year?"

"Hard to say," he said, standing and walking Paul toward the door. "They're going to call back the guys with seniority first." The supervisor's voice was heavy and tired.

• • •

Walking towards his car across acres of parking lot, Paul could hear the robins that had recently returned. Their sounds usually cheered him, would send him into reveries of fishing trips and long camping weekends. Now he hated the birds. On the drive home he thought of all the things he had bought on credit: a house, a car, furniture, a bedroom set, a stereo. Slowly paying them off over months, he had always thought of these things as his. Now he realized they weren't. He thought of his wife and his kids. Though he tried to fight them, the tears slid down his cheeks.

• • •

For the first six months he collected unemployment and looked for work. During the second month of the layoff, he drove down the lakeshore to check on the status of his application at one of the power plants where he'd heard there was an opening. When he arrived, the head of human resources told him that they'd lost his application, but he could fill out another one. Angry, Paul drove home. Waking the next morning with no new prospects, he drove back to the power plant and filled out another application. His wife began to encourage him to apply for jobs out-of-state.

• • •

Most mornings Paul would drink coffee while Sandy would get Katy ready for kindergarten. He closed the morning paper. "Same damn jobs as yesterday," he reported.

Sandy waited in front of the microwave, didn't say anything. When it beeped, she removed a bowl of hot cereal and walked it over to Michael's highchair. Paul watched his wife.

• • •

Just last night they lay in bed together, and he remembered how cold the space had felt between them. And he thought that he couldn't hold her to comfort her (and himself) because she had never really wanted this. She had always wanted to move out of the Upper Peninsula to a big city where things were happening. And though he really didn't want to, they had planned on moving to Minneapolis. Then Katy was born. When Katy was about one year old, Paul's dad got him a job at the mines, which meant good money and stability. He never knew how Sandy felt about the job— he just took it because that's what he assumed a father should do. They had never really talked about their hardships but instead tiptoed through weeks of polite silences that, like aspirin, masked their pain more than healed it.

"I'm cold," she had said, but he'd only rolled over, thinking that somehow her words were simply a reproach to his new habit of turning the thermostat down at night.

• • •

For the most part the kitchen was quiet—the clink of Katy's spoon in her bowl, Michael's little rebellious whines. Through the vents Paul heard the furnace. The blower wheel dragged, screeched and then finally picked up momentum; he could tell that the motor was dying.

"It's snowing," Katy squealed. She jumped up from her seat and pushed the curtain back.

Paul looked out the window and could see the lazy flakes floating down. It reminded him of Christmas, and he opened the paper again to see if he had overlooked anything.

"They go away when they touch the grass," Katy said, her voice disappointed.

"You'll have plenty of snow soon enough," Sandy said. "Now eat up, the bus will be here soon."

Katy sat down again and ate a few bites while her mother watched. Sandy smiled at her. Michael began to cry, and she wiped his face with a small washcloth. Suddenly, Paul stood and wrestled the entire newspaper down into a tight ball and then shoved it into the wastebasket. Everyone including the baby looked at him. Conscious of himself, Paul opened the refrigerator and bent down to look inside.

"My cousin had ten years in, and he hasn't been called back yet," Sandy announced.

When Paul closed the refrigerator the bottles in the door shelves rattled around.

"We have to do something soon," she said. Her back was to him; Michael was finally eating.

"Some of these jobs I can get don't pay what I made at the mines," he said after a few seconds.

She nodded and kept feeding Michael.

• • •

Paul walked Katy out to the bus stop. She tried to catch a snowflake, told him that she wanted to take one to school.

That night another couple stopped by and haggled a hundred dollars off the price of their sofa and recliner.

• • •

By the next Monday the ground had frozen and snow covered the lawn. Paul walked Katy to the bus stop. The children called to her and she ran ahead.

Ignoring Paul, the children talked about sledding and snowmen and the upcoming holidays. Paul noticed one girl standing separate from the rest, closer to the blacktop. Tall, she looked older, maybe in third or fourth grade. He watched her staring down the road. The way she stood suggested that she knew something that the other children didn't or had decided that what they did know was childish. After a few minutes she tensed and then turned quickly to look down the street. Seeing other kids straggling out of their dri-veways making their way leisurely, she yelled, "The bus!" When they began to run she seemed satisfied and turned to watch the road again.

Paul leaned forward and could see the dim headlights coming toward them. Though he didn't want this world to end he could see that it was already dissolving. The children began to shrug their book bags into place and pick up their lunch buckets. They didn't speak, but drifted one behind the other into a little line, the tallest girl in front.

"Bye Katy, I love you. Have a good day at school," Paul said, his voice rising into sweetness.

"I love you too, Daddy."

The bus moaned to a stop in front of them, and the door sighed open. The children began to march up the stairs and file back to find their seats. The driver nodded to Paul and then scanned the children in his overhead mir-ror. When he was satisfied, he worked the clutch and gas, and the bus grunted its way up through the gears and then dropped out of sight over a hill.

Paul walked home cutting a path over the snowy sidewalk. He hoped to have some kind of work before the holidays. He had heard that some out-of-work miners, especially those that had been through the last layoff, were driving over to Iron Mountain, a small town about two hours away. The press operators had been on strike at the *Iron Mountain Gazette* for the past year, and the newspaper owners were offering anyone who'd cross the line twelve dollars an hour. Paul thought about going, but he heard the way the men in town talked about the scabs. They called them thieves, and now and again Paul overheard groups of men talking about individual scabs, saying, "I know where he lives." Unknown assailants jumped one man in his driveway late at night, but he swore to reporters from his hospital bed in Marquette that he'd only been visiting relatives in Iron Mountain. Windows had been smashed out of other houses, and one car was drenched in gasoline and set on fire. Paul was frightened by the situation but in some ways felt he'd never have to get into it. Unlike many miners, he had other skills to fall back on— he was certified in both HV/AC repair and welding. He felt pretty sure that he would find work. *Still, I'd cross a line if I had to* he thought.

• • •

The next Monday another two inches had accumulated on the ground. The back screen door rattled, and Paul looked out the window as a squall whipped snow across their yard. A small voice droned through the radio speaker listing the few cancellations for the morning—church events mostly.

"This ain't bad enough to cancel school," Paul announced. He circled a job in the newspaper. A local chain hotel was hiring a maintenance worker—starting pay was six dollars an hour. He also glanced through the real estate section to see what apartments were available. Seeing the same advertisements he closed the paper and watched Sandy feed Michael. He felt the heaviness that had settled between them. They didn't talk beyond common courtesies—hadn't made love in weeks.

Later while he was helping Katy into her winter coat, Paul heard the telephone ring. Michael jumped from a small nap he had fallen into in his highchair. Sandy answered the phone and then nodded to Paul, her face tinged with a slight smile.

"It's for *Paul Wolfe*," she whispered.

He took the phone, could feel his heart thumping through his ribs.

"Hello?"

"Hello, Paul? This is Martin Rose of Gren&Dell Incorporated in Milwaukee. You sent us an application a couple months back, and we have some openings now. You're a welder, right?"

"Yeah, I'm certified." He heard his own voice rising, becoming almost childlike. Sandy stared at him from across the room, her hand closed over Katy's.

"Good, can you come down this Friday for an interview?"

"I think so." Paul's voice was hesitant. Milwaukee was a five-hour drive.

"We're starting guys at fourteen bucks an hour, and we pay overtime."

"I can be there."

The man told him where to make reservations and to call him as soon as he arrived on Friday. When Paul hung up the phone he danced Sandy around the room.

• • •

Katy missed her bus, so they bundled up Michael and drove to the school together. Paul was excited, and the rear end of the car fishtailed around corners.

"Careful Paul, not too fast," Sandy said.

"Oh, we're fine. Just gotta turn the wheel into the slides." He pumped the brakes and came to a stop at one of the three traffic lights in town.

"I think it would be fun to live in a big city—so much to do," Sandy said.

"Milwaukee's good size."

"We could go to some concerts . . ." Her voice trailed off and she unbuckled her seatbelt. Quietly, she turned around and checked on Michael in his car seat.

"I don't have it yet," Paul said, his eyes fixed on the snowy road.

"How far is Negaunee from Milwaukee?" Sandy asked as she buckled herself back in.

"About five hours."

Paul noticed that she was quiet the rest of the way to the school and then home.

• • •

That night they found each other lying in the darkness and celebrated with skin and mouths. Afterwards they cooled quietly in silence. He wanted to ask her how she really felt about possibly moving, but he thought he might disturb their perfect evening. *Better not to bring it up* he thought.

• • •

Sandwiched between two letters from collection agencies, a Gren&Dell brochure arrived with Thursday's mail. Standing by the mailbox, Paul examined the cover. About fifty employees were posed outside of the company headquarters in Madison. They struck Paul as clean people—standing straight, smiling, each with the index finger of their right hands held out in front of them to let everyone know that Gren&Dell was number one. In the background the mirrored window of the building reflected their backs, suggesting that they were only whole people because the company was behind them. He read the caption below: "Gren&Dell Inc.—helping you dig in to your future." Later, when Paul was reading through the brochure at the kitchen table, he saw a picture of the welding line where the earth-moving machines filed by. On the same page someone (probably a secretary at Gren&Dell) had pasted a sticky note with an arrow pointing to one of the welders on the line. Above the arrow was written "you!"

• • •

He left early on Friday morning. Coming into Wisconsin he watched the trees fade away into acres of farmland. The tops of cut cornstalks peeked up through the snow like stubble. To either side of him and ahead he could look out for miles. Then, nearing Green Bay, he saw the fields rise into overpasses and factories.

• • •

As the interstate wound around the city, Paul noticed exits that looked familiar to him, and he remembered family vacations from his boyhood. Every January his father had always taken the family to Green Bay for a little getaway—a chance to swim in a pool and eat in restaurants. Though his mother had wanted to save enough to go to Florida at least once, his father insisted on the yearly trip into Wisconsin, which always drained their meager vacation account.

Paul could picture his mother sitting by the pool with her sad eyes. And his father came to mind, too. Always going into the sauna, or into the whirlpool, or diving into the deep end—despite the posted signs. This, after the three-and-a-half-hour drive of his father pointing out the same tourist traps and his mother sighing. He remembered that his parents never really had spoken on car trips (or any other time), but instead just looked out their separate windows. When Paul turned sixteen his parents did begin to talk more than they ever had—sometimes yelling.

His mother now lived in Duluth with her second husband. His father, still living in Negaunee, would be leaving for his winter trip to Green Bay in about a month.

Paul wondered if he and Sandy talked enough. He decided he would call her as soon as he got to the motel and ask her if she really even wanted to move to Milwaukee. *If she doesn't, we won't* he thought, but somewhere in the seventy miles between Green Bay and Milwaukee the impulse to call her faded away.

• • •

As Paul drove into Milwaukee the snow vanished, and everything became brick, steel, and asphalt. Hundreds of road signs overwhelmed him and he had a difficult time following the directions to the motel. He nearly missed one exit when a man dragging a sled full of mufflers down the interstate's shoulder distracted him. As he pulled into the motel's parking lot, he was still thinking about him. He wondered if he was homeless.

• • •

Paul set his suitcase down in his motel room and picked up the phone. He dialed a number from a slip of paper in his wallet.

"Yeah?" said a tired voice on the other end. It was not the same person he had spoken to earlier in the week. This voice was not as friendly.

"Yes, hi. This is Paul Wolfe. I got an interview today."

"Hold on." Paul could hear the man shuffling through some papers. "I don't have you down here."

"I'm not down?" Paul had trouble taking a breath, could feel his lungs constricting.

"No. What were you coming in for?"

"Welding." His voice was high, and he tried to clear his throat.

"Are you in Milwaukee?"

"Yes."

For a few seconds Paul heard nothing.

"All right, get here by one thirty."

"Where?" Again his voice was timid.

"Jesus, didn't they tell you anything? Take I-43 out of Milwaukee and follow it to Highway 83. Stay on 83 for ten or fifteen miles, and you'll see us on the left. You can't miss it. Just look for the Gren&Dell cars."

Paul scrambled for pen and paper and wrote down the directions. "Got it."

"All right." The man hung up.

Though at first he started to worry, he soon shrugged off the incident for what it was—a paperwork mistake. Someone had misplaced him. He had seen it happen many times at the mines—lost vacation requests, delayed pay raises, deceased spouses left on insurance policies. These were common occurrences. He looked in the mirror, cinched up his tie, and walked out to his car.

• • •

Although traffic on the interstate wasn't heavy he still felt crowded by the many eighteen-wheelers passing him. Cars eventually began to honk at him, and he noticed that he was only going fifty miles an hour. As he sped up to seventy, he missed his exit. He had to drive three miles before he could find another exit and get back on the interstate in the other direction. Glancing down he saw that it was already after one o'clock.

• • •

Without a layer of snow over them, the fields on Highway 83 struck Paul as sad and barren. The overcast sky ran all the way down to the horizon. On the edges of black fields crouched tilted barns and houses with abandoned cars rusting around them.

Ahead, Paul spotted a small cloud of dust on the right shoulder of the highway, which slowly became a teenager on a dirt bike. He began to wonder if he was on the right road; he couldn't imagine that a Gren&Dell plant was out in the middle of farm country. He decided he would signal for the rider to stop, ask him if he was on the right highway but, barely slowing, the kid dropped his right leg, leaned into a sharp turn, and raised a ribbon of dust as he sped down a gravel driveway.

Where the hell am I? Paul thought. He drove for a few more miles, haunted by the feeling that he should turn around, go back to the motel, start over.

But he had nowhere to go from here, no other directions. He had this one road, which he wasn't even sure anymore was Highway 83. Slowing, he looked for road signs, but the shoulders were bare, nothing to see except miles of telephone wires.

Just before he was about to turn around and backtrack to see if he had missed any obvious driveways, he finally saw a white building coming up on the left side of the road. Four white station wagons with Gren&Dell painted on the front doors were parked around it. He pulled into the driveway and parked near the back of the lot next to a black truck with Indiana plates. His heartbeat finally slowed.

• • •

Opening the door to the warehouse Paul immediately made eye contact with a bearded man across the room who indicated with a snap of his head that he should sit down in the chair next to the door. The bearded man was standing next to another man, both in white shirts, and they were watching a small forklift stacking boxes. The driver was smooth and handled his loads with precision. After five minutes, he saw the bearded man signaling for the forklift driver to cut the engine and get out. The driver, dressed in jeans and a camouflage jacket, followed the other two men to a picnic table about ten feet from Paul. The bearded man set down what looked like an application onto a neatly stacked pile. His mouth moved, and the man in the camouflage jacket nodded.

After about a minute, the man in the camouflage jacket started towards the door. Paul smiled at him and spotted the dull gray remainder of a black eye above his left cheek.

The man with the beard walked over soon after. "You the one thirty?"

"Yeah, I'm Paul Wolfe," he said, standing. They shook hands.

"What do you do?"

"Welder," Paul said. He looked at the pile of applications in the neat stack. "Are there still positions left?"

"If there's nothing left in welding we can get you in somewhere else." He walked towards the picnic table and Paul followed. He could feel heat spreading throughout his forehead.

"This is going to go kind of fast, we got a lot of guys to hire by Monday."

Paul nodded and felt a little relieved that the interview would be brief.

A balding man sat at the picnic table, a laptop computer open in front of him. He looked up at Paul and then pointed to a box full of applications. "Find yours. They're pretty close to alphabetical."

"His name's Paul Wolfe," the man with the beard said, then turned and walked across the warehouse floor and disappeared behind a wall.

Paul went down to the W's but couldn't find his application. Anxious, he began to sort through the papers one by one starting from the top. He felt a drop of sweat roll down the side of his ribs.

"What's your social security number?" the balding man asked.

Paul recited it as he searched a second time through the applications and could hear the man keying the numbers in.

Another man walked over, a man Paul hadn't seen before. "How many after him?" he asked, motioning to Paul as he pulled a bench out so he could sit. Paul recognized the man's voice from the phone call in the motel.

The balding man stopped and looked at the clipboard. "About fourteen," he reported.

The new man exhaled loudly.

"Found it," Paul said, relieved. He could see the bearded man walking back towards him.

"Found it? Good." He took the application from Paul's hand and gave it to the balding man, who nodded slightly. "Follow me," he said.

Paul followed him to the other side of the warehouse. Behind the wall he saw a small welding station. Pieces of steel were scattered across the floor, but he noticed that a few pieces had been set in vises near a welding table.

"Put that gear on," the bearded man said, his hand pointing to a box under the table. His words were demanding, but his voice was soft.

Paul slipped a heavy leather apron over his head, tightened a mask on his brow, and pulled the thick gloves over his hands. They were damp inside.

The bearded man saw that he was ready. "All right, I made four different seams—ones you'd typically find on the line. Weld them together."

Paul looked over the seams. None looked too difficult, just a few tight corners. Snapping his neck, he flipped the mask down over his face, and everything darkened to a small rectangle. For a few seconds he could only see the silhouette of the steel, but then he pulled the trigger, and his eyes began to follow the bright spot of the arc as it slid down the seams. Between welds he checked his work, trying to be fast but accurate. For the last weld he kneeled to get at a tricky corner. Flipping his mask up he saw that the bearded man was already checking the other welds.

"I can clean them up a bit," Paul said. He looked around for a steel brush.

"No, they look fine."

He took off the gloves, and the man extended his hand down to him. Paul could feel tension and torque in his palm and fingers and knew that the man wanted more than to congratulate him; he was trying to pull him to his feet. He let his body relax, began to rise, and then slipped out of the sweaty grip. His head cracked against the bottom of a vise. Ignoring the hot pain, he scrambled to his feet.

"You all right?"

Paul nodded. His head throbbed.

Walking back toward the picnic table, he saw that the other men were chuckling, and he wondered if they had seen. Another man in jeans and a blaze orange hunting shirt was hunched over the box of applications. He wasn't chuckling.

The bearded man set Paul's application on the neatly stacked pile. "We'll need you to start Monday at six," he said. He shook his hand one last time and then walked over near the new man. "Finding your application all right?"

Paul couldn't hear the other man's answer—only the murmur of words.

"We'll do your W-4 information Monday," the balding man at the laptop said without looking up.

"Do I come here?" Paul asked.

"No." The man looked up. His face wrinkled as he thought for a moment. "Do you still have your brochure?"

He nodded. He could picture it on the bedside table back in the motel.

"Okay, map on the back will take you to our downtown plant."

"All right, I'll see you Monday then," Paul said. He began to walk toward the door.

"Hey?"

Paul turned and saw the balding man looking at him seriously. "When you get there, just drive through the gates. We'll be looking for your car. Red Cavalier, right?"

Paul nodded, guessing that they had tight security.

"Good, see you Monday then." The man turned back to his screen.

• • •

When he arrived back at his motel he called Sandy and told her the good news. Then he explained his plan. He would stay in the motel for the week and start the new job. During the evenings he would look for a decent apartment, something they could live in until their old house sold and they could look for another. During the week she should have her brothers help her pack up the house so he could drive back the following weekend and move the whole family down.

She started to cry.

"What's wrong, honey?" he asked. He hadn't heard her cry in years.

"It's just so much . . . so fast," she said in between shaking breaths. "I mean . . . it's almost the holidays . . . my family's up here . . . your dad."

"Now I shouldn't take the job? Why the hell did I drive all the way down here?" He could hear the frustration in his own voice and tried to keep it from rising into anger.

"No, you have to take it . . . I know that. It's just a lot to think about. I'll be o.k.—I just need to adjust." Her voice shook less.

He told her that he could stay in Milwaukee during the week and come home on the weekends, at least until after the holidays.

"No, I'll be o.k.. I just need to think about everything for a while," she said.

He told her he'd call again on Sunday. As he hung up he felt he should have kept talking with her. *She'll figure this out for herself* he finally decided.

• • •

He spent Saturday looking for an apartment. Confident, he circled eight prospects in the newspaper. Although he reached six of the landlords by phone he was only able to get to three of his scheduled showings. Driving through the city confused him: the one-way streets, the chaos of signs, the streets without signs. Of the apartments he did get to, two were too small. After seeing the third, which turned out to be an efficiency, he drove back to the motel. He decided that he had all week to look for apartments.

• • •

On Sunday he called home and spoke with Sandy. She told him she felt better about moving and said her brothers were coming on Tuesday to help her begin packing up the house.

"I won't mind moving out of this town," she told him. "I bet there are a lot of colleges and universities around Milwaukee. I could take a few courses."

"I didn't know you still thought about going back to school."

"I enjoyed the few classes I took before Katy was born," she said.

Paul was happy for her, although he thought her voice still sounded quiet and sad. After about a half hour he told her that he would call again on Wednesday. She wished him luck with the job.

• • •

Driving into the buildings of the downtown the next morning reminded him of the time he had fished the gorge, where the Ontonagon River is flanked on either side by two hundred-foot cliffs. The river he was in now, however, bubbled with flashing brake lights, and the windows of early morning offices shined in the cliff faces. *Jesus, does everyone in Wisconsin come into Milwaukee for work?* he wondered. According to the back of the brochure, the Gren&Dell plant was on fifth, and Paul had only jerked his way to tenth by 5:40. By the time he finally crossed Sixth Street, he looked at his dashboard and saw the green 6:05 glowing back at him. Five minutes late on his first day.

He slammed his fist into the dashboard, regretting it before it even landed. His index finger split open at the knuckle. Looking up from the small bead of blood, he saw the Gren&Dell plant and he could tell something near the entrance wasn't right. His mind focused the details slowly. *Ah Christ* he thought. A crowd of people was standing in front of the gate, and police cars were parked near the high fence that ran along the sidewalk. *This can't be a strike.* The driver in front of him slammed on his brakes, and Paul just barely kept from rear-ending him. Two cars up, another driver had his signal on to turn into the crowd of people, and Paul saw that it was the black truck from his interview on Friday.

In front of the gate to the plant about fifty angry strikers shook signs and shouted. In the parking lot beyond the strikers, Paul could see white Gren&Dell cars and, beyond that, men in white shirts were moving about in a small eddy near the canopy of the plant. *Those bastards didn't even tell me* Paul thought. He then thought of his family and knew he had to cross the line. There was nothing for him back in Negaunee except minimum wage or waiting out the months— maybe years—of the layoff. If he didn't drive through the gates and take this job, it might be a long time before he and his family could live in a house again. They had grown used to the things that come with a good job—a nice television, newer clothes, two cars, vacations. A good job had helped shape him and Sandy into the people they were, and he wasn't sure that the people they would become without a good job would still want to be together. That's what scared him the most, he wasn't sure who he was anymore. For months he'd felt uprooted, torn from his name; everything he believed himself to be left him when he punched out from the mines that last time back in the spring. The sudden anonymity had fueled his rush to find another good job as soon as possible. More than anything he was afraid of the changes not having a good job would bring. *If I don't take this I could lose everything,* he thought.

The black truck rolled slowly towards the open gates, and the strikers yelled into the windshield. Paul watched their individual faces break out of the surface of the mob like whitecaps on Lake Superior. He had seen these faces before, though none of these men had ever probably been to Neguanee.

These were the faces he'd always seen at company softball games, on the edges of parades, or scattered down beaches surrounded by their children. Most of them were good men, and Paul realized that they were angry because they, like him, were becoming less who they were with each scab that slipped by.

A fire barrel on the sidewalk was still throwing up flames, and Paul pictured the men who had stood around it through the cold overnight shift of the strike. Their wives, he imagined, had driven thermoses of coffee and soup to them. Their children, like his own, were in school, unsuspecting, waiting for Christmas. *These guys are the same as me,* he realized.

The bearded man from his interview ran out a few yards from under the canopy and spoke into a walkie-talkie. Suddenly, the police near the gate formed a line like a breakwall and began to push the strikers back, and their desperate, yelling faces disappeared behind the uniforms. Punching the gas, the driver of the black truck drove the rest of the way through the gates, but not before a brick arced up out of the mob.

As the brick shattered the rear window out of the black truck, Paul thought of his wife. *She cried,* he suddenly remembered. When he had told her that Gren&Dell had hired him, she had cried. That she had later stopped crying, and had even said that she wanted to move, didn't matter to him. Her first reaction had not been relief or excitement, but sadness. Her crying was probably the most honest gesture either of them had made in months, maybe years.

The cars in front of him began to lurch forward, past the plant, and Paul knew he had to decide whether or not to drive through the gates. As he looked at the men he began to feel guilt—a heavy burn in his spine. Everything these men understood themselves to be was at risk, and Paul felt sorry for them and their families. He also felt the danger in the air; somebody was going to get hurt today. *Courses?* he thought. *If Sandy had wanted to take courses, she could have done that at the college back home.* He didn't know what his wife was thinking, and he decided he couldn't drive through the gates until he did.

• • •

As Paul drove past the plant he kept his eyes straight ahead, and the strikers ized that his entire body was shaking. Inside, Paul handed the cashier the last of his bills. The teenager sighed, but cracked open a few rolls of quarters and counted out twelve dollars worth. Paul closed his fist around the money and then walked across the parking lot where he huddled into the small shelter of a telephone booth. Setting the coins in stacks across the top of the phone he thought about how he would start the conversation. Down the street he could see another car rolling slowly up to the gates. Two police officers were trying to pull a striker off of the hood. Paul dropped the first few quarters in and dialed before he really knew what he was going to say. After the first ring he decided he was simply going to talk with his wife honestly. He wanted to tell her how afraid he felt—of everything. He wanted to tell her that he didn't know what he was doing and that he needed her help. He felt the warmth from his tears. Looking down the street he saw a striker holding his right arm and a police officer waving a nightstick in his face.

To Body to Chicken

XU XI

—for Maggie H

"To chicken, that should be a verb," Teresa said. The teacher asked if she was thinking of chickening out, or even funky-chickening, "the dance for losers," was what he said, chuckling to himself. Teresa Teng Lai-sin shook her head, not comprehending either expression. What she was mulling over at English class that day was the Cantonese verb "jouh," which the dictionary defined as "to do." To do chicken, meaning, to be a prostitute, sounded clumsy. To chicken, she decided. That made more sense. She explained as best she could in her halting English.

It was already 2007 when our story began so this was not the famous Teresa Teng, romantic singer of yore, although our heroine's mother had been an ardent fan and thus her daughter was named. *You're joking, right?* The manager at Big Boy Massage in Tsimshatsui laughed, the first day she came to work there, not believing it was really her name. Now, everyone at work called her Teng Lai-gwan, the singer's more familiar Chinese name.

But at English class that afternoon, in an airless office above a noodle shop near her job, Teresa didn't care what her name was.

The teacher was a young Norwegian who spoke with a clipped, exact accent. "No," he said. "To chicken is not a verb. What you mean is to *be* a chicken." He paused, momentarily flummoxed, and added. "Although in English, that has a different meaning."

Teresa groaned. "So difficult. Need so many words to say one thing."

At work that evening, things were quiet for the first hour or so and she took the opportunity to review her lesson. If what the teacher said was true, then perhaps "to body" wasn't a verb either. *I body you,* she had wanted to say earlier, when asked to construct a sentence with a newly learned verb, but chose chicken instead because it was provocative, something the teacher seemed to like. *She chicken because she want to make a lot money.* The rest of the class had laughed in apparent comprehension; the teacher frowned.

"Twenty-five," the manager called Teresa's number. "Half part feet and one part body," he instructed in Cantonese. The customer at the front counter was a thin blonde woman. Teresa brought her to the massage chair, where she prepared the water for a foot soak. "It's so peaceful in here," the woman said, as she leaned back into the undulating wooden rollers and dipped both feet into the basin below. "Such a nice way to end a long day of sightseeing." Teresa smiled. "I come back few minutes, O.K.?" "O.K.," the customer said, closing her eyes.

Halfway through her full body massage, the customer raised her head. "Can I ask how you learned to do this? You're very good."

"Thank you very much," Teresa replied. Teresa knew Americans expected thanks for compliments, not that she minded since they tipped generously, but it was just odd. "I learn from Master Teacher."

"Here?"

"Yes. I am Hong Kong girl."

"You speak good English. Did you learn it at school?"

"I take English lessons now, because of job. Many foreign customers speak English."

"Mmmh," said the woman who put her head back down and was silent for the rest of her seventy-five minutes, this one and a half "part" as a session was called, fifty minutes being the unit, which cost HK $225, the equivalent of U.S. $29, a steal by many standards.

In fact, Teresa had studied English at school, the way everyone else had, something she never admitted to tourists, who wouldn't know anyway. Her school had been Chinese-medium, where the English teachers were not native speakers and some might even have considered "to body" quite an acceptable verb.

• • •

At each class, since she'd started these English lessons two months ago, her weekly assignment was to use a new word in a sentence. The first two weeks had been devoted to concrete nouns, and Teresa wondered whether "oil" could be considered concrete, given its liquid state. To describe what she did at work she said *I help you push oil,* which was how the industry's language translated from Chinese, but the teacher suggested that "rub" might be a better verb to use for "oil." After four lessons, Teresa concluded that English was nothing like in the dictionary.

But as she signed out of work that night, *I body you* echoed in her head. She had wanted to ask the teacher earlier whether or not this was correct, but he was generally so morose and stern that she felt questions were not very welcome.

Her father was up, unfortunately, when she arrived home.

"Late enough for you, hah? Young lady, one night you're going to be raped wandering around in the city like that."

"Please A-Ba. I'm tired."

"Of course you're tired! This 'night-style' work is always tiring. Lucky your mother's 'passed over life' so she doesn't have to cry in this life for you."

"Shut your mouth, can you? Just for one night? Besides it's late. Come on, I'll take you to the bedroom."

She helped him out of his chair and led her half-blind father to his room. Her older brother was already asleep, but Teresa knew A-Ba sometimes suffered from insomnia and would stumble his way back into the living room just to annoy her. *I body you*—like the ohm of Zen—as she made sure her father was properly situated. *I body you.*

It was around five a.m. when a commotion woke her. Teresa peered out the window of their flat and saw the police leading away the woman who lived two doors down. Her brother joined her at the window. "So finally nabbed, huh? I figured they would."

"What're you on about?"

"Hey, don't you know anything? She's a chicken girl. Everybody knew. She as good as hung out a shingle."

Their father spoke from behind, making them both jump. "How dare she spoil our neighborhood!" He stumbled his way to the front door and opened it. "Chicken girl!" He yelled into the dark of the corridor. "Keep her away!" But the lift door had already closed on the arrested party.

Teresa followed her father out, and placed a hand on his shoulder to calm him. He shook it away. "Don't touch me! My own daughter is just as bad as a chicken girl!" He groped his way back into the flat, and shut the door in her face. Her brother opened it seconds later.

And what would she have done if her brother hadn't been home? On her way to work later that afternoon, Teresa pondered the question. There she had been, in just a thin nightgown out in public, and did her father even care? Her brother, her only sibling, was a security guard who worked varying shifts, often overnight. She dreaded being at home alone with A-Ba and sometimes stayed out after work at the open-all-nights until dawn, her excuse being that work ended late and she was too tired to travel the hour-long bus ride home. Her father believed she slept at quarters at work and she did not tell him otherwise. He wasn't all bad, really, but if only he weren't so unreasonably nasty when he got in his moods. He once told her that at Dai Gor, the Chinese name for Big Boy, literally, 'older brother,' the dai gors she'd meet would all be no-good losers who would only be after her body.

I body you. I body you. The bus sped along the highway towards the terminus by the harbor.

• • •

The manager buzzed her in the back room. "Twenty-five, will you do a gwailo?"

"Feet or body?"

"Both."

"Do I have to? I'd really rather not."

"All the guys have customers. Look, I'll explain our rules and personally come by to check."

"Do I get extra?"

"Twenty."

One of the other girls said, "Go on, do it. If he likes you he'll leave a bigger tip. The guys always do, just like the women give the guys more also."

Teresa said O.K., but when she saw the customer, she immediately regretted her decision. He was massive, like the Terminator or Hulk. Feet were fine and she had foot massaged many male customers of various nationalities, and even done a few full bodies for the Japanese and Korean men who found their way to Big Boy. This, however, was her first body for a white foreigner since she started here eight months ago.

On top of everything, he was the chatty type, and, she noticed, spoke English with a strange accent, stretching out sounds in a way she hadn't heard before, not like the English, American or Australian customers she was now used to hearing. He didn't look European either, she didn't think.

The customer was saying. "I'm from Tennessee do you know where that is?"

Teresa was leaning into his back, trying her best to manipulate his waist bone, which was difficult to locate. It wasn't fat, just muscle, way too much muscle. He probably worked out in the gym all the time, or took steroids, or both.

"No, I don't know where?"

"In the good ol' U.S. OF A. You been there?"

"Not yet. One day I go. Your home, how to spell?"

He told her, then added. "They'd love you back home."

The manager called in English from outside the curtain. "No problem in there?"

"No problem," she replied.

"Miss," Tennessee asked. "Would you mind using a little oil?"

Dead, she thought, *I'm dead on fire.* And right after the manager had left as well, timing never being his strong suit. "Er, not allowed," she said.

The man lifted the back of the cover-up shirt all customers were required to wear for cross-gender massages. "My skin's awful dry, especially in the back." He pointed at the flaking skin around his waist. "Just a little please."

Teresa hesitated. Normally, it was no problem if she pushed oil on a man's neck or shoulders when doing a head massage. For full body oil however, only male staff could do that for a man. He seemed decent enough, though, not a haam saap lo, "accidentally" trying to cop a feel. Saying "don't tell manager," she grabbed the bottle of oil and rubbed a little on his dry skin, and then quickly covered him up again. "Thank you, Miss," he said. "I'll take care of you later, promise."

He was good to his word too, she decided, when she emptied her tip box later. A crisp green fifty was in there, and she was sure it was from him. Yet on her way home aboard the bus that night, she couldn't help feeling bad. *I body.* Ohm. *I body.* Ohm. She did not chicken. No, she did not.

• • •

Teresa was off the next day and she took her father to dimsum brunch at their neighborhood tea house. An elderly couple and several women from their building were at the next table.

"Did you hear?" one of the women began. "Chicken girl made bail."

The man of the couple snorted. "Police are no good. They make the chickens themselves and let them out! Half her customers are cops, everyone knows that. The arrest was just for show."

His wife nudged his elbow. "Wei, shut up. No one wants to hear your dirty words."

"It doesn't matter," one of the women said. "Speaking 'white,' we all know she deserves our scorn. If she didn't own her place, a landlord would have thrown her out ages ago." Seeing Teresa and her father, the woman acknowledged them. "Uncle, I hope you weren't too disturbed the other night."

He squinted at the next table. "Ah, Mrs. Woo, isn't it? Kind of you to ask. No, my son and daughter closed the window and kept the noise out. They're good children, not like that one."

Teresa nodded and did not say anything.

The rest of the day, she took care of the laundry and grocery shopping for the week. Most days, she cooked dinner before heading out to work, which her father and brother could heat up in the microwave, but on her day off, she could eat with family. Lately, though, she found this a chore, wanting instead to study her English lessons, see friends, do anything rather than trap herself at home with him. She said so to her brother that night while the two of them cleaned up after dinner.

"I get tired, you know. Massage is hard work physically."

"Change jobs then if it's too much."

"After all the time I spent learning the trade? No way. I like it most of the time, but I'd just like a little space for myself."

Her brother glanced at their father, who was in front of the television. "He's nodded off already."

"Typical," she said.

"So go out. I'll stay with him." He handed her a bowl to dry. "You shouldn't let A-Ba get you, you know. He's just lonely. And cranky because he's arthritic," he added, grinning.

She dried the bowl and set it back in place on the kitchen shelf. "Where should I go at this hour?"

"That I can't tell you."

She took a walk in the park below their public housing estate. The evening was cool and winter was definitely in the air. Teresa liked the cold. It was less exhausting at work than in summer. Less disgusting too, what with some of the sweaty customers who came in when the weather was hot. Big Boy was a good place to work for now, better than the previous center, which had been one step up from a chicken farm. Her brother had warned her—*it'll be rough*—when she first said she wanted to learn massage. Then, she had dreams of working at one of the fancy hotel spas or ladies salons, where the rich tai tais went, but she soon discovered that the ladder was a long, slow climb.

I body you. English lessons were a step up to a better position.

• • •

When Tennessee showed up the next day, asking for number twenty five, Teresa blanched. The manager accommodated his request without asking her. When she objected he said, "It's only foot today, and he behaved, didn't he?" She acquiesced, because business was slow and turning away a customer, no matter how good her reasons, was frowned upon.

"I looked for you yesterday," Tennessee said as he dipped his feet into the basin.

Teresa set the massage chair on high and pretended to busy herself. "Right temperature?" She asked, not looking up from the tap.

"Just perfect." He leaned back.

While his feet were soaking, her colleague who had seen the customer follow her, said. "Got yourself a boyfriend?"

"Shut your mouth. You know me better than that."

"To body is like that. Brings out the worst in you."

"Get lost."

But as she began on his left foot, after first wrapping the right in a warm towel, a deep unease cut through her. *I body you.* The words took on new meaning, and she didn't at all like what they implied.

Tennessee asked to raise the massage couch up from its prone position. "So's I can speak to you more easily," he explained.

She knelt beside his head and adjusted the lever. He turned to watch.

"Miss, you have a name?"

"Twenty-five."

"You're not just some number." Because she hesitated, he teased. "Come on, otherwise I'll call you Fairy Girl, 'cos you're as pretty as a fairy tale."

Against her better judgment, but because he hadn't tried to touch her, she told him. "Teresa."

"Like my mother."

She was back at the foot of the couch and had begun in on his left foot. "Really?"

"Yeah." He laughed quietly. "My sisters and I, we used to call her Mother Teresa."

That made her laugh too because she understood him. "Is your mother in," she stopped, trying to remember how to say where he came from. "Ten-Nussy?"

He shook his head. "No, she died last year."

The customer was quiet for several minutes after that and Teresa wished she knew what to say. She thought of appropriate Chinese expressions—*you have a hard time passing on*—but somehow, when she tried to frame the words in English they didn't come out right. How did you express sympathy to a stranger in a foreign tongue? Teresa concentrated on her work and remained silent as well.

Finally, she said. "My mother die . . . had died last year too. Cancer."

Tennessee stuck his head up and looked directly at her. "Oh honey, I'm sorry. You're much too young for that. My mother, she was just old and it was time. I'm very, very sorry for your loss."

She nodded, then looked up at him and smiled. "I sorry you too."

"Thank you, Teresa."

At the end of the session, Tennessee said he was leaving in the morning and discreetly handed her a folded hundred-dollar bill. She hesitated, because it was against the rules. "Go on," he said softly, flicking it towards her, "take it. I won't tell." She did. Later, she saw that he'd also left her another fifty, one of the old violet banknotes that were gradually being phased out.

• • •

She was already on board the bus when her brother's text message bleeped. *Got to work tonight. Someone's out sick. Sorry I couldn't let you know earlier.* Teresa flipped her cell shut. *Dead.* Her father would be in a mean mood for sure.

A-Ba was dozing in front of the television when she returned, his dinner half eaten. Teresa wrapped up the remainder and put it into the fridge. She was about to wake him, but then decided to sit a moment first, before having to listen to him carp. She was thinking how wrong she'd been about Tennessee, who really was just a nice man making polite conversation, and a very generous customer. An extra hundred! And no cut to Big Boy. Nothing her father said tonight should matter.

She glanced at his sleeping form. He looked peaceful, the way he used to when Ma would massage his legs while he dozed. A-Ba's legs tended to cramp. The heavy work at construction sites didn't help, although since the accident that nearly blinded him, he'd been on disability. And a royal pain.

A-Ba shifted. A faint smile lit his lips and it looked to Teresa as if he were holding a conversation, his lips moving, then stopped, and then moving again. She gazed at his legs, roughened skin, but muscular, lean, still strong. Then, she began to massage his knee joints, tentatively at first. When he didn't awaken, she pressed harder, working her fingers around the calf muscles, pulling at them, loosening the tightness, expertly feeling for the problem spots. *Lai-sin,* she thought she heard him murmur. Her mother's name, and hers. "Beautiful spirit" was how she explained her name to the teacher at the first English class, although later, when she looked up "sin" in the dictionary, she saw it also meant "fairy."

After about ten minutes, her father opened his eyes. "You?"

"If not me then who?" She pressed his knee joints with both hands and tapped his legs as she would a customer. "There, you're done."

He nodded, groggy, then looked around. Teresa said, "I've put away your dinner already."

"Oh." He blinked. "I'll go to bed then."

"Okay." She helped him out of his chair and led him to safety.

Before she went to her room for the night, she dusted the altar where the death photo hung. The frame was slightly askew, angling her mother's face in such a way that made her look especially kind. For a moment, she wanted to play one of Ma's old Teresa Teng tapes, just like old times, when Ma would sing along. She didn't though since it was too late and would disturb the neighborhood. Tomorrow, perhaps.

Tennessee, flying home in the morning. Teresa brought her English workbook into the bedroom to study before sleeping. Next lesson was to use a new place name in a sentence. She thought for a bit and then wrote: *The man from Tennessee said his mother had died last year, so I say I sorry him too.*

3

NON-FICTION, HISTORIES, AND MEMOIRS

from Life in the Iron Mills (or The Korl Woman)

REBECCA HARDING DAVIS

A cloudy day: do you know what that is in a town of iron-works? The sky sank down before dawn, muddy, flat, immovable. The air is thick, clammy with the breath of crowded human beings. It stifles me. I open the window, and, looking out, can scarcely see through the rain the grocer's shop opposite, where a crowd of drunken Irishmen are puffing Lynchburg tobacco in their pipes. I can detect the scent through all the foul smells ranging loose in the air.

The idiosyncrasy of this town is smoke. It rolls sullenly in slow folds from the great chimneys of the iron-foundries, and settles down in black, slimy pools on the muddy streets. Smoke on the wharves, smoke on the dingy boats, on the yellow river,—clinging in a coating of greasy soot to the house-front, the two faded poplars, the faces of the passers-by. The long train of mules, dragging masses of pig-iron through the narrow street, have a foul vapor hanging to their reeking sides. Here, inside, is a little broken figure of an angel pointing upward from the mantel-shelf; but even its wings are covered with smoke, clotted and black. Smoke everywhere! A dirty canary chirps desolately in a cage beside me. Its dream of green fields and sunshine is a very old dream,—almost worn out, I think.

From the back-window I can see a narrow brick-yard sloping down to the river-side, strewed with rain-butts and tubs. The river, dull and tawny-colored, (la belle rivière!) drags itself sluggishly along, tired of the heavy weight of boats and coal-barges. What wonder? When I was a child, I used to fancy a look of weary, dumb appeal upon the face of the negro-like river slavishly bearing its burden day after day. Something of the same idle notion comes to me to-day, when from the street-window I look on the slow stream of human life creeping past, night and morning, to the great mills. Masses of men, with dull, besotted faces bent to the ground, sharpened here and there by pain or cunning; skin and muscle and flesh begrimed with smoke and ashes; stooping all night over boiling caldrons of metal, laired by day in dens of drunkenness and infamy; breathing from infancy to death an air saturated with fog and grease and soot, vileness for soul and body. . . .

. . . I want you to hide your disgust, take no heed to your clean clothes, and come right down with me,—here, into the thickest of the fog and mud and foul effluvia. I want you to hear this story. There is a secret down here, in this nightmare fog, that has lain dumb for centuries: I want to make it a real thing to you. You, Egoist, or Pantheist, or Arminian, busy in making straight paths for your feet on the hills, do not see it clearly,—this terrible question which men here have gone mad and died trying to answer. I dare not put this secret into words. I told you it was dumb. These men, going by with drunken faces and brains full of unawakened power, do not ask it of Society or of God. Their lives ask it; their deaths ask it. There is no reply. I will tell you plainly that I have a great hope; and I bring it to you to be tested. It is this: that this terrible dumb question is its own reply; that it is not the sentence of death we think it, but, from the very extremity of its darkness, the most solemn prophecy which the world has known of the Hope to come. . . .

. . . This house is the one where the Wolfes lived. There were the father and son,—both hands, as I said, in one of Kirby & John's mills for making railroad-iron,—and Deborah, their cousin, a picker in some of the cotton-mills. The house was rented then to half a dozen families. The Wolfes had two of the cellar-rooms. The old man, like many of the puddlers and feed-ers of the mills, was Welsh,—had spent half of his life in the Cornish tin-mines. You may pick the Welsh emigrants, Cornish miners, out of the throng passing the windows, any day. They are a trifle more filthy; their muscles are not so brawny; they stoop more. When they are drunk, they neither yell, nor shout, nor stagger, but skulk along like beaten hounds. . . . Their lives . . . incessant labor, sleeping in kennel-like rooms, eating rank pork and molasses, drinking—God and the distillers only know what; with an occasional night in jail, to atone for some drunken excess. Is that all of their lives?—of the por-tion given to them and these their duplicates swarming the streets to-day?—nothing beneath?—all? So many a political reformer will tell you,—and many a private reformer, too, who has gone among them with a heart tender with Christ's charity, and come out outraged, hardened. . . .

A heap of ragged coats was heaved up, and the face of a young girl emerged, staring sleepily at the woman.

"Deborah," she said, at last, "I'm here the night."

"Yes, child. Hur's welcome," she said, quietly eating on.

The girl's face was haggard and sickly; her eyes were heavy with sleep and hunger: real Milesian eyes they were, dark, delicate blue, glooming out from black shadows with a pitiful fright.

"I was alone," she said, timidly.

"Where's the father?" asked Deborah, holding out a potato, which the girl greedily seized.

"He's beyant,—wid Haley,—in the stone house." (Did you ever hear the word *jail* from an Irish mouth?) "I came here. Hugh told me never to stay me-lone."

"Hugh?"

"Yes."

A vexed frown crossed her face. The girl saw it, and added quickly,—

"I have not seen Hugh the day, Deb. The old man says his watch lasts till the mornin'."

The woman sprang up, and hastily began to arrange some bread and flitch in a tin pail, and to pour her own measure of ale into a bottle. Tying on her bonnet, she blew out the candle.

"Lay ye down, Janey dear," she said, gently, covering her with the old rags. "Hur can eat the potatoes, if hur's hungry."

"Where are ye gain', Deb? The rain's sharp."

"To the mill, with Hugh's supper."

"Let him bide till th' morn. Sit ye down."

"No, no,"—sharply pushing her off. "The boy'll starve."

She hurried from the cellar, while the child wearily coiled her self up for sleep. The rain was falling heavily, as the woman, pail in hand, emerged from the mouth of the alley, and turned down the narrow street, that stretched out, long and black, miles before her. Here and there a flicker of gas lighted an uncertain space of muddy footwalk and gutter; the long rows of houses, except an occasional lager-bier shop, were closed; now and then she met a band of mill-hands skulking to or from their work. . . .

As Deborah hurried down through the heavy rain, the noise of these thousand engines sounded through the sleep and shadow of the city like far-off thunder. The mill to which she was going lay on the river, a mile below the city-limits. It was far, and she was weak, aching from standing twelve hours at the spools. Yet it was her almost nightly walk to take this man his supper, though at every square she sat down to rest, and she knew she should receive small word of thanks.

Perhaps, if she had possessed an artist's eye, the picturesque oddity of the scene might have made her step stagger less, and the path seem shorter; but to her the mills were only "summat deilish to look at by night."

The road leading to the mills had been quarried from the solid rock, which rose abrupt and bare on one side of the cinder-covered road, while the river, sluggish and black, crept past on the other. The mills for rolling iron are simply immense tent-like roofs, covering acres of ground, open on every side. Beneath these roofs Deborah looked in on a city of fires, that burned hot and fiercely in the night. Fire in every horrible form: pits of flame waving in the wind; liquid metal-flames writhing in tortuous streams through the sand; wide caldrons filled with boiling fire, over which bent ghastly wretches stirring the strange brewing; and through all, crowds of half-clad men, looking like revengeful ghosts in the red light, hurried, throwing masses of glittering fire. It was like a street in Hell. Even Deborah muttered, as she crept through, "'T looks like t' Devil's place!" It did,—in more ways than one.

She found the man she was looking for, at last, heaping coal on a furnace. He had not time to eat his supper; so she went behind the furnace, and waited. . . .

• • •

If you could go into this mill where Deborah lay, and drag out from the hearts of these men the terrible tragedy of their lives, taking it as a symptom of the disease of their class, no ghost Horror would terrify you more. A reality of soul-starvation, of living death, that meets you every day under the besotted faces on the street,—I can paint nothing of this, only give you the outside outlines of a night, a crisis in the life of one man: whatever muddy depth of soul-history lies beneath you can read according to the eyes God has given you.

Wolfe, while Deborah watched him as a spaniel its master, bent over the furnace with his iron pole, unconscious of her scrutiny, only stopping to receive orders. Physically, Nature had promised the man but little. He had already lost the strength and instinct vigor of a man, his muscles were thin, his nerves weak, his face (a meek, woman's face) haggard, yellow with consumption. In the mill he was known as one of the girl-men: "Molly Wolfe" was his *sobriquet.* He was never seen in the cockpit, did not own a terrier, drank but seldom; when he did, desperately. He fought sometimes, but was always thrashed, pommeled to a jelly. The man was game enough, when his blood was up: but he was no favorite in the mill; he had the taint of school-learning on him,—not to a dangerous extent, only a quarter or so in the free-school in fact, but enough to ruin him as a good hand in a fight.

For other reasons, too, he was not popular; . . . silent, with foreign thoughts and longings breaking out through his quietness in innumerable curious ways: this one, for instance. In the neighboring furnace-buildings lay great heaps of the refuse from the ore after the pig-metal is run. *Korl* we call it here: a light, porous substance, of a delicate, waxen, flesh-colored tinge. Out of the blocks of this korl, Wolfe, in his off-hours from the furnace, had a habit of chipping and moulding figures,—hideous, fantastic enough, but sometimes strangely beautiful: even the mill-men saw that, while they jeered at him. It was a curious fancy in the man, almost a passion. The few hours for rest he spent hewing and hacking with his blunt knife, never speaking, until his watch came again,—working at one figure for months, and, when it was finished, breaking it to pieces perhaps, in a fit of disappointment. A morbid, gloomy man, untaught, unled, left to feed his soul in grossness and crime, and hard, grinding labor.

I want you to come down and look at this Wolfe, standing there among the lowest of his kind, and see him just as he is, that you may judge him justly when you hear the story of this night. I want you to look back, as he does every day, at his birth in vice, his starved infancy; to remember the heavy years he has groped through as boy and man,—the slow, heavy years of constant, hot work. So long ago he began, that he thinks sometimes he has worked there for ages. There is no hope that it will ever end. Think that God put into this man's soul a fierce thirst for beauty,—to know it, to create it; to be—something, he knows not what—other than he is. There are moments when a passing cloud, the sun glinting on the purple thistles, a kindly smile, a child's face, will rouse him to a passion of pain,—when his nature starts up with a mad cry of rage against God, man, whoever it is that has forced this vile, slimy life upon him. With all this groping, this mad desire, a great blind intellect stumbling through wrong, a loving poet's heart, the man was by habit only a coarse, vulgar laborer, familiar with sights and words you would blush to name. Be just: when I tell you about this night, see him as he is. Be just,—not like man's law, which seizes on one isolated act, but like God's judging angel, whose clear, sad eye saw all the countless cankering days of this man's life, all the countless nights, when, sick with starving, his soul fainted in him, before it judged him for this night, the saddest of all. . . .

• • •

"Here, some of you men!" said Kirby, "bring up those boards. We may as well sit down, gentlemen, until the rain is over. It cannot last much longer at this rate."

"Pig-metal,"—mumbled the reporter,—"um! coal facilities,—um! hands employed, twelve hundred,—bitumen,—um!—all right, I believe, Mr. Clarke;—sinking-fund,—what did you say was your sinking-fund?"

"Twelve hundred hands?" said the stranger, the young man who had first spoken. "Do you control their votes, Kirby?"

"Control? No." The young man smiled complacently. "But my father brought seven hundred votes to the polls for his candidate last November. No force-work, you understand,—only a speech or two, a hint to form themselves into a society, and a bit of red and blue bunting to make them a flag. The Invincible Roughs, I believe that is their name. I forget the motto: 'Our country's hope,' I think." . . .

The men began to withdraw the metal from the caldrons. The mills were deserted on Sundays, except by the hands who fed the fires, and those who had no lodgings and slept usually on the ash-heaps. The three strangers sat still during the next hour, watching the men cover the furnaces, laughing now and then at some jest of Kirby's.

"Do you know," said Mitchell, "I like this view of the works better than when the glare was fiercest? These heavy shadows and the amphitheatre of smothered fires are ghostly, unreal. One could fancy these red smouldering lights to be the half-shut eyes of wild beasts, and the spectral figures their victims in the den."

Kirby laughed. "You are fanciful. Come, let us get out of the den. The spectral figures, as you call them, are a little too real for me to fancy a close proximity in the darkness,—unarmed, too."

The others rose, buttoning their over-coats, and lighting cigars.

"Raining, still," said Doctor May, "and hard. Where did we leave the coach, Mitchell?"

"At the other side of the works.—Kirby, what's that?"

Mitchell started back, half-frightened, as, suddenly turning a corner, the white figure of a woman faced him in the darkness,—a woman, white, of giant proportions, crouching on the ground, her arms flung out in some wild gesture of warning.

"Stop! Make that fire burn there," cried Kirby, stopping short. The flame burst out, flashing the gaunt figure into bold relief.

Mitchell drew a long breath.

"I thought it was alive," he said, going up curiously.

The others followed.

"Not marble, eh?" asked Kirby, touching it.

One of the lower overseers stopped.

"Korl, Sir."

"Who did it?"

"Can't say. Some of the hands; chipped it out in off-hours."

"Chipped to some purpose, I should say. What a flesh-tint the stuff has! Do you see, Mitchell?"

"I see."

He had stepped aside where the light fell boldest on the figure, looking at it in silence. There was not one line of beauty or grace in it: a nude woman's form, muscular, grown coarse with labor, the powerful limbs instinct with some one poignant longing. One idea: there it was in the tense, rigid muscles, the clutching hands, the wild, eager face, like that of a starving wolf's. Kirby and Doctor May walked around it, critical, curious. Mitchell stood aloof, silent. The figure touched him strangely.

"Not badly done," said Doctor May. "Where did the fellow learn that sweep of the muscles in the arm and hand? Look at them! They are groping,—do you see?—clutching: the peculiar action of a man dying of thirst."

"They have ample facilities for studying anatomy," sneered Kirby, glancing at the half-naked figures.

"Look," continued the Doctor, "at this bony wrist, and the strained sinews of the instep! A working-woman,—the very type of her class."

"God forbid!" muttered Mitchell.

"Why?" demanded May. "What does the fellow intend by the figure? I cannot catch the meaning."

"Ask him," said the other, dryly. "There he stands,"—pointing to Wolfe, who stood with a group of men, leaning on his ash-rake.

The Doctor beckoned him with the affable smile, which kind-hearted men put on when talking with these people.

"Mr. Mitchell has picked you out as the man who did this,—I'm sure I don't know why. But what did you mean by it?"

"She be hungry."

Wolfe's eyes answered Mitchell, not the Doctor.

"Oh-h! But what a mistake you have made, my fine fellow! You have given no sign of starvation to the body. It is strong,—terribly strong. It has the mad, half-despairing gesture of drowning."

Wolfe stammered, glanced appealingly at Mitchell, who saw the soul of the thing, he knew. But the cool, probing eyes were turned on himself now,—mocking, cruel, relentless.

"Not hungry for meat," the furnace-tender said at last.

"What then? Whiskey?" jeered Kirby, with a coarse laugh.

Wolfe was silent a moment, thinking.

"I dunno," he said, with a bewildered look. "It mebbe. Summat to make her live, I think,—like you. Whiskey ull do it, in a way."

417

The young man laughed again. Mitchell flashed a look of disgust some-where,—not at Wolfe.

"May," he broke out impatiently, "are you blind? Look at that woman's face! It asks questions of God, and says, 'I have a right to know.' Good God, how hungry it is!"

They looked a moment; then May turned to the mill-owner:—

"Have you many such hands as this? What are you going to do with them? Keep them at puddling iron?"

Kirby shrugged his shoulders. Mitchell's look had irritated him.

"Ce n'est pas mon affaire. I have no fancy for nursing infant geniuses. I suppose there are some stray gleams of mind and soul among these wretches. The Lord will take care of his own; or else they can work out their own sal-vation. I have heard you call our American system a ladder, which any man can scale. Do you doubt it? Or perhaps you want to banish all social ladders, and put us all on a flat table-land,—eh, May?"

The Doctor looked vexed, puzzled. Some terrible problem lay hid in this woman's face, and troubled these men. Kirby waited for an answer, and, receiving none, went on, warming with his subject.

"I tell you, there's something wrong that no talk of 'Liberté' or 'Égalité' will do away. If I had the making of men, these men who do the lowest part of the world's work should be machines, nothing more,—hands. It would be kindness. God help them! What are taste, reason, to creatures who must live such lives as that?" He pointed to Deborah, sleeping on the ash-heap. "So many nerves to sting them to pain. What if God had put your brain, with all its agony of touch, into your fingers, and bid you work and strike with that?"

"You think you could govern the world better?" laughed the Doctor.

"I do not think at all."

"That is true philosophy. Drift with the stream, because you cannot dive deep enough to find bottom, eh?"

"Exactly," rejoined Kirby. "I do not think. I wash my hands of all social problems,—slavery, caste, white or black. My duty to my operatives has a nar-row limit,—the pay-hour on Saturday night. Outside of that, if they cut korl, or cut each other's throats, (the more popular amusement of the two,) I am not responsible."

The Doctor sighed,—a good honest sigh, from the depths of his stomach.

"God help us! Who is responsible?"

"Not I, I tell you," said Kirby, testily. "What has the man who pays them money to do with their souls' concerns, more than the grocer or butcher who takes it?"

"And yet," said Mitchell's cynical voice, "look at her! How hungry she is!" . . .

"Money has spoken!" [Mitchell] said, seating himself lightly on a stone with the air of an amused spectator at a play. "Are you answered?"—turning to Wolfe his clear, magnetic face. . . . He looked at the furnace-tender as he had looked at a rare mosaic in the morning; only the man was the more amusing study of the two.

"Are you answered? Why, May, look at him! 'De profundis clamavi.' Or, to quote in English, 'Hungry and thirsty, his soul faints in him.' And so Money sends back its answer into the depths through you, Kirby! Very clear the answer, too! . . . Now, Doctor, the pocket of the world having uttered its voice, what has the heart to say? You are a philanthropist, in a small way,—n'est ce pas? Here, boy, this gentleman can show you how to cut korl better,—or your destiny. Go on, May!" . . .

He went to Wolfe and put his hand kindly on his arm. Something of a vague idea possessed the Doctor's brain that much good was to be done here by a friendly word or two: a latent genius to be warmed into life by a waited-for sun-beam. Here it was: he had brought it. So he went on complacently:—

"Do you know, boy, you have it in you to be a great sculptor, a great man?—do you understand?" (talking down to the capacity of his hearer: it is a way People have with children, and men like Wolfe,)—"to live a better, stronger life than I, or Mr. Kirby here? A man may make himself anything he chooses. God has given you stronger powers than many men,—me, for instance."

May stopped, heated, glowing with his own magnanimity. And it was magnanimous. The puddler had drunk in every word, looking through the Doctor's flurry, and generous heat, and self-approval, into his will, with those slow, absorbing eyes of his.

"Make yourself what you will. It is your right."

"I know," quietly. "Will you help me?"

Mitchell laughed again. The Doctor turned now, in a passion,—

"You know, Mitchell, I have not the means. You know, if I had, it is in my heart to take this boy and educate him for"—

"The glory of God, and the glory of John May."

May did not speak for a moment; then, controlled, he said,—

"Why should one be raised, when myriads are left?—I have not the money, boy," to Wolfe, shortly.

"Money?" He said it over slowly, as one repeats the guessed answer to a riddle, doubtfully. "That is it? Money?"

"Yes, money,—that is it," said Mitchell, rising, and drawing his furred coat about him. "You've found the cure for all the world's diseases.—Come, May, find your good-humor, and come home. This damp wind chills my very bones. Come and preach your Saint-Simonian doctrines to-morrow to Kirby's hands. Let them have a clear idea of the rights of the soul, and I'll venture next week they'll strike for higher wages. That will be the end of it. . . .

"Besides," [he] added, "it would be of no use. I am not one of them. . . . Reform is born of need, not pity. No vital movement of the people's has worked down, for good or evil; fermented, instead, carried up the heaving, cloggy mass. Think back through history, and you will know it. What will this lowest deep-thieves, Magdalens, negroes—do with the light filtered through ponderous Church creeds, Baconian theories, Goethe schemes? Some day, out of their bitter need will be thrown up their own light-bringer,—their Jean Paul, their Cromwell, their Messiah."

• • •

[It is "his right" to keep the money she has stolen from Mitchell, Deb tells Hugh.]

His right! The word struck him. Doctor May had used the same. He washed himself, and went out to find this man Mitchell. His right! Why did the chance word cling to him so obstinately? . . .

He did not deceive himself. Theft! That was it. At first the word sickened him, then he grappled with it. Sitting there on a broken cart-wheel, the fading day, the noisy groups, the church-bells' tolling passed before him like a panorama, while the sharp struggle went on within. This money! He took it out, and looked at it. If he gave it back, what then? He was going to be cool about it.

People going by to church saw only a sickly mill-boy watching them quietly at the alley's mouth. They did not know that he was mad, or they would not have gone by so quietly: mad with hunger; stretching out his hands to the world, that had given so much to them, for leave to live the life God meant him to live. His soul within him was smothering to death; he wanted so much, thought so much, and knew—nothing. There was nothing of which he was certain, except the mill and things there. Of God and heaven he had heard so little, that they were to him what fairy-land is to a child: something real, but not here; very far off. His brain, greedy, dwarfed, full of thwarted energy and unused powers, questioned these men and women going by, coldly, bitterly. . . . Was it not his right to live as they,—a pure life, a good, true-hearted life, full of beauty and kind words? He only wanted to know how to use the strength within him. His heart warmed, as he thought of it. He suffered himself to think of it longer. If he took the money?

Then he saw himself as he might be, strong, helpful, kindly. The night crept on, as this one image slowly evolved itself from the crowd of other thoughts and stood triumphant. He looked at it. As he might be! What wonder, if it blinded him to delirium,—the madness that underlies all revolution, all progress, and all fall?

You laugh at the shallow temptation? You see the error underlying its argument so clearly,—that to him a true life was one of full development rather than self-restraint? that he was deaf to the higher tone in a cry of voluntary suffering for truth's sake than in the fullest flow of spontaneous harmony? I do not plead his cause. I only want to show you the mote in my brother's eye: then you can see clearly to take it out. . . .

. . . Do you want to hear the end of it? You wish me to make a tragic story out of it? Why, in the police-reports of the morning paper you can find a dozen such tragedies: hints of shipwrecks unlike any that ever befell on the high seas; hints that here a power was lost to heaven,—that there a soul went down where no tide can ebb or flow. Commonplace enough the hints are. . . .

Doctor May, a month after the night I have told you of, was reading to his wife at breakfast from this fourth column of the morning-paper: an unusual thing,—these police-reports not being, in general, choice reading for ladies; but it was only one item he read.

"Oh, my dear! You remember that man I told you of, that we saw at Kirby's mill?—that was arrested for robbing Mitchell? Here he is; just listen:—'Circuit Court. Judge Day. Hugh Wolfe, operative in Kirby & John's Loudon Mills. Charge, grand larceny. Sentence, nineteen years hard labor in penitentiary.'—Scoundrel! Serves him right! After all our kindness that night! Picking Mitchell's pocket at the very time!"

His wife said something about the ingratitude of that kind of people, and then they began to talk of something else.

Nineteen years! How easy that was to read! What a simple word for Judge Day to utter! Nineteen years! Half a lifetime!

Hugh Wolfe sat on the window-ledge of his cell, looking out. His ankles were ironed. Not usual in such cases; but he had made two desperate efforts to escape. "Well," as Haley, the jailer, said, "small blame to him! Nineteen years' imprisonment was not a pleasant thing to look forward to." Haley was very good-natured about it, though Wolfe had fought him savagely.

"When he was first caught," the jailer said afterwards, in telling the story, "before the trial, the fellow was cut down at once,—laid there on that pallet like a dead man, with his hands over his eyes. Never saw a man so cut down in my life. Time of the trial, too, came the queerest dodge of any customer I ever had. Would choose no lawyer. Judge gave him one, of course. Gibson it was. He tried to prove the fellow crazy; but it wouldn't go. Thing was plain as day-light: money found on him. 'Twas a hard sentence,—all the law allows; but it was for 'xample's sake. These mill-hands are gettin' onbearable. When the sentence was read, he just looked up, and said the money was his by rights, and that all the world had gone wrong. That night, after the trial, a gentleman came to see him here, name of Mitchell,—him as he stole from. Talked to him for an hour. Thought he came for curiosity, like. After he was gone, thought Wolfe was remarkable quiet, and went into his cell. Found him very low; bed all bloody. Doctor said he had been bleeding at the lungs. He was as weak as a cat; yet, if ye'll b'lieve me, he tried to get a-past me and get out. I just carried him like a baby, and threw him on the pallet. Three days after, he tried it again: that time reached the wall. Lord help you! he fought like a tiger,—giv' some terrible blows. Fightin' for life, you see; for he can't live long, shut up in the stone crib down yonder. Got a death-cough now. 'T took two of us to bring him down that day; so I just put the irons on his feet. There he sits, in there. Goin' to-morrow, with a batch more of 'em. That woman, hunchback, tried with him,—you remember?—she's only got three years. 'Complice. But she's a woman, you know. He's been quiet ever since I put on irons: giv' up, I suppose. Looks white, sick-lookin'. It acts different on 'em, bein' sentenced. Most of 'em gets reckless, devilish-like. Some prays awful, and sings them vile songs of the mills, all in a breath. That woman, now, she's desper't'. Been beggin' to see Hugh, as she calls him, for three days. I'm a-goin' to let her in. She don't go with him. Here she is in this next cell. I'm a-goin' now to let her in.". . .

• • •

It was market day. The narrow windows of the jail looked down directly on the carts and wagons drawn up in a long line, where they had unloaded. He could see, too, and hear distinctly the clink of money as it changed hands, the busy crowd of whites and blacks shoving, pushing one another, and the chaffering and swearing at the stalls. Somehow, the sound, more than anything else had done, wakened him up,—made the whole real to him. He was done with the world and the business of it. He let the tin fall, and looked out, pressing his face close to the rusty bars. How they crowded and pushed! And he,—he should never walk that pavement again! There came Neff Sanders, one of the feeders at the mill, with a basket on his arm. Sure enough, Neff was married the other week. He whistled, hoping he would look up; but he did not. He wondered if Neff remembered he was there,— if any of the boys thought of him up there, and thought that he never was to go down that old cinder-road again. Never again! He had not quite understood it before; but now he did. Not for days or years, but never!—that was it.

How clear the light fell on that stall in front of the market! and how like a picture it was, the dark-green heaps of corn, and the crimson beets, and golden melons! There was another with game: how the light flickered on that pheasant's breast, with the purplish blood dripping over the brown feathers! He could see the red shining of the drops, it was so near. In one minute he could be down there. It was just a step. So easy, as it seemed, so natural to go! Yet it could never be—not in all the thousands of years to come—that he should put his foot on that street again! He thought of himself with a sorrowful pity, as of some one else. There was a dog down in the market, walking after his master with such a stately, grave look!—only a dog, yet he could go backwards and forwards just as he pleased: he had good luck! Why, the very vilest cur, yelping there in the gutter, had not lived his life, had been free to act out whatever thought God had put into his brain; while he—No, he would not think of that! He tried to put the thought away, and to listen to a dispute between a countryman and a woman about some meat; but it would come back. He, what had he done to bear this?

Then came the sudden picture of what might have been, and now. He knew what it was to be in the penitentiary,—how it went with men there. He knew how in these long years he should slowly die, but not until soul and body had become corrupt and rotten,—how, when he came out, if he lived to come, even the lowest of the mill-hands would jeer him,—how his hands would be weak, and his brain senseless and stupid. He believed he was almost that now. He put his hand to his head, with a puzzled, weary look. It ached, his head, with thinking. He tried to quiet himself. It was only right, perhaps; he had done wrong. But was there right or wrong for such as he? What was right? And who had ever taught him? He thrust the whole matter away. A dark, cold quiet crept through his brain. It was all wrong; but let it be! It was nothing to him more than the others. Let it be! . . .

• • •

"It is best. Deb, I cannot bear to be hurted any more."

"Hur knows," she said, humbly.

"Tell my father good-bye; and—and kiss little Janey."

423

She nodded, saying nothing, looked in his face again, and went out of the door. As she went, she staggered.

"Drinkin' to-day?" broke out Haley, pushing her before him. "Where the Devil did you get it? Here, in with ye' and he shoved her into her cell, next to Wolfe's, and shut the door.

Along the wall of her cell there was a crack low down by the floor, through which she could see the light from Wolfe's. She had discovered it days before. She hurried in now, and, kneeling down by it, listened, hoping to hear some sound. Nothing but the rasping of the tin on the bars. He was at his old amusement again. Something in the noise jarred on her ear, for she shivered as she heard it. Hugh rasped away at the bars. A dull old bit of tin, not fit to cut korl with.

He looked out of the window again. People were leaving the market now. A tall mulatto girl, following her mistress, her basket on her head, crossed the street just below, and looked up. She was laughing; but, when she caught sight of the haggard face peering out through the bars, suddenly grew grave, and hurried by. A free, firm step, a clear-cut olive face, with a scarlet turban tied on one side, dark, shining eyes, and on the head the basket poised, filled with fruit and flowers, under which the scarlet turban and bright eyes looked out half-shadowed. The picture caught his eye. It was good to see a face like that. He would try to-morrow, and cut one like it. *To-morrow!* He threw down the tin, trembling, and covered his face with his hands. When he looked up again, the daylight was gone.

Deborah, crouching near by on the other side of the wall, heard no noise. He sat on the side of the low pallet, thinking. Whatever was the mystery which the woman had seen on his face, it came out now slowly, in the dark there, and became fixed,—a something never seen on his face before. The evening was darkening fast. The market had been over for an hour; the rumbling of the carts over the pavement grew more infrequent: he listened to each, as it passed, because he thought it was to be for the last time. For the same reason, it was, I suppose, that he strained his eyes to catch a glimpse of each passer-by, wondering who they were, what kind of homes they were going to, if they had children,—listening eagerly to every chance word in the street, as if—. . .—as if he never should hear human voices again.

It was quite dark at last. The street was a lonely one. The last passenger, he thought, was gone. No,—there was a quick step: Joe Hill, lighting the lamps. Joe was a good old chap; never passed a fellow without some joke or other. He remembered once seeing the place where he lived with his wife. "Granny Hill" the boys called her. Bedridden she was; but so kind as Joe was to her! kept the room so clean!—and the old woman, when he was there, was laughing at "some of t' lad's foolishness." The step was far down the street; but he could see him place the ladder, run up, and light the gas. A longing seized him to be spoken to once more.

"Joe!" he called, out of the grating. "Good-bye, Joe!"

The old man stopped a moment, listening uncertainly; then hurried on. The prisoner thrust his hand out of the window, and called again, louder; but Joe was too far down the street. It was a little thing; but it hurt him,—this disappointment.

"Good-bye, Joe'" he called, sorrowfully enough.

"Be quiet!" said one of the jailers, passing the door, striking on it with his club.

Oh, that was the last, was it?

There was an inexpressible bitterness on his face, as he lay down on the bed, taking the bit of tin, which he had rasped to a tolerable degree of sharpness, in his hand, . . .

. . . I think in that one hour that came then he lived back over all the years that had gone before. I think that, all the low, vile life, all his wrongs, all his starved hopes, came then, and stung him with a farewell poison that made him sick unto death. . . .

The hour was over at last. The moon, passing over her nightly path, slowly came nearer, and threw the light across his bed on his feet. He watched it steadily, as it crept up, inch by inch, slowly. It seemed to him to carry with it a great silence. He had been so hot and tired there always in the mills! The years had been so fierce and cruel! There was coming now quiet and coolness and sleep. His tense limbs relaxed, and settled in a calm languor. The blood ran fainter and slow from his heart. He did not think now with a savage anger of what might be and was not; he was conscious only of deep stillness creeping over him. At first he saw a sea of faces: the mill-men,—women he had known, drunken and bloated,—Janey's timid and pitiful,—poor old Deb's: then they floated together like a mist, and faded away, leaving only the clear, pearly moonlight. . . .

• • •

Nothing remains to tell that the poor Welsh puddler once lived, but this figure of the mill-woman cut in korl. I have it here in a corner of my library. I keep it hid behind a curtain,—it is such a rough, ungainly thing. Yet there are about it touches, grand sweeps of outline, that show a master's hand. Sometimes,—tonight; for instance,—the curtain is accidentally drawn back,

425

and I see a bare arm stretched out imploringly in the darkness, and an eager, wolfish face watching mine: a wan, woeful face, through which the spirit of the dead korl-cutter looks out, with its thwarted life, its mighty hunger, its unfinished work. Its pale, vague lips seem to tremble with a terrible question. "Is this the End?" they say,—"nothing beyond?—no more?" Why, you tell me you have seen that look in the eyes of dumb brutes,—horses dying under the lash. I know.

The deep of the night is passing while I write. The gas-light wakens from the shadows here and there the objects which lie scattered through the room: only faintly, though; for they belong to the open sunlight. As I glance at them, they each recall some task or pleasure of the coming day. A half-moulded child's head; Aphrodite; a bough of forest-leaves; music; work; homely frag-ments, in which lie the secrets of all eternal truth and beauty. Prophetic all! Only this dumb, woeful face seems to belong to and end with the night. I turn to look at it. Has the power of its desperate need commanded the dark-ness away? While the room is yet steeped in heavy shadow, a cool, gray light suddenly touches its head like a blessing hand, and its groping arm points through the broken cloud to the far East, where, in the flickering, nebulous crimson, God has set the promise of the Dawn.

—The Atlantic Monthly, *April 1861*

from In Fields and Factories

DOROTHY DAY

OUR STAND ON STRIKES, JULY 1936

Let us be honest, let us say that fundamentally, the stand we are taking is not on the ground of wages and hours and conditions of labor, but on the fundamental truth that men should be treated not as chattels, but as human beings, as "temples of the Holy Ghost." When Christ took on our human nature, when He became man, He dignified and ennobled human nature. He said, "The Kingdom of Heaven is within you." When men are striking, they are following an impulse, often blind, often uninformed, but a good impulse—one could even say an inspiration of the Holy Spirit. They are trying to uphold their right to be treated not as slaves, but as men. They are fighting for a share in the management, for their right to be considered partners in the enterprise in which they are engaged. They are fighting against the idea of their labor as a commodity, to be bought and sold.

Let us concede that the conditions at the RCA Victor plant down in Camden, where a strike involving 13,000 men started last month, are not bad conditions, and that wages and hours are not bad. There is probably a company union which is supposed to take care of such conditions and complaints, but it perpetuates the enslavement of the worker.

Let us concede that the conditions of the seamen are not so atrocious as the *Daily Worker* contends. Let us get down to the fundamental point that the seamen are striking for: the right to be considered partners, sharers in responsibility, the right to be treated as men and not as chattels.

Is it not a cause worth fighting for? Is it not a cause which demands all the courage and all the integrity of the men involved? *Let us be frank and make this our issue.*

Let us be honest and confess that it is the social order which we wish to change. The workers are never going to be satisfied, no matter how much pay they get, no matter what their hours are. And it is to reconstruct the social order that we are throwing ourselves in with the workers, whether in factories or shipyards or on the sea.

The popes have hit the nail on the head: "No man may outrage with impunity that human dignity which God Himself treats with reverence. . . . Religion teaches the rich man and the employer that their work people are not their slaves; that they must respect in every man his dignity as a man and as a Christian; that labor is an honorable employment: and that it is shameful and inhuman to treat men like chattels to make money by, or to look upon them merely as so much muscle or physical power."

These are fundamental principles which the A.F. of L. has neglected to bring out. They have based their appeal on enlightened self-interest, a phrase reeking with selfishness and containing a warning and a threat. A warning to the workers of the world that they are working for themselves alone, and not as "members one of another." One can see how it has worked out in this country. What percentage of the workers are organized? Only a fraction. And how has the highly organized workman cared for his poorer brother? There has grown up an aristocracy of labor so that it is an irksome fact that brick-layers receive more than farmers in the necessary goods of this world—in goods which we should strive for in order that we may have those God-given means to develop to the full and achieve the Kingdom of Heaven.

We are not losing sight of the fact that our end is spiritual. We are not losing sight of the fact that these better conditions of labor are means to an end. But the labor movement has lost sight of this fact. The leaders have for-gotten such a thing as a philosophy of labor. They have not given to the worker the philosophy of labor, and they have betrayed him.

And the inarticulate rank and file throughout the world are rising up in rebellion, and are being labeled Communists for so doing, for refusing to accept the authority of such leaders, which they very rightly do not consider just authority. They intuitively know better than their leaders what they are looking for. But they have allowed themselves to be misled and deceived.

We have so positive a program that we need all our energy, we have to bend all our forces, material and spiritual, to this end, to promulgate it. Let us uphold our positive program of changing the social order.

But let us, too, examine the Communist means to the end which they claim they are working for, a true brotherhood of man. We do not talk about a classless society, because we acknowledge functional classes as opposed to acquisitive classes.

We agree with this end, but we do not agree on the means to attain it.

The Communists say: "All men are our brothers except the capitalists, so we will kill them off." They do not actually believe in the dignity of man as a human being, because they try to set off one or another class of men and say, "They are not our brothers and never will be. So let us liquidate them." And then to point their argument they say with scorn, "Do you ever think to convert J. P. Morgan, or Rockefeller, or Charlie Schwab?"

They are protesting against man's brutality to man, and at the same time they perpetuate it. It is like having one more war to end all wars. We disagree with this technique of class war, without which the Communist says the brotherhood of man can never be achieved.

"Nothing will be achieved until the worker rises up in arms and forcibly takes the position that is his," the Communist says. "Your movement, which trusts to peaceful means, radical though it may seem, is doomed to failure."

We admit that we may seem to fail, but we recall to our readers the ostensible failure of Christ when He died on the Cross, forsaken by all His followers. Out of the failure a new world sprang up. We recall to our readers the folly of the Cross St. Paul talks about.

When we participate in strikes, when we go out on picket lines and distribute leaflets, when we speak at strike meetings, we are there because we are reaching the workers when they are massed together for action. We are taking advantage of a situation. We may not agree that to strike was the wise thing to do in that particular case. We believe that the work of organization must be thorough before any strike action occurs, unless indeed the strike is a spontaneous one which is the outcome of unbearable conditions.

We oppose all use of violence as un-Christian. We do not believe in persuading scabs with clubs. They are workers, too, and the reason they are scabs is because the work of organization has been neglected.

We oppose the misuse of private property while we uphold the right of private property. The Holy Father says that "as many as possible of the workers should become owners," and how else in many cases except by developing the cooperative ideal?

While we are upholding cooperatives as a part of the Christian social order, we are upholding at the same time unions, as organizations of workers wherein they can be indoctrinated and taught to rebuild the social order. While we stress the back-to-the-land movement so that the worker may be "deproletarianized," we are not going to leave the city to the Communists.

Month by month, in every struggle, in every strike, on every picket line, we shall do our best to join with the worker in his struggle for recognition. We reiterate the slogan of the old I.W.W.'s: "An injury to one is an injury to all." St. Paul says, "When the health of one member of the Mystical Body suffers, the health of the whole body is lowered."

We are all members, one of another, in the Mystical Body of Christ, so let us work together for Christian solidarity.

MEMORIAL DAY IN CHICAGO, JULY 1937

On Memorial Day, May 30, 1937, police opened fire on a parade of striking steel workers and their families at the gate of the Republic Steel Company, in South Chicago. Fifty people were shot, of whom ten later died; one hundred others were beaten with clubs.

Have you ever heard a man scream as he was beaten over the head by two or three policemen with clubs and cudgels? Have you ever heard the sickening sounds of blows and seen people with their arms upraised, trying to protect their faces, stumbling blindly to get away, falling and rising again to be beaten down? Did you ever see a man shot in the back, being dragged to his feet by policemen who tried to force him to stand, while his poor body crumpled, paralyzed by a bullet in the spine?

We are sickened by stories of brutality in Germany and Russia and Italy. A priest from Germany told me of one man who came to him whose back was ridged "like a washboard," by the horrible beatings he had received at the hands of the German police in concentration camps. I shudder with horror at the thought of the tortures inflicted on Catholics, Protestants, Jews, and Communists in Germany today.

And here in America, last month, there was a public exhibition of such brutality that the motion-picture film, taken by a Paramount photographer in a sound truck, was suppressed by the company for fear that it would cause riots and mass hysteria, it was so unutterably horrible.

I am trying to paint a picture of it for our readers because so many did not read the story of the Memorial Day "riot" in Chicago in front of the Republic Steel Mills.

Try to imagine the mass of people—men, women, and children—picketing, as they have a right to do, coming up to the police line and being suddenly shot into, not by one hysterical policeman, but by many. Ten were killed and one hundred were taken to the hospital wounded. Tear gas and clubs supplied by the Republic Steel Company were used.

I am trying to picture this scene to our readers because I have witnessed these things firsthand, and I know the horror of them. I was on a picket line when the "radical" squad shot into the line and pursued the fleeing picketers down the streets, knocking them down and kicking and beating them. I, too, have fled down streets to escape the brutality and vicious hatred of the "law" for those whom they consider "radical." And by the

430

police anyone who protests injustice, who participates in labor struggles, is considered a radical.

Two years ago I wrote an account in the *Catholic Worker* of two plain-clothesmen beating up a demonstrator. I told of the screams and the crumpling body of the man as two men who had dragged him into a hallway beat him up against the wall, aiming well-directed blows at his face, smashing it to a pulp.

We protested this to the Police Commissioner, and our protest was respected and acted upon.

We are repeating the protest against the Chicago massacre because the only way to stop such brutality is to arouse a storm of protest against it.

On whom shall the blame be laid for such a horrible spectacle of violence? Of course, the police and the press in many cases lay the blame on the strikers. But I have lived with these people, I have eaten with them and talked to them day after day. Many of them have never been in a strike before, many of them were marching in the picket line, as in a supplicatory procession, for the first time in their lives. They even brought children on that line in Chicago.

Shall we blame only the police? Or shall we blame just Tom Girdler of the Republic Steel Company? God knows how he can sleep comfortably in his bed at night with the cries of those strikers, of their wives and children, in his ears. He may not hear them now in the heat of battle, but he will hear them, as there is a just God.

Or shall we blame the press, the pulpit, and all those agencies who form public opinion, who have neglected to raise up their voices in protest at injustice and so have permitted it? In some cases, the press have even instigated it so that it would come to pass. Inflammatory, hysterical headlines about mobs, about expected riots, do much to arouse the temper of the police to prepare them for just what occurred. The calm, seemingly reasonable stories of such papers as the *Herald Tribune* and the *Times,* emphasizing the violence and the expectation of violence, do much to prepare the public to accept such violence when it comes to pass.

In that case we all are guilty inasmuch as we have not "gone to the workingman" as the Holy Father pleads and repeats. Inasmuch as we have not inclined our hearts to him, and sought to incline his to us, so that we could work together for peace instead of war, inasmuch as we have not protested such murder as was committed in Chicago—then we are guilty.

One more sin, suffering Christ, worker Yourself, for You to bear. In the garden of Gethsemane, You bore the sins of all the world—You took them on

Yourself, the sins of those police, the sins of the Girdlers and the Schwabs, of the Graces of this world. In committing them, whether ignorantly or of their own free will, they piled them on Your shoulders, bowed to the ground with the weight of the guilt of the world, which You assumed because You loved each of us so much. You took them on Yourself, and You died to save us all. Your Precious Blood was shed even for that policeman whose cudgel smashed again and again the skull of that poor striker, whose brains lay splattered on the undertaker's slab.

And the sufferings of those strikers' wives and children are completing Your suffering today.

Have pity on us all, Jesus of Gethsemane—on Tom Girdler, those police, the souls of the strikers, as well as on all of us who have not worked enough for "a new heaven and a new earth wherein justice dwelleth."

BLOOD ON OUR COAL

A long time ago I read a Russian story about a mother and daughter who earned their living by sewing. They sat by a window and rested their eyes by lifting them from their work now and then to survey the scene outside. Then someone came and built a house right next to their window, which rose like a massive wall and shut out the light and sun and air. They worked in sorrow for many years. Then the wall was demolished, and when it was gone, they grieved for it. They had come to enjoy being shut in by the tenement next door! I remember how extraordinary this gloomy story seemed to me.

Once a migrant worker said to me fervently, "There's nothing I like better than getting out in that hot field and chopping cotton." He meant it, too, with the hot sun on his back and the vast field all around, and silent men, women, and children working down the long rows around him—a long, endless, stupefying work that identifies the man with the field he works in.

Down in Derry, Pennsylvania, in the soft-coal regions, almost worked out now, a miner told me after we had talked together for several days, "Miners don't want to do anything else. They don't want to be farmers. Many of them that leave their work and try something else go back to it again." And I suppose it's true.

The entire industrial world has so little to offer, what with its cannibalism, its competition, that the men go back to their black holes and their nine hours a day underground, six days a week, and begin to take pride in its hazards, its own unique misery.

"It's black down there," he said. "No light but what you carry on your hat." How can men love darkness rather than light? How can men choose such an occupation except that they have been forced to it?

It is not so many hundred years ago that the only way they could get miners was to make bondsmen of them. Technically they were not slaves, but they were bonded over to the owners of the mines—men, women, and children—and if they tried to escape they were beaten back to work.

How much do we meditate on coal and its uses? There is a limited amount of it in the earth; many of the mines in Pennsylvania are worked out now, leaving ghost towns. The forests, too, are cut down so fast we will have neither wood nor coal, looking at things from the long view. Yet it is not with any knowledge of organic farming, the necessity for tree planting, the use of other forms of energy, that miners revolt against this form of labor. They revolt because it is inhuman, it demands too much of a man. If they do not leave it for other work it is because that other work, whether it is farming for profit or working in factories, is also inhuman and "takes it all out of a man."

People want to know what this present coal strike is about. It is about shorter hours, for one thing—instead of the fifty-four-hour weeks the men work now. And it is about the welfare fund. Up to this time there have been no pensions, no recreation, no education, no adequate medical services. The need for such a fund is evidenced by these figures: Every year some 1,500 miners are killed; some 60,000 to 70,000 are injured, many of them so badly they are thrown on the scrap heap.

When we can read figures like these, when we read of the inhuman suffering of the workers, when we remember the blood that is on our coal, we know what the Holy Father means when he says that the world has lost a sense of sin. Not personal sin, but *social sin*. When priests do not cry out for the workers, try to share with the workers their poverty, then surely this is what the Holy Father means when he speaks of the devitalization of the Church. They are dead branches indeed.

"All the way to heaven is heaven, because Christ said, 'I am the Way.'" And work should be part of heaven, not part of hell. In the black underground caverns where the miners lose all light of day—month after month, from early fall till late spring—there is a glimpse of "everlasting night where no order is and everlasting horror dwelleth." We want to change man's work; we want to make people question their work; is it on the way to heaven or hell?

Man gains his bread by his work. It is his bread and wine. It is his life. We cannot emphasize the importance of it enough. We must emphasize the holiness of *work*, and we must emphasize the sacramental quality of *property*, too. That means the property of the poor. They have very little of it. We know that it is dangerous, it corrupts, it is almost a testing ground in this life of attachment and detachment. We must love it as a sample of God's providence and goodness and we must be ready to give it up.

The Holy Father says we must deproletarize the workers. That is, we must get them out of the wage-slave class and into the owner class. One very good reason is that a man loves what is his, and has a sense of responsibility for it, almost a sacramental sense in regard to his house, his land, and his work on them.

When we talk about property, we do not think of stocks and bonds, shares in coal mines, the property of the gentlemen hunters in their red coats and silk top hats whom we saw prancing by on Thanksgiving morning. They have no respect for property. For example, it turns out that the farmers around Pennsylvania only own their ground plow-deep. They do not know this until they begin to object to the mining operations which undermine their homes and cause them to settle in the cave-ins so prevalent throughout the state. When the operators finish taking out all the coal in a given place they start to retreat, taking out pillars of wood and pillars of coal. The roof falls in and the ground above settles. This goes on all through that region, and the farmer who objects is told he can pay for all the coal which the miners would have been able to mine from his acres.

There is no respect for property here. So why do we talk of fighting Communism on the grounds that it does away with private property? We have done that very well ourselves in this country. Or because Communism denies the existence of God? We do not see Christ in our brothers in the mines, in our brother John L. Lewis. We deny Christ here. And what about that other argument about the use of force? We live in an age of war, and the turning of the wheels of industry, the very working of the mines depends on our wars.

We heard Louis Budenz speak at the Harrisburg forum as we passed through on our way to the mining sections, and one of his messages to Catholics was this warning: that the Communists would try to foment anticlericalism and divide the people from the hierarchy.

There is really no need of their doing it. It is already an accomplished fact. Pope Pius XI himself said, "The workers of the world are lost to the Church."

Our good readers absolve us from any charges of anticlericalism as they read these rather severe articles on the church and work. They know that the wish of our heart is to bring closer together the priest and the people. There is a great division between the two, and one of the very reasons for the Catholic Worker's existence is to bridge this gap.

from Loaves & Fishes

DOROTHY DAY

CHAPTER 1: A KNOCK AT THE DOOR

It is a joy to me to sit in front of a window and write in this way, in my little two-room apartment on Ludlow Street. This is in an old slum section of New York (the Lower East Side) which is not yet being boarded up or demolished.

The day is very hot, but my windows, facing east, look out on a back yard with a bare tree, an ailanthus tree—the tree of heaven. Down in the next yard are a maple and some bushes.

The sun pours in on the rooms, which are freshly painted. Next door, two other rooms face onto the yard. In these four rooms there are at present five of us: besides me, a girl just out of prison; a seventeen-year-old school-girl, a runaway; a serious young college student of twenty-one whose commitment to the intellectual life means her ideas may overflow into action; and a girl on vacation from a hospital for the poor in Montreal, where she gives her services to the crippled and the destitute.

Yes, it is a joy to write in these surroundings. But it is a confinement, too: the ailanthus tree, bare though it may be, yet reaches up bonily in this New York canyon of back yards for a bit of air and sunlight.

My mind goes back. I am reminded of an apartment much like this one, four rooms deep, at East Fifteenth Street and Avenue A, where I was living when I started the *Catholic Worker* with Peter Maurin. All those old houses are torn down now, but there was a row of them then along the narrow street, occupied mostly by Germans and Italians.

I was living with my younger brother, John, and Teresa, his Spanish wife. Our kitchen looked out on a back yard where there were no ailanthuses—that tough weed of a tree—but fig trees, carefully cultivated and guarded by Italians, who corseted them in hay and burlap against the cold during the winter. In the summer the trees bore fruit. There were peach trees, privet hedges growing as high as trees, and rows of widow's tears. Petunias and marigolds gave us a small riot of color—and delightful fragrance, too, whenever the rain washed the air clear of the neighborhood cooking smells.

We were in the third year of the depression. Roosevelt had just been elected President. Every fifth adult American—twelve million in all—was unemployed. No smoke came from the factories. Mortgages on homes and farms were being foreclosed, driving more people to the city and loading them onto the already overburdened relief rolls. In New York long, bedraggled breadlines of listless men wound along city streets. On the fringes, by the rivers, almost every vacant lot was a Hooverville, a collection of jerry-built shanties where the homeless huddled in front of their fires.

An air of excitement, of impending social change, with the opportunity to implement our social ideas, buoyed up all who were young and had ideas. We met, we talked endlessly, feeling that this was the time to try new things. I had just come back from Washington, where I was covering the story of the Hunger March of the Unemployed Councils for *Commonweal* and the story of the Farmers' Conference for *America*. I had been a journalist most of my days, and I was earning my living by freelance writing of articles about the social order.

Sitting in the kitchen one afternoon, I was working on a book about the unemployed—it was to be a novel—when a knock came at the door. Tessa was just starting supper. John was getting ready to go to work—he was a copy boy on a Hearst paper at the time. They were both twenty years old and expecting their first baby. Tessa had a warm, radiant look, a glowing look. John was more reserved.

Tessa, who was always very hospitable, welcomed the man at the door. A short, broad man (he was fifty-seven, I found out later, but my first impression was that he was older) came in and started talking at once—casually, informally, almost as though he were taking up a conversation where it had been left off., There was a gray look about him: he had gray hair, cut short and scrubby; gray eyes; strong features; a pleasant mouth; and short-fingered, broad hands, evidently used to heavy work, such as with a pick and shovel. He wore the kind of old clothes that have so lost their shape and finish that it's impossible to tell whether they are clean or not. But Peter Maurin, agitator and soon to be founder of what came to be known as the Catholic Worker movement, was, as I later learned, always neat.

Tessa went on with her work and the newcomer stood before me, declaiming one of what John named his "Easy Essays":

People go to Washington
asking the government
to solve their economic problems,

while the Federal government
was never intended
to solve men's economic problems.
Thomas Jefferson says that
the less government there is,
the better it is.
If the less government there is,
the better it is,
then the best kind of government
is self-government.
If the best kind of government
is self-government,
then the best kind of organization
is self-organization.
When the organizers try
to organize the unorganized,
then the organizers
don't organize themselves.
And when the organizers
don't organize themselves,
nobody organizes himself,
and when nobody organizes himself
nothing is organized.

He actually spoke this way, using repetition to make his points. He phrased these points so simply that they sounded like free verse (and to this day people talk about "Peter's verses").

Tamar, my little daughter, had been calling me from the next room. She was down with measles, and she wanted orange juice and me. For his part, Peter wanted a listener and a disciple, so he went on talking to a doctor who had just come in. When the doctor left, he talked to the plumber, to the gas-man reading the meter, to Tessa at the kitchen sink, and to John, while he was shaving before the kitchen mirror.

I learned from Tessa that he had actually come to see me. Tessa had a wonderful serenity, but I felt torn apart. The doctor, Tamar, and Peter, all wanted my undivided attention at this moment, and I was dulled by my own fatigue as well. Peter had come a few times before to see if I was back from Washington, and Tessa had welcomed him; but John, solid American that he was, had not been so sure whether Peter was someone I would want to see or a crackpot from Union Square. Peter had told Tessa—his French accent made him hard to understand at first—that he had read articles I wrote in Catholic magazines and had come to suggest I start a newspaper to bring about "clarification of thought." Clarification was the first "point" in his program. Men must think before they act. They must study. "There could be no revolution without a theory of revolution," he had quoted Lenin as saying, and what he himself was interested in was the "green revolution," the back-to-the-land revolution, not the red one, which emphasized industry. It was because I had just come back from Washington that he had delivered to me his "People go to Washington" essay, but in my mixed roles as cook, dishwasher, nurse, and mother, as well as writer, it was hard for me to grasp what he said immediately.

It was a long time before I really knew what Peter was talking about that first day. But he did make three points I thought I understood: founding a newspaper for clarification of thought, starting houses of hospitality, and organizing farming communes. I did not really think then of the latter two as having anything to do with me, but I did know about newspapers. My father and three brothers worked on them all their adult lives. When I was eleven, we children had started to type out a little family newspaper. We all liked to write, and I had been taught early to write personally, subjectively, about what I saw around me and what was being done.

• • •

Tamar was not very sick. She was content for a few days to play with dolls and kittens and modeling clay, and Peter took advantage of my confinement at home to come back and continue my indoctrination.

"He who is not a Socialist at twenty has no heart, and he who is a Socialist at thirty has no head," he was fond of quoting from a French author. Since I had been a Socialist in college, a Communist in the early twenties, and now a Catholic since 1927, I had a very definite point of view about poverty, unemployment, and my own vocation to try to do something about it all. I had no doubts about the Church. It was founded upon Saint Peter, that rock, who yet thrice denied his Master on the eve of His crucifixion. And Jesus had compared the Church to a net cast into the sea and hauled in, filled with fishes, both good and bad. "Including," one of my non-Catholic friends used to say, "some blowfish and quite a few sharks."

Peter Maurin spoke to me often of his ideas about hospitality, a concept I understood well because I had lived so long on the Lower East Side of New York—and the poor are noted for their hospitality. "There is always enough for one more," my brother's Spanish mother-in-law used to say. "Everyone just take a little less." Poor families were always taking in other needy ones. So, when Peter began talking about what "we need," it sounded clear and logical:

> The Catholic unemployed
> should not be sent to the Muni [municipal lodging house].
> The Catholic unemployed
> should be given hospitality
> in Catholic Houses of Hospitality.
> Catholic Houses of Hospitality
> are known in Europe
> under the name of hospices.
> There have been hospices in Europe
> since the time of Constantine.
> Hospices are free guest houses;
> hotels are paying guest houses.
> And paying guest houses or hotels
> are as plentiful
> as free guest houses or hospices
> are scarce.
> So hospitality, like everything else,
> has been commercialized.
> So hospitality, like everything else,
> must now be idealized.

Some of Peter's other ideas were less readily understandable, but his verses probably helped people grasp the sense and spirit of what he had to say. He fancied himself a troubadour of God, going about the public squares and street corners indoctrinating his listeners by a singsong repetition, which certainly caught their attention. Being a born teacher, he did not hesitate to repeat his ideas over and over again. He even suggested to the young students and unemployed who flocked around him and accompanied him to Columbus Circle that there should be a sort of antiphonal chant. Peter would sing out, "To give and not to take," and the chorus would respond, "That is what makes man human," and so on, through the entire essay.

He was good as bread. He was not gay or joyful, as others have described him, but he was a truly happy man, with the happiness a man feels when he has found his vocation in life and has set out on the way and is sure of himself: and sure, too, that others are searching for and willing to undertake their task in life, striving not only to love God and their brother but to *show* that love. Peter had faith in people as well as in ideas, and he was able to make them feel his faith in them, so that they gained confidence and overcame the sense of futility that so plagues the youth of today. In fact, he gave me so great a faith in the power of his ideas that if he had said, "Go to Madison Square Garden and speak these ideas," I would have overcome all sense of fear and would have attempted such a folly, convinced that, though it was the "folly of the Cross" and doomed to failure, God Himself could take this failure and turn it into victory.

Certainly there was nothing in Peter's physical appearance to impress his hearers. His dusty, unpressed, ill-fitting suit bulged with books and pamphlets; yet he gave no impression of carelessness, for he invariably wore a felt hat (not too wide-brimmed), a shirt (rough-dried), a tie, and sturdy shoes. He was not the bearded, sandaled, hatless fanatic—he had no appearance of an apostle. Neither was he establishing a personality cult; it was the primacy of the spiritual that Peter always emphasized. He was happy when people listened to him, yet he did not want people to follow him because of the influence he himself exerted but only because of the strength and beauty of the idea.

The idea of poverty, for instance. How glowing a thing it is in Franciscan literature, and how many illusions people have about it! But Peter *lived* it. He literally possessed nothing. He lived in an old hotel on the Bowery where he paid fifty cents a night for his lodging. He ate, when he had the money, in the "horse markets" of the Bowery, cheap cafés serving stew and hot weak coffee, very sweet. He was used to living on soup and bread.

Among his ideas it was the one of publishing a paper which most immediately appealed to me. "But how can it be done without money?" I wanted to know.

"In the Catholic Church one never needs any money to start a good work," Peter replied. "People are what are important. If you have the people and they are willing to give their work—that is the thing. God is not to be outdone in generosity. The funds will come in somehow or other."

Did he really say this? I cannot be sure now, and I suspect that he passed over my question about money—it was not needed in the Church. The important thing was work.

I had been reading the life of Rose Hawthorne Lathrop. She was a daughter of Nathaniel Hawthorne, the nineteenth-century American novelist. Rose, with her husband, had become a convert in 1891. She had started a cancer hospital for the poor and homeless—such institutions were a rarity in those days—in three dark, airless rooms down on the East Side. Her beginnings had been as humble as ours would be if I started the work Peter wanted. Indeed, when Rose herself fell ill with grippe, her very first patient had to take care of her. But from that simple start her work had grown until there are now a half dozen of those hospitals, run by the Dominicans, scattered around the country. A new order of nuns, wearing the Dominican habit, came into being as a result.

Reading about Rose Hawthorne Lathrop and listening now to Peter so inspired me that I was quite ready to believe that in the Church no money was necessary. I was all for plunging right in. After all, I had a typewriter and a kitchen table and plenty of paper and plenty to write about. The thing was to find a printer, run off the first issue and go out on the streets and sell it. Beginnings are always exciting.

CHAPTER 2: EVERYONE'S PAPER

Someone once said that it took me from December until May to bring out the paper. The truth is that I agreed at once. The delay was due chiefly to the fact that Peter, in his optimism about funds, was relying on a priest he knew who had a very plush rectory uptown on the West Side. His clerical friend would give us a mimeograph machine, paper, and space in the rectory basement. None of these were forthcoming—they had been only optimistic notions of Peter's.

But in the meantime Peter was educating me. I had had a secular education, he said, and he would give me a Catholic outline of history. One way to study history was to read the lives of the saints down the centuries. Perhaps he chose this method because he had noticed my library, which contained a life of St. Teresa of Avila and her writings, especially about her spiritual foundations, and a life of St. Catherine of Siena. "Ah, there was a saint who had an influence on her times!" he exclaimed. Then he plunged into a discussion of St. Catherine's letters to the Popes and other public figures of the fourteenth century, in which she took them to task for their failings.

The date I had met Peter is clear in my mind because it was just after the feast of the Immaculate Conception, which is on December 8. I had visited the national shrine at Catholic University in Washington to pray for the hunger marchers. I felt keenly that God was more on the side of the hungry, the ragged, the unemployed, than on the side of the comfortable churchgoers who gave so little heed to the misery of the needy and the groaning of the poor. I had prayed that some way would open up for me to do something, to line myself up on their side, to work for them, so that I would no longer feel that I had been false to them in embracing my new-found faith.

The appearance of Peter Maurin, I felt with deep conviction, was the result of my prayers. Just as the good God had used the farmer Habakkuk to bring the mess of food intended for the reapers to Daniel in the lions' den, so had He sent Peter Maurin to bring me the good intellectual food I needed to strengthen me to work for Him.

I learned shortly how he had happened to come to see me. He had heard of me on a visit to *Commonweal*, our famous New York weekly edited by laymen. It had been started by Michael Williams, a veteran journalist, who had worked in San Francisco on the same paper with my father years before. Peter had also been told of my conversion by a redheaded Irish Communist with whom he struck up a conversation on a bench in Union Square. The Irishman told Peter that we both had similar ideas—namely, that the Catholic Church had a social teaching which could be applied to the problems of our day. So Peter set out to find me.

Now he had someone to whom he could propound his program. He must have proposed it many times before, at Social Action conferences, in visits to public figures and chancery offices around the country. But he seemed to have got nowhere. It might have been his shabbiness, it might have been his thick accent, that prevented him from getting a hearing.

Perhaps it was because of my own radical background that Peter brought me a digest of the writings of Kropotkin one day, calling my attention especially to *Fields, Factories and Workshops*. He had gone over to the Rand School of Social Science for this, and carefully copied out the pertinent passages. He also liked *Mutual Aid* and *The Conquest of Bread*.

I was familiar with Kropotkin only through his *Memoirs of a Revolutionist*, which had originally run serially in the *Atlantic Monthly*. (Oh, far-off day of American freedom, when Karl Marx could write for the morning *Tribune* in New York, and Kropotkin could not only be published in the *Atlantic*, but be received as a guest in the homes of New England Unitarians, and in Jane Addams's Hull House in Chicago!)

Peter came day after day. He brought me books to read and the newest of his phrased writings. There was to be no end to my learning.

One day I chanced upon Peter in his friend's uptown church. I had dropped in to say a few prayers. After some minutes I looked up. There was Peter, sitting in front of the Blessed Sacrament, evidently in deep meditation.

He seemed totally unconscious of the presence of anyone else in the church. He sat there in silence. Every now and then he would nod his head, and gesticulate with his hands, as though he were making one of his points to the Presence before Whom he sat so quietly. I did not want to disturb him.

Also, in my subconscious I was probably tired of his constant conversation. His line of thought, the books he had given me to read, were all new to me and all ponderous. There was so much theory. I had read about Kropotkin the man, his life and adventures. In a way, they told me much. I was not sure I wanted to know more. Peter read Kropotkin's theoretical works. It was the idea, the abstract thought, that got him and that he hoped would get me.

Sitting there thinking back over the past weeks, I had to face the fact that Peter was hard to listen to. I would tune in on some concert, some symphony, and beg him to be still. Tessa and I both loved music, but Peter seemed to have no ear for it. He would be obedient for a time. But soon he would look at my forbidding face and, seeing no yielding there, he would go over to the gentler Tessa. Pulling a chair close to hers and leaning almost on the arm, he would begin to talk. He was incorrigible. Yet we were growing to love him, to greet him warmly when he came, to press food on him, knowing that he ate only one meal a day.

His willingness to talk to any visitor who dropped in, however, was a boon to us; it released us for our various chores. I, for example, could run into the front room to my typewriter and get some work done. I recall one visitor in particular, who came quite often, a sculptor named Hugh—a tall man, heavy and quiet, with big brown eyes. He used to take out a flute and play while Peter talked to him.

"You are quite right, Peter," he would say every now and then, nodding absently. Then he would go right on piping his simple tunes. He startled us one day, when a woman friend of ours came to call, by remarking after she had left that she used to come to his studio and sit in the nude on the mantelpiece. We concluded that she must have resembled some model who had once posed for him.

Usually by ten or eleven we urged our visitors to go. We were at home with them and felt free to send them on their way. On mild nights, Hugh and Peter would go on to Union Square to sit on a park bench. There they would continue their conversation—if it could be called that—with Hugh playing his flute, and Peter, gesticulating, haranguing him with his discussion of history, his analysis of ideas, old and new, and, in doing so, perhaps rehearsing his lessons for me for the next day.

Placidly, Tessa awaited her baby, and I went on with my freelancing. In the evenings, my brother and I (John was working days now) would talk over plans for the paper with Peter, who knew nothing at all about journalism. He would supply the ideas, and we would get out the paper for the "man in the street."

My mind and heart were full of the part I had to play, self-centered creature that I was. I planned the makeup and the type, and what stories I would write to go with Peter's easy essays. I don't think we even consulted Peter as to whether he liked the title we had given to his writings in the paper, "Easy Essays." He was so happy over the coming incarnation of his ideas in print that he never expressed himself on the subject. But he well knew that, in spite of the title, his essays were anything but easy. Like those in the Gospel, his were hard sayings—hard to work out in everyday life.

Having become convinced of this after several weeks, I went, on the advice of Father Joseph McSorley, former provincial of the Paulist Society and my good spiritual adviser at the time, to the Paulist Press. For an edition of two thousand copies, I was told, the price would be fifty-seven dollars.

I decided to wait until I had the cash in hand before getting out the first issue. I didn't want to run up any debts. I did no installment buying, although I didn't mind being late with the rent or skimping on groceries to speed the accumulation of enough money to pay the first bill. Father McSorley helped a lot by finding work for me to do. Father Harold Purcell gave me ten dollars, and Sister Peter Claver brought me a dollar, which someone had just given to her.

All that winter Peter had come back and forth from Mt. Tremper in upstate New York, but by April he was in town all the time. Our plans were shaping up. Yet Peter was plainly not too well pleased with the way the paper was going.

I had sent my copy to the printer—news accounts of the exploitation of Negroes in the South, and the plight of the sharecroppers; child labor in our own neighborhood; some recent evictions; a local strike over wages and hours; pleas for better home relief, and so on—and we were waiting for proofs.

When they came we cut them out and started making a dummy, pasting them up on the eight pages of a tabloid the size of the Nation, writing headlines, and experimenting with different kinds of type. Peter looked over what I had written as it came back from the printer. I could see that, far from being happy about it, he was becoming more and more disturbed. One day, while looking over some fresh proofs, he shook his head. His expression was one of great sadness.

"It's everyone's paper," he said. I was pleased. I thought that was what we both wanted. "And everyone's paper is no one's paper," he added with a sigh.

He rose without another word and went out the door. Later we learned indirectly that he had gone back upstate. It was some time before we heard from him again.

We kept hoping that he would be on hand for that historic May Day in 1933 when we ventured out in Union Square to sell the first issue. He wasn't. A friendly priest sent three young men to accompany me. One of them was Joe Bennett, a tall, gangling blond boy from Denver, who was to work closely with us for some months. The day was bright and warm and beautiful. The square was packed with demonstrators and paraders, listening to speeches, carrying on disputes among themselves, or glancing through the great masses of literature being given out or sold, which so soon were litter on the ground.

The two younger men, intimidated and discouraged by the slighting comments of the champions of labor and the left, soon fled. Religion in Union Square! It was preposterous! If we had been representing Jehovah's Witnesses, we might have had a friendlier reception. But people associated with the Roman Catholic Church! Joe Bennett and I stuck it out, reveling in the bright spring sunshine. We did not sell many papers, but we did enjoy the discussions into which we were drawn. One Irishman looked at the masthead and rebuked us for the line which read "a penny a copy." We were in the pay of the English, he said. Next month we changed it to "a cent a copy" just to placate the Irish.

We knew Peter would not have let this go without making a point. He would have said, "When an Irishman met an Irishman a thousand years ago, they started a monastery. Now, when an Irishman meets an Irishman, you know what they start!" Then he would have gone on with a long discourse on Gaelic culture, on how it was the Irish who kept civilization alive through the Dark Ages, and on and on, until his adversary would have forgotten all about his heat over the penny.

Another protest came from a Negro, who pointed out that the two workers on our masthead, standing on either side of our title, the *Catholic Worker*, were both white men. One had a pick and the other had a shovel. "Why not have one white and the other colored?" he wanted to know.

We thought it was a good suggestion. Before our next issue came out we found an artist who made a new masthead for us, a white man and a colored man, each with his implements of toil, clasping hands, with the figure of Christ in the background, uniting them. Joe Bennett and I sat on park benches that first day, got our first touch of sunburn, and gradually relaxed. In spite of our small sales and the uncertain prospects for the future, it was with a happy feeling of accomplishment that I returned to East Fifteenth Street that evening.

But I missed Peter Maurin. We had been so excited at the idea of launching a new paper, small though it was, and we had had so many details to attend to, that there was not much time to miss him before the paper came out. But now I did. His absence gave me an uneasy feeling, reminding me that our paper was not reflecting his thought, although it was he who had given us the idea.

Then, for a while, I was too busy again to think much about it. Copies had to be mailed out to editors of diocesan papers and to men and women prominent in the Catholic world. Mail began to come in praising our first effort. Some letters even contained donations to help us continue our work. I was lightheaded with success. We had started. Tessa's baby was born the week after the *Catholic Worker* was launched. A few days later my brother got a job editing the small-town paper in Dobbs Ferry, up the Hudson River, and moved his family there.

At the same time a barbershop on the street floor below our apartment became empty. I could see that it would be ideal for an office. It was a long shop, and narrow. In back of it was a bedroom, and beyond that a kitchen. A door opened on the back yard, and the paved space in front of the garden made an ideal spot for an outdoor sitting room where we could receive guests and even serve afternoon tea. So, with a few pieces of secondhand furniture—a desk, a table, a filing case, and a couple of chairs—we made still another start.

More and more people began to come. Two constant visitors at the office of the *Catholic Worker* were a thin, shabby, and rather furtive-looking pair whom Peter had picked up in Union Square earlier in the spring before he went away. To him they represented "the worker." They would listen to him untiringly and without interrupting. They were the beginning of an audience, something to build on—not very promising, but something. After one of Peter's discussions in the square, they usually followed him to my place, where, if there was not a bit of change forthcoming, there were at least bread and sweet tea. Peter would say each time, "They have no place to sleep." He was sure that I would produce the dollar needed for two beds on the Bowery. But often there was no dollar, so they stayed for lunch instead.

All the while Peter was in the country I was visited regularly by the pair of them. They always announced themselves before I opened the door: "Dolan and Egan here again." It got so that my personal friends, knowing how exasperated I was becoming at having my time taken up, used to call out upon arriving, "Dolan and Egan here again."

Thus it was with repressed impatience that I heard one day a knock on the door of my apartment above the barbershop. I stood there, braced for the familiar greeting. When it did not come, I opened the door anyway—there stood Peter Maurin.

"Peter! Where have you been?" My relief was so great that my welcome was ardent. "Where were you on May Day? Thousands of people in Union Square and not a sign of Peter!"

"Everyone's paper is no one's paper," he repeated, shaking his head. Peter seemed rested and not so dusty as usual. His gray eyes told me that he was glad to be back. While I prepared coffee and soup and put out the bread, he went on and on, and I let him, content to wait until he was eating his soup to tell him all that had been happening. When his mouth was full he would listen.

I got no explanation from him as to why he had gone away. The closest he came to it was to say wryly, with a shrug, "Man proposes and woman disposes." But he looked at me and smiled and his eyes warmed. I could see that he was happy to be back and ready to get on with his mission. He was full of patience, ready to look at me now: not as a Catherine of Siena, already enlightened by the Holy Spirit, but as an ex-Socialist, ex-I.W.W., ex-Communist, in whom he might find some concordance, some basis on which to build. But unions and strikes and the fight for better wages and hours would remain my immediate concern. As St. Augustine said, "The bottle will still smell of the liquor it once held." I continued on this track until Peter had enlightened my mind and enlarged my heart to see further, more in accord with the liberty of Christ, on which St. Paul was always speaking.

Peter took up right where he had left off, pulling a book from his pocket to continue my schooling. It might have been an encyclical on St. Francis of Assisi; or something by Eric Gill, writer, sculptor, artist, craftsman, living at that time in a community in England; or the short book *Nazareth or Social Chaos* by Father Vincent McNabb, O.P., who had encouraged that community. It was only gradually, through many conversations, that I came to understand enough of his thinking to realize why he considered the stories in the first issue of *The Catholic Worker* inadequate.

He often spoke of what he called "a philosophy of work." "Work, not wages-work is not a commodity to be bought and sold" was one of his slogans. "Personal responsibility, not state responsibility" was another. A favorite source of his was *The Personalist Manifesto* by Emmanuel Mounier, which he would go around extemporaneously translating from the French for the benefit of any who would listen. He finally persuaded Father Virgil Michel, a Benedictine priest of St. John's Abbey, in Minnesota, to translate it. Peter got it published. "A personalist is a *go-giver*, not a *go-getter*," he used to say. "He tries to give what he has instead of trying to get what the other fellow has. He tries to be good by doing good to the other fellow. He has a social doctrine of the common good. He is alter-centered, not self-centered."

Much later, when I had a look at that first issue, I could see more clearly what bothered Peter. We had emphasized wages and hours while he was trying to talk about a philosophy of work. I had written of women in industry, children in industry, of sweatshops and strikes.

"Strikes don't strike me!" Peter kept saying, stubbornly. It must have appeared to him that we were just urging the patching-up of the industrial system instead of trying to rebuild society itself with a philosophy so old it seemed like new. Even the name of the paper did not satisfy him. He would have preferred *Catholic Radical*, since he believed that radicals should, as their name implied, get at the root of things. The second issue of the paper, the June-July number, showed that we had been talking things over. My editorial said:

> Peter Maurin (whose name we misspelled in the last issue) has his program, which is embodied in his contribution this month. Because his program is specific and definite, he thinks it is better to withdraw his name from the editorial board and continue his contact with the paper as a contributor.

Then came Peter's editorial:

> As an editor, it will be assumed that I sponsor or advocate any reform suggested in the pages of the *Catholic Worker*. I would rather definitely sign my own work, letting it be understood what I stand for.
>
> My program stands for three things: Round-table discussions is one and I hope to have the first one at the Manhattan Lyceum the last Sunday in June. We can have a hall holding 150 people for eight hours for ten dollars. I have paid a deposit of three. I have no more money now but I will beg the rest. I hope everyone will come to this meeting. I want Communists, radicals, priests, and laity. I want everyone to set forth his views. I want clarification of thought.

The next step in the program is houses of hospitality. In the Middle Ages it was an obligation of the bishop to provide houses of hospitality or hospices for the wayfarer. They are especially necessary now and necessary to my program, as halfway houses. I am hoping that someone will donate a house rent-free for six months so that a start may be made. A priest will be at the head of it and men gathered from our round-table discussions will be recruited to work in the houses cooperatively and eventually be sent out to farm colonies or agronomic universities. Which comes to the third step in my program. People will have to go back to the land. The machine has displaced labor. The cities are overcrowded. The land will have to take care of them.

My whole scheme is a Utopian, Christian communism. I am not afraid of the word *communism*. I am not saying that my program is for everyone. It is for those who choose to embrace it. I am not opposed to private property with responsibility. But those who own private property should never forget it is a trust.

This succinct listing of his aims was not even the lead editorial. Perhaps it sounded too utopian for my tastes; perhaps I was irked because women were left out in his description of a house of hospitality, where he spoke of a group of men living under a priest. In addition to Peter's editorial, there were several of his easy essays. In one, recommending the formation of houses of hospitality and farming communes, he wrote in his troubadour mood:

We need round-table discussions
to keep trained minds from becoming academic.

We need round-table discussions
to keep untrained minds from being superficial.

We need round-table discussions
to learn from scholars
how things would be, if they were as they should be.
We need round-table discussions
to learn from scholars
how a path can be made
from things as they are
to things as they should be.

We need houses of hospitality
to give to the rich
the opportunity to serve the poor.

We need houses of hospitality
to bring the Bishops to the people
and the people to the Bishops.

We need houses of hospitality
to bring back to institutions
the technique of institutions.

We need houses of hospitality
to bring social justice
exercised in Catholic institutions.
The unemployed need free rent.
They can have that
in an agronomic university.

The unemployed need free fuel.
They can get that
in an agronomic university.

The unemployed need free food.
They can raise that
in an agronomic university.

The unemployed need to acquire skill.
They can do that
in an agronomic university.

There were other articles on more mundane matters. One stated that readers had contributed $156.50. That, with what money I got from freelancing, would keep us going. There was also a report on distribution: papers were being mailed out all over the country in bundles of ten or twenty; Dolan and Egan had been selling on the streets (they kept the money to pay for their "eats and tobacco"); and I too had embarked on the great adventure of going out to face up to "the man in the street."

So we continued through the summer. Since this was the depression and there were no jobs, almost immediately we found ourselves a group, a staff, which grew steadily in numbers. Joe Bennett, our first salesman, was still with us. Soon we were joined by Stanley Vishnewski, a seventeen-year-old Lithuanian boy from the Williamsburg section of Brooklyn who used to walk to New York over the bridge every day and then twenty-five blocks uptown to Fifteenth Street. He sold the paper, too, and ran errands and worked without wages despite the urging of his father, a tailor, that he ought to be looking for a job. (Stanley has remained with us ever since.) A young girl, a journalism student at Columbia and a graduate of Manhattanville, also joined us at about this time.

There were also Dan Irwin, an unemployed bookkeeper, and Frank O'Donnell, who had been working as a salesman, selling people things they didn't really want, and who had a guilty conscience about it. Then there was Big Dan. I remember how he came in the first time, groaning and shouting, and, when asked what we could do for him, he bellowed, "I'd like to soak my feet!" He had been walking the streets all day, looking for a job. His shoes were worn and shabby, and did not fit him, and since it had been raining, they were wet and shrunken besides. I brought out a washtub of hot water. He gratefully took off his socks, which were full of holes, and gingerly, one after the other, put his feet into the hot water, roaring his delight. I was thinking of the time Jesus washed the feet of His apostles and then told them, "As I have done to you, so you do also." But I couldn't bring myself to do any more than offer the tub of hot water, soap, and towels. It would have been too embarrassing.

Anyone who came in was always invited to the meal being served in the kitchen—we ate in shifts when the room would not hold us all—so Big Dan stayed that evening. Between mouthfuls he told us that he had been sleeping around the piers on the waterfront. He had been eating out of garbage cans as he did not want to stay with his sister—who was perfectly ready to keep him—because she had so many kids and he had such a big appetite.

One thing Peter used to love to say—and he said it that night to Big Dan—was "People are always looking for a job. What I say is 'Fire the bosses! Fire the bosses!'"

This slogan enchanted Big Dan. He would have liked to see the boss put in *his* place, walking the streets, looking for a job. He no doubt pictured himself sitting in a fine office, in the act of "firing the boss" while he himself was gainfully employed doing nothing. His eyes sparkled as he looked at Peter.

"The boss offers his employees stock in the company and the worker gets stuck!" Peter shouted gleefully. It was hard to imagine anyone having the stock to get stuck with in those days, but he loved the word play, laughing at his own wit, which often failed to get across. The idea of being proud to be poor, however, was something that straightened Dan's shoulders. He came back early the next morning to pick up a bundle a papers to sell in Union Square. He had a reason now to stand on a street corner in touch with the passers-by.

A *Daily Worker* salesman would shout, "Read the *Daily Worker!*" Big Dan would counter with "Read the *Catholic Worker* daily!" He had a big voice and shouting slogans gave him a chance to use it. He also had a smile people could not resist. He sold lots of papers and was the best public-relations man we could have had. Besides selling on Fourteenth Street, he also ventured uptown, where he sold in front of Macy's and in front of the midtown church of St. Francis of Assisi on Thirty-first Street. One time he saw me on my way to midday Mass and began to yell, "Read the *Catholic Worker!* Romance on every page!" On another occasion he roared, "Read the *Catholic Worker*—and here comes the editor down the street."

An unemployed girl named Mary Sheehan who joined our group also had a taste for badinage. She made the most of her keen wit in selling papers, relishing her street-corner encounters. Once a comrade jeered at her, "I know your Cardinal! He gets drunk with his housekeeper every Saturday night."

Mary snapped back, "And doesn't that show how democratic he is!"

When there was too much of this sort of play going on, Peter would at first look a little puzzled. Then he would become withdrawn. "Too much kidding, too much joshing," he would say. When things got noisy around the office, he would wander off to Union Square to find someone else to listen to him.

That summer Peter performed with gusto his role as a troubadour of God. During dinner he talked—or rather he chanted—and his essays made a pleasant accompaniment to our meals.

One of them, "A Case for Utopia," which we printed later in our paper, is especially pertinent today:

> The world would be better off
> if people tried to become better,
> and people would become better
> if they stopped trying to become better off.
> For when everyone tries to become
> better off nobody is better off.
> But when everyone tries to become better

everybody is better off.
Everyone would be rich
if nobody tried to become richer,
and nobody would be poor
if everybody tried to be the poorest.
And everybody would be what he ought to be
if everybody tried to be
what he wants the other fellow to be.

Peter would go on to tell how Mirabeau said there were three ways to make a living—begging, stealing, and working. "But stealing is against the law of God and the law of man. Begging is against the law of man, but not against the law of God. Work, on the other hand, is against neither the law of God nor the law of man. But they say there is no work to do. There is *plenty* of work to do." His voice would rise, for this was a clarion call with Peter. "But there are no wages. Well, people do not need to work for wages. They can offer their services as a gift."

At first, Big Dan looked at Peter with astonishment. But noticing our own respectful attention, he ate—and, I think, listened. He heard Peter's ideas often enough to make them, however grudgingly, a part of his life. He never did quite get the idea of working without wages; his little income from selling the paper on the street meant a lot to him. He could tell his sister he was working for board and room, and he had a few coins now to jingle in his pocket.

"To work without wages!" Here was the saying that made people turn away, shrugging their shoulders. How hard this was to take! We none of us realized how much feeling of class war there was in our attitudes, how much resentment, how much readiness to assume that everyone was trying to take advantage of the worker, to get all he could out of him.

Even now I often think, "What an inspired attitude Peter took in his painful and patient indoctrination—and what a small part of it we accepted." He had the simplicity of an Alyosha, a Prince Mishkin. He accepted gratefully what people offered, finding plenty of work to do, always taking the least place—and serving others.

Navigating North Jersey by CPS
(Class Positioning System)

JENNIFER GILLAN

In my New Jersey hometown, the cool kids spent their weekend evenings cruising in their used Camaros and Chargers. This popular pastime involved driving aimlessly up and down the main drags of various suburban towns. Although I would have gladly participated had I been cool enough to be asked, I preferred driving purposefully and with a specific direction in mind. My destination was metaphorical—away from my working-class roots and the blue-collar town that broadcast my working-class origins.

A child of the post-war era of immigrant mobility, my mother made a dramatic jump from the working poor into the middle class. From her outsider's vantage point, the middle class was a singular entity. Coming of age in a blue-collar suburb, I learned of the complexity of the gradations within the working and middle class. Leaving behind the Italian immigrant ghetto in urban Paterson, my mother went to college and graduate school and then married a middle-class, fourth-generation Irish American. This trajectory, she believed, positioned her children as solidly middle class. When we interacted with kids outside our town, my brother and I were reminded that our status as working poor once removed made more difference to our class categorization than in whatever economic bracket my parents' tax return might have placed us. We would find that our young adulthood would not be marked by the kind of dramatic class catapulting many in my mother's generation experienced. Instead, we faced a slow climb through the various levels of the lower-middle and middle-middle class.

A popular children's record branded the 1970s as the "Free-to-Be-You-and-Me" decade, but we experienced it as an era of increasing conformity and class stagnation. No matter how far removed my mother believed our childhoods to be from hers, my brother and I found that the kids with a well-established middle-class pedigree perceived us as working class. Rooted neither in the working-poor Italian world into which my mother was born, nor the middle-class American world in which we had happened to live, my brother and I lived in the space between.

• • •

Just where we would be located on the class continuum was made more complicated by the irregularity of town and county borders in North Jersey. One main street in our town, for instance, is also a thoroughfare that begins at Paterson's Rent-a-Wreck, wedged on a bank of the polluted Passaic River, and ends after a stretch of Ridgewood houses that look as if they have appeared on the cover of *Martha Stewart Living*. In between, the street bisects blue-collar Hawthorne and middle-class Glen Rock. Of course, such simple class categorizations are misleading; although each town has a dominant class identity, each also includes some neighborhoods weighing in at different class levels. We even have a few streets of *Father Knows Best* colonials in the part of Hawthorne that is adjacent to Glen Rock, a town that has a few more upscale neighborhoods where it abuts Ridgewood. That village, in turn, has some mansions on its border with the wealthy enclave of HoHoKus. As the richest people I knew lived in these two towns, I would often say to anyone who was hazy about Jersey geography that I lived in a town near Ridgewood. I hoped they would assume mine was a clone of that upscale community or, better yet, confuse Hawthorne with HoHoKus.

Depending on how you look at it, Hawthorne is one town away from the urban blight of Paterson or one or two towns away from the suburban bliss of Glen Rock and Ridgewood. Hawthorne is the last town in the working-class county of Passaic, a proximity that to my mind made it practically part of the middle- to upper-middle-class county of Bergen. While Paterson is the city right next door, I never mentioned that fact to my college friends, stressing instead that Hawthorne is just thirty to forty minutes from Manhattan.

My desire to be associated with the towns on the higher end of the suburban spectrum manifested itself in the way I gave friends directions to our house. To get there from a major highway, they either had to take an indirect route that eventually ambled past Nabisco's suburban industrial park or a more direct urban one that snaked around the Marcal paper mill. If I chose the latter route, I would have to tell them that the bridge to Hawthorne was located "right after the Rent-a-Wreck and the Tip Top Tavern." Those urban poor landmarks were just a few of the gems they would have to pass as they navigated the bowels of Passaic County with its industrial sites and blue-collar towns. The most prominent landmark along the way would be Marcal, located as it was at the intersection of the local highway and the interstate. Rising up from below the interstate's elevated supports, Marcal asserted itself through its smokestack's frequent expulsions of noxious gases, making it seem rough, red-faced and ready to fight.

A major problem with this urban route was the fact that the Marcal exit was actually designated by a sign reading, "Paterson/ Hawthorne"; thus, if my friends went this way, the distinction I was hoping to maintain would collapse. As I wanted my visitors to see our house as closer to the middle-class suburbs, I obviously preferred the route that would lead them down a tree-lined highway and allow them to "take the Ridgewood exit after Nabisco." Perched pleasantly on a large grassy lot, the Nabisco "bakery," the daily producer of 400 lbs. of cookies, crackers, and snack foods, has nothing in common with the angry red brick factories in downtown Paterson. It is more like something that the 1970s architect dad on TV's *The Brady Bunch* would have designed. Without any visible smokestacks, Nabisco sugarcoats the production process by covering its factory with a coat of paint that resembles the super sweet buttercream icing on birthday party sheet cakes. With bands of baby blue accents as decoration, Nabisco's "Fair Lawn Bakery" is pure suburban confection. Perhaps its corporate leaders learned the strategy of emphasizing the fantastical over the actual from its competitor Keebler, whose trademark cookie-baking elves lived and worked in a hollow tree and were cuter and clearly more appealing to consumers than real factory workers and workplaces. Ernie Keebler, TV spokeself for The Hollow Tree: the Elfin Cookie and Cracker Corps., branded the cookies to be Uncommonly Good and a 1967 lyric assured consumers, "They're baked in magic ovens, and there's no factory. Hey!"

Although elfless, Nabisco is still a suburban-friendly factory, even adopting the color scheme of many of the tiled bathrooms in our neighborhood. Given how Nabisco's pleasant façade elides the mind-numbing labor that has taken place inside the factory, it was easy for me to imagine its production process as a more elaborate version of baking cookies with my mother. Making baked goods all day, the workers at Nabisco must have loved their jobs, or so I believed as a kid. No such fantasy could be spun about dark and gritty Marcal. The best I could do was to imagine it as a dragon of sorts, a fantasy encouraged by its sizzling neon red sign and synchronized spouting smokestacks. By my teens, I was no longer ignorant of the history of factory work that had almost slain my grandfather; I could recognize, therefore, that while my mother was the only one in her family who had done a stint at Marcal, the grim building was the same kind in which her parents labored away their adult lives.

• • •

These acts of redirection were my ways of steering people away from an awareness of my family history, attempts to bypass my connection to factories and workers. Of course, no matter what I did, I couldn't change the fact that my family was defined by the proximity of factories, both literally and familially.

With these generational and geographical ties to its factories, I found it almost impossible to distance myself from Paterson. Although it seemed like another country, downtown Paterson was less than a ten minute drive from our house. To get there, we had to cross the Passaic River, a place where my Italian grandfather once swam that had since been contaminated with industrial run-off. There were several bridges from which we could choose, but when I was a little kid my favorite was the steel girder one. I came to think of it as the road to Oz because on the Paterson side there was the door to a factory out of which would emerge fantastical creatures I called the bluemen. Employees of one of Paterson's dye works, these men did not become alive to me as workers until later. Seeing one of the bluemen was like spotting an elusive animal during a safari. They were often the color of the *Yellow Submarine* Blue Meanies. They didn't seem real to me and their position as exploited workers didn't register, although it should have given my own family history. When we crossed the rickety, clanking bridge leading into the factories, I didn't consider how blue dye seeped into the skin of these workingmen too poor for insurance and too precariously employed to accrue or take sick days. I was busy calculating the odds of spotting one. I had no idea what the bluemen did in that factory; nor did it occur to me to see Grandpa in them. His factory days had ended before I could remember. The Italians of his generation had either died or retired, and many of their children had moved up in the world—some to skilled blue-collar work and others to white collar professions. By the time I made these crossings with my mother, the Italian American factory workers had been replaced by immigrants and working poor of Black and Latino descent.

I am sure that the bluemen saw me only as a generic white suburban girl who stared at them out of the window of her mother's car—sealed and protected not only within the Blue Beetle, but also inside a safe, suburban world. I doubt they would have seen my mother as one of them either, as the sheen of color overlaying her skin was much less dramatic than theirs. While the brown and black skin beneath the blue dye corresponded to separate boxes on standard questionnaires, my mother checked "white," despite her olive skin. Of course, doing so did not immediately grant her access to all the aspects of white privilege. Her parents were immigrant factory hands and as a young woman she had also worked in the Marcal factory to earn money for college.

To secure a firmer lock on the white check box and to distance herself from the dye works and mills, my mother spent her college years seeking out suburban boyfriends whose homes were filled with factory-produced name-brand products, but whose minds had never contemplated the conditions under which the workers in such factories labored. My father was one of those boys from the leafy green suburbs. Together they would have children whose skin would give them a more solid claim on that white box.

My hold on that box was less firm than my mother assumed it would be. To shore it up, I felt the need to surround myself with other boxes—the kinds in which brand names were packaged. While I eventually learned that *Kleenex* was better than Marcal, my fondness for Nabisco baked goods never faded. My working-class origins never did either.

Despite my mother's attempts at putting some distance between her children and factories, they still defined my childhood. It wasn't that we could see them from our house, but rather that although we couldn't, the smell still lingered. It was not the infamous stench of New Jersey's industrial sectors or even the sweet combination of cocoa and vanilla that sometimes did waft over our neighborhood and make us hungry for Nabisco's *Chips Ahoy!*; rather, it is a metaphoric odor, a residue of sorts that seeped into me sometime in childhood and lingered long after I left those suburban streets behind. Wherever I went, my lack of distance from factory work seemed to be sniffed out by the class-conscious kids in the upper-middle-class worlds into which college had propelled me. Even if I stocked my shelves with the brand names that pronounced my conformity to cookie-cutter middle class American tastes, they immediately picked up the scent of my familial factory ties.

It wasn't until I became a scholarship student at an elite college that I really understood what people meant by "the smell of money." I know the phrase is not supposed to refer to specific smells, but rather to an aura that comes from careful social training and a seemingly innate ability to glide gracefully through all worldly negotiations. My experience of the "smell of money" was more literal and had everything to do with a person's consumption of brand name products. Money smelled like *Tide*-scented clothes that were always *Downy* soft; *Crest* white teeth bathed in minty and *Herbal Essences* hair that made people want to say, *"Gee Your Hair Smells Terrific."* My family used none of these products. Being barely one generation removed from factory work meant that our pantry was stocked with a lot of plain white boxes whose only ornamentation was their black lettered product names. In our pantry the s-a-l-t-i-n-e-s and s-a-l-t, and other generics outnumbered the name-brand packages; although, my brother and I often did lobby successfully for boxes of *Captain Crunch* and *Quisp* cereal.

Somewhere in the aisles of *Stop & Shop* I learned to shift my allegiance from people to products, experiencing class not in terms of labor and production, but in relation to leisure and consumption. I felt stamped by the

Good Housekeeping seal of approval when I ate *Pepperidge Farm* boxed 3-layer cakes at my American grandmother's no matter how inferior they tasted to my Italian grandma's plain cakes covered in a simple mixture of anisette, almond extract, and confectioner's sugar. I even loved the bowls of *Spaghetti Os* that my American grandmother dished out despite the fact that my Italian grandma spoiled me with homemade Italian pasta. The only explanation for how a kid whose taste buds delighted in the flavors of vine-ripe tomatoes and freshly picked basil could also have savored *Spaghetti Os* was that it wasn't bitter tomato ketchup that I tasted, but rather the sweetness of name-brand acceptance. Eating processed food made me feel deliciously ordinary and satisfyingly middle class.

To my eternal shame, I could only offer my private love to my cookie- and cake-baking Italian grandma, while I pledged my public allegiance to my American grandmother as she served me plates of *Vienna Fingers* and pie tins filled with *M&Ms*. Even though today they sell them in the gourmet section of the supermarket, Grandma's anisette balls were definitely not cookies that any self-respecting kid would pluck out of her *Brady Bunch* lunch box in the school cafeteria. Although at 4' 10", Grandma was elf-like, she could never make cookies that would silently brand me with the Keebler elves' seal of uncommon goodness. I learned early that a lunch box stocked with brand name cookies put you on the ground floor of the grammar school social hierarchy. Of course, your ascent to higher levels involved other factors and a houseful of brand names, but you weren't even in the building if your family ate homemade or bought generic. Instead, you found yourself perpetually on the outside looking in, consigned with the other generic kids to the bargain basement annex.

Believing it was the only way I could ever get inside, I denied my familial connection to my Italian working-poor grandparents and their immigrant garden, to Marcal and the factories, silk mills, and ghettos of Paterson. Transforming myself into a *Brady Bunch* American would, I assumed when I was a teenager, be as easy as sending my friends on the Nabisco route to our house.

• • •

Whether you take the suburban or the urban route to Hawthorne, you have to cross Diamond Bridge, a structure that is less a bridge than a stretch of road elevated to accommodate the train tracks that link Ridgewood, Glen Rock, Hawthorne, and Paterson. Aptly named, Diamond Bridge is indicative of the view of my grandparents and other immigrants like them that

Hawthorne was a land of riches. Acquiring the down payment necessary to relocate there would be the crowning achievement in their hardworking lives, thereby, guaranteeing a clear and brilliant future for their children. Once on the Hawthorne side, they believed that all distances would be bridgeable.

• • •

I crossed over but have never gotten to the other side. Even though I have long since moved away from my blue-collar home town, leaving behind its pastimes, décor, and dialect, I still bear its identity marks.

I like to believe that I have mostly rid myself of my Jersey accent, but people always seem to pick it out. Having worked since college on refining my speech, I have at least learned how to control my pronunciation of Hawthorne. Everyone who lives there calls it "Whore-thorn," but I stress the first syllable instead, adding a Midwestern inflection and carefully enunciating it as "Haw-thorne." I usually add "like Nathaniel Hawthorne," as if it were a quaint New England village rather than a blue-collar town desperate to put some more distance between itself and working-poor Paterson.

from *Bound for Glory*

WOODY GUTHRIE

CHAPTER XI: BOY IN SEARCH OF SOMETHING

I was thirteen when I went to live with a family of thirteen people in a two-room house. I was going on fifteen when I got me a job shining shoes, washing spittoons, meeting the night trains in a hotel up in town. I was a little past sixteen when I first hit the highway and took a trip down around the Gulf of Mexico, hoeing figs, watering strawberries, picking mustang grapes, helping carpenters and well drillers, cleaning yards, chopping weeds, and moving garbage cans. Then I got tired of being a stranger, so I stuck my thumb in the air again and landed back in the old home town, Okemah.

I found me a job at five dollars a week in a push-button service station. I got a letter twice a week as regular as a clock from Papa out on the Texas plains. I told him everything I thought and he told me everything he was hoping. Then, one day, he wrote that his burns had healed up enough for him to go to work, and he'd got him a job managing a whole block of property in Pampa, Texas.

In three days I was standing in the little office shaking his hand, talking old times, and all about my job with him as general handyman around the property. I was just past my seventeenth birthday.

Pampa was a Texas oil boom town and wilder than a woodchuck. It traveled fast and traveled light. Oil boom towns come that way and they go that way. Houses aren't built to last very long, because the big majority of the working folks will walk into town, work like a horse for a while, put the oil wells in, drill the holes down fifteen thousand feet, bring in the black gushers, case off the hot flow, cap the high pressure, put valves on them, get the oil to flowing steady and easy into the rich people's tanks, and then the field, a big thick forest of drilling rigs, just sets there pumping oil all over the world to run limousines, factories, war machines, and fast trains. There's not much work left to do in the oil fields once the boys have developed it by hard work and hot sweat, and so they move along down the road, as broke, as down and out, as tough, as hard hitting, as hard working, as the day they come to town.

The town was mainly a scattering of little old shacks. They was built to last a few months; built out of old rotten boards, flattened oil barrels, buckets, sheet iron, crates of all kinds, and gunny sacks. Some were lucky enough to have a floor others just the dusty old dirt. The rent was high on these shacks. A common price was five dollars a week for a three roomer. That meant one room cut three ways.

Women folks worked hard trying to make their little shacks look like something, but with the dry weather, hot sun, high wind, and the dust piling in, they could clear and wipe and mop and scrub their shanty twenty-four hours a day and never get caught up. Their floors always was warped and crooked. The old linoleum rugs had raised six families and put eighteen kids through school. The walls were made out of thin boards, one inch thick and covered over with whatever the women could nail on them: old blue wallpaper, wrapping paper from the boxcars along the tracks, once in a while a layer of beaver board painted with whitewash, or some haywire color ranging from deep-sea blue through all of the midnight blues to a blazing red that would drive a Jersey bull crazy. Each family usually nailed together some sort of a chair or bench out of junk materials and left it in the house when they moved away, so that after an even thirty-five cents worth of hand-made wash benches, or an old chair, or table had been left behind, the landlord hired a sign painter to write the word "Furnished" on the "For Rent" sign.

Lots of folks in the oil fields come in from the country. They heard about the high wages and the great number of jobs. The old farm has dried up and blowed away. The chickens are gone dry and the cows have quit laying. The wind has got high and the sky is black with dust. Blow flies are taking the place over, licking off the milk pails, falling into the cream, getting hung up in the molasses. Besides that, they ain't no more work to do on the farm; can't buy no seed for planting, nor feed for the horses and cows.

Hell, I can work. I like to work. Born working. Raised working. Married working. What kind of work do they want done in this oil boom town? If work is what they want done, plowing or digging or carrying something, I can do that. If they want a cellar dug or some dirt moved, I can do that. If they want some rock hauled and some cement shoveled, I can do that. If they want some boards sawed and some nails drove, hell's bells, I can do that. If they want a tank truck drove, I can do that, too, or if they want some steel towers bolted up, give me a day's practice, and I can do that. I could get pretty good at it. And I wouldn't quit. Even if I could, I wouldn't want to.

Hell with this whole dam layout! I'm a-gonna git up an' hump up, an' walk off of this cussed dam place I Farm, toodle-do. Here I come, oil town! Hundred mile down that big wide road.

Papa's new job was the handling of an old ramshackle rooming house, right on the main street; built out of corrugated iron on a framework of two by four scantlings, and cut up into little stalls called rooms. You couldn't hardly lay down to sleep in your room without your head scraping the wall at one end and your feet sticking out in the hall. You could hear what was taking place in the six stalls all around you, and it was a pretty hard matter to keep your mind on your own business for trying to listen in on the rooms on each side of you. The beds made so much racket it sounded like some kind of a factory screaking. But there was a rhythm and a song in the scraping and the oil boom chasers called it "the rusty bedspring blues." I got so good at this particular song that I could rent a flop in a boom-town hotel, and go to my room and just set there and listen a minute, and then guess within three pounds of the other roomers' weight, just by the squeek of the springs.

My dad run one of these houses. He tended to a block of property where girls rented rooms: the girls that follow the booms. They'd come in to look for work, and they'd hit the rooming house so as to set up a home, and straighten out their citizenship papers with the pimps, the McGimps, the other girls, and the old satchels that acted as mothers of the flock. One of Papa's boarders, for instance, was an old lady with gray hair dyed as red as the side of a brick barn, and her name was Old Rose. Only there never was a rose that old. She'd been in all of the booms, Smackover, Arkansas, Cromwell, Oklahoma, Bristow, Drumright, Sand Springs, Bow Legs, and on to East Texas, Kilgore, Longview, Henderson, then west to Burke-Burnett, Wichita Falls, Electra, and farther west, out on the windy plains, around Panhandle. Amarillo, and Pampa. It was a thriving business, boom chasing; and this old rusty sheet-iron rooming house could have been in any of these towns, and so could Old Rose.

Come to think of it, I've been in every one of these towns. I might of slept in this old rooming house a dozen times around over the country, and it was awful high-priced sleeping. I might of paid out a lot of them sheets of iron. And the girls that stayed here, they might of paid out a truck load or two of them two by fours. The usual price is about five dollars a week. If a girl is working, that is not so much, but if she's out of a job, it's a lot of money. She knows that the officers might grab her by the arm any time for "Vag," for it's a jail house offense to be a-loafing in a boom town.

I remember one little girl that come in from the country. She blowed into town one day from some thriving little church community, and she wasn't what you'd call a good looking girl, but she wasn't ugly. Sort of plump, but she wasn't a bit fat. She'd worked hard at washing milk buckets, doing housework, washing the family's clothes. She could milk an old Jersey cow. Her face and her hands looked like work. Her room in the rooming house wasn't big enough to spank a cat in. She moved in, straightened it up, and gave it a sweeping and a dusting that is headline news in a oil boom town. Then she washed the old faded window curtains, changed the bed and dresser around every way to see how it looked best, and tacked pretty pictures on her wall.

She didn't have any extra clothes with her. I wondered why; something went haywire at home, maybe. Maybe she left home in a hurry. Guess that's what she done. She just thought she'd come into town and go to work in a café or hotel or in some body's house, and then when she got her first week's pay, she'd get what things she needed, and add to them as she went along. She wasn't a town girl. You could tell that. Everything about her looked like the farm, and the outhouses and barns, and the pastures, and wide-open spaces, and the cattle grazing, and the herds of sheep, or like looking out across the plains and seeing a hard-working cowhand rolling down across the country on a fat bay mare. Some way or another, her way of talking and the words that she knew just didn't seem to connect up with this oil-smeared, gasoline-soaked, whiskey-flavored, wild and fast-moving boom town. No cattle; no milk buckets. Nothing about raising an early garden, or putting on a big-brim straw hat and driving a speckled mare and a black hoss to a hay rake. I guess she was just a little bit lost. The other girls flocked in to see her, walking on high-heel shoes, with a bottle or two of fingernail paint, some cigarets, different flavors of lipstick, and a half a pint of pale corn whiskey. They jabbered and talked a blue streak. They giggled and snickered, and hollered, Oh, Kid, this, and Oh, Kid, that. Everything they said was funny and new, and she would set, listen, soak it all in, but she didn't talk much. She didn't know much to talk about. Didn't smoke, and didn't know how to use that fingernail paint. Hadn't seen the picture show lately. Once in a great while she'd get up and walk across the floor and straighten up something that had got pushed over, or remark that she had to scrape the grease and dirt off of her two-burner hot plate.

When the girls had gone off to their rooms, she'd take a good look around over her room to see if it was neat enough, and if it was she'd sometimes take a little walk down the old dark hall, out into the back yard that stood about ankle deep in junk and garbage. You'd run onto her every once in a while out there. You'd catch her with a handful of old sacks and papers, carrying them in a high north wind out to the alley to put them in the trash box; sometimes she'd smile at you and say, "I just thought I'd pick up a few of these papers."

She's thinking it's over a week now since I paid my room rent. Wonder what the landlord will do? Wonder if I'd grab the broom and pitch in and sweep out the hall, and go and carry a few buckets of water and mop it, wonder if he'd care? Maybe it'll get under his skin, and he might give me a job of keeping it up.

She'd come to the office where Papa was, and she'd set down and turn through the magazines and papers, looking at all of the pictures. She liked to look at pictures of the mountains. Sometimes she'd look at a picture for two or three minutes. And then she'd say, "I'd like to be there."

She'd stand up and look out the window. The building was just one story. It was all right down on the ground. The sidewalk went past the door, and all of the oil field boys would crowd up and down the street, talking, staggering, in their work clothes, khaki pants and shirts smeared with crude oil, blue overhalls soaked with grease and covered with thick dust, salted and flavored with sweat. They made good money. The drillers drawed as high as twenty-five dollars a day. Boy, that was a lot of money. They wasted most of it. Whooped it off on slot machines and whiskey. Fights broke out every few minutes up and down the street. She could see the mob gang up. She could see a couple of heads bobbing up and down and going around in the middle. Pretty soon everybody would be beating the hound out of everybody else, choked, wet with blood and hot sweat. You could hear them breathing and cussing a block away. Then the fight would bust up and the men would come down the sidewalk, their clothes tore all to pieces, hats lost, hair full of mud and dirt, whiskey broke.

She was new in town, I knew that because she held back a little when a fist fight broke out. She just didn't much want to jump into that crazy river of oil field fist fighters. She might have liked it if she'd known the people better, but she didn't know anybody well enough to call them friend. It was plumb dangerous for a strange girl even to go from one joint to the other looking for a job, so she waited till her money was all gone and her room rent was about two weeks behind. Then she went to a few places and asked for work. They didn't need her. She wasn't experienced. She went back several times. They still didn't need her. She was flat.

She got acquainted with a one-eyed girl. The one-eyed girl introduced her to a truck driver. The truck driver said he might find her a job. He would come in every day from the fields with a yarn about a job that he was trying to get her. The first few days they usually met in the office or hall and he would tell her all about it. But he'd have to wait another day or two to see for sure. The day come along when they didn't happen to meet in the office or hall, so he had to go to her room to tell her about something else that looked like a job for her. He made this a regular habit for about a week and she turned up at the office one day with seven dollars and fifty cents to pay on her rent. This was a big surprise to my dad, so he got curious. In fact he stayed curious. So he thought he would do a little eavesdropping around over the hotel to see what was going on. One day he saw her go off uptown with the one-eyed girl. In about an hour they come back with their hats in their hands, brushing their hair back out of their eyes, talking and saying that they was awful tired. The one-eyed girl took her down the hall and they went into a room. Papa tiptoed down to the door and looked through the keyhole. He could see everything that was going on. The one-eyed girl took out a teaspoon and put something in it. He knew then what it was. The girl struck a match and held it under the spoon, and heated it real hot. That's one way of fixing a shot of dope—morphine. Sometimes you use a needle, sometimes you sniff it, sometimes you eat it, sometimes you drink it. The main idea seems to be any old way to get it into your system.

He pushed the door open and run in while they was trying to take the dope. He grabbed the works away from the one-eyed girl and bawled both of them out good and proper, telling how terrible it was to get on the stuff. They cried and bawled and talked like a couple of little babies, and swore up and down that neither of them used it regular, they didn't have the habit. They just bought it for fun. They didn't know. The girl from the country never tasted it. She swore that she never would. They all talked and cried some more and promised never to touch the junk again.

But I stayed around there. I noticed how that girl with the one eye would come and go, and come and go, feeling one minute like she was the queen of the whole wide world, all smiles, laughing and joking; and then she'd go and come again, and she'd be all fagged out, tired and footsore, broke, hungry, lonesome, blue, and her eyes sunk way back, her hair tangled. This kept up after Dad took away her morphine apparatus, and after all of her big promises to layoff the stuff. The farm girl never showed the least signs of being on dope, but the truck driver brought a little bottle of whiskey along with him after he got to knowing her better, and through the partition I heard them drinking.

467

Mister truck driver ate his meals in a little greasy wall restaurant right next door. He introduced her to the boss of the joint, a man with TB, about six foot four inches tall, skinny and humped as a spider. He had studied to be a preacher, read most of the books on the subject, and was bootlegging liquor in his eating place.

He gave the girl a job in the kitchen of this place, where she done all of her work, his work, and run over two or three swampers and helpers trying to keep the place from falling down, and all of the boards on the roof, and all of the meals cooked and served. It was so hot I don't see how she stood it. I more or less went into and out of these places because Papa was looking after them. Personally, I never have been able to figure out how anybody ate, slept, or lived around in this whole firetrap.

He give her one dollar a day to hang around there. He didn't call it a job, so he didn't have to pay her much. But he said if she wanted to hang around, he'd pitch her a dollar every night just to show her that his heart was on the right side.

The whole rooming house had been added onto a little at a time by moving old odd shacks onto the lot, till it had about fifty stalls. None of them were ever painted. Like a bunch of match-boxes strung along; and some of them housed whole families with gangs of kids, and others sheltered several men in one room where there was fifteen or twenty cots in a one-bed space, dirty, bed-buggy, slick, slimy, and otherwise not fit to live in or around.

It was my job to show folks to their rooms, and show the rooms to the people, and try to convince them that they was really rooms. One day when I was out bungling around with a mattress and a set of rusty bed springs, I chanced to hear a couple having more or less of a two-cylinder celebration in one of the rooms.. I knew that the room was supposed to be vacant. Nobody was registered in there. The door was shut and the thumb-latch was throwed. I had a sneaking idea of what was up.

Through a knothole in the shack, I saw a half a pint of hot whiskey setting up on the old dirty dresser, and it was about eighty-nine percent drunk up. The bed didn't have a sheet on it, or any kind of covers, just the bare mattress. It was a faded pink mixed with a running brownish green, trimmed around with a bed-bug tan color soaked into the cloth. The TB boss of the little café and the bootleg store was setting on the side of the bed with the country girl. Both of them had had a few out of the bottle. He was talking to her and what he said had been said too often before by other men like him to put into quote. You've had lots of trouble lately, haven't you? You look kinda sad. Even when you smile or laugh, it stays in your eyes. It never goes away. I've noticed it a lot since you've been around me lately. You're a good girl. I've read lots of books and studied about people. I know.

She said she liked to work.

He told her that she had a pretty face.

You got pretty eyes, even if they are sad. They're blue. Sad and blue.

She said she wasn't feeling so bad now since she had a job.

He said he wished that he could pay her more than a dollar. He said she made a good hand. He didn't feel like working very hard. It was too hot for him in his condition with the low roof.

I could hear him breathe and could hear the rattling in his lungs. His face was pale, and when he rubbed his hand over his chin the red blood would show through his skin. He said, I feel better when I got you around.

She said that she was going to buy a few little things.

Where do your folks live at? Must have run away from home once. Tell me what caused it.

Her family lived thirty-five miles away in Mobeetie. Thirty-five or forty miles. She never did know just how far. Times got hard. And the farm gets awful lonesome when the sun comes up or when it goes down. A family argument got started and she got mad at her folks. So she bought a bus ticket. Hit the oil fields. Heard lots about oil fields. Said they paid good wages, find always was needing somebody to work in them.

You've got a job right where you are. Just as long as you want it. I know you'll learn as you keep working. I don't think my dollar is entirely wasted. This fall is going to be good, and you'll know my business better, and I'll pay you better. We'll get an old man to be dishwasher. It's too much for you when business get rushing.

Her hand was resting on the mattress and he looked down at it and said, "It looks nice and clean, and I don't want the strong lye soap and the hot dishwater to make it all red and dry the skin out. Cause it to chap. Break open. Bleed." He put his hand on hers and give it a good friendly squeeze. He rubbed real slow up and down her arm with the back of his hand just barely touching her skin, and they stopped talking. Then he took her hand and folded his fingers between hers and pulled her hand from the mattress and took the weight from her arm in such a way that she fell back across the bed. He held her hand and he bent over and kissed her. And then he kissed her again. They kept their mouths together for a long time. He rolled over against her, and she rolled up against him. She had good firm muscles on her shoulders and her back, and he felt each one of them, going from one to the other. Her green café uniform was fresh washed and ironed so that it shined

469

where the light struck it, and where it curved to fit her body. Several times be rubbed across the belt that tied in a big bow knot above her hips and be pulled the sash and the knot came loose. The uniform started coming open a little at the front and by the touch of his hand he laid it half open almost without her knowing it. His hands was long and his fingers was slim and he'd turned the pages of lots of books, and he took the first two long fingers of his right hand and caught the thickness of the uniform between them, and with a twist of his wrist he turned the rest of the dress back. He played and felt of both of her breasts, his fingers walking from first one and then the other like some kind of a big white spider. His TB caused him to make a loud spitty noise when be breathed in and out, and he was breathing faster all of the time.

I heard the sound of somebody's feet walking down the old boardwalk, and I took a quick glance down and out of the door, and saw some body's shadow coming. I was standing on the steel frame of an iron folding cot, and I jumped down from my lookout for a minute. It was my dad. He said he had to go to the bank and for me to come and watch the office. There was a couple there to look at a room and the room had to be fixed up before they moved in. Needed linens. I stood there for about ten seconds not saying a thing. My dad looked sort of funny at me. I didn't let on. Lust stood there straining my ears through that wall, and wondering what I was a-missing. But, shucks, I knew. Yeah, I knew, it was just exactly like all of the rest of them, and I wasn't a-missing out on nothing.

About thirty minutes later and along about dark, after the couple had been well rented and well roomed, and the linens had been put on for them, I took a flying high dive back out to the old board wall and knothole and climbed up and took a last look. But they had left. Nothing left to tell the tale but the prints of her hips sunk way down deep in the mattress.

• • •

I'll never feel as funny as the day I walked into the office and found Papa behind the flowery curtain, setting on the edge of the bed holding his face in his hands.

"Matter?" I asked him.

His finger pointed to the top of the dresser, and I found a check made out to me for a dollar and fifty cents.

At first I grinned and said, "Guess mebbe it's some o' my oil money a-rollin' in."

My blood turned to cold slush oil when my eyes saw on the corner of the check the name and address of the Insane Asylum in Norman, Oklahoma.

I set down by the side of Papa and put my arm around him.

The letter said that Nora B. Guthrie had died some days ago. Her death was a natural death. Because she only knew my address in Okemah, they were sending me the balance of her cash account.

Papa was wiping his eyes red with his knuckles, trying to quit crying. I patted him on the back and held the check down between my knees, reading it again.

I walked over across the tracks, uptown to the bank, not wanting to cash the check in our neighborhood. The man in the bank window could tell by my face that I was nervous and scared, and everybody standing in line was anxious for me to move on out of their way. I seen their hands full of checks, pink, tan, yellow, and blue ones. My face turned a pale and sickly color, and my throat was just a wadding of dry cotton, and my eyes got hazy, and my whole life went through my head. It took every muscle in my body to pick up that dollar bill and fifty-cent piece. Somewhere on the outskirts of town, a high whining fire whistle seemed to be blowing.

• • •

I got a job selling root beer. It was just a big barrel with a coil running around inside of it, and it cost you a nickel for me to pull the handle, unless you was a personal friend of mine, in which case I'd draw you off a mug free.

Prohibition was on and folks seemed like they were dry. The first day that I was there, the boss come around and said, "Oh, here's your day's pay. We pay every day here, because we may have to close up any day. Business is rushing and good right now, but nobody can tell.

"Another thing I want to show you is about this little door right down here under the counter. You see this little door? Well, you push this trigger right here, just like that, and then you see the door comes open. Then you see inside. There's some little shelves. On these little shelves, as I suppose you see, are some little bottles. These little bottles are two ounces. They are fifty cents a bottle. They are a patented medicine, I think, and it's called Jamaica Ginger, or plain Jake-a mixture of ginger and alcohol. The alcohol is about ninety-nine percent. So now, in case anybody comes in with their thumbnail busted or ankle sprung, or is snake bit, or has got ancestors, or the hoof and mouth disease, or is otherwise sick and has got fifty cents cash money on him, get the fifty cents and then reach down here and give him one of these little bottles of Jake. Be sure to put the money in the register."

While I worked there only about a month, I saved up four dollars, and to boot I got an inside view of what the human race was drinking.

You couldn't tell any more about the rot-gut called whiskey than you could about the Jake. It was just about as poison. Lots of people fell over dead and was found scattered here and yonder with different kinds of whiskey poisoning. I hated prohibition on that account. I hated it because it was killing people, paralyzing them, and causing them to die like flies. I've seen men set around and squeeze that old pink canned heat through an old dirty rag, get the alcohol drained out of it, and then drink it down. The papers carried tales about the men that drunk radiator alcohol and died from—rust poisoning. Others came down with the beer head. That's where your head starts swelling up and it just don't quit. Usually you take the beer head from drinking home brew that ain't made right, or is fermented in old rusty cans, like garbage cans, oil drums, gasoline barrels, and slop buckets. It caused some of the people to die. They even had a kind of beer called Old Chock that was made by throwing everything under the sun into an old barrel, adding the yeast and sugar and water to it, and letting her go. Biscuit heels, corn-bread scraps, potato leavings, and all sorts of table scraps went into this beer. It IS a whitish, milky, slicky-looking bunch of crap. But especially down in Oklahoma I've seen men drive fifteen miles out in the country just to get a hold of a few bottles of it. The name Chock come from the Choctaw Indians. I guess they just naturally wanted to celebrate some way or another, and thought a little drink would fire them up so's they'd break loose, forget their worries, and have a good time.

When I was behind the counter, men would come in and purchase bay rum, and I'd get a look into their puffy, red-speckled faces, and their bleary, batty eyes, that looked but didn't see, and that went shut, but never slept, that closed, but never rested, and dreamed but never arrived at a conclusion. I would see a man come in and buy a bottle of rubbing alcohol, and then buy a bottle of coke and go out and mix it half and half, hold his breath, wheeze for a few seconds, and then waddle on away.

One day my curiosity licked me. I said that I was going to taste a bottle of that Jake for myself. Man ought to be interested. I drawed up about a half a mug of root beer. It was cold and nice, and I popped the little stopper out of one of the Jake bottles, and poured the Jake into the root beer. When that Jake hit that beer, it commenced to cook it, and there was seven civil wars and two revolutions broke out inside of that mug. The beer was trying to tame the Jake down and the Jake was trying to eat the beer up. They sizzled and boiled and sounded about like bacon frying. The Jake was chasing the little bubbles and the little bubbles was chasing the Jake, and the beer spun like a whirlpool in a big swift river. It went around and around so fast that it made a little funnel right in the middle. I waited about twenty minutes for it to settle down. Finally it was about the color of a new tan saddle, and about as quiet as it would get. So I bent over it and stuck my ear down over the mug. It was spewing and crackling like a machine gun, but I thought I'd best to drink it before it turned into a waterspout or a dust storm. I took it up and took it down, and it was hot and dry and gingery and spicy, and cloudy, and smooth, and windy and cold, and threatening rain or snow. I took another big swallow and my shirt come unbuttoned and my insides burnt like I was pouring myself full of home-made soapy dishwater. I drank it all down, and when I woke up I was out of a job.

from *Rivethead*

BEN HAMPER

PROLOGUE

D ead rock stars are singin' for me and the boys on the Rivet Line tonight. Hendrix. Morrison. Zeppelin. The Dead Rock Star catalog churnin' outta Hogjaw's homemade boom box. There's Joplin and Brian Jones and plenty of Lynyrd Skynyrd. Dead Rock Stars full of malice and sweet confusion. Tonight and every night they bawl. The Dead Rock Stars yowling at us as we kick out the quota.

We're all here. Department 07, Blazer/Suburban Line—factory outpost FF-15 stenciled in black spray paint on the big iron girder behind Dougie's workbench. We're building expensive trucks for the General Motors Corp. We've come back once again to tussle with our parts and to hear the Dead Rock Stars harmonize above the industrial din.

The music of the Dead Rock Stars bursts from a ledge on Dougie's workbench—our hideaway for Hogjaw's stereo. Just before the start of every shift, Dougie goes through the complicated ritual of threading the cords and speaker wires from the stereo down a hollow leg in his workbench and into the plug at the base of the water fountain behind his job. The camouflage must be perfect. It is against company policy to use a General Motors electrical outlet as a source to summon up Dead Rock Stars. Only battery-powered radios are allowed.

Originally Hogjaw complied with this rule. It wasn't easy. Due to the enormous power demand of his radio creation, the Jaw was forced to lug a car battery into work with him every shift. You would see him strainin' his way through the parking lot every afternoon, a lunch bucket curled under one arm and his trusty Delco Weatherbeater hoisted on top of his other shoulder. Trailing behind him would be a couple of riveters with their arms locked around the speaker boxes—pallbearers bringin' around the tombs of the Dead Rock Stars.

This went on for a month or so before the security guards decided to halt the parade. Car batteries were declared illegal. Apparently the guards had concluded that it was a mighty dangerous precedent to allow workers to enter the plant premises with the batteries of their automobiles stashed on their shoulders. After all, whose heads would be in the vise if one of these sonic blasters pulled an overload up on the assembly line and spewed a load of battery acid into the eyes and ears of the screw brigade? Dead Rock Stars? Dead Shoprats? Not on *my* goddamn beat.

As for the popularity of Dead Rock Stars on the Rivet Line, I've settled upon this private theory. The music of the Dead Rock Stars is redundant and completely predictable. We've heard their songs a million times over. In this way, the music of the Dead Rock Stars infinitely mirrors the drudgery of our assembly jobs. Since assembly labor is only a basic extension of high school humdrum, it only stands to reason that the same wearied hepsters who used to dodge economics class for a smoke in the boys' room would later in life become fossilized to the hibernatin' sound tracks of their own implacable youth. Let the eggheads in economics have David Byrne and Laurie Anderson. The rivetheads be needin' their "Purple Haze" and "Free Bird" just like tomorrow needs today.

It's mob rule, and the mob demands Dead Rock Stars in their choir loft. Of course this arrangement provides for a fair amount of bitching from line-mates in our area who hold no sacred allegiance to the songs of the rockin' deceased.

For example, there's Dick, the left-side rear spring man. He works directly across from Dougie, travelin' a nightly path that requires him to take the max-imum dose of Dead Rock Star thud. It's nothing unusual to spot Dick takin' a deep drag from one of his ever-present Winstons while gazin' head-on into the boom box with this buggered glint in his eye and this twisted grimace on his face that almost pleads aloud for some kind of transistor malfunction, tweeter meltdown or any other variety of holy intervention.

Eddie and Jehan prefer rap music. On occasion, Jehan brings in his own battery-powered blaster and engages in this furious battle-of-the-blare with Hogjaw's almighty boom box. The Kings of Rap vs. The Dead Rock Stars vs. The Steady Clang of Industry. It makes for quite the raucous stew—sorta like pluggin' your head into the butt end of a Concorde during acceleration mode.

Management's stance on all of this usually boils down to a simple mat-ter of see no evil, hear no evil. If the guy in the tie can't actually *see* the vis-ible evidence of how you're wastin' millions of corporate dollars, he's most often inclined to let the music flow. It keeps him off the hook. He doesn't have to play killjoy. He can dummy up and pretend that all those guitar solos he hears screechin' through the middle of the night are only happy by-products of a contented work force. His boss will love him, his wife will love him, his men will like him and the Company will somehow stagger on. Industry on the march. Bravo!

But even in victory, there's often a price to pay. Let us not forget that General Motors has already informed the work force that there won't be any profit sharing to spread around this year. Too much waste. Too many buyouts. Too few pennies. And I imagine those damn utility bills are way out of sight too.

Oh well, what can I say? I'm just sitting here waiting for the next chassis to arrive. I'm tapping my toes to the beat of the Dead Rock Stars. Ten feet to my right, I can hear the trickle of untold billions bein' sucked outta the corporate coffers through the base of the water fountain behind Dougie's workbench.

I'm thinking that rock stars, even dead ones, don't come cheap.

CHAPTER 1

I was seven years old the first time I ever set foot inside an automobile factory. The occasion was Family Night at the old Fisher Body plant in Flint where my father worked the second shift.

General Motors provided this yearly intrusion as an opportunity for the kin of the work force to funnel in and view their fathers, husbands, uncles and granddads as they toiled away on the assembly line. If nothing else, this annual peepshow lent a whole world of credence to our father's daily grumble. The assembly line did indeed stink. The noise was very close to intolerable. The heat was one complete bastard. Little wonder the old man's socks always smelled like liverwurst bleached for a week in the desert sun.

For my mother, it was at least one night out of the year when she could verify the old man's whereabouts. One night a year when she could be reasonably assured that my father wasn't lurchin' over a pool table at the Patio Lounge or picklin' his gizzard at anyone of a thousand beer joints out of Dort Highway. My father loved his drink. He wasn't nearly as fond of labor.

On this night, the old man was present. I remember my mother being relieved. If he hadn't been there, it would have been difficult for her to explain to my little brother and me why we had made this exhaustive trek through Satan's playpen just to ogle a bunch of oily strangers and their grinnin' lineage.

After a hundred wrong turns and dead ends, we found my old man down on the trim line. His job was to install windshields using this goofy apparatus with large suction cups that resembled an octopus being crucified.

476

A car would nuzzle up to the old man's work area and he would be waiting for it, a cigarette dangling from his lip, his arms wrapped around the windshield contraption as if it might suddenly rebel and bolt off for the ocean. Car, windshield. Car, windshield. Car, windshield. No wonder my father preferred playin' hopscotch with barmaids. This kind of repetition didn't look like any fun at all.

And here, all of this time, I had assumed that Dad just built the vehicles all by his lonesome. I always imagined that building adult cars was identical to building cars in model kits. You were given a large box with illustrated directions, a clutter of fenders, wheels and trunk lids, and some hip-high vat of airplane glue. When one was finished, you simply motioned to some boss-type in the aisle: "Hey, bring me another kit and make it a god damn Corvette this time!"

We stood there for forty minutes or so, a miniature lifetime, and the pattern never changed. Car, windshield. Car, windshield. Drudgery piled atop drudgery. Cigarette to cigarette. Decades rolling through the rafters, bones turning to dust, stubborn clocks gagging down flesh, another windshield, another cigarette, wars blinking on and off, thunderstorms muttering the alphabet, crows on power lines asleep or dead, that mechanical octopus squirming against nothing, nothing, NOTHINGNESS. I wanted to shout at my father "Do something else!" Do something else or come home with us or flee to the nearest watering hole. DO SOMETHING ELSE! Car, windshield. Car, windshield. Christ, no.

Thank God that, even at age seven, I knew what I was going to be when I grew up. There wouldn't be any car-windshield cha-cha awaiting me. I was going to be an ambulance driver, the most glamorous calling in the world. I would spend my days zooming from one mangled calamity to the next. I would have full license to poke my face into the great American bucket seat bloodfest. The metallic crunch, the spiderweb of cracked glass (no doubt installed by my zombied father), the stupid eyeballs of the ripped and ravaged, the blood and guts of the accordion carnage. Ah, yes. To engage the sweet wail of the sirens. To scoop teeth from out of the dashboard. That would be the life. Everything my mother insisted we avoid when we passed a wreck. "Boys, don't look out the window," she would tremble. I always looked. I had to look.

My mind was set. Someday I'd be an ambulance driver. I would eat at McDonald's every night. I would buy a house right across the street from Tiger Stadium. My old man was nuts. Car, windshield, car, windshield: what kind of idiot occupation was that?

As far as I remember, we never returned for another Family Night. It was just as well, for in all likelihood, we'd never have spotted my father. He had this habitual lean for the nearest exit. As soon as my grandmother lined him up for another job, he'd disappear into an eternal crawl for the coldest mug of beer in town. He took turns being a car salesman, a milkman, a construction worker, a railroad hand, a house painter, a mechanic and a landscaper. Each time the suds would devour his sense of duty, he'd get canned or simply quit, and back he'd come to his lumpy retreat on the living room sofa. My grandmother would be less than pleased.

Frequently mixed in with these dashed occupations were the inevitable sojourns back to the assembly line. It was not the least bit uncommon for a man to be fired at one factory on a Friday and be given the red carpet treatment at another automotive facility across town on Monday. If this is Tuesday, this must be Buick. If this is Thursday, how 'bout AC Spark Plug. During the sixties there were ten or so factories in Flint workin' three shifts per day and in this kind of boomtown climate even the beggars could afford to be choosers. "Sign here, Mr. Beerbreath. So glad to have you collapse on our doorstep."

I can't recall how many times my old man spun through the revolving doors of General Motors. However, around the house, we could always sense when Dad was cleaving through the factory rut. He would enter the house with this bulldog grimace. He'd gobble his meal, arise, put on one of his Arnie Palmer golf sweaters and whisk off for a troll through publand. Often, he wouldn't return for days. Then, suddenly one morning, there he'd be—reekin' of Pabst and pepperoni, passed out in a fetal position on the sofa, wearin' the same cool duds he left home in.

Not surprisingly, this led to a fair amount of friction between my mother and father. I could hear them early in the morning, their ferocious bitching driftin' through the heater vent up and into the bedroom I shared with three of my brothers.

It didn't take a marriage counselor or referee to sift to the bottom of these parental showdowns. Propped up in my bunk, I could easily discern the irrationality of my old man's barbs and the meek desperation of my mother's rebuttals. My father insisted that my mother was yanking the family against him. "You're turnin' the whole bunch of them into goddamn mama's boys!" the old man would rant. "Everyone of them acts like I'm some kind of villain."

Meanwhile, my mother would score with a hefty uppercut of fact. "Don't blame me, Bernard. Maybe if you hung around the house more than two nights a month the kids might get to know you." My old man abhorred the truth. It was like some horrible, foreign diction that ripped at his core. The car payment was truth. The telephone bill was truth. The six sleeping children, plus the one sitting bolt upright in his bed, were truth. Worst of all, the cars and windshield were truth.

Cars, windshields. Cars, fenders. Cars, whatever. The ongoing shuffle of the shoprat. It wasn't as if this profession was a plague that appeared out of nowhere to ensnare my old man. Quite the opposite was true. His daddy was a shoprat. His daddy's daddy was a shoprat. Perhaps his daddy's daddy's daddy would have been a shoprat if only Hank Ford would have dreamed this shit up a little sooner.

My old man's mother had been a shoprat. The same with Uncle Jack and Uncle Gene and Uncle Clarence. Ditto dear old Aunt Laura. My mother's dad had been a shoprat. (If you're wondering what happened to my mother's mother and her sense of duty—well, Christ, somebody had to stay home and pack this clan a lunch.)

Right from the outset, when the call went out for shoprats, my ancestors responded in almost Pavlovian compliance. The family tree practically listed right over on its side with eager men and women grasping for that great automotive dream.

My great-grandfather got the wheel rollin'. In 1910, he began his twenty-year tenure down on Industrial Avenue piecing together mobilized buggies. This was a period right after the invention of the gas-powered engine and long before the introduction of freeway sniping. My great-grandfather would have hung in there longer, but he bumped heads in the thirties with something called the Depression.

My grandfather hired on in 1930. He rode out the turbulence of the Depression and worked as a skilled tradesman for thirty-two years at Buick. He had no plans to retire, but the cancer took him down at age fifty-two. He died one week to the day after he cashed his first pension check.

My other grandfather hitched his way from Springfield, Illinois, to the Vehicle City in 1925. He put in forty years, from Babe Ruth to the Beatles, as an inspector at the Chevrolet Engine plant. He always claimed that the only reason he retired was his disdain for the new breed of autoworkers in the sixties. He referred to them as "candy-asses." I assumed he was remarking about some inedible new brand of chocolate bar.

During the war, my grandmother helped build machine guns at the AC Spark Plug factory. She later switched over to working on aircraft out on Dort Highway. To this day, my grandmother still helps me change the oil in my Camaro.

My Aunt Laura and her husband Jack put in a combined sixty-five years at the AC plant and the Buick Foundry. Uncle Jack was well known for his lust for overtime, often volunteering to work double shifts and sixteen-hour days. This may provide a valuable clue as to why they never had any children.

For sheer longevity, my Uncle Clarence outdistanced everyone in the family tree. From 1919 till 1964, an amazing span of forty-five years, he answered the whistle over at the Buick Engine plant.

Forty-five years! That's longer than the life expectancy of over two-thirds of the world's population. Forty-five years! Shit, just imagine—from a cradle down in Dixie to his hunched-over demise on the potty—Elvis Presley never even lived that long. Forty-five years! After all of that, what do they give you for a retirement gift? A grandfather clock? An iron lung? A bronzed calendar the size of a Yugo?

With a heritage like that you'd think my old man would have had enough grit and grind floatin' through his gene pool to practically assure his pod development as a full-bloomin' archetype of the species. A purebred shoprat, begotten from sperms that jingle, jangle, jingle to the jungle strains of Greaseball Mecca. The fair-haired boy in the rhinestone coveralls. Spawn of labor. Self-winding fetus with the umbilical lasso looped around the blue-collared neckbone of Mr. Goodwrench.

Apparently, the old man wasn't much for heritage. He tumbled out of the family tree, urinated on it, and never looked back. For him, General Motors was nothing more than a recurring nuisance, an occasional pit stop where he could tidy up his bankroll before troopin' out on another aimless binge.

It was unfortunate that my father couldn't combine his love for beer and his dependence on pocket money into one workable formula. After all, he wasn't the only palooka in the family who tipped toward the tap-per. The majority of my ancestors were heavy drinkers. Excluding my grandmother, all of them imbibed frequently as hard-laborin' shoprats are wont to do.

My mother's dad was especially skilled at juggling work and play. Monday morning through Friday afternoon he was the consummate provider. Straight home from work, dinner, the evening news and immediately into bed at 7:00 p.m. He arose each weekday at 3:30 a.m., fixed himself some black coffee, turned on the kitchen radio, smoked a handful of Lucky Strikes and waited to leave for work at a quarter to five. This regimen never varied one iota in the forty years he worked for GM.

Come the quittin' whistle on Friday afternoon, a colossal metamorphosis took place. So long, shoprat. Hello, hooligan. As my mother tells it, they never caught more than a staggerin' glimpse of my grandfather on any given weekend. He occasionally dropped in for a quick supper whereupon he would substitute the dinner hour for an excuse to denounce my grandma's cooking, castigate the children and generously mutter "goddamn-it-alls" for the benefit of the rest of the defective universe.

My grandfather surely could be an ornery bastard, but it should be thusly noted that he was always there to answer the bell. He had a wife and three kids to house and feed. He turned the trick daily. He may have had a passionate lust for booze, but it never interfered with his job at General Motors. When he retired, he was a very wealthy man. Devotion, responsibility and duty to the Corporation. The bottle was never far away, but it always rode shotgun.

Seeing as how my old man constructed this formula completely ass-back-wards, the entire burden of support fell solely into my mother's lap. While the old man was off baby-sitting barstools, it was left up to my mom to raise and provide for eight kids.

Throughout my youth, my mother worked two jobs a day. Nine to five, she was a medical secretary at a doctor's office. She walked the two miles to work each day because we were too broke to afford a car. By night, she worked as a medical records transcriber, pounding the dictaphone machine for Hurley Hospital in the tiny, makeshift office in the corner of the living room.

It was unfortunate for my old man that my mother was such a strict and loyal Catholic. Consequently, my mother wasn't allowed to practice the pill and the baby faucet was allowed to leak on unabated. The final tally showed five boys and three girls of which I was the eldest. Eight was indeed enough. In fact, eight was plainly too goddamn many. Every time the stork paid a visit, he left a new bundle of joy for my mother and a fresh load in the chamber of the gun pointed at my old man's skull.

It seemed with each new addition to our family, my father slid further and further away from accountability. He liked children, he just didn't have the space for a clan of his own. It was like the cars and the windshield. The equation never balanced out. The undertow of all this repetition was a rid-dle he could never hope to untangle.

By the age of ten, I realized that my old man was not soon to be con-fused with Ward Cleaver. I was hip to all his ploys and well aware of his flair for bullshit. His boozin' never particularly bothered me. I figured if my father wanted to go get plowed, it was his decision.

What bothered me was my old man's insistence on fabricating dreadful transparent lies. We both knew what he was up to so why not just 'fess up and admit the obvious.

I surely would have respected him more if he'd only come up to me on those occasions of rabid thirst and said, "Look, son. I feel like some kind of suffocatin' beast. The world is knockin' me around something awful and it's only fuckin' proper that I find a bar at once. I want to get smashed. I want to play footsies with the locals. I want to sing like Dean Martin. I want to drink until they start clickin' the lights off and on, and then I wanna weave home and collapse into bed with the weight of the world slidin' off the sheets. You may not understand any of this now, but someday you'll have a world of your own to contend with."

My friends were always amused with my old man's approach to the duties of fatherhood. Most of their fathers were dedicated shoprats, shackled to some factory titty like hornets to honey. Their fathers wouldn't miss a day's work if their spinal cords were severed. Obedience to the Corporation. An honest day's pay for an honest day's toil. Car, bumper. Car, door latch. Car, dipstick.

For them, my father was the mold breaker—the curious renegade who dared to scrunch himself up in fetal bliss, smack dab in the middle of the workday, snoozin' off the effects of another nocturnal creepy-crawl.

After school, we would tiptoe past him, snickering back and forth at the behemoth in full slumber. You had to be very cautious. To awaken the old man from his beer coma would earn you an immediate pass to have your head dislodged. Sometimes, just for laughs, I'd get as close as I possibly dared and jut my middle finger right in his face. The poor bastard was like some dormant circus geek and he never even knew it. Of course, my friends preferred to catch my old man in his glorious prime. This usually occurred whenever I'd have a friend over for the night. My old man would weave in while we were watchin' some late-night horror flick and immediately take over the entertainment. After a full night of drinkin', there was nothin' my old man enjoyed more than a captive audience for his sloshed bar chatter. Even if he was playin' to a crowd comprised of two sleep-starved ten-year-olds.

There were the stories about how he broke said pool stick over said chiseler's head and how the babes he hung with had chests the size of pony kegs ("They'd be through with you boys before you ever got it unzipped," he'd chuckle), and how he knew Tiger great Denny McLain on a first-name basis, and how Denny better watch his shit cuz these mob pricks were no one to try and slip a change-up by, and how he was rapin' the local bookies with his expertise at pickin' the over and under.

It went on and on. Typically, he would conclude these drunken seminars with horrible denunciations of the black race. My old man was a master of deflecting his own guilt onto anyone other than himself. The blacks were his favorite dumping ground. He would blame them for everything. He'd make all these demented assertions about how Hitler was stopped too early because once he ditched all the Jews, he was gonna wipe out the niggers. Fine fodder for festerin' ten-year-old minds. We preferred hearin' about large breasts and the woes of Denny McLain.

Despite the racial garbage, my friends all agreed that my old man's beer blather beat the shit out of listenin' to their fathers whine about what was on television and how the lawn needed trimmin'. Their fathers were as robotic in their home life as they were about their factory jobs. It was as if the shop had hollowed them out and replaced their intestines with circuit breakers. Car, tailpipe. Food, pork chop. Car, brake pad. Rent, Friday. Car, hubcap. Life, toothpaste.

Mike Gellately's father was a good example. Almost every evening after dinner I headed over to Mike's house. He would greet me at the side door, and we'd trail through the kitchen on our way up to his bedroom.

Without fail, Mr. Gellately would be propped at the kitchen table—a six-pack of Blue Ribbon at his right elbow, an overloaded ashtray at his left. He would be staring straight ahead at the kitchen sink, and his faithful radio would be stationed in front of him, forever tuned in to the Detroit Tigers or Red Wings. Sip, puff, belch. Occasionally, he would startle the homestead by muttering a random "shit" or "fuck." That would be the extent of his nightly vocabulary.

Neither Mike nor I understood the first thing about our fathers. They were like the living dead. Their patterns differed: Mike's old man held a job most of the time, my old man was on some kind of less-paying treadmill— but their ruts were terribly predictable. We grew to hate our fathers.

By the time I approached teenhood, I no longer wanted to be an ambulance driver. I didn't know what the hell I wanted to be. Mike always suggested that we become disc jockeys. I never argued. A disc jockey would certainly lead a glamorous life. Anything had to be better than the cadaver shuffle the factories were peddlin' our fathers.

Even the neighborhood we lived in was a by-product of General Motors. During the boom years of the twenties, houses had to be constructed in order to keep up with the influx of factory workers arriving from the South to find jobs. General Motors built their own little suburb on the north side of Flint. In keeping with their repetitive nature, all the houses were duplicates.

Our neighborhood was strictly blue-collar and predominantly Catholic. The men lumbered back and forth to the factories while their wives raised large families, packed lunch buckets and marched the kids off to the nuns.

483

My family was no exception. From the very beginning, I was raised a good Catholic boy. Catholic church, Catholic school, Catholic home, Catholic drone. I was baptized, confirmed, anointed, and tattooed with ashes all in the hope that one day I might have a spot reserved for me on that glorious flotilla up to the heavens.

No matter how tight the budget was at home, my mother always managed to scrape up the necessary funds to provide for our Catholic education. It was never intended that I grow up to be anything other than a good Catholic man—a steady churchgoer with a steady factory income, a station wagon parked under the elms and a wife with an automatic door on her womb.

St. Luke's Elementary provided a very capable boot camp environment for those who would later deposit themselves in the rigid bustle of factory life. The education-through-intimidation technique favored there was not unlike the jarhead gang mentality of the General Motors floorlords. Our fathers' overseers were brutes with clipboards, sideburns, and tangled rhetoric. Our overseers, the sisters of St. Luke's, were brutes with clipboards, sideburns, and tangled rosaries.

A pattern was developing. During the seventh and eighth grades at St. Luke's, the nuns divided the students into groups according to intelligence and behavior. There were three groups: the obedient eggheads, the bland robots of mediocrity, and, my group, the who-gives-a-shit-hey-have-you-heard-the-new-Cream-album-yet-yup-my-daddy's-a-stinkin'-shoprat-too clan.

Being a proud underachiever of the latter grouping, I was relieved of much of the pressure to succeed in life and was left with my drowsy peers to clog up the classroom while we awaited our almost certain fate as future factory nimwits. Not much was expected of us and we went out of our way to ensure that was how it would remain. Consequently, the nuns cut us a great deal of slack figuring that for every Einstein and Aristotle flipped out of the cookie cutter there had to be a couple mental dwarves available to assemble a life's procession of Buicks and Impalas for those on the road to high places.

Of course this method of reasoning didn't exactly jibe with our parents' outlook on destiny. At report card time, our folks would raise all kinds of hell while cringing over our grades. I suppose it only makes sense that every mom and pop wants more for their tuition dollar than a series of lazy failures guaranteed to pave the lane right into the turd dump of the assembly line. You could achieve that predestination at any public school and save the family till a lootful.

My folks were no exception. My mother would gaze at my report card and the color would leave her face. It was like a slap to the head—a horrible betrayal on my part considering the long hours of work she had put in to assure her son a fine Catholic education.

"An E in Math, a D in History and Science, a D- IN RELIGION?" my mother would howl. "How could any child who attends mass SIX days a week possibly do so poorly in Religion?"

I would make a pathetic attempt to switch to the highlights. "Look, Mom, I did raise my Self-Conduct mark from a D to a C-. And I did receive passing grades in Music and Gym."

"Music and Gym? MUSIC AND GYM! Just what is that supposed to tell me? That you have a secure future singing the national anthem at basketball games? Just wait until your father takes a look at this mess."

I could wait. If there was one thing I detested, it was my old man preachin' to me about my shortcomings as a model Catholic youth. It was such a bad joke. What the hell qualified him to criticize anything I did? I felt that he should reserve his critiques for matters that more closely coincided with his niche in life. Education? Shit. He should have stuck to advising me on the proper methods of wife cheating and check forging and navigating a car with triple vision. And what about the studied art of smoking an entire Winston without ever removing it from your mouth or the precious knack of impersonating a morgue stiff for forty-eight consecutive hours on the living room sofa. This was the kind of heavy data no nun could ever pass along.

I was my father's seed. Technically, I guess that was reason enough for him to meddle with my grade situation.

"You think you're hot shit, don't you, son?" my father would begin. I would shrug nervously. "You think you've got a pretty soft thing going for yourself. Am I right?" I would shake my head slowly.

"Well, the way I see it, you ain't nothin' but a bad actor. You may be snowin' your mother, but I can smell your game a mile away. You wanna play wiseass with me and I'll knock you down a few pegs. Anytime you feel like you can take the old man, I'll be right here. Anytime you wanna wear the pants in the family, you just let me know. I'll be more than willing to put my foot right up your ass. Understand, son?"

"Yes," I would mumble enraged and full of regrets. If only I were eight inches taller and had a reckless set of balls. I could envision myself springing from the interrogation seat and sucker-punching my old man right in the chops. "Here, sweet father of mine, take this busted lip as a loving token of

485

my esteemed adulation and let this punt to the rib cage serve as a loving reminder that your eldest son worships the ground you piss on."

But back to reality or, at least, my father's version of such. "Now, son, you must realize that your mother and I have worked very hard to see that you receive some proper schooling. All this report card tells me is that you don't give a good goddamn one way or the other. You keep this shit up and you'll be just like half the other morons in this city who end up spinnin' their wheels and suckin' some heavy ass down at Chevrolet or over at Buick. You can clown it up now, but you'll be laughin' out of the other side of your mouth once the blisters appear and some bastard starts leanin' over your shoulder with another bumper to fasten down."

I heard this speech often during my formative years. I came to refer to it as my old man's "State of the Hometown" address. Do as I say, not as I did, kid. My friends received similar pronouncements from their fathers. The factories weren't looking for a few good men. They were dragging the lagoon for optionless bumpkins with brats to feed and livers to bathe. An educated man might hang on for a while, but was apt to flee at any given whistle. That wasn't any good for corporate continuity. GM wanted the salt of the earth, dung-heavers, flunkies and leeches—men who would grunt the day away void of self betterment, numbed-out cyborgs willing to swap cerebellum loaf for patio furniture, a second jalopy and a tragic carpet ride deboarding curbside in front of some pseudo-Tudor dollhouse on the outskirts of town.

Which is to say that being a factory worker in Flint, Michigan wasn't something purposely passed on from generation to generation. To grow up believing that you were brought into this world to follow in your daddy's footsteps, just another chip-off-the-old-shoprat, was to engage in the lowest possible form of negativism. Working the line for GM was something fathers did so that their offspring wouldn't have to.

In the case of my ancestry, we had been blessed with this ongoing cycle of martyrs. Men who toiled tirelessly in an effort to provide their sons and daughters with a better way of living. Unfortunately, at the same time, our family was also cursed by a steady flow of uninspired descendants who scoffed at alternative opportunity and merely hung around waitin' for the baton to be passed from crab claw to puppy paw.

By deftly flunking my way through St. Luke's Junior High, I was already exhibiting symptoms of one who was pointing squarely to the loading dock of the nearest General Motors outpost. Even my father was accurate with his diagnosis. Another Hamper banging at the gate of idiot industry with a ten-foot scowl and a forehead fresh for stampin'. I could practically hear my great-grandfather yelpin' from his crypt: "Not another one! Hey, don't any of you pricks wanna become lawyers or somethin'? Huh? ʜᴜʜ?" Silent decades drifted by choking on indecision. "Well, piss on ya, I'm going back to sleep. Car, windshield. Car, fuel pump. Car, ignition switch. Car, zzzzzz . . ."

THE SHOP FOOD MATCH GAME

Hey, just for kicks. Here's the directions: simply match the food listings in the numbered column with the corresponding taste sensations in the lettered column. No fair approaching a shoprat for assistance. Scoring: 9 or 10 correct—ready to dine on the set of a snuff movie. 7 or 8 correct—consider moving to the Republic of Mylanta. 5 or 6 correct—too wimpy to have a beer gut. Less than 5—pray that you never become blue collar.

1. Mashed Potatoes	A. Construction Paper
2. Beans & Franks	B. Alan Trammel's Sweat Socks Immediately After a Doubleheader
3. Reuben Sandwich	C. Sunoco High Octane 260
4. Chicken Soup	D. Airplane Glue
5. Tater Tots	E. Embalming Fluid
6. Turkey	F. Sam Kinison's Shower Mat
7. Coney Dogs	G. Squirrel Death
8. Patty Melt	H. Golfball Skins
9. Cole Slaw	I. Collie dung
10. Salisbury Steak	J. Grated Crickets

ANSWERS: 1-D, 2-C, 3-B, 4-E, 5-H, 6-F, 7-G, 8-A, 9-J, 10-I

from *The Undertaking*

THOMAS LYNCH

[A]n emotionally potent and spiritually stimulating intersection of the living and the dead. In death and its rituals, they see the leveled playing field so elusive in life. Whether we bury our dead in Wilbert Vaults, leave them in trees to be eaten by birds, burn them or beam them into space; whether choir or cantor, piper or jazz band, casket or coffin or winding sheet, ours is the species that keeps track of our dead and knows that we are always outnumbered by them. Thus immigrant Irish, Jews of the diaspora, Black North Americans, refugees and exiles and prisoners of all persuasions, demonstrate, under the scrutiny of demographers and sociologists, a high tolerance, almost an appetite, for the rites and ceremonies connected to death.

Furthermore, this approval seems predicated on one or more of the following variables: the food, the drink, the music, the shame and guilt, the kisses of aunts and distant cousins, the exultation, the outfits, the heart's hunger for all homecomings.

The other exception to the general abhorrence of funerals is, of course, types of my own stripe whose lives and livelihoods depend on them. What sounds downright oxymoronic to most of the subspecies—a good funeral— is, among undertakers, a typical idiom. And though I'll grant some are pulled into the undertaking by big cars and black suits and rumors of riches, the attrition rate is high among those who do not like what they are doing. Unless the novice mortician finds satisfaction in helping others at a time of need, or "serving the living by caring for the dead" as one of our slogans goes, he or she will never stick it. Unless, of course, they make a pile of money early on. But most of us who can afford to send our kids to the orthodontist but not to boarding school, who are tied to our brick and mortar and cash-flow worries, who live with the business phone next to our beds, whose dinners and intimacies are always being interrupted by the needs of others, would not do so unless there were satisfactions beyond the fee schedule. Most of the known world could not be paid enough to embalm a neighbor on Christmas or stand with an old widower at his wife's open casket or talk with a leukemic mother about her fears for her children about to be motherless. The ones who last in this work are the ones who believe what they do is not only good for the business and the bottom line, but good, after everything, for the species.

A man that I work with named Wesley Rice once spent all of one day and all night carefully piecing together the parts of a girl's cranium. She'd been murdered by a madman with a baseball bat after he'd abducted and raped her. The morning of the day it all happened she'd left for school dressed for picture day—a schoolgirl dressed to the nines, waving at her mother, ready for the photographer. The picture was never taken. She was abducted from the bus stop and found a day later in a stand of trees just off the road a township south of here. After he'd raped her and strangled her and stabbed her, he beat her head with a baseball bat, which was found beside the child's body. The details were reported dispassionately in the local media along with the speculations as to which of the wounds was the fatal one—the choking, the knife, or the baseball bat. No doubt these speculations were the focus of the double postmortem the medical examiner performed on her body before signing the death certificate *Multiple Injuries*. Most embalmers, faced with what Wesley Rice was faced with after he'd opened the pouch from the morgue, would have simply said "closed casket," treated the remains enough to control the odor, zipped the pouch, and gone home for cocktails. It would have been easier. The pay was the same. Instead, he started working. Eighteen hours later the girl's mother, who had pleaded to see her, saw her. She was dead, to be sure, and damaged; but her face was hers again, not the madman's version. The hair was hers, not his. The body was hers, not his. Wesley Rice had not raised her from the dead nor hidden the hard facts, but he had retrieved her death from the one who had killed her. He had closed her eyes, her mouth. He'd washed her wounds, sutured her lacerations, pieced her beaten skull together, stitched the incisions from the autopsy, cleaned the dirt from under her fingernails, scrubbed the fingerprint ink from her fingertips, washed her hair, dressed her in jeans and a blue turtleneck, and laid her in a casket beside which her mother stood for two days and sobbed as if something had been pulled from her by force. It was the same when her pastor stood with her and told her, "God weeps with you." And the same when they buried the body in the ground. It was then and always will be awful, horrible, unappeasably sad. But the outrage, the horror, the heartbreak belonged, not to the murderer or the media or the morgue, each of whom had staked their claims to it: It belonged to the girl and to her mother. Wesley had given them the body back. "Barbaric" is what Jessica Mitford called this "fussing over the dead body." I say the monster with the baseball bat was barbaric. What Wesley Rice did was a kindness.

And, to the extent that it is easier to grieve the loss that we see, than the one we imagine or read about in papers or hear of on the evening news, it was what we undertakers call a good funeral.

It served the living by caring for the dead.

But save this handful of the marginalized—poets and preachers, foreigners and undertakers—few people not under a doctor's care and prescribed powerful medications, really "appreciate" funerals. Safe to say that part of the American Experience, no less the British, or the Japanese or Chinese, has been to turn a blind eye to the "good" in "goodbye," the "sane" in "sadness," the "fun" in "funerals."

Thus the concept of merging the highest and best uses of land, which came to me high over California, seemed an idea whose time had come. The ancient and ongoing duty of the land to receive the dead aligned with the burgeoning craze in the golf business led, by a post-modem devolution, to my vision of a place where one could commemorate their Uncle Larry and work on their short game at the same time—two hundred acres devoted to memories and memorable holes; where tears wept over a missed birdie comingled with those wept over a parent's grave. A *Golfatorium!* It would solve, once and for all, the question of Sundays—what to do before or after or instead of church. The formerly harried husband who always had to promise he'd do the windows "next weekend" in order to get a few holes in during good weather, could now confidently grab his golf shoes and Big Berthas and tell his wife he was going to visit his "family plot." He might let slip some mention of "grief work" or "unfinished business" or "adult-child issues still unresolved." Or say that he was "having dreams" or was feeling "vulnerable." What good wife would keep her mate from such important therapy? What harm if the cure includes a quick nine or eighteen or twenty-seven holes if the weather holds?

So began the dialogue between my selves: the naysayer and the true believer—there's one of each in every one of us. I read my poems in L.A., chatted up the literary set, waxed pithy and beleaguered at the book signings and wine and cheese receptions. But all along I was preoccupied by thoughts of the Golfatorium and my mother dying. When, after the reading at the Huntington Library, I asked the director where would she go if she had four days free in Southern California, she told me "Santa Barbara" and so I went.

There are roughly ten acres in every par four. Eighteen of those and you have a golf course. Add twenty acres for practice greens, club house, pool and patio, and parking and two hundred acres is what you'd need. Now divide the usable acres, the hundred and eighty, by the number of burials per acre—one thousand—subtract the greens, the water hazards, and the sand traps, and you still have room for nearly eight thousand burials on the front nine and the same on the back. Let's say, easy, fifteen thousand adult burials for every eighteen holes. Now add back the cremated ashes scattered in sand-traps, the old marines and swabbies tossed overboard in the water hazards and the Italians entombed in the walls of the club house, and it doesn't take a genius to come to the conclusion that there's gold in them there hills!

You can laugh all you want, but do the math. Say it costs you ten thousand an acre and as much again in development costs—you know, to turn some beanfield into Roseland Park Golfatorium or Arbordale or Peachtree. I regard as a good omen the interchangeability of the names for golf courses and burial grounds: Glen Eden and Grand Lawn, like Oakland Hills or Pebble Beach could be either one, so why not both? By and large we're talking landscape here. So two million for property and two million for development, the club house, the greens, the watering system. Four million in up-front costs. Now you install an army of telemarketers-slash-memorial counselors to call people during the middle of dinner and sell them lots at an "introductory price" of, say, five hundred a grave—a bargain by any standard—and *cha-ching* you're talking seven point five million. Add in the pre-arranged cremations at a hundred a piece and another hundred for scattering in the memorial sandtraps and you've doubled your money before anyone has bought a tee time or paid a greens fee or bought golf balls or those overpriced hats and accessories from your pro shop. Nor have you sold off the home lots around the edges to those types that want to live on a fairway in Forest Lawn. Building sights at fifty thousand a pop. Clipping coupons is what you'd be. Rich beyond any imagination. And that's not even figuring how much folks would pay to be buried, say, in the same fairway as John Daly or Arnold Palmer. Or to have Jack Nicklaus try to blast out of your sand-trap. And think of the gimmicks—tree burial for a hole in one, select tee times for the pre-need market. And the package deals: a condo on the eighteenth hole, six graves on the par-three on the front nine, dinner reservations every Friday night, tennis lessons for the missus, maybe a video package of you and your best foursome for use at your memorial service, to aid in everyone's remembrance of the way you were, your name and dates on the wall of the nineteenth hole where your golf buddies could get a little liquored up and weepy all in your memory. All for one low price, paid in a way that maximized your frequent-flier miles.

The impulse to consolidate and conglomerate, to pitch the big tent of goods and services is at the heart of many of this century's success stories. No longer the butcher, the baker, the candlestick maker, we go to supermarkets where we can buy meats, breads, motor oils, pay our light bill, rent a video, and do our banking, all in the one stop. Likewise the corner gas station sells tampons and toothpaste (of course, no one comes out to check your oil, nor can the insomniac behind the glass wall fix your brakes or change your wiper blades). Our churches are no longer little chapels in the pines but crystal cathedrals of human services. Under one roof we get day care and crisis intervention, bible study and columbaria. The great TV ministries of the eighties—the Bakkers and Swaggarts and Falwells—were theme parks and universities and hospital complexes that flung the tax-free safety net of God over as much real estate as could be bought. Perhaps the tendency, manifest in many of today's mega-churches, to entertain rather than to inspire, to wow rather than to worship, proceeds from the intelligence, gained generations back, that the big top needed for the tent revival and the three-ring circus was one and the same. Some of these televangelists went to jail, some ran for president, and some rode off into the sunset of oblivion. But they seemed to be selling what the traffic would bear. A kind of one-stop shopping for the soul, where healing, forgiveness, a time-share in the Carolinas, musical ministry, water parks, and pilgrimages to the Holy Land can all be put on one's Visa or Mastercard.

In the same way the Internet is nothing if not an emergent bazaar, a global mall from which one can shop the shelves of a bookstore in Galway, order a pizza or some dim sum, talk dirty to strangers bored with their marriages, and check the demographics of Botswana all without budging from—this would have sounded daft twenty years ago—the "home office."

Thus the paradigm of dual-purpose, high-utility, multitasking applications had taken hold of the market and my imagination.

This had happened to me once before.

Years back before the cremation market really—I can't help this one—heated up, I dreamed a new scheme called "Cremorialization." It was based on the observation that those families who elected to cremate their dead, much as those who buried theirs, felt a need to memorialize them. But unlike earth burial where the memorial took the form of a stone—informative but silent and otherwise useless—those who reduced the dead to ashes and bone fragments seemed to be cheered by the thought that something good might come of something bad, something useful might proceed from what they saw as otherwise useless. Such notions have root in what has been called the Protestant ethic that honors work and utility. The dead, they seemed to be saying, ought to get off their dead ashes and be good for something beyond the simple act of remembrance.

This is the crowd who can always be counted on to say "such a shame" or "what a waste" when they see a room full of flowers at one end of which is a dead human body. The same flowers surrounding a live human body hosting a tea for the visiting professor are, for the most part, "perfectly lovely." Or when the body amid the gladioli is one recovering from triplets, say, or triple bypass surgery, the flowers are reckoned to be "how very thoughtful." But flowers surrounding a casket and corpse are wasteful and shameful—the money better spent on "a good cause." This notion, combined with cremation, which renders the human corpse easily portable—ten to twelve pounds on average—and easily soluble with new age polymers and resins, brought me to the brainstorm years ago of the dead rising from their ashes, doing their part again—Cremorialization. Rather than dumbly occupying an urn, what old hunter wouldn't prefer his ashes to be used to make duck decoys or clay pigeons? The dead fisherman could become a crank-bait or plastic worms, perhaps given, with appropriate ceremony, to a favorite grandson. The minister's wife, ever the quiet and dignified helpmate, could be resurrected as a new tea service for the parsonage, her name etched tastefully into the saucers. Bowlers could be mixed into see-through bowling balls, or bowling pins, or those bags of rosin they are always tossing. Ballroom dancers could be ocarinas, cat lovers could be memorial kitty litter. The possible applications were endless. The ashes of gamblers could become dice and playing chips, car buffs turned into gear shift knobs or hood ornaments or whole families of them into matching hubcaps. After years spent in the kitchen, what gourmand could resist the chance to become a memorial egg-timer, their ashes slipping through the fulcrum in a metaphor of time. Bookends and knickknacks could be made of the otherwise boring and useless dead. And just as the departed would be made more valuable by becoming something, what they became would be more valuable by placing the word "memorial" in front of it.

We always kept the ashes in a closet—those that weren't picked up by the family or buried or placed in a niche. After ten years I noticed we'd accumulated several dozen unclaimed . . .

DAVE MARSH

I

This old town is where I learned about lovin'
This old town is where I learned to hate
This town, buddy, has done its share of shoveling
This town taught me that it's never too late
—Michael Stanley, "My Town"

When I was a boy, my family lived on East Beverly Street in Pontiac, Michigan, in a two-bedroom house with blue-white asphalt shingles that cracked at the edges when a ball was thrown against them and left a powder like talc on fingers rubbed across their shallow grooves. East Beverly ascended a slowly rising hill. At the very top, a block and a half from our place, Pontiac Motors Assembly Line 16 sprawled for a mile or so behind a fenced-in parking lot.

Rust-red dust collected on our windowsills. It piled up no matter how often the place was dusted or cleaned. Fifteen minutes after my mother was through with a room, that dust seemed thick enough for a finger to trace pointless, ashy patterns in it.

The dust came from the foundry on the other side of the assembly line, the foundry that spat angry cinders into the sky all night long. When people talked about hell, I imagined driving past the foundry at night. From the street below, you could see the fires, red-hot flames shaping glowing metal.

Pontiac was a company town, nothing less. General Motors owned most of the land, and in one way or another held mortgages on the rest. Its holdings included not only the assembly line and the foundry but also a Fisher Body plant and on the outskirts, General Motors Truck and Coach. For a while, some pieces of Frigidaires may even have been put together in our town, but that might just be a trick of my memory, which often confuses the tentacles of institutions that monstrous.

In any case, of the hundred thousand or so who lived in Pontiac, fully half must have been employed either by GM or one of the tool-and-die shops and steel warehouses and the like that supplied it. And anybody who earned his living locally in some less directly auto-related fashion was only fooling himself if he thought of independence.

My father worked without illusions, as a railroad brakeman on freight trains that shunted boxcars through the innards of the plants, hauled grain from up north, transported the finished Pontiacs on the first leg of the route to almost anywhere Bonnevilles, Catalinas and GTOs were sold.

Our baseball and football ground lay in the shadow of another General Motors building. That building was of uncertain purpose, at least to me. What I can recall of it now is a seemingly reckless height—five or six stories is a lot in the flatlands around the Great Lakes—and endless walls of dark greenish glass that must have run from floor to ceiling in the rooms inside. Perhaps this building was an engineering facility. We didn't know anyone who worked there, at any rate.

Like most other GM facilities, the green glass building was surrounded by a chain link fence with barbed wire. If a ball happened to land on the other side of it, this fence was insurmountable. But only very strong boys could hit a ball that high, that far, anyhow.

Or maybe it just wasn't worth climbing *that* particular fence. Each August, a few weeks before the new models were officially presented in the press, the finished Pontiacs were set out in the assembly-line parking lot at the top of our street. They were covered by tarpaulins to keep their design changes secret—these were the years when the appearance of American cars changed radically each year. Climbing *that* fence was a neighborhood sport because that was how you discovered what the new cars looked like, whether fins were shrinking or growing, if the new hoods were pointed or flat, how much thinner the strips of whitewall on the tires had grown. A weird game, since everyone knew people who could have told us, given us exact descriptions, having built those cars with their own hands. But climbing that fence added a hint of danger, made us feel we shared a secret, turned gossip into information.

The main drag in our part of town was Joslyn Road. It was where the stoplight and crossing guard were stationed, where the gas station with the condom machine stood alongside a short-order restaurant, drugstore, dairy store, small groceries and a bakery. A few blocks down, past the green glass building, was a low brick building set back behind a wide, lush lawn. This building, identified by a discreet roadside sign, occupied a long block or two. It was the Administration Building for all of Pontiac Motors—a building for executives, clerks, white-collar types. This building couldn't have been more than three-quarters of a mile from my house, yet even though I lived on East Beverly Street from the time I was two until I was past fourteen, I knew only one person who worked there.

In the spring of 1964, when I was fourteen and finishing eighth grade, rumors started going around at Madison Junior High. All of the buildings on our side of Joslyn Road (possibly east or west of Joslyn, but I didn't know directions then—there was only "our" side and everywhere else) were about to be bought up and torn down by GM. This was worrisome, but it seemed to me that our parents would never allow that perfectly functioning neighborhood to be broken up for no good purpose.

One sunny weekday afternoon a man came to our door. He wore a coat and tie and a white shirt, which meant something serious in our part of town. My father greeted him at the door, but I don't know whether the businessman had an appointment. Dad was working the extra board in those years, which meant he was called to work erratically—four or five times a week, when business was good—each time his nameplate came to the top of the big duty-roster board down at the yard office. (My father didn't get a regular train of his own to work until 1966; he spent almost twenty years on that extra board, which meant guessing whether it was safe to answer the phone every time he actually wanted a day off—refuse a call and your name went back to the bottom of the list.)

At any rate, the stranger was shown to the couch in our front room. He perched on that old gray davenport with its wiry fabric that bristled and stung against my cheek, and spoke quite earnestly to my parents. I recall nothing of his features or of the precise words he used or even of the tone of his speech. But the dust motes that hung in the air that day are still in my memory, and I can remember his folded hands between his spread knees as he leaned forward in a gesture of complicity. He didn't seem to be selling anything; he was simply stating facts.

He told my father that Pontiac Motors was buying up all the houses in our community from Tennyson Street, across from the green glass building, to Baldwin Avenue—exactly the boundaries of what I'd have described as our neighborhood. GM's price was more than fair; it doubled what little money my father had paid in the early fifties. The number was a little over ten thousand dollars. All of the other houses were going, too; some had already been sold. The entire process of tearing our neighborhood down would take about six months, once all the details were settled.

The stranger put down his coffee cup, shook hands with my parents and left. As far as I know, he never darkened our doorstep again. In the back of my mind, I can still see him through the front window cutting across the grass to go next door.

"Well, *we're* not gonna move, right, Dad?" I said. Cheeky as I was, it didn't occur to me this wasn't really a matter for adult decision-making—or rather, that the real adults, over at the Administration Building, had already made the only decision that counted. Nor did it occur to me that GM's offer might seem to my father an opportunity to sell at a nice profit, enabling us to move some place "better."

My father did not say much. No surprise. In a good mood, he was the least taciturn man alive, but on the farm where he was raised, not many words were needed to get a serious job done. What he did say that evening indicated that we might stall awhile—perhaps there would be a slightly better offer if we did. But he exhibited no doubt that we would sell. And move.

I was shocked. There was no room in my plans for this . . . rupture. Was the demolition of our home and neighborhood—that is, my life—truly inevitable? Was there really no way we could avert it, cancel it, *delay* it? What if we just plain *refused to sell?*

Twenty years later, my mother told me that she could still remember my face on that day. It must have reflected extraordinary distress and confusion, for my folks were patient. If anyone refused to sell, they told me, GM would simply build its parking lot—for that was what would replace my world—around him. If we didn't sell, we'd have access privileges, enough space to get into our driveway, and that was it. No room to play, and no one there to play with if there had been. And if you got caught in such a situation and didn't like it, then you'd really be in a fix, for the company wouldn't keep its double-your-money offer open forever. If we held out too long, who knew if the house would be worth anything at all. (I don't imagine that my parents attempted to explain to me the political process of condemnation, but if they had, I would have been outraged, for in a way, I still am.)

My dreams always pictured us as holdouts, living in a little house surrounded by asphalt and automobiles. I always imagined nighttime with the high, white-light towers that illuminated all the other GM parking lots shining down upon our house—and the little guardhouse that the company would have to build and man next door to prevent me from escaping our lot to run playfully among the parked cars of the multitudinous employees. Anyone reading this must find it absurd, or the details heavily derivative of bad concentration-camp literature or maybe too influenced by the Berlin Wall, which had been up only a short time. But it would be a mistake to dismiss its romanticism, which was for many months more real to me than the ridiculous reality—moving to accommodate a *parking lot*—which confronted my family and all of my friends' families.

If this story were set in the Bronx or in the late sixties, or if it were fiction, the next scenes would be of pickets and protests, meaningful victories and defeats. But this isn't fiction—everything set out here is as unexaggerated as I know how to make it—and the time and the place were wrong for any serious uproar. In this docile midwestern company town, where Walter Reuther's trip to Russia was as inexplicable as the parting of the Red Sea (or as forgotten as the Ark of the Covenant), the idea that a neighborhood might have rights that superseded those of General Mo tors' Pontiac division would have been regarded as extraordinary, bizarre and subversive. Presuming anyone had had such an idea, which they didn't—none of my friends seemed particularly disturbed about moving, it was just what they would *do*.

So we moved, and what was worse, to the suburbs. This was catastrophic to me. I loved the city, its pavement and the mobility it offered even to kids too young to drive. (Some attitude for a Motor City kid, I know.) In Pontiac, feet or a bicycle could get you anywhere. Everyone had cars, but you weren't immobilized without them, as everyone under sixteen was in the suburbs. In the suburb to which we adjourned, cars were *the* fundamental of life—many of the streets in our new subdivision (not really a neighborhood) didn't even have sidewalks.

Even though I'd never been certain of fitting in, in the city I'd felt close to figuring out how to. Not that I was that weird. But I was no jock and certainly neither suave nor graceful. Still, toward the end of eighth grade, I'd managed to talk to a few girls, no small feat. The last thing I needed was new goals to fathom, new rules to learn, new friends to make.

So that summer was spent in dread. When school opened in the autumn, I was already in a sort of cocoon, confused by the Beatles with their paltry imitations of soul music and the bizarre emotions they stirred in girls.

Meeting my classmates was easy enough, but then it always is. Making new friends was another matter. For one thing, the kids in my new locale weren't the same as the kids in my classes. I was an exceptionally good student (quite by accident—I just read a lot) and my neighbors were classic underachievers. The kids in my classes were hardly creeps, but they weren't as interesting or as accessible as the people I'd known in my old neighborhood or the ones I met at the school bus stop. So I kept to myself.

In our new house, I shared a room with my brother at first. We had bunk beds, and late that August I was lying sweatily in the upper one, listening to the radio (WPON-AM, 1460) while my mother and my aunt droned away in the kitchen.

Suddenly my attention was riveted by a record. I listened for two or three minutes more intently than I have ever listened and learned some thing that remains all but indescribable. It wasn't a new awareness of music. I liked rock and roll already, had since I first saw Elvis when I was six, and I'd been reasonably passionate about the Ronettes, Gary Bonds, Del Shannon, the Crystals, Jackie Wilson, Sam Cooke, the Beach Boys, and those first rough but sweet notes from Motown: the Miracles, the Temptations, Eddie Holland's "Jamie." I can remember a rainy night when I tuned in a faraway station and first heard the end of the Philadelphia Warriors' game in which Wilt Chamberlain scored a hundred points and then found "Let's Twist Again" on another part of the dial. And I can remember not knowing which experience was more splendid.

But the song I heard that night wasn't a new one. "You Really Got a Hold on Me" had been a hit in 1963, and I already loved Smokey Robinson's voice, the way it twined around impossibly sugary lines and made rhymes within the rhythms of ordinary conversation, within the limits of everyday vocabulary.

But if I'd heard those tricks before, I'd never understood them. And if I'd enjoyed rock and roll music previously, certainly it had never grabbed me in quite this way: as a lifeline that suggested—no, insisted—that these singers spoke *for* me as well as to me, and that what they felt and were able to cope with, the deep sorrow, remorse, anger, lust, and compassion that bubbled beneath the music, I would also be able to feel and contain. This intimate revelation was what I gleaned from those three minutes of music, and when they were finished and I climbed out of that bunk and walked out the door, the world looked different. No longer did I feel quite so powerless, and if I still felt cheated, I felt capable of getting my own back, some day, some way.

II (MARSH)

It seems I've been playing your game way too long
And it seems the game I've played has made you strong
—Jimmy Cliff, "Trapped"

That last year in Pontiac, we listened to the radio a lot. My parents always had. One of my most shattering early memories is of the radio blasting when they got up—my mother around four-thirty, my father at five. All of my life I've hated early rising, and for years I couldn't listen to country music without being reminded almost painfully of those days.

But in 1963 and 1964, we also listened to WPON in the evening for its live coverage of city council meetings. Pontiac was beginning a decade of racial crisis, of integration pressure and white resistance, the typical scenario. From what was left of our old neighborhood came the outspokenly racist militant anti-school busing movement.

The town had a hard time keeping the shabby secret of its bigotry even in 1964—Pontiac had mushroomed as a result of massive migration during and after World War II. Some of the new residents, including my father, came from nearby rural areas where blacks were all but unknown and even the local Polish Catholics were looked upon as aliens potentially subversive to the community's Methodist piety.

Many more of the new residents of Pontiac came from the South, out of the dead ends of Appalachia and the border states. As many must have been black as white, though it was hard for me to tell that as a kid. There were lines one didn't cross in Michigan, and if I was shocked, when visiting Florida, to see separate facilities labeled "White" and "Colored," as children we never paid much mind to the segregated schools, the lily-white suburbs, the way that jobs in the plants were divided up along race lines. The ignorance and superstition about blacks in my neighborhood were as desperate and crazed in their own way as the feelings in any kudzu-covered parish of Louisiana.

As blacks began to assert their rights, the animosity was not less, either. The polarization was fueled and fanned by the fact that so many displaced Southerners, all with the poor white's investment in racism, were living in our community. But it would be foolish to pretend that the situation would have been any more civilized if only the natives had been around. In fact the Southerners were often regarded with nearly as much condescension and antipathy as blacks—race may have been one of the few areas in which my parents found themselves completely in sympathy with the "hillbillies."

Racism was the great trap of such men's lives, for almost everything could be explained by it, from unemployment to the deterioration of community itself. Casting racial blame did much more than poison these people's entire concept of humanity, which would have been plenty bad enough. It immobilized the racist, preventing folks like my father from ever realizing the real forces that kept their lives tawdry and painful and forced them to fight every day to find any meaning at all in their existence. It did this to Michigan factory workers as effectively as it ever did it to dirt farmers in Dixie.

The great psychological syndrome of American males is said to be passive aggression, and racism perfectly fit this mold. To the racist, hatred of blacks gave a great feeling of power and superiority. At the same time, it allowed him the luxury of wallowing in self-pity at the great conspiracy of rich bastards and vile niggers that enforced workaday misery and let the rest of the world go to hell. In short, racism explained everything. There was no need to look any further than the cant of redneck populism, exploited as effectively in the orange clay of the Great Lakes as in the red dirt of Georgia, to find an answer to why it was always the *next* generation that was going to get up and out.

Some time around 1963, a local attorney named Milton Henry, a black man, was elected to Pontiac's city council. Henry was smart and bold; he would later become an ally of Martin Luther King, Jr., of Malcolm X, a principal in the doomed Republic of New Africa. The goals for which Henry was campaigning seem extremely tame now, until you realize the extent to which they *haven't* been realized in twenty years: desegregated schools, integrated housing, a chance at decent jobs.

Remember that Martin Luther King would not take his movement for equality into the North for nearly five more years, and that when he did, Dr. King there faced the most strident and violent opposition he'd ever met, and you will understand how inflammatory the mere presence of Milton Henry on the city council was. Those council sessions, broadcast live on WPON, invested the radio with a vibrancy and vitality that television could never have had. Those hours of imprecations, shouts and clamor are unforgettable. I can't recall specific words or phrases, though, just Henry's eloquence and the pandemonium that greeted each of his speeches.

So our whole neighborhood gathered round its radios in the evenings, family by family, as if during wartime. Which in a way I guess it was—surely that's how the situation was presented to the children, and not only in the city. My Pontiac junior high school was lightly integrated, and the kids in my new suburban town had the same reaction as my Floridian cousins: shocked that I'd "gone to school with niggers," they vowed they would die—or kill—before letting the same thing happen to them.

This cycle of hatred didn't immediately elude me. Thirteen-year-olds are built to buck the system only up to a point. So even though I didn't dislike any of the blacks I met (it could hardly be said that I was given the opportunity to *know* any), it was taken for granted that the epithets were essentially correct. After all, anyone could see the grave poverty in which most blacks existed, and the only reason ever given for it was that they liked living that way.

But listening to the radio gave free play to one's imagination. Listening to music, that most abstract of human creations, unleashed it all the more. And not in a vacuum. Semiotics, the New Criticism and other formalist approaches have never had much appeal to me, not because I don't recognize their validity in describing certain creative structures but because they emphasize those structural questions without much consideration of content. And that simply doesn't jibe with my experience of culture, especially popular culture.

The best example is the radio of the early 1960s. As I've noted, there was no absence of rock and roll in those years betwixt the outbreaks of Presley and Beatles. Rock and roll was a constant for me, the best music around, and I had loved it ever since I first heard it, which was about as soon as I could remember hearing anything.

In part, I just loved the sound—the great mystery one could hear welling up from "Duke of Earl," "Up on the Roof," "Party Lights"; that pit of loneliness and despair that lay barely concealed beneath the superficial bright spirits of a record like Bruce Channel's "Hey Baby"; the nonspecific terror hidden away in Del Shannon's "Runaway." But if that was all there was to it, then rock and roll records would have been as much an end in themselves—that is, as much a dead end as TV shows like *Leave It to Beaver* (also mysterious, also—thanks to Eddie Haskell—a bit terrifying).

To me, however, TV was clearly an alien device, controlled by the men with shirts and ties. Nobody on television dressed or talked as the people in my neighborhood did. In rock and roll, however, the language spoken was recognizably my own. And since one of the givens of life in the outlands was that we were barbarians, who produced no culture and basically consumed only garbage and trash, the thrill of discovering depths within rock and roll, the very part that was most often and explicitly degraded by teachers and pundits, was not only marvelously refreshing and exhilarating but also in essence liberating—once you'd made the necessary connections.

It was just at this time that pop music was being revolutionized—not by the Beatles, arriving from England, a locale of certifiable cultural superiority, but by Motown, arriving from Detroit, a place without even a hint of cultural respectability. Produced by Berry Gordy, not only a young man but a *black* man. And in that spirit of solidarity with which hometown boys (however unlike) have always identified with one another, Motown was mine in a way that no other music up to that point had been. Surely no one spoke my language as effectively as Smokey Robinson, able to string together the most humdrum phrases and effortlessly make them sing.

That's the context in which "You Really Got a Hold on Me" created my epiphany. You can look at this coldly—structurally—and see nothing more than a naked marketing mechanism, a clear-cut case of a teenager swaddled in and swindled by pop culture. Smokey Robinson wrote and sang the song as much to make a buck as to express himself; there was nothing of the purity of the mythical artist about his endeavor. In any case, the emotion he expressed was unfashionably sentimental. In releasing the record, Berry Gordy was mercenary in both instinct and motivation. The radio station certainly hoped for nothing more from playing it than that its listeners would hang in through the succeeding block of commercials. None of these people and institutions had any intention of elevating their audience, in the way that Leonard Bernstein hoped to do in his *Young People's Concerts* on television. Cultural indoctrination was far from their minds. Indeed, it's unlikely that anyone involved in the process thought much about the kids on the other end of the line except as an amorphous mass of ears and wallets. The pride Gordy and Robinson had in the quality of their work was private pleasure, not public.

Smokey Robinson was not singing of the perils of being a black man in this world (though there were other rock and soul songs that spoke in guarded metaphors about such matters). Robinson was not expressing an experience as alien to my own as a country blues singer's would have been. Instead, he was putting his finger firmly upon a crucial feeling of vulnera - bility and longing. It's hard to think of two emotions that a fourteen-year-old might feel more deeply (well, there's lust . . .), and yet in my hometown expressing them was all but absolutely forbidden to men. This doubled the shock of Smokey Robinson's voice, which for years I've thought of as falsetto, even though it really isn't exceptionally high-pitched compared to the spec- tacular male sopranos of rock and gospel lore.

"You Really Got a Hold on Me" is not by any means the greatest song Smokey Robinson ever wrote or sang, not even the best he had done up to that point. The singing on "Who's Loving You," the lyrics of "I'll Try Something New," the yearning of "What's So Good About Goodbye" are all at least as wor- thy. Nor is there anything especially newfangled about the song. Its trembling blues guitar, sturdy drum pattern, walking bass and call-and-response voice arrangement are not very different from many of the other Miracles records of that period. If there is a single instant in the record which is unforgettable by itself, it's probably the opening lines: "I don't like you / But I love you . . ."

The contingency and ambiguity expressed in those two lines and Robin son's singing of them was also forbidden in the neighborhood of my youth, and forbidden as part and parcel of the same philosophy that propounded racism. Merely calling the bigot's certainty into question was revolutionary—not merely rebellious. The depth of feeling in that Miracles record, which could have been purchased for 69¢ at any K-Mart, overthrew the premise of racism, which was that blacks were not as human as we, that they could not feel—much less express their feelings—as deeply as we did.

When the veil of racism was torn from my eyes, everything else that I knew or had been told was true for fourteen years was necessarily called into question. For if racism explained everything, then without racism, not a single commonplace explanation made any sense. *Nothing* else could be taken at face value. And that meant asking every question once again, including the banal and obvious ones.

For those who've never been raised under the weight of such addled philosophy, the power inherent in having the burden lifted is barely imaginable. Understanding that blacks weren't worthless meant that maybe the rest of the culture in which I was raised was also valuable. If you've never been told that you and your community are worthless—that a parking lot takes precedence over your needs—perhaps that moment of insight seems trivial or rather easily won. For anyone who was never led to expect a life any more difficult than one spent behind a typewriter, maybe the whole incident verges on being something too banal for repetition (though in that case, I'd like to know where the other expressions of this story can be read). But looking over my shoulder, seeing the consequences to my life had I not begun questioning not just racism but all of the other presumptions that ruled our lives, I know for certain how and how much I got over.

That doesn't make me better than those on the other side of the line. On the other hand, I won't trivialize the tale by insisting upon how fortunate I was. What was left for me was a raging passion to explain things in the hope that others would not be trapped and to keep the way clear so that others from the trashy outskirts of barbarous America still had a place to stand—if not in the culture at large, at least in rock and roll.

Of course it's not so difficult to dismiss this entire account. Great revelations and insights aren't supposed to emerge from listening to rock and roll records. They're meant to emerge only from encounters with art. (My encounters with Western art music were unavailing, of course, because everyone of them was prefaced by a lecture on the insipid and worthless nature of the music that I preferred to hear.) Left with the fact that what happened to me did take place, and that it was something that was supposed to come only out of art, I reached the obvious conclusion. You are welcome to your own.

Horatio Alger Must Die
(from *Dude, Where's My Country?*)

MICHAEL MOORE

Perhaps the biggest success in the war on terror has been its ability to distract the nation from the Corporate War on Us. In the two years since the attacks of 9/11, American businesses have been on a punch-drunk rampage that has left millions of average Americans with their savings gone, their pensions looted, their hopes for a comfortable future for their families diminished or extinguished. The business bandits (and their government accomplices) who have wrecked our economy have tried to blame it on the terrorists, they have tried to blame it on Clinton, and they have tried to blame it on us.

But, in fact, the wholesale destruction of our economic future is based solely on the greed of the corporate mujahedeen. There is a master plan, my friends, each company has one, and the sooner you can get over not wanting to believe it, or worrying that to believe it puts you in the ranks of the nutters who thrive on conspiracy theories, then the sooner we have a chance of stopping them. Their singular goal is to take enough control over our lives so that, in the end, we'll be pledging allegiance, not to a flag or some airy notions of freedom and democracy, but to the dictates of Citigroup, Exxon, Nike, GE, GM, P&G, and Philip Morris. It is their executives who now call the shots, and you can go vote and protest and cheat the IRS all you want to get back at them, but face it: You are no longer in charge. You know it and they know it, and all that remains is the day when it will be codified onto a piece of paper, the Declaration of the Corporate States of America.

"We hold these truths to be self-evident: that all men and women and their underaged children are created equally to serve the Corporation, to provide its labor without question, to accept whatever remuneration without complaint, and to consume its products without thought. In turn, the Corporation will provide for the common good, secure the defense of the nation, and receive the bulk of the taxes taken from the people . . ."

It doesn't really sound that absurd anymore, does it? The takeover has happened right under our noses. We've been force-fed some mighty powerful "drugs" to keep us quiet while we're being mugged by this lawless gang of CEOs. One of these drugs is called fear and the other is called Horatio Alger.

The fear drug works like this: You are repeatedly told that bad, scary people are going to kill you, so place all your trust in us, your corporate leaders, and we will protect you. But since we know what's best, don't question us if we want you to foot the bill for our tax cut, or if we decide to slash your health benefits or jack up the cost of buying a home. And if you don't shut up and toe the line and work your ass off, we will sack you—and then just try to find a new job in this economy, punk!

That shit is so scary, of course we do what we are told, mind our Ps and Qs in our dreary cubicles, and fly our little American flags to show that yes, boss, we believe in your War on Terror.

The other drug is nicer. It's first prescribed to us as children in the form of a fairy tale—but a fairy tale that can actually come true! It's the Horatio Alger myth. Alger was one of the most popular American writers of the late 1800s (one of his first books, for boys, was called Ragged Dick). Alger's stories featured characters from impoverished backgrounds who, through pluck and determination and hard work, were able to make huge successes of themselves in this land of boundless opportunity. The message was that anyone can make it in America, and make it big.

We're addicted to this happy rags-to-riches myth in this country. People elsewhere in other industrialized democracies are content to make a good enough living to pay their bills and raise their families. Few have a cutthroat desire to strike it rich. If they have a job that lets them go home after seven or eight hours of work and then gives them the standard four to eight weeks of paid vacation every year, they're relatively happy. And with their governments providing health care, good free schools, and a guaranteed pension to live well in old age, they're even happier.

Sure, some of them may fantasize about making a ton more money, but most people outside the U.S. don't live their lives based on fairy tales. They live in reality, where there are only going to be a few rich people, and you are not going to be one of them. So get used to it.

Of course, rich people in those countries are very careful not to upset the balance. Even though there are greedy bastards among them, they've got some limits placed on them. In the manufacturing sector, for example, British CEOs make twenty-four times as much as their average workers—the widest gap in Europe. German CEOs only make fifteen times more than their employees, while Swedish CEOs get thirteen times as much. But here in the U.S., the average CEO makes 411 times the salaries of their blue collar workers. Wealthy

Europeans pay up to 65 percent in taxes and they know better than to bitch too loud about it or the people will make them fork over even more.

In the United States, we are afraid to sock it to them. We hate to put our CEOs in prison when they break the law. We are more than happy to cut their taxes even as ours go up!

Why is this? Because we drank the Kool-Aid. We bought into the drug, the lie that we, too, could some day be rich. So we don't want to do anything that could harm us on that day we end up millionaires. The American carrot is dangled in front of us all our lives, and we believe that we are almost within reach of making it.

It's so believable because we have seen it come true. A person who comes from nothing goes on to strike it rich. There are more millionaires now than ever before. This increase in the number of millionaires has served a very useful function for the rich because it means in every community there's at least one person prancing around as the rags-to-riches poster child, conveying the not-so-subtle message: "SEE! I MADE IT! YOU CAN, TOO!!"

It is this seductive myth that led so many millions of working people to become investors in the stock market in the 1990s. They saw how rich the rich got in the 1980s and thought, hey, this could happen to me!

The wealthy did everything they could to encourage this attitude. Understand that in 1980, only 20 percent of Americans owned a share of stock. Wall Street was the rich man's game and it was off-limits to the average Joe and Jane. And for good reason—the average person saw it for what it was, a game of risk, and when you are trying to save every dollar so you can send the kids to college, games of chance are not where you place your hard-earned money.

Near the end of the eighties, though, the rich were pretty much tapped out with their excess profits and could not figure out how to make the market keep growing. I don't know if it was the brainstorm of one genius at a brokerage firm or the smooth conspiracy of all the well-heeled, but the game became, "Hey, let's convince the middle class to give us their money, and we can get even richer!"

Suddenly, it seemed like everyone I knew jumped on the stock market bandwagon, putting their money in mutual funds or opening up 401(k)s. They let their unions invest all their pension money in stocks. Story after story ran in the media about how everyday, working people were going to be able to retire as near-millionaires! It was like a fever that infected everyone. No one wanted to be left behind. Workers immediately cashed their paychecks and called their broker to buy more stocks. Their broker! Ooh, it felt so good . . . after working your ass off all week at some miserable, thankless job, you could still feel that you were a step ahead, and a head above, because you had your own personal broker! Just like the rich man!

Soon, you didn't even want to be paid in cash. Pay me in stock! Put it in my 401(k)! Call my broker!

Then, each night, you'd pore over the stock charts in the newspaper as one of the all-finance-news-all-the-time cable channels blared in the background. You bought computer programs to map out your strategy. There were ups and downs but mostly ups, lots of ups, and you could hear yourself saying, "My stock's up 120 percent! My worth has tripled!" You eased the pain of daily living imagining the retirement villa you would buy some day or the sports car you could buy tomorrow if you wanted to cash out now. No, don't cash out! It's only going to go higher! Stay in for the long haul! Easy Street, here I come!

But it was a sham. It was all a ruse concocted by the corporate powers-that-be who never had any intention of letting you into their club. They just needed your money to take them to that next level, the one that insulates them from ever having to actually work for a living. They knew the Big Boom of the 1990s couldn't last, so they needed your money to artificially inflate the value of their companies so their stocks would reach such a phantasmal price that, when it was time to cash out, they would be set for life, no matter how bad the economy got.

And that's what happened. While the average sucker was listening to all the blowhards on CNBC tell him that he should buy even more stock, the ultra rich were quietly getting out of the market, selling off the stocks of their own company first. At the same time they were telling the public—and their own loyal employees—that they should invest even more in the company because forecasters were predicting even more growth, the executives were dumping their own stocks as fast as they could.

In September 2002, *Fortune* magazine released a staggering list of these corporate crooks who made off like bandits while their company's stock prices had dropped 75 percent or more between 1999 and 2002. They knew the downturn was coming, so these executives secretly cashed in while their own employees and common shareholders either bought up more stock ("Look, honey, we can get GM now really cheap!") or held on to their rapidly depleting "worth" in the hopes that it would bounce back ("It has to! It always has before! They say you have to be in the market for the long haul!").

At the top of the list of these evildoers was Qwest Communications, At its peak, Qwest shares traded at nearly $40. Three years later the same shares

were worth $1. Over that period, Qwest's director, Phil Anschutz, and its for-
mer CEO, Joe Nacchio, and the other officers made off with $2.26 billion—sim-
ply by selling out before the price hit rock bottom. My corporate overlords
here at AOL Time Warner stuffed their pockets with $1.79 billion. Bill Joy and
Ed Zander and their friends at Sun Microsystems? $1.03 billion. Charles
Schwab of, yes, Charles Schwab, took home just over $350 million all by him-
self. The list goes on and on and covers every sector of the economy.

With their man Bush in the White House, and the economy pushed
about as far as it could go, the market took a wallop. It was at first massaged
with that old chestnut that "the market is cyclical—don't take your money
out, folks, it will come back up, just as it always does." And so the average
investor stayed in, listening to all the rotten advice. And the market kept
going down, down, down—so low that you looked insane if you took your
money out. It HAD to have bottomed out by now, so just hang tight. And
then it just went down further, and before you knew it, your money was
gone, gone, gone.

Over four trillion dollars was lost in the stock market. Another trillion
dollars in pension funds and university endowments is now no longer there.

But here's what's still here: rich people. They are still with us and they
are doing better than ever. They laughed all the way to the Swiss bank over
the scam of the millennium. They pulled it off, mostly legally, and if they
bent the law here and there, no problem, there aren't more than a small handful of them behind bars as I write this. The rest, they're on the private beach
with the well-groomed sand.

So, here's my question: After fleecing the American public and destroying the American dream for most working people, how is it that, instead of
being drawn and quartered and hung at dawn at the city gates, the rich got
a big wet kiss from Congress in the form of a record tax break, and no one
says a word? How can that be?

I think it's because we're still addicted to the Horatio Alger fantasy drug.
Despite all the damage and all the evidence to the contrary, the average
American still wants to hang on to this belief that maybe, just maybe, he or
she (mostly he) just might make it big after all. So don't attack the rich man,
because one day that rich man may be me!

Listen, friends, you have to face the truth: You are never going to be rich.
The chance of that happening is about one in a million. Not only are you
never going to be rich, but you are going to have to live the rest of your life
busting your butt just to pay the cable bill and the music and art classes for
your kid at the public school where they used to be free.

And it is only going to get worse. Whatever benefits you may have now are going to get whittled down to nothing. Forget about a pension, forget about Social Security, forget about your kids taking care of you when you get old because they are barely going to have the money to take care of themselves. And don't even think about taking a vacation, because odds are your job won't be there when you get back. You are expendable, you have no rights, and, by the way, "what's a union?"

I know, many of you don't think it's that bleak. Sure, times may be tough, but you think you'll survive. You'll be that one person who somehow escapes the madness. You are not going to give up the dream of some day having your slice of the pie. In fact, some of you believe the whole pie might some day be yours.

I have some news for you: You're not even going to get to lick the plate. The system is rigged in favor of the few, and your name is not among them, not now and not ever. It's rigged so well that it dupes many otherwise decent, sensible, hard-working people into believing that it works for them, too. It holds the carrot so close to their faces that they can smell it. And by promising that one day they will be able to eat the carrot, the system drafts an army of consumers and taxpayers who gladly, passionately, fight for the rights of the rich, whether it means giving them billions in tax breaks while they send their own children into dilapidated schools, or whether it means sending those children off to die in wars to protect the rich man's oil. Yes, that's right: The workers/consumers will even sacrifice the lives of their own flesh and blood if it means keeping the rich fat and happy because the rich have promised them that some day they can join them at the table!

But that day never comes, and by the time the working stiff has this figured out, he's in an old-age home spewing a lot of bitter mumbo jumbo about authority and taking it out on the aide who is just trying to empty his sorry bedpan. There might have been a more humane way to spend his final days, but the money that would have financed that was spent by him on all that fantastic AOL Time Warner and World Com stock—and the rest was spent by the government on that outer space weapons system that never did quite seem to work.

If you are still clinging to the belief that not all of Corporate America is that bad, consider these three examples of what our good captains of industry have been up to of late.

First, are you aware that your company may have taken a life insurance policy out on you? Oh, how nice of them, you say? Yeah, here's how nice it is:

During the past twenty years, companies including Disney, Nestle, Procter & Gamble, Dow Chemical, JP Morgan Chase, and WalMart have been secretly taking out life insurance policies on their low- and mid-level employees *and then naming themselves—the Corporation—as the beneficiary!* That's right: When you die, the company—not your survivors—gets to cash in. If you die on the job, all the better, as most life insurance policies are geared to pay out more when someone dies young. And if you live to a ripe old age, even long after you've left the company, the company still gets to collect on your death. The money does not go to help your grieving relatives through hard times or to pay for the funeral and burial; it goes to the corporate executives. And regardless of when you croak, the company is able to borrow against the policy and deduct the interest from its corporate taxes.

Many of these companies have set up a system for the money to go to pay for executive bonuses, cars, homes, trips to the Caribbean. Your death goes to helping make your boss a very happy man sitting in his Jacuzzi on St. Barts.

And what does Corporate America privately call this special form of life insurance?

Dead Peasants Insurance.

That's right. "Dead Peasants." Because that's what you are to them—peasants. And you are sometimes worth more to them dead than alive. (It's also sometimes referred to as "Dead Janitors" insurance.)

When I read about this in the *Wall Street Journal* last year, I thought I had mistakenly picked up one of those parody versions of that newspaper. But, no, this was the real deal, and the writers, Ellen Schultz and Theo Francis, told some heartbreaking stories of employees who died and whose families could have used the money.

They wrote of a man who died at twenty-nine of complications of AIDS, who had no life insurance of his own. His family received no death benefits, but CM Holdings, the parent company of the music store where he worked, collected $339,302 at his death.

Another CM Holdings policy was taken out on an administrative assistant who earned $21,000 a year, who died from Amyotrophic Lateral Sclerosis (Lou Gehrig's disease). According to the Journal story, the company turned down a request from her grown children, who cared for her during her illness, to help buy a $5,000 wheelchair so they could take their mother to church. When the woman died in 1998 the company received a payout of $180,000.

Some of the companies—Wal-Mart among them—have stopped the practice. Some states have enacted laws banning "Dead Peasants" policies, and others are considering similar actions. And numerous lawsuits have been filed against companies by survivors of deceased employees seeking to be named the beneficiaries of the policies. But, for now, the policies continue at many companies. Is yours one of them? You might want to find out. It's good to know that, after you die, your corpse could in fact mean a new Porsche for the chairman.

· · ·

Still not convinced that the rich could care less about you? Here's another example of just how little you mean to your corporate masters once they've got your vote and your obedience. Congress is considering a bill that will let companies put less money into your pension funds if you work in a blue-collar job because, they say, as a result of the filthy, unsafe working conditions they've created for you, you aren't going to live that long anyway. So companies don't need to really be planning to give you all your retirement money because, heck, you ain't going to be around to use it! You'll be dead because they didn't install enough ventilation, or they made you work so hard you'll be lucky if you're not coughing up blood by the time you're fifty-eight. So why make them set aside all this pension money for you?

What's even more disgusting about this legislation is that it is backed by unions such as the UAW who want to see the pension money used now in the form of higher wages for their workers. But the numbers don't add up: Blue-collar workers who are union members actually live longer than nonunion industrial workers because they are paid better and have good health benefits. People with more money who have access to health care tend to stick around longer in this life and thus need more, not less, money put into pensions to support them during their lengthy retirements.

· · ·

The third example of how expendable you are comes from our good friends in the Bush administration's Environmental Protection Agency. They have a plan called the "Senior Death Discount." Corporate polluters have complained for a long time about how the government figures the actual cost, in human lives, of their poisoning of the air and water. The EPA develops its regulations—and establishes fines—in part by calculating how many people will die as a result of the pollution. So, they came up with a number for the actual "worth" of a human life—$3.7 million. (See, you are worth millions, after all!)

But the business community complained. They said, "No way are all these schmucks worth nearly $4 million!" So, the Bush EPA came up with a neat little math trick: They said, O.K., in order to reduce your costs and your efforts to clean up your pollution, we'll now say that anyone over seventy is only worth $2.3 million. After all, they're almost finished anyway, and they aren't producing anything for you anymore, so their lives just aren't worth as much.

That's when critics coined the policy the "Senior Death Discount." The elderly protested, and EPA Director Christie Whitman claimed the agency would stop using the calculation. And then she resigned.

So, you slaved your life away, you worked long hours, you gave everything you had to help your company earn record profits. When you went into the voting booth you voted for their Republican (and Democratic) candidates just like they asked you to—and after you retired, this is the thanks you got. A senior discount—not just at the movies or at McDonald's, but on your, very life.

• • •

Look, I don't know how to put it any gentler than to say that these bastards who run our country are a bunch of conniving, thieving, smug pricks who need to be brought down and removed and replaced with a whole new system that we control. That is what democracy is supposed to be about—we, the people, in fucking charge. What happened to us? Perhaps we never were really in charge and those words just sounded good at Independence Hall on that sweltering day in 1776. Maybe if the Founding Fathers had air conditioning and a corporate jet they never would have written such a foolish thing. But they did, and that's what we're left to work with.

So how did we let the bad people win out, the ones who would've been blowing George III back then if they had half a chance? When are we going to get this country and its economy in our hands, electing representatives who will split the pie fairly and see that no one gets more than their fair share?

Instead, what we have are sad realities like this one: the two bosom buddies, George W. Bush (CEO of America), and Kenneth Lay (Chairman of Enron, the seventh largest company in the U.S.). Before its collapse, Houston-based Enron was raking in a monstrous $100 billion a year, mostly by trading contracts for commodities including oil, gas, and electricity around the world. The increasingly deregulated energy market was a gold mine for the company, which was known for aggressive deal-making.

Lay, affectionately nicknamed "Kenny Boy" by Bush, was never shy about public displays of friendship. Enron donated $736,800 to Bush from 1993 on.

Between 1999 and 2001, CEO Lay raised $100,000 for his pal, and personally contributed $283,000 to the Republican National Committee. Lay also graciously gave candidate Bush use of the Enron corporate jet during the presidential campaign so he could fly his family around the country and talk about his plan to "restore dignity to the White House."

This friendship was truly a two-way street. Bush interrupted an important campaign trip in April 2000 to fly back to Houston to watch Lay throw out the first pitch at the Astros opening day game at the new Enron Field. Who said men aren't sentimental?

After Bush became president, he invited Lay to come to Washington to personally conduct the interviews of people who would serve in the Bush administration, primarily for high-level positions in the Energy Department—the very regulatory agency overseeing Enron.

Harvey Pitt—the chairman of the Securities and Exchange Commission at the time—was a former lawyer for Enron's accountant, Arthur Andersen. Lay and the Andersen team also worked to make sure that accounting firms would be exempt from numerous regulations and would not be held liable for any "funny bookkeeping"—arrangements that would come in handy later.

The rest of Lay's time in Washington was spent next door with his old buddy, Vice President Dick Cheney. The two formed an "energy task force" responsible for drafting the country's new "energy policy," a policy that could affect virtually all of Enron's business dealings. Cheney and/or his aides met with Enron executives at least six times during this period, but no one knows the full extent of the meetings because Cheney has refused to make public the records of those meetings. Meanwhile, Enron's wheeler-dealers were cooking up schemes to manipulate an energy crisis in California that would end up adding millions to their own pockets.

Does any of this ring a bell? You may have forgotten, with all the military distractions that have taken the focus off of Enron, that this was one of the greatest corporate scandals in the history of the United States. And it was committed by one of the "president's" closest friends. I'm sure Bush thanks God every night, for the War on Terror!, 9/11, Afghanistan, Iraq, and the Axis of Evil all but assured that Enron would disappear from the news and from the minds of the voting public. This scandal should have resulted in Bush's early impeachment and removal from our White House, but fate often has a way of working in Bush's favor and letting him escape the consequences of his actions. As I've pointed out before, when you've had three run-ins with the law, as he has, and never spent a single night in jail, you have the lucky touch, and for people like him it rarely goes away.

But I, for one, will not forget Enron, and neither should you. It's an event that goes beyond corporate malfeasance to a concerted plan to wreck our economy and elect political hacks who would protect them in their scheme to attack America from within.

When things were good at Enron, they were very, very good. Lay and other high-ranking honchos took home huge paychecks, and enjoyed generous expense accounts and lavish perks. The sweet life at Enron helped them afford to make significant donations to politicians in both major parties— politicians who were able to ensure that the regulatory climate stayed very, very sympathetic to Enron's interests. According to the Center for Responsive Politics, Enron gave nearly $6 million to the Republican and Democratic parties since 1989, with 74 percent going to the Republicans. This meant that when Congress began investigating Enron at the beginning of 2002, 212 of the 248 members of the House and Senate on the investigating committees had taken campaign contributions from Enron or its crooked accountant, Arthur Andersen.

Even lower-level Enron employees thought they had a good deal going: They sat back and watched their retirement plans, heavily invested in Enron stock, grow and grow.

But the company's phenomenal success was fleeting . . . and fraudulent. Much of Enron's profitability was achieved through the creation of shell partnerships, and was propped up by dubious (and possibly criminal) accounting practices. It's unclear how much of the true story will ever be known, as important documents were shredded before investigators could see them.

By the fall of 2001, the pyramid scheme that was Enron imploded. And while the rest of the country was in a state of shock over 9/11, Enron executives were busy bailing out, selling stocks, and shredding documents.

And a national crisis didn't stop them from reaching out to their buddies in the Bush administration. Calls were placed by Enron executives to Commerce Secretary Don Evans and then-Treasury Secretary Paul O'Neill, seeking help as the company was on the brink of collapse. Evans and O'Neill said they did nothing when Enron told them of the company's shell game and impending failure, and the administration proudly used that as evidence that no special favors were granted to one of the president's biggest supporters.

That's right—they were proud of doing nothing while millions of Americans were swindled. And the fleecing was made possible to a large degree by the Bush administration's willingness to let Enron run amok.

When he finally had to go before the press, George W. Bush tried to distance himself from his old friend and said, essentially, "Ken who?" Bush explained that his good buddy wasn't really a good buddy, but was instead just some businessman from Texas. "He [Kenny Boy] was a supporter of Ann Richards in my run [for governor] in 1994!" Bush told the media. (In fact, Lay contributed almost four times as much money to Bush's campaign for governor.)

When Enron officially went bankrupt in December 2001, Wall Street pundits and investors throughout the country were stunned.

But "bankrupt" has a different meaning for Enron's top executives than it does for the rest of us. The company's bankruptcy filing in 2001 shows 144 top executives received a total of $310 million in compensation and another $435 million in stock. That's an average of over $2 million each in compensation and another $3 million in stock.

And while the big guns counted their millions, thousands of Enron workers lost their jobs and much of their savings. Enron had established three savings plans for its employees and at the time of the bankruptcy, 20,000 of them were members of these plans. Sixty percent of the plans were made up of Enron stock. When the stock evaporated to pennies from an August 2000 high of $90, these employees were left with next to nothing. Losses in 401(k) plans totaled more than $1 billion.

But huge losses from the Enron collapse extended far beyond its employees, to thousands of others who owned Enron stock in public retirement funds, which, according to a *New York Times* article, lost at least $1.5 billion.

And the Enron collapse sent the entire stock market into a down turn, with a negative ripple effect that is still being felt today.

But as I write this, in the summer of 2003, fewer than two dozen people have been charged with Enron-related crimes. Five of those have entered into plea agreements and are awaiting sentencing, and fifteen others are awaiting trial.

No charges have been filed against former Chairman Ken Lay or CEO Jeff Skilling.

So, what do we do?

The only true value your life has to the wealthy is that they need your vote every election day in order to get the politicians they've funded into office. They can't do that by themselves. This damnable system of ours that allows for the country to be run by the will of the people is a rotten deal for them as they represent only 1 percent of "the people." You can't get tax cuts for the rich passed when the rich don't have enough votes to pull it off. This is why they truly hate democracy: because it puts them at the distinct disadvantage of being in the smallest of the smallest minorities. So they need to somehow dupe or buy off 50 percent of the people to get the majority they need to run the show. That is no simple task. The easy part is buying the politicians, first with campaign donations, then with special favors and perks once in office, and then with a good-paying consulting job once out of office. And the best way to ensure that your politician always wins is to give money to both sides, which is what nearly every corporate PAG does.

Fooling the majority of the voters into voting for the rich man's candidate (or candidates) is much harder, but they've proven it can be done. Getting the media to repeat your words as if they were truth, with hardly a question being asked, is one method. As we've seen, scaring people works well, too. As does religion. The rich have thus had a hardcore army of conservatives, right-wingers, and Christian Coalition-types to act as their foot soldiers. It's an odd marriage of sorts because the rich, by and large, are neither conservative nor liberal, neither right nor left, nor are they devout Christians or Jews. Their real political party is called Greed, and their religion is Capitalism. But they are more than happy to see millions of poor whites and even millions more middle-class people cheerfully pulling the lever in the voting booth for the candidates who will only screw these poor-white and middle-class people once they're in office.

So, our challenge, our mission, is to find ways to reach out to these millions of working people and show them how they are voting against their own best interests. It took the bankruptcy of Enron before thousands of its conservative employees, many of whom have said they proudly voted for George W. Bush and the Republicans, woke up. How many of them do you think will be voting for Ken Lay's best friend in the next election? But that's a painful way to build an opposition party. These otherwise good people should not be punished because they thought Rush Limbaugh and Tom DeLay were looking out for them. They were deceived and used. I truly believe that when they find out about tricks like dead peasants insurance and the senior death discount, when they learn what this latest tax cut has cost them in the form of reduced services and higher local taxes, they will wise up and be mad, very mad. And once they realize their name will never be Horatio Alger and that fairy tales are for children, they will grow up—and rise up—mighty fast.

NOTES AND SOURCES

The statistics for corporate compensation come from: "Executive Pay," John A. Byrne et al., *Business Week*, May 6, 2002; "Executive Pay: A Special Report," Alan Cowell, the *New York Times*, April 1, 2001. The *Business Week* report also noted: "In the past decade, as rank-and-file wages increased 36 percent, CEO pay climbed 340 percent, to $11 million." *Fortune*'s report on corporate crooks, "You Bought, They Sold," was published September 2, 2002. You can view it online at www.fortune.com. "The bulk of the information in the section on Dead Peasants Insurance, as was noted in the text, comes from the great work of Ellen E. Schultz and Theo Francis. "Valued Employees: Worker Dies, Firm Profits—Why?" appeared in the *Wall Street Journal* on April 19, 2002. Other subsequent reports include "Companies Gain a Death Benefit," Albert B. Crenshaw, the *Washington Post*, May 36, 2002; and "Bill to Limit Dead Peasants Policies Ignored to Death," L.M. Sixel, *Houston Chronicle*, October 4, 2002.

To find out more about the bill in Congress that would let companies put less money into the pension funds of blue-collar workers, see "Bill Reduces Blue-Collar Obligations for Pension," Mary Williams Walsh, the *New York Times*, May 6, 2003. You can read more about the "Senior Death Discount" controversy in "Life: The Cost-Benefit Analysis," John Tierney, the *New York Times*, May 18, 2003. If you would like more specific information on Ken Lay's contributions to the Bush campaign, or if you're looking for information on campaign donations in general, check the excellent people at the Center for Responsive Politics, www.opensecrets.org. Information on Bush's use of the Enron jet see "Enron: Other Money in Politics Stats," Center for Responsive Politics, November 9, 2001; and "Flying High on Corporations," *Capital Eye*, Winter 2000. Reports of Bush's quick detour from campaigning to see Lay throw the opening pitch at Houston's Enron Field appeared in "Bush Visits Top Contributor for Houston Baseball Bash," Megan Stack, *Associated Press*, April 7, 2000. For more on "Kenny Boy's" role in "helping" Bush select people for the new administration and his part in Cheney's "Energy Task Force," see "Mr. Dolan Goes to Washington," James Bernstein, *Newsday*, January 4, 2001; "Bush Advisers on Energy Report Ties to Industry," Joseph Kahn, the *New York Times*, June 3, 2001; "Power Trader Tied to Bush Finds Washington All Ears," Lowell Bergman and Jeff Gerth, the *New York Times*, May 25, 2001; "Bush Energy Paper Followed Industry Path," Don van Natta and Neela Banerjee, the *New York Times*, March 27, 2002; "Judge Questions U.S. Move in Cheney Suit," Henri E. Cauvin, the *Washington Post*, April 18, 2003. Additional information about Enron can be found in the following: Richard A. Oppel

Jr., "Enron Corp. Files Largest U.S. Claim for Bankruptcy," the *New York Times*, December 3, 2001; Steven Pearlstein & Peter Behr, "At Enron, the fall came quickly; complexity, partnerships kept problems from public view," the *Washington Post*, December 2, 2001; Leslie Wayne, "Enron, preaching deregulation, worked the statehouse circuit," the *New York Times*, February 9, 2002; John Schwartz, "The cast of characters in the Enron drama is lengthy, and their relationships complex," the *New York Times*, January 13, 2003; Jim Drinkard & Greg Farrell, "Enron made a sound investment in Washington," *USA Today*, January 24, 2002; Stephen Labaton, "Balancing deregulation and Enron," the *New York Times*, January 17, 2002; Jerry Hirsch, et al., "Safeguards failed to detect warnings in Enron debacle," the *Los Angeles Times*, December 14, 2001; Mary Flood, "The Fall of Enron," *Houston Chronicle*, February 5, 2003; Jerry Hirsch, "Energy execs gain millions in stock sales," the *Los Angeles Times*, June 13, 2001; Stephanie Scar, "Wealth of options," *Boston Herald*, September 30, 2002; Jake Tapper, "Secret hires warned Enron," *Salon*, January 20, 2002; Ben White and Peter Behr, "Enron paid creditors $3.6 billion before fall; filing also details payments to executives," the *Washington Post*, June 18, 2002; Jim Yardley, "Big burden for ex-workers of Enron," the *New York Times*, March 3, 2002; Eric Berger, "Enron facing pension lawsuit," *Houston Chronicle*, June 26, 2003; Steven Greenhouse, "Public funds say losses top $1.5 billion," the *New York Times*, January 29, 2002; Mary Flood, et al., "Far from finished," *Houston Chronicle*, June 22, 2003. Enron and Andersen's political donations and the conflicts of interest they ultimately caused in the government's "investigations" are discussed in Don Van Natta Jr., "Enron or Andersen made donations to almost all their congressional investigators," Don Van Natta Jr., the *New York Times*, January 25, 2002. Information on Enron's attempts to hide its law breaking, and the Bush administration's decision to do nothing about the impending collapse can be found in: "Shredded papers key in Enron case," Kurt Eichenwald, the *New York Times*, January 28, 2002; "Ken who?" Bennet Roth, et al., *Houston Chronicle*, January 11, 2002; "Bush aide was told of Enron's plea," Dana Milbank, the *Washington Post*, January 14, 2002; "Number of contacts grows," H. Josef Herbert, *Associated Press*, January 12, 2002. "President" Bush's attempt to deny his close friendship with Ken Lay are documented, first and foremost, in the transcript of a question-and-answer session with reporters on January 10, 2002. This can be found at www.whitehouse.gov. Also see "Ken who?" Bennet Roth, et al., *Houston Chronicle*, January 11, 2002, "Enron spread contributions on both sides of the aisle," Don van Natta Jr., the *New York Times*, January 21, 2002 and "Despite President's Denials, Enron & Lay Were Early Backers of Bush," Texans for Public Justice (www.tpj.org). January 11, 2002.

Green Onions

BOOKER T. & THE MG'S, 1962 BY AL YOUNG

"Dress the part," American humorist and realist George Ade used to say, "and the role plays itself." The dress was laboratory garb, which mostly meant a clean, crisply starched white lab coat. Whether you chose to wear a dress shirt or tie beneath it was strictly a personal matter, but everybody on the job, intentionally or not, eventually developed some kind of relationship with this uniform.

As for me, I was a lab aide, one of two at the Laboratory for Comparative Biology out in Richmond, California. Our job was to wash chemical glassware and other apparatus such as test tubes, beakers, flasks, pipettes, crucibles, weighing bottles, and so forth. We were also responsible for the sterilization of certain articles and solutions, and this usually involved subjecting them to high temperatures in the autoclave. Washing was done in an acid bath solution and for this you wore heavy rubber gloves and a hooded mask. That acid solution was something else; the fumes alone slowly ate away your clothing and you had to be extra careful about rinsing all traces of it from your skin. I used to have nightmares about the stuff.

Lab aides were flunkies; the maintenance crew of the scientific world. You were the one they pulled over to assist in the preparation or analysis of experiments of any kind. One day you might find yourself running organic substances or samples through the centrifuge machine; another day you might be sitting at a table or bench, stringing or snapping green beans or chopping up the stems of green onions. It was a gig that was anything but dull, and I must say I never worked around so many lab-coated eccentrics as I did the year I spent at LCB, which was housed in the lab wing of Kaiser Hospital in working class Richmond. Anything was likely to happen and usually did.

Booker T. and the MG's came out with "Green Onions" the year I started work there and it was always playing on the jukebox either at the A&W Root Beer franchise across the street, or at Gray's Club a little further down on Cutting Boulevard, or at the Slick Chick, a cryptic greasy spoon, along the same strip. There was also a chili joint, whose name I've forgotten, where I'd go for lunch with Ethel Holmes, the older black woman who was the other fulltime lab aide in this operation. We'd sit there—a Louisianan and a

Mississippian—munching on our chili beans and rice, talking that drowsy stuff Southerners and ex-Southerners slip into whenever they get together, listening to Booker T. Jones, Steve Cropper, and the rest of the MG's laying down that jumping, bluesy Memphis sound in the background.

"Green Onions" was on the radio, on the jukeboxes and, subliminally it seems, on everybody's mind. If you paid close attention—as I did at the time, for I was also gigging weekends in coffee houses and cabarets; singing and playing guitar—you could hear how this particular tune with its mesmerizing vamp was influencing pop music. You couldn't get away from "Green Onions," and the fact that it was an instrumental probably lengthened its life considerably. An elderly gentleman at a neighborhood house party told me, "How come it look like everything else seem to come and go, but people still crazy 'bout 'Green Onions'? You in the music business, so explain that to me if you can."

I couldn't explain it, but I did know it was infectious. The Gray's Club I speak of was about as elemental as they came. The sign out front was hand-lettered and semi-literate. The "s" in Gray's had been brushed on in such a way that it looked bigger than the rest of the name, and the letterer hadn't bothered painting in an apostrophe. Wes Jacobs, who was one of two black lab assistants at LCB, used to call it the Gray S Club, and that name stuck. Wes was a Buffaloan who, like me, had done time in Detroit and Ann Arbor. "Hey," he'd say, "they're throwin' another one of those Blue Monday parties over at the Gray S Club. What say we jump in there and pick up on some of those free turnip greens and cornbread and blackeyed peas and fried chicken?" And that's what we'd do after work some Mondays. They'd be advertising blues singer Jimmy McCracklin, scheduled for Friday and Saturday night, but guess what they'd be playing on the jukebox?

Whenever I'd show up anyplace in my lab coat, and expecially if I wore a tie, which I did sometimes just to bolster the old ego or give my low status a momentary, arbitrary facelift, people behind the counters would of often—usually after making change—say something like, "You know, Doctor, I been feelin' this funny pain right up under my ribs for 'bout a week now. Like, when I breathe, that's when I feel it sharpest. What you reckon I oughtta do?"

At first, I'd trip all over myself trying to explain how I really wasn't a doctor and, look, you better have that checked out because it sounds serious to me. But after awhile, I came to realize it was the look of me, and only the look of me, they were responding to. That white lab coat was what rounded out the effect. Soon I'd change my tune, and when they'd hit me with their medical problems, I'd finger the pencil in my lab coat chest pocket, look away thoughtfully and say, "Take two aspirin, get a few good nights' sleep, get some exercise and then tell me how you feel."

And, by Godfrey, it worked!

There was a fellow we'll call Janocz who'd come to the States from Hungary after the 1956 uprising by way of Brazil. Somewhere along the line, probably some moon drenched night on a Rio beach, he'd got it in his head he was going to be a doctor of something. By the time he'd begun becoming an American citizen, he was working with one of the top biologists at LCB. One afternoon I happened to be present when the boss—a chunky woman, thoroughly lovable, with a round, Germanic face framed by a severe, short bowl-cut hairdo—asked Janocz to rattle off the valence of some chemical element. He, uh, he, uh, wasn't sure what she meant or, rather, what the valence should've been, uh—That's when Janocz got busted down to the level of rat keeper for the resident toxicologist, an Austrian who, because he didn't hold a degree in medicine from an American school, had to travel the back roads and byways of the profession he'd been trained for. I remember he'd spent a lot of time on Tahiti and, at some point, had actually met the English novelist Somerset Maugham, or, rather—depending on which version of the story he was dishing out of a particular morning or afternoon—he had spent some time with the real-life woman who had served as the model for the prostitute-become-religious-convert in Maugham's famous short story, "Rain." Joan Crawford portrayed her in *Sadie Thompson,* the movie based on that story. Either way, the good doctor was a voracious reader and lover of literature who was enamoured of the fact that Maugham, like himself, had been trained as a physician. He too had literary ambitions and planned some day to knock out a few short stories or maybe a novel or two about his own adventures and travels. For the time being, he was the LCB toxicologist—the Rat Man, we called him—and the one Dr. Allen farmed you out to assist when you started messing up and your lab future was growing uncertain.

I myself grew rather fast and loose in my handling of lab protocol as the months wore on, so that one reckless mid-morning Dr. Allen, brandishing her steely, businesslike grin, asked me to submit my schedule. That was the tip-off. When she asked you to submit a schedule—which was what she'd asked of Janocz—you could be certain you were skating on thin ice, indeed. Discipline around LCB, for lower-level workers anyway, was anything but tight. With your hands pushed down into the pockets of your lab coat and, wearing the proper expression of authority, you could mingle leisurely and roam at large. Such roaming, if you didn't look out, was apt to get you in trouble.

I should perhaps explain that the facilities of the Laboratory for Comparative Biology were spread around the immediate neighborhood. The main facility, for example, was where my work was headquartered, but I had occasion sometimes dozens of times a day, to walk across the street and make use of the autoclave, or to deliver specimens to the Rat Man or to pick up equipment that needed cleaning from any of several associates who ran mini-labs on that side of Cutting Boulevard. Further down the block was a storage and warehouse building. Another lab aide named Ken—one of two so named; both of them hired after Ethel and I had gotten on—used to go with me down there on one errand or another, and sometimes we'd linger and joke around for the fun of it. Or else Wes Jacobs and I would make a run over to Cutter Glass Labs or some other scientific firm along the Bay, on business, of course, and always with the blessings and under the unquestionable protection of our official uniforms.

It was Janocz, though, who took the cake when it came to abusing lab coat privileges. He actually had the nerve to wear his lab coat to work mornings, and he was fond of carrying a little black leather bag. Whenever Janocz got stopped for speeding by some highway patrolman, all he had to do was blush or look flustered, then point to his black bag on the car seat beside him and say, "Oh, officer, I must have gotten carried away in the face of this emergency." And the patrolman would inevitably presume him to be an M.D. of some kind and wave the little imposter on. Janocz was almost unstoppable. It took me a long time to catch on to his clever gambit of arriving late to the job, loosening his tie, then disappearing with a clipboard into one of the back rooms where he and his boss had some manner of experiment set up. That way, should Dr. Allen come looking for him, he could always emerge from his hideaway, breathless and tousled, and give her the impression that he'd been on the scene all along, taking care of business.

At the time, I was in my early twenties. Everything was serious, but not too serious. A college dropout and would-be writer, I was busiest of all with life itself and the process of getting it lived. The idea here was to hold down enough of a day job to eat and meet the rent of $75 a month and to drop into a cookie jar the earnings I picked up from music gigs on the weekends and part-time disk-jockeying at a local radio station nights.

Along the way I gathered enough mental notes to paper a book on that lab experience, which will always be punctuated with blasts from Booker T. and the MG's "Green Onions." Now I'm forced to realize that I was the one who was green at one end and sprouting at the other. And while shedding one layer after another, I was getting to know the world in ways that never paid off so much materially as they did experientially. It never occurred to me then, for instance, that there would have to be no fewer than a thousand chapters in this imagined volume devoted to that year, for the Laboratory for Comparative Biology—whose personnel came from the States, Europe, Japan, India, China, Canada, Australia, and the Middle East—was nothing but a complex crew of biological space cadets. Once their ship was off the ground, they had proceeded to cajole, color, rank, playoff against, condemn, investigate, experiment, consort, and fall in love with one another like any other random batch of humans being human.

Sometimes, even now, years later, I like to get together with Wes Jacobs, a staunch survivor of that era, and talk about the time Dr. Allen—who used to get juiced at lab parties—did a striptease, or the time when ethanol theft grew to such proportions that she had to send down a order that its use be strictly regulated. I've never forgotten that it was chemist and former winemaker Jack Murchio who introduced me to the work of novelist George P. Elliot and the writings of Alfred Döblin, the German Expressionist novelist who wrote *Alexanderplatz Berlin*. It was also around that time that I heard Ken Fishler play piano—the other of those lab aides named Ken—long before he joined with his singing wife to form the duo known as Bobbi & I, and also before he went on the road with singer Anita O'Day.

Betcha you never played "Green Onions," Kenny. But I did. I stole and stuck it—vamp chords, that is—directly into a song arrangement. That was around the time in my life when things started falling into place, when being around systematic processes of analysis infiltrated some mindless part of me to the point where I'd get flashes now and then, usually when showering to go to work, that we were all formed of earth and spirit and had as our goal the realization that, like a rainbow of flames in a Bunsen burner, we were emanating from the same ignited pilot.

Acknowledgments

I would like to thank the following good folks who helped, suffered, and stuck by me throughout the long process of putting this book together and finally getting it published.

First and foremost, and without whom this anthology would have never seen the light of day, I would like to thank Allan Kornblum, Chris Fischbach, Molly Mikolowski, Anitra Budd, and author extraordinaire Allison Adelle Hedge Coke at Coffee House Press.

Another invaluable person for this project was my longtime friend, colleague, and working-class pal Kathleen Zamora, who did an incredible job pulling all of these pieces together, gathering initial permissions, checking them in, and getting this entire book onto disk. She has always been my rock in this process, and I am very grateful. Thanks also to my son, Shane M. Liebler, who helped with the initial readings of *Working Words*'s nineteenth-century literature while he was an intern at St. Bonaventure University. I offer much thanks to Kathleen Garrett for the inclusive and wonderful working-class bibliography she started compiling in my Labor Studies course at Wayne State University long ago, and to my longtime friend and comrade in the working-class literary arts' struggle, Dr. Larry Smith at Fireland College of Bowling Green State University in Huron, Ohio, who always gave me courage and comfort when the going got tough.

The following good folks offered me much assistance in the completion of this process, and I want to let them all know I am indeed grateful for their friendship and their full support of me and this project: Aran Ruth, Jeff Rosen, Al Kooper, Michael Moore, Philip Levine, Mike Dutkewych, Jim Daniels, Maria Mazziotti Gillan, Brendan and Shelby L. Maidment, Ben "Rivethead" Hamper, Edward Sanders, Lolita Hernandez, Barry Wallenstein, Joel Martin, Matty Lee, Dave Marsh, Joe Henry, Peter Coyote, and Anne Feeney.

Last, but certainly not least, I want to give all thanks and praise to my dear wife and friend of over forty years, Pamela Liebler, who had to endure much wailing and gnashing of teeth throughout the long process of pulling this book together. She really deserves much more than this little acknowledgment can express for being there for me through all these years.

Biographies

MAGGIE ANDERSON is the author of four books of poems, most recently *Windfall: New and Selected Poems,* published in 2000. Anderson is also the editor of the new and selected poems of Louise McNeill and co-editor of *Learning by Heart: Contemporary American Poetry about School* and *A Gathering of Poets.* Until her retirement in 2009, Maggie Anderson was a professor of English and faculty member in the Northeast Ohio MFA program at Kent State University, where she directed the Wick Poetry Center and edited the Wick Poetry Series of the Kent State University Press.

ANTLER, former poet laureate of Milwaukee, is author of *Factory* (City Lights, 1980), *Last Words* (Ballantine, 1986), *Subterranean Rivulet, Your Great-Great Grand-father's Puberty Boners, Open Bible with a Gun on It, Exclamation Points Ad Infinitum,* and *Ever-Expanding Wilderness.* His work also appears in anthologies, including *Poets Against the War, Poets on 9/11,* and *Reclaiming the Heartland: Lesbian and Gay Voices from the Midwest.* When not wildernessing or traveling to read his poems, he lives along the Milwaukee River in Milwaukee, Wisconsin.

ALVIN AUBERT is a poet, educator, editor, short story writer, and drama-tist. He founded *Obsidian: Black Literature in Review* in 1975. He taught African American literature and creative writing at both the State University of New York (1970–1979) and later at Wayne State University (1979–1993). His books of poetry include *Against the Blues* (1972), *Feeling Through* (1976), *South Louisiana: New and Selected Poems* (1985), *If Winter Come: Collected Poems 1967–1992,* and *Harlem Wrestler and Other Poems* (1995). He retired from Wayne State in 1993 after thirty-three years of teaching.

AMIRI BARAKA (né LeRoi Jones) is the author of more than forty books of essays, poems, drama, music history, and criticism. A political activist and one of the founders of the Black Arts Movement, Baraka's works include a study on African American music, *Blues People* (1963); the play *Dutchman* (1963); and *Selected Poetry of Amiri Baraka/LeRoi Jones* (1979). He has taught at Yale, Columbia, and the State University of New York at Stony Brook. Baraka is Professor Emeritus at the State University of New York at Stony Brook and the former poet laureate of New Jersey.

JAN BEATTY is a poet whose works include *Boneshaker* (2002), *Mad River* (1995), and *Red Sugar* (2008). *Ravenous*, her limited edition chapbook, won the 1995 State Street Prize. Beatty's poetry has appeared in anthologies published by Oxford University Press, University of Illinois Press, and University of Iowa Press. For the past thirteen years, she has hosted and produced *Prosody*, a public radio show on NPR-affiliate WYEP-FM featuring the work of national writers. Beatty directs the creative writing program at Carlow University, where she runs the Madwomen in the Attic writing workshops and teaches in the MFA program.

DANIEL BERRIGAN, SJ is the author of fourteen volumes of poetry and numerous books of commentary and interpretations of key books in the Bible. His first volume of poetry, *Time Without Number* (1957), whose publication occurred at the suggestion of poet Marianne Moore, was nominated for the National Book Award and awarded the prestigious Lamont Prize for Poetry by the American Academy of Arts and Letters. His collected poems, *And the Risen Bread*, was published by the Fordham University Press.

LAURA BOSS was a first-prize winner in PSA's Gordon Barber Poetry Contest. Founder and editor of *Lips* poetry magazine, her awards for her own poetry also include an ALTA (funded through the NEA) and three fellowships in creative writing (poetry) from the NJSCA. Her books of poetry include *Stripping* (1982), *On the Edge of the Hudson* (CCC, 1986), *Reports from the Front* (CCC, 1995), and *Arms: New and Selected Work* (Guernica Editions, 1999). Her poetry has appeared in the *New York Times*.

MELBA JOYCE BOYD is the author of several books of poetry. She has won numerous awards for her work, including the Michigan Council for the Arts Individual Artist Award. She was commissioned to write the official poem for the Charles H. Wright Museum of African American History. She is the author of two biographies, including *Wrestling with the Muse: Dudley Randall and the Broadside Press* (Columbia University Press), which received the 2005 Black Caucus of the American Library Association Book Honor for Nonfiction. She is professor and chair of the Department of Africana Studies at Wayne State University and lives in Detroit with her family.

JEANNE BRYNER was born in Appalachia and grew up in Newton Falls, Ohio. A retired registered nurse, her books in print are *Breathless; Blind Horse: Poems; Eclipse: Stories; Tenderly Lift Me: Nurses Honored, Celebrated and Remembered;* and *No Matter How Many Windows.* Her poetry has been adapted for the stage and performed in Ohio, West Virginia, New York, California, Kentucky, and the Fringe Festival in Edinburgh, Scotland. She has received fellowships from Bucknell University, the Ohio Arts Council, and the Vermont Studio Center. "Turn the Radio to a Gospel Station" appeared in *Our Working Lives: Short Stories of People and Work* (Bottom Dog Press, 2000) and *Eclipse: Stories* (Bottom Dog Press, 2003).

BONNIE JO CAMPBELL was born in Kalamazoo, Michigan, and is the author of two short story collections, *Women & Other Animals* (1999) and *American Salvage* (2009); and the novel *Q Road* (2002). Campbell lives in Kalamazoo with her husband, Christopher Magson, and teaches fiction at Pacific University in Forest Grove, Oregon, in the low-residency MFA program. In 2010, *American Salvage* was a finalist for both the National Book Award and the National Book Critics Circle Award.

MICHAEL CASEY's first book, *Obscenities,* was in the Yale Younger Poet Series in 1972. His later books are *Millrat, The Million Dollar Hole, Raiding a Whorehouse,* and *Permanent Party.* His writing has appeared in the *Los Angeles Times* and the *New York Times.* He teaches at Northern Essex Community College in Haverhill, Massachusetts.

WILLA CATHER (1873–1947) is an American novelist noted for her books about immigrants struggling to make a living in the Midwest during the late nineteenth century. She wrote twelve novels, including *My Antonia* (1918), *O Pioneers!* (1913), *The Song of the Lark* (1915), and *Death Comes to the Archbishop* (1927).

HAYAN CHARARA was born in Detroit, Michigan, to immigrant parents and lived in New York City for many years. He is the author of two books of poetry, *The Alchemist's Diary* (Hanging Loose Press) and *The Sadness of Others* (Carnegie Mellon Press). He now lives and teaches in Texas. He is also a woodworker.

ANDREI CODRESCU is a Romanian-born American poet, novelist, essayist, screenwriter, and commentator for National Public Radio. His publications include several books of poetry, including *License to Carry a Gun* (1970), *Alien Candor: Selected Poems, 1970–1995*, and *Jealous Witness* (Coffee House Press, 2008); essay collections, including *The Devil Never Sleeps and Other Essays* (2000); and three novels, including *Messiah* (1999). He was the MacCurdy Distinguished Professor of English at Louisiana State University from 1984 until his retirement in 2009.

WANDA COLEMAN is a Los Angeles-based poet and performer. Since the late 1970s, Coleman has published eight books, including *Art in the Court of the Blue Fag* (1977) and *Hand Dance* (1993). Colman has received numerous awards, including an Emmy for writing in 1976 and a Guggenheim Fellowship for poetry in 1984. Distinguishing herself from other African American writers from the South and the East, Coleman sees herself as a distinctly West Coast writer. Despite her ambivalent relationship with Los Angeles, she remains dedicated to depicting the varied lives in the city, giving voice to the dispossessed, making visible the invisible, and putting a human face on anonymous statistics.

DAVID CONNOLLY was born and raised in South Boston and served in Vietnam with the Eleventh Armored Cavalry Regiment of the u.s. Army. He is the author of the prose and poetry collection *Lost in America*. Dave was a member of the Retail Clerks International Union as a teenager and holds a lifetime membership card from Local 2222 of the International Brotherhood of Electrical Workers. He is proud of his thirty-two years of active service for them as a union man and a steward.

CARLOS CORTEZ (1923–2005) was an extraordinary artist, poet, printmaker, photographer, songwriter, and lifelong political activist. His mother was a German socialist pacifist, and his father was a Mexican Indian organizer for the Industrial Workers of the World (iww), also known as the Wobblies. Carlos was a Wobblie until he died. He spent two years in prison for refusing to "shoot at fellow draftees" during World War ii. He authored several books of poetry, and is best known for large linocut poster-portraits of activists and labor organizers such as Joe Hill, Ricardo Flóres Magón, Lucy Parsons, and Ben Fletcher.

JAYNE CORTEZ was born in Arizona, grew up in Los Angeles, California, and currently lives in New York City. She is the author of ten books of poems and has performed her poetry with music on nine recordings. Her books include *Pisstained Stairs and the Monkey Man's Wares* (Phrase Text, 1969), *Coagulations: New and Selected Poems* (Thunder's Mouth Press, 1984), and *Jazz Fan Looks Back* (Hanging Loose Press, 2002). She is co-founder and president of the Organization of Women Writers of Africa and has had a long career as a social activist.

STEPHEN CRANE (1871–1900) is an American author whose unromanticized war novel, *The Red Badge of Courage* (1895), brought him international fame. Crane's first novel, *Maggie: A Girl of the Streets*, was a milestone in the development of literary naturalism. His manuscript was turned down by publishers, who considered its realism too "ugly." Crane printed the book at his own expense, borrowing the money from his brother. In its inscription Crane warned that "it is inevitable that you be greatly shocked by this book but continue, please, with all possible courage to the end." The story of the descent of a slum girl in turn-of-the-century New York into prostitution was first published under the pseudonym of Johnston Smith.

JIM DANIELS is the author of three collections of short fiction and thirteen collections of poetry, including, most recently, *Having a Little Talk with Capital P Poetry* (Carnegie Mellon University Press) and *From Milltown to Malltown*, a collaborative book with photographer Charlee Brodsky and writer Jane McCafferty (Marick Press), both published in 2010. He received the Tillie Olsen Creative Writing Award from the Working-Class Studies Association in 2007.

REBECCA HARDING DAVIS (1831–1910) was an American novelist. Her early non-fiction pieces, particularly those collected under the title *Life in the Iron Mills* (1861), and her first novel, *Margaret Howth* (1862), foreshadowed the naturalistic techniques of later nineteenth-century writers by showing how a dismal environment can warp personal character.

DOROTHY DAY (1897–1980) was a socialist and founder of the Catholic Worker Movement, which joined radical social reform with the Roman Catholic faith in a movement for social justice and peace. Day wrote for the socialist magazine *New York Call*, co-edited the famous radical magazine *Masses*, and co-founded *The Catholic Worker*. Day's autobiography, *The Long Loneliness*, was published in 1952. Day was inducted into the National Women's Hall of Fame in Seneca Falls, New York, on October 5, 2001.

GERI DIGIORNO is founder and director of the Petaluma Poetry Walk. Her book, *White Lipstick*, was published by Red Hen Press.

DIANE DI PRIMA is the author of more than forty books of poetry and prose. Her work has been translated into over twenty languages. An expanded edition of her *Revolutionary Letters* will be released by Last Gasp Press in 2010. She lives and works in San Francisco.

SUE DORO was born in 1937 in Berlin, Wisconsin. She is the daughter of a welder and a homemaker and has been writing since she was twelve. She has had three books published: *Of Birds and Factories; Heart, Home, and Hard Hats;* and most recently *Blue Collar Goodbyes*. She lives in Oakland, California, and edits a free support and informational newsletter, *Pride and a Paycheck*. Funded by the San Francisco Foundation, the goal of the publication is to help under-employed women, and those systemically forced off welfare, find and be successful in high-paying, blue-collar skilled and semi-skilled careers with benefits. She is the mother of six and a retired machinist.

BOB DYLAN is widely regarded as America's greatest living popular song-writer. Much of his best-known work is from the 1960s, when his musical shadow was so large that he became a documentarian and reluctant figure-head of American unrest. Millions of young people embraced his song "The Times They Are A-Changin'" during that era of extreme change. More broadly, Dylan is credited with expanding the vocabulary of popular music into the heady realms of politics/social commentary, philosophy, and a kind of stream of consciousness, absurdist humor that defies easy description. This lyrical innovation has occurred within the context of Dylan's steadfast devotion to the richest traditions of American song, from folk and country/blues to rock 'n' roll and rockabilly, to Gaelic balladry, gospel, and even jazz, swing, and Broadway. In addition to his legendary songwriting, he is the author of two books: *Chronicles: Volume One* and *Tarantula*.

W. D. EHRHART teaches English and history at the Haverford School in Haverford, Pennsylvania. He lives in Philadelphia with his wife Anne and daughter Leela.

EMINEM is the stage name of Detroit-based rapper and celebrity Marshall Mathers III. He has released several albums, including *The Slim Shady LP* (1999), *The Eminem Show* (2002), and *Recovery* (2010). In addition, Mathers starred in the semi-autobiographical film *8 Mile* and subsequently became the first rapper to win an Oscar for Best Song (for the film's "Lose Yourself"). Mathers is also one of the first white rappers to garner both critical acclaim and respect within the genre.

ANNE FEENEY is based in Pittsburgh, Pennsylvania, and is the granddaughter of an intrepid mineworkers' organizer, who also used music to carry the message of solidarity to working people. After two decades of community activism and regional performances at rallies, Anne took her message on the road. Since 1991, Anne has traveled to the frontlines in more than forty states, Canada, Mexico, Ireland, and Sweden. Her anthem "Have You Been to Jail for Justice?" is performed by Peter, Paul and Mary. Dubbed the "minister of culture" in the movements for economic and social justice and human rights, Anne is "the best labor singer in North America," according to Utah Phillips.

VIEVEE FRANCIS has published work and has work forthcoming in several journals and anthologies, including *Margie, Crab Orchard Review, Callaloo*, and *The Best American Poetry 2010*. In 2009 she recieved a Rona Jaffe Foundation Writer's Award, and was the 2009/2010 Alice Lloyd Hall Scholars Program Poet in Residence at the University of Michigan. A Cave Canem Fellow, she is married to poet Matthew Scott Olzmann.

STEWART FRANCKE was born in Saginaw, Michigan, and is a singer and songwriter. His albums include *Where the River Meets the Bay* (1995); he is also the author of *Between the Ground & God* (2006), a collection of his lyrics and writing. A bone marrow transplant survivor, Stewart has been recognized by the Points of Light Foundation for his personal work in cancer patient support. The Stewart Francke Leukemia Foundation was presented the prestigious Partnership in Humanity Award by the Detroit Newspapers, and he was named Volunteer of the Year by the National Marrow Donor Program in 2002. In 2009 he was awarded a Lifetime Achievement Award from the Saginaw County Cultural Arts Commission. He fronts his own soul band at venues across the country.

CYNTHIA GALLAHER is author of three collections of poetry: *Earth Elegance, Swimmer's Prayer,* and *Night Ribbons.* She is also featured in various anthologies, such as *Stand Up Poetry: An Expanded Anthology* (University of Iowa Press), and is a recipient of a recent Community Arts Assistance Program grant in theater from the City of Chicago.

JENNIFER GILLAN is an Associate Professor in the English Department at Bentley College in Waltham, Massachusetts. With Maria Mazziotti Gillan, she is the coeditor of three award-winning multicultural anthologies. Their fourth collection, *Italian American Writers on New Jersey,* co-edited with Edi Giunta, was published by Rutgers University Press in 2003. Her articles on race, class, and assimilation have appeared in *American Literature, American Drama, African American Review, Cinema Journal, MOSAIC, North Dakota Quarterly,* and *Arizona Quarterly,* among others.

MARIA MAZZIOTTI GILLAN won the American Book Award for her latest book, *All That Lies Between Us.* She is the founder/executive director of the Poetry Center at Passaic County Community College in Paterson, New Jersey. She is also director of the creative writing program and professor of poetry at Binghamton University, SUNY. She has published eleven books of poetry, including *The Weather of Old Seasons* (Cross-Cultural Communications) and *Italian Women in Black Dresses* (Guernica Editions). She is co-editor, with her daughter Jennifer, of four anthologies: *Unsettling America, Identity Lessons,* and *Growing Up Ethnic in America* (Penguin/Putnam); and *Italian American Writers on New Jersey* (Rutgers). She is the editor of the *Paterson Literary Review.*

KATHLEEN GLYNN has been the Executive Producer of Dog Eat Dog Films, Inc. since 1989, and has produced several films, including Michael Moore's films *Roger and Me* (1989), *Bowling for Columbine,* which received the Academy Award in 2003 for best documentary, and most recently, the critically acclaimed documentary *Fahrenheit 9/11,* which won the Palme d'Or at the 2004 Cannes Film Festival. She won an Emmy Award and the Montreaux Television Festival's Rose d'Or for Moore's TV *Nation.* Also with Moore, she co-wrote *Adventures in a TV Nation.* Along with Mr. Moore, she also formed the Center for Alternative Media and Culture, a private foundation that has awarded hundreds of grants to filmmakers and organizations that seek to correct injustice in the world.

MARIELA GRIFFOR is the author of *Exiliana* (Luna Publications) and *House* (Mayapple Press). She was born in the city of Concepcion in southern Chile. She is co-founder of the Institute for Creative Writers at Wayne State University and publisher of Marick Press. Her work has appeared in periodicals across Latin America and the United States. She is a Joel Oppenheimer Scholar at New England College and is Honorary Consul of Chile in Detroit, Michigan.

WOODY GUTHRIE (1912–1967) was a writer and performer of folk and labor songs. Guthrie composed "This Land Is Your Land," a song many call an unofficial national anthem. His songs include messages of unity and brotherly love and remain anthems of the poor and broken. Guthrie is the author of the classic autobiography *Bound for Glory*. He was inducted into both the Songwriters' Hall of Fame and the Rock and Roll Hall of Fame and Museum in Cleveland.

FRANCES ELLEN WATKINS HARPER (1825–1911) was an African American writer, lecturer, and political activist, who promoted abolition, civil rights, women's rights, and temperance. She helped found, or held high office in, several national progressive organizations. She is best remembered today for her poetry and fiction, which preached moral uplift and counseled the oppressed on how to free themselves from their demoralized condition.

BILL HARRIS is playwright, novelist, and poet. Harris has had two books of poetry published: *The Ringmaster's Array* and *Yardbird Suite: Side One*. His published plays include *Stories about the Old Days*, *Riffs*, and *Coda*, which was written with funding from a Guggenheim Foundation Award. Harris is a professor at Wayne State University.

STEPHEN HAVEN's book of poems, *Dust and Bread* (Turning Point, 2008), was selected by the Ohio Poetry Day Association as co-winner in a competition to recognize the best book published by an Ohio poet in 2008. He was named Co-Ohio Poet of the Year in 2009. Haven is also the author of an earlier collection of poems, *The Long Silence of the Mohawk Carpet Smokestacks* (West End Press, 2004), and of the memoir *The River Lock: One Boy's Life along the Mohawk* (Syracuse University Press, 2008). He directs the MFA program in poetry and creative non-fiction at Ashland University in Ashland, Ohio.

ALLISON HEDGE COKE's books include *Dog Road Woman* (winner of the American Book Award) and *Off-Season City Pipe,* poetry (Coffee House Press); *Rock Ghost, Willow, Deer,* a memoir; and *Blood Run,* a free-verse play. Hedge Coke's edited collections include *Sing, Ahani,* and *Effigies.* She regularly performs at international poetry festivals, including events in Colombia, Venezuela, Argentina, Canada, and Jordan. Hedge Coke spent her youth and young adult life working in factories, sharecropping tobacco and sweet potato fields, migrant picking citrus, working construction (heavy equipment, carpentry, and demolition), and working waters as a commercial fisher. Hedge Coke currently serves as the Reynolds Chair of Poetry and Writing at the University of Nebraska at Kearney.

JOE HENRY For more than two decades as a solo artist and Grammy-winning producer, Joe Henry has worked with some of the most celebrated names in music, including Ornette Coleman, Elvis Costello, Allen Toussaint, T-Bone Burnett, Don Byron, Solomon Burke, Brad Mehldau, Madonna, and Ani DiFranco. *Blood from Stars,* his new album, is his eleventh studio album. He lives in Pasadena, grew up in the Detroit metro area, and attended Oakland University.

LOLITA HERNANDEZ, born and raised in Detroit, is the author of *Autopsy of an Engine and Other Stories from the Cadillac Plant* (Coffee House Press), winner of the PEN Beyond Margins Award. She also is the author of two chapbook collections of poems: *Quiet Battles* (Wayne State University Writers Forum) and *snakecrossing* (Ridgeway Press). All her writing is influenced by the rhythms and language of her Trinidad and St. Vincent family and tempered by over thirty years as a UAW worker, twenty-one of them at the Cadillac Plant in Detroit. She now teaches in the creative writing department of the University of Michigan Residential College and is working on her first novel.

LABAN CARRICK HILL is a poet, novelist, and non-fiction writer who is the co-director and co-founder of the Ghana Poetry Project, a nonprofit arts organization promoting literacy and literary culture in Africa. He is the author of numerous books for children, young adults, and adults, including *Harlem Stomp!,* which was a 2004 National Book Award Finalist.

EDWARD HIRSCH, who has had some hard jobs, has published five books of poems, including *Wild Gratitude* (1986) and *Lay Back the Darkness* (2003), and three books of prose, among them *How to Read a Poem: and Fall in Love with Poetry* (1999), a national bestseller. His most recent book is *The Living Fire: New and Selected Poems* (2010).

MIKHAIL HOROWITZ is the author of *Big League Poets* (City Lights, 1978) and two collections of poetry. His performance pieces have been featured on eight CDs, including *The Blues of the Birth*, a collection of his jazz fables, and the anthology album *Bring It On Home, Vol. II* (Columbia Records). He's painted fences at a horse farm, worked as a moving man and in mailrooms, movie theaters, and newspaper offices, and currently impersonates an editor in the Bard College Publications Office.

MURRAY JACKSON grew up in Detroit, Michigan, and attended Wayne State University. He served as founding president of Wayne County Community College from 1967–1970, and was a professor emeritus of higher education at the University of Michigan, where he taught from 1971–1991. His books include *Watermelon Rinds & Cherry Pits* (Broadside Press, 1991), *Woodland Sketches: Scenes from Childhood* (X-Press Productions, 1990), and his final collection *Bob Weaving Detroit* (Wayne State University Press, 2004). He passed away in 2002.

X. J. KENNEDY, in his own words, is a poet "for three separate audiences: children, college students (who use textbooks), and that small band of people who still read poetry." His first book of poetry, *Nude Descending a Staircase*, won the Lamont Award of the Academy of American Poets. He is the author of many collections of poetry for young people, including *One Winter Night in August, and Other Nonsense Jingles* (1975) and *Talking Like the Rain: A Read-to-Me Book of Poems*, with Dorothy M. Kennedy (1992). His latest book is *In a Prominent Bar in Secaucus: New and Selected Poems, 1955–2007* (Johns Hopkins University Press, 2007). Kennedy is also the author of several textbooks.

AL KOOPER is one of the giants of 60s rock and beyond. In addition to co-writing the classic mid-60s pop-rock song, "This Diamond Ring" (though it was written as an R&B number), he was a session man on some of the most important records of the decade, including Bob Dylan's "Like a Rolling Stone." Kooper also joined and led the Blues Project and Blood, Sweat & Tears. He played on two classic blues-rock albums in conjunction with his friend Mike Bloomfield. As a producer at Columbia, he signed the British Invasion act, the Zombies, just in time for them to complete the best LP in their entire history; and still later, Kooper discovered Lynyrd Skynyrd and produced their best work. Kooper has toured the world and is the author of the popular and acclaimed autobiography *Backstage Passes & Back Stabbing Bastards: Memoirs of a Rock 'N' Roll Survivor.*

DORIANNE LAUX was born in Augusta, Maine, in 1952. She worked as a sanatorium cook, a gas station manager, a maid, and a donut holer before receiving a B.A. in English from Mills College in 1988. Laux is the author of several collections of poetry, including *Facts About the Moon* (W. W. Norton & Company, 2006), *Smoke* (BOA Editions Ltd., 2000), *What We Carry* (1994), and *Awake* (1990). Among her awards are a Pushcart Prize, an Editor's Choice III Award, and a fellowship from the NEA. Laux has taught at the University of Oregon's program in creative writing. She now lives with her husband, poet Joseph Millar, in Raleigh, North Carolina, where she serves on the faculty at North Carolina State University's MFA program.

LI-YOUNG LEE is an Asian American poet born in Jakarta, Indonesia, to Chinese parents. Lee's father, personal physician to Mao Zedong while in China, moved his family to Indonesia and helped to found Gamaliel University. Lee has taught at Northwestern University and the University of Iowa. He has written several poetry collections, including *Book of My Nights* (2001), *The City in Which I Love You* (1990), and *Rose* (1986). His memoir, *The Winged Seed: A Remembrance* (1995), received an American Book Award from the Before Columbus Foundation. His awards include a Lannan Literary Award and a Whiting Writer's Award; grants from the Illinois Arts Council, the Commonwealth of Pennsylvania, the Pennsylvania Council on the Arts, and the NEA; and a Guggenheim Foundation fellowship. Lee currently resides in Chicago, Illinois.

CHRISTOPHER T. LELAND is a professor of English and director of creative writing at Wayne State University. His books include *The Book of Marvels* (1989), *Letting Loose* (1996), and *The Creative Writer's Style Guide: Rules and Advice for Writing Fiction and Creative Non-Fiction* (2002). He has a new collection of short stories forthcoming from the Wayne State University Press in 2011.

PHILIP LEVINE was born in 1928 and raised in Detroit, the son of Russian-Jewish immigrants. He was educated in the public schools of Detroit and also attended Wayne State University. After a succession of industrial jobs, including punching in at Chevy Gear & Axle and running jack hammer at Detroit Transmission, Levine left Detroit to teach part-time at the University of Iowa, which enabled him to attend the Iowa Writer's Workshop. He taught literature and writing at Fresno State for over thirty years. Levine has won both a National Book Award and a Pulitzer Prize. His books include *On the Edge* (1964), *What Work Is: Poems* (1991), and *The Mercy: Poems* (1999). His most recent book is the 2009 *News of the World*.

M. L. LIEBLER is an internationally known and widely published Detroit poet, university professor, literary arts activis, and arts organizer, and the author of more than a dozen books, including the award-winning *Wide Awake in Someone Else's Dream* (Wayne State University Press, 2008), which features poems written in and about Russia, Israel, Germany, Alaska, and Detroit. *Wide Awake* won both the Paterson Poetry Prize for Literary Excellence and the American Indie Book Award for 2009. In 2005, he was named St. Clair Shore's (his hometown) first poet laureate. Liebler has read and performed his work in Israel, Russia, China, France, the U.K., Macao, Italy, Germany, Spain, Finland, Turkey, and most of the fifty states. Liebler has taught English, American Studies, Labor Studies, Canadian Studies, and World Literature at Wayne State University in Detroit since 1980, and he is the founding director of both the National Writer's Voice Project in Detroit and the Springfed Arts: Metro Detroit Writers Literary Arts Organization. He was recently selected as Best Detroit Poet by the *Detroit Free Press* and Detroit's *Metro Times,* and he is the nation's first ever artist in residence for a public library at the Chelsea District Library for 2008–2009. In 2010, he received the Barnes & Noble *Poets & Writers* Writers for Writers Award with Maxine Hong Kingston and Junot Diaz. Learn more about him at www.mlliebler.com.

SHIRLEY GEOK-LIN LIM is a professor in the English department at the University of California, Santa Barbara. She received her Ph.D. from Brandeis University in 1973, and has also taught internationally at the National University of Singapore, NIE of Nanyang Technological University, and most recently as Chair Professor at the University of Hong Kong. She is the author of five books of poems; three books of short stories; two books of criticism, *Nationalism and Literature* (1993) and *Writing South/East Asia in English: Against the Grain* (1994); a book of memoirs, *Among the White Moon Faces: An Asian-American Memoir of Homelands* (1996), and a novel, *Joss and Gold* (2001). Lim is currently at work on a study of gender and nation in Asian American representations.

HENRY WADSWORTH LONGFELLOW (1807–1882) is one of the most popular American poets of the nineteenth century, a storyteller whose works are still cited today—or parodied. Longfellow's works range from sentimental pieces such as "The Village Blacksmith" to translations of Dante. Among his most interesting works are *Evangeline* (1847), a narrative poem of the former French colony of Acadia, and *The Song of Hiawatha* (1855), noted for its singsong meter and shamanistic rhythm.

BRET LOTT is the author of twelve books, including 2008's *Ancient Highway* and the Oprah Book Club Selection *Jewel*. "Work" is from his first collection of stories, *A Dream of Old Leaves* (Viking, 1989). He teaches at the College of Charleston and lives with his wife, Melanie, in Hanahan, South Carolina.

THOMAS LUX's most recent book is *God Particles* (Houghton Mifflin Harcourt, 2008) and *The Cradle Place* (Houghton Mifflin Harcourt, 2004). He currently holds the Bourne Chair in Poetry at the Georgia Institute of Technology and runs their Poetry at Tech program. Thomas Lux was born in Northampton, Massachusetts, the son of a milkman and a Sears & Roebuck switchboard operator, neither of whom graduated from high school. Lux was raised in Massachusetts on a dairy farm.

THOMAS LYNCH was born in Detroit, Michigan. In 1973 he graduated from mortuary school, and in 1974 he took over a funeral home in Milford, Michigan, where he has worked ever since. Lynch began writing poetry about his work and in 1987 published the critically acclaimed *Skating with Heather Grace*. He has published two other volumes of poetry, *Grimalkin and Other Poems* (1994) and *Still Life in Milford* (1998), and a collection of essays, *The Undertaking: Life Studies from the Dismal Trade* (1997). His most recent book is a novella and stories entitled *Apparitions & Late Fictions* (W. W. Norton & Company, 2010).

DAVE MARSH is a music critic who attended Wayne State University, became a formative editor of *Creem* magazine, and wrote for various publications such as *Newsday*, the *Village Voice*, and *Rolling Stone*. Marsh also edited *Rock and Roll Confidential*, a newsletter about rock music and social issues. His other credits include being Bruce Springsteen's quasi-official biographer, with a total of four books published. Marsh's books include *Born to Run: The Bruce Springsteen Story* (1979), *Glory Days: Bruce Springsteen in the 1980s* (1987), and *Sly and the Family Stone: An Oral History* (1998). Marsh has also been involved in organizing and maintaining the Rock and Roll Hall of Fame in Cleveland, Ohio.

CAROLINE MAUN, Assistant Professor of English at Wayne State University in Detroit, Michigan, is the editor of *The Collected Poems of Evelyn Scott* (National Poetry Foundation, 2005), a collection of poetry, *The Sleeping* (Marick Press, 2006), and a chapbook of poetry, *Cures and Poisons* (Pudding House Press, 2009). Her work as a poet and critic has appeared in the *Mississippi Quarterly*, the *Emily Dickinson Journal*, the *Yeats-Eliot Review*, the *Adirondack Review*, *Third Wednesday*, and *Raving Dove*.

MICHAEL MCCLURE has long been noted for the popularity of his dynamic poetry performances. At the age of twenty-two he gave his first poetry reading at the legendary Six Gallery event in San Francisco, where Allen Ginsberg first read *Howl*. Today McClure is more active than ever, writing and performing his poetry at festivals, colleges, and clubs across the country. Michael McClure is "the role model for Jim Morrison," as the *Los Angeles Times* characterized him, and he has found sources in music from Thelonious Monk and Miles Davis to the composer Terry Riley, with whom his poetry readings frequently share a bill. He is the author of several books of poetry and writing from New Directions, and he currently records and performs with Ray Manzarek of the Doors.

RAY MCNIECE is a poet, actor, singer, educator, and the author of five poetry books: *Dis, The Bone-Orchard Conga, The Road that Carried Me Here, Song that Fathoms Home,* and *Wet Sand Raven Tracks: New Haiku.* He is also the author of theater works and music/poetry collaborations. He was the voice of Woody Guthrie in WCPN/NPR's award-winning radio documentary *Hard Travellin'.* "Grandfather's Breath" was originally published in *Red Brick Review.* Learn more about him at www.raymcniece.com.

TONY MEDINA is the author of thirteen books. His poetry, fiction, and essays appear in over eighty anthologies and publications. Associate Professor of Creative Writing at Howard University, Medina's most recent books are *I and I: Bob Marley* and *My Old Man Was Always on the Lam.* His collection, *Broke on Ice,* is forthcoming through Willow Books, a division of Aquarius Press.

D. H. MELHEM is the author of eight books of poetry, including *New York Poems, Rest in Love, Conversation with a Stonemason,* and *Country.* As a novelist, she published *Patrimonies,* a trilogy, comprising *Blight, Stigma,* and *The Cave;* as a scholar, *Gwendolyn Brooks* and *Heroism in the New Black Poetry;* as an editor, two anthologies, including *A Different Path;* as a playwright, a musical drama, *Children of the House Afire,* produced in New York; as a creative writing teacher, *Reaching Exercises;* and more than seventy essays. Among her numerous awards for poetry and prose are an American Book Award, a RAWI Lifetime Achievement Award, and fellowships from the National Endowment for the Humanities and the Fondation Ledig-Rowohlt in Switzerland. Her eighth poetry collection, *Art and Politics / Politics and Art,* was published by Syracuse University Press in 2010. Learn more about him at www.dhmelhem.com.

GARY METRAS's books of poems include *Until There Is Nothing Left, Destiny's Calendar,* and *The Night Watches.* His poems, essays, and reviews have appeared in the *Boston Review of Books, English Journal, Poetry, Rosebud,* and *Yankee.* The son of a bricklayer, he has worked as tobacco picker, mason's tender, short order cook, air traffic controller, book store manager, and English teacher in high school and college.

JOSEPH MILLAR's first book, *Overtime,* was a finalist for the Oregon Book Award, and his poems won an NEA fellowship in 2003. For many years he lived in the San Francisco Bay area and worked as a telephone installation foreman.

MICHAEL MOORE was born in Flint, Michigan, and is an Academy Award-winning director and author. Moore's politically charged documentaries include *Roger & Me* (1989), *Bowling for Columbine* (2002), *Fahrenheit 9/11* (2004), and *Sicko* (2007). He has also written and starred in two television shows, TV *Nation* and *The Awful Truth*. Moore's books include *Stupid White Men* (2001) and *Dude, Where's my Country?* (2003). Moore's films have won several awards, including an Oscar for Best Documentary for *Bowling for Columbine* and a Palme d'Or at Cannes for *Fahrenheit 9/11*. Moore lives with his wife, producer Kathleen Glynn, in northern Michigan.

MARK NOWAK is a documentary poet, social critic, and labor activist, whose writings include *Shut Up Shut Down* (afterword by Amiri Baraka), a *New York Times* "Editor's Choice," and the recently published book on coal mining disasters in the U.S. and China, *Coal Mountain Elementary* (2009). Nowak founded the Union of Radical Workers and Writers, and his projects with them have included the unionization of a Borders bookstore and an essay in the *Progressive* on the plight of big box chain and independent bookstore workers.

ANNE-MARIE OOMEN is the author of *Pulling Down the Barn* and *House of Fields* (Wayne State University Press), both Michigan Notable Books, as well as *Uncoded Woman* (Milkweed Editions). She has also published two chapbooks of poetry, *Seasons of the Sleeping Bear* and *Moniker* (with Ray Nargis), and is a featured poet in *New Poems of the Third Coast: Contemporary Michigan Poetry*. *An American Map* is her new collection of essays from the Wayne State University Press's Made in Michigan Writers Series.

CLIFFORD ODETS (1906–1963) was an American socialist playwright, film screenwriter, and social protester. His famous labor-based plays were *Waiting for Lefty* and *Awake & Sing*. He later turned to Hollywood to write screenplays. He died in Los Angeles in 1963.

MATTHEW OLZMANN currently directs InsideOut's Citywide Poets, an intensive after-school poetry workshop for teenage writers in Detroit.

RICHARD PEABODY, a prolific poet, fiction writer, and editor, is an experienced teacher and activist in the Washington, DC community. He is editor of *Gargoyle Magazine* (founded in 1976) and has published a novella, two books of short stories, six books of poems, and an e-book. He has edited and co-edited nineteen anthologies, including *Mondo Barbie*, *Mondo Elvis*, *Conversations with Gore Vidal*, *A Different Beat: Writings by Women of the Beat Generation*, and *Kiss the Sky: Fiction and Poetry Starring Jimi Hendrix*. Peabody teaches fiction writing for the Johns Hopkins Advanced Studies program. You can find out more about him at www.gargoylemagazine.com/richard/richard.html.

JEFF PONIEWAZ teaches "Literature of Ecological Vision" and a course that presents Whitman and Ginsberg as parallel American bards via the University of Wisconsin—Milwaukee. His book, *Dolphin Leaping in the Milky Way*, praised by Ginsberg for its "impassioned prescient Whitmanesque/ Thoreauvian verve and wit," won him a Discovery Award from PEN, the international writers' organization. His last name, pronounced "poe-nYEAH-vAHsh," is Polish for "because."

MINNIE BRUCE PRATT's most recent book of poetry, *The Dirt She Ate: Selected and New Poems* (University of Pittsburgh Press), received a Lambda Literary Award. Her previous book, *Walking Back Up Depot Street*, also from Pitt, was named Best Lesbian/Gay Book of the Year by *ForeWord: The Magazine of Independent Bookstores and Booksellers*. Her work, *Crime Against Nature*, was chosen as the Lamont Poetry Selection by the Academy of American Poets. She received a 2005 Fellowship in Poetry from the New Jersey State Council on the Arts. She can be reached at www.mbpratt.org.

DUDLEY RANDALL (1914–2000) was the first poet laureate of Detroit (1981–2000) and the author of six books of poetry: *Poem Counterpoem* (with Margaret Danner), *Cities Burning*, *After the Killing*, *More to Remember*, *Love You*, and *A Litany of Friends*. He was the founding editor/publisher of Broadside Press and the editor of numerous anthologies of black poetry. His poetry has been translated into many languages, including Russian.

KEVIN RASHID was for nineteen years a groundskeeper at Wayne State University. Recently, he moved inside to become the curriculum coordinator of Wayne State's honors program and administrator of undergraduate research. He has taught creative writing at wsu, for the Poetry Club at Cass Tech High School, for the InsideOut program, and at Detroit Southwest Mental Health's Outpatient Clinic for the Writer's Voice. He has been published in several books and journals, including *The Academy of American Poet's New Voices 1989–1998*, *Abandon Automobile: Detroit City 2001*, *The Maxis Review 2001* and *2002*, and *Arab Detroit: From Margins to Mainstream*.

JOHN R. REED is Distinguished Professor of English at Wayne State University in Detroit. He has written several books on Victorian and Modern subjects from Emily Dickinson to William Thackeray. His newest scholarly book is *Dickens's Hyperrealism* (Ohio State University Press, 2010). He is also an acclaimed poet and author of several books, including *A Gallery of Spiders* (Ontario Review Press), *Life Sentences* (Wayne State University Press), *Dear Ruth* (Ridgeway Press), and others.

JUDITH ROCHE is a poet. Her book, *Wisdom of the Body*, won a 2007 American Book Award. Roche has worked in collaboration with visual artists on several public art projects, which are installed in the Seattle area. Roche is Literary Arts Director Emeritus for the One Reel, an arts producing company, and teaches poetry workshops. Though she lives and writes in Seattle, she is still and always a Detroiter in her heart.

TRINIDAD SANCHEZ, JR. (1943–2006), poet and activist, was born in Pontiac, Michigan. Sanchez entered the Society of Jesus as a Jesuit brother in Detroit, Michigan, where he worked with young offenders and prison inmates. He remained in the order for twenty-seven years. Sanchez received several awards during his lifetime and was given the President's Peace Commission Art of Peace Award posthumously in 2007. His works include *Why Am I So Brown?* (1991) and *Jalapeño Blues* (2006).

ED SANDERS is an American poet, singer, social activist, environmentalist, author, and publisher, and has been a longtime member of the band the Fugs. Sanders received a Guggenheim Fellowship in poetry in 1983, and an NEA fellowship in poetry for 1987. His works include *The Family* (1971), *Investigative Poetry* (1976), and *America: A History in Verse* (2000); his *Thirsting for Peace in a Raging Century, Selected Poems 1961–1985* (Coffee House Press) won an American Book Award in 1988. Sanders lives in Woodstock, New York.

JOHN SAYLES is an American film director and screenwriter. He graduated from Williams College and wrote short stories and novels, including *Union Dues* (1977), before becoming a screenwriter for Roger Corman. He made his directorial debut with the acclaimed *Return of the Secaucus Seven* (1980). He explored social and political issues in films such as *Lianna* (1983), *Matewan* (1987), *Eight Men Out* (1988), *City of Hope* (1991), *Lone Star* (1996), and *Sunshine State* (2002). He also directed the children's movie *The Secret of Roan Inish* (1994).

MICHAEL SHAY's fiction and essays have been published in *Northern Lights, High Plains Literary Review, Colorado Review, Owen Wister Review, Visions, High Plains Register*, and *In Short*, a Norton anthology of brief creative non-fiction. His book of short fiction, *The Weight of a Body*, was published in 2006 by Ghost Road Press. He was co-editor of the 2003 anthology *Deep West: A Literary Tour of Wyoming*. Michael is the literature, visual, and performing artists' program specialist for the Wyoming Arts Council in Cheyenne.

VIVIAN SHIPLEY is a Connecticut State University Distinguished Professor and editor of *Connecticut Review*. Vivian Shipley teaches at Southern Connecticut State University. In 2010, an eighth book of poetry, *All of Your Messages Have Been Erased*, was published by Southeastern Louisiana University, and a sixth chapbook, *Greatest Hits: 1974–2010*, is forthcoming from Pudding House Press. Raised in Kentucky, with a Ph.D. from Vanderbilt, she was inducted into the University of Kentucky Hall of Fame for Distinguished Alumni in April 2010.

BETSY SHOLL is the author of seven books of poetry, most recently *Rough Cradle* (Alice James Books, 2009). She teaches in the MFA in writing program at Vermont College.

LARRY SMITH was born in the industrial Ohio Valley in the 1940s. Smith has worked as a steel mill laborer, a high school teacher, a college professor, and a writer. A graduate of Mingo Central High School, Muskingum College, and Kent State University, he is the director of the Firelands Writing Center and editor-in-chief of Bottom Dog Press, Inc. Smith is also the father of three adult children, and is married to Ann Smith, a professor emerita of nursing at the Medical College of Ohio. He is the author of numerous works, including eight books of poetry, three books of fiction, and two literary biographies of Kenneth Patchen and of Lawrence Ferlinghetti. Recently retired, he may be reached at BGSU Firelands College, where he still teaches writing, literature, and film. His most recent book is *The Long River Home: A Novel* (Working Lives Series, Bottom Dog Press, 2009).

MARC KELLY SMITH is an American poet and the creator and founder of the poetry slam movement, for which he received the nickname "Slam Papi." Smith's several books include *Crowdpleaser* (1996) and *The Spoken Word Revolution* (2003). Smith's poetry has been featured in *Hammer's Magazine, Chicago Magazine, The Outlaw Bible of American Poetry,* and *Aloud! Voices from the Nuyorican Poets Cafe,* which won the 1994 American Book Award. Smith continues to host and perform at the Uptown Poetry Slam in Chicago, now in its twenty-first year.

LAMONT B. STEPTOE was born and raised in Pittsburgh, Pennsylvania, is the author of twelve collections of poetry, and has edited two collections of poetry by the late South African poet, Dennis Brutus. Steptoe is a poet, publisher, and photographer. In 2005, he was the recipient of the American Book Award for his collection, *A Long Movie of Shadows.* In 2006, he was awarded a Pew Fellowship in the Arts and inducted into the International Hall of Fame for Writers of African Descent by the Gwendolyn Brooks Center at Chicago State University. Steptoe's most recent collections are *Crowns and Halos, Oracular Rumblings,* and *Stiltwalking.* He is the founder and publisher of Whirlwind Press and a Vietnam veteran. Steptoe's work has appeared in over one hundred anthologies, and he regularly reads throughout the United States as well as overseas. He has read his work in Den Haag, Netherlands, the countries of Nicaragua and France, and most recently in Mumbai, India.

QUINCY TROUPE is a poet, performer, and editor. His books of poetry include *Transcircularities: New and Selected Poems* (2002), *Avalanche: Poems* (1996), and *Skulls along the River* (1984). He is also the author of *Miles: The Autobiography* (1989), which received an American Book Award, and the memoir, *Miles and Me: A Memoir of Miles Davis* (2000). Among his honors and awards are fellowships from the National Foundation for the Arts, the New York Foundation for the Arts, and a grant from the New York State Council on the Arts. In 2010, Troupe was awarded a Lifetime Achievement Award from the Before Columbus Foundation. He has taught at the University of California at San Diego and Columbia University. He was the first official poet laureate of the state of California. Troupe lives with his wife, Margaret, and son Porter, in La Jolla, California.

JEFF VANDE ZANDE teaches English at Delta College in Midland, Michigan. His stories have been collected in a full-length collection, *Emergency Stopping and Other Stories* (Bottom Dog Press). Individual stories have appeared in *Coe Review, Existere, Iron Horse Literary Review,* and *Matrix,* among others. He has two novels: *Into the Desperate Country* (March Street Press) and *Landscape with Fragmented Figures* (Bottom Dog Press). In 2010, Whistling Shade Press released his novella, *Threatened Species and Other Stories.* He maintains a website at www.jeffvandezande.com.

ANCA VLASOPOLOS has published the award-winning novel *The New Bedford Samurai,* the award-winning memoir *No Return Address: A Memoir of Displacement,* a collection of poems, *Penguins in a Warming World,* three poetry chapbooks, a detective novel, *Missing Members,* and over two hundred poems and short stories. She was nominated for the Pulitzer for *The New Bedford Samurai* and was nominated several times for the Pushcart Award in poetry and fiction. She is associate editor of *Corridors Magazine.*

MICK VRANICH was born downriver from Detroit. He was one of two in 1970 to earn a master's in the new Creative Writing program at Wayne State University. During six years of college, he was a general laborer at Zug Island, scrapballer and hooker at Great Lakes Steel, and squaring shear operator at Ford Stamping Plant, before spending a year in Europe. In San Francisco from 1973 to 1980, he worked as a Teamster delivering auto parts. Vranich released five collections of poetry, including *Idols of Fear*—thirty-four poems (New Alliance Records, Los Angeles)—and six recordings of his music and words. *The Bottom of Time,* with his band K-9, was released in 2009. He wrote and played guitar for forty-five years, and through his performances was an activist for Native American justice, Vietnam veterans, Food Not Bombs, and the Earth. He lived in Detroit with his mate, painter Sherry Hendrick, and worked as a carpenter.

DIANE WAKOSKI is an American poet who is associated with the "deep image" poets and the Beats. She has published over forty books of poetry, including *Emerald Ice: Selected Poems, 1962–1987* (1988) and the four volumes of her Archaeology of Movies and Books sequence, *Argonaut Rose* (1998), *The Emerald City of Las Vegas* (1995), *Jason the Sailor* (1993), and *Medea the Sorceress* (1991). A book of essays, *Toward a New Poetry*, was published in 1980. She is best known for a series of poems collectively known as "The Leather Jacket Diaries." She won the prestigious William Carlos Williams Award for her book *Emerald Ice*. Wakoski teaches creative writing at Michigan State University.

BARRY WALLENSTEIN is the author of five books of poetry. He is a professor of literature and creative writing at City College in New York and is an editor of *American Book Review*.

MARY ANN WEHLER holds an MFA in poetry from Vermont College. She has two books of poetry, *Walking Through Deep Snow* and *Throat*. Mary Ann has been teaching poetry, writing, and reading for over a decade.

JOSEPH E. WEIL was born and raised in Elizabeth, New Jersey, where he attended St. Mary of the Assumption grade school and high school. For over twenty years, Weil worked on the graveyard shift at various factories, mainly at National Tool and Manufacturing in Kenilworth, New Jersey. During this time, he became involved in hosting poetry readings in both New Jersey and New York, and founded the literary magazine *Black Swan*. Weil is currently a lecturer in the creative writing department at Binghamton University. He has published three books of poetry: *Painting the Christmas Trees* (Texas Review Press), *What Remains* (Night Shade Press), and *The Plumber's Apprentice* (NYQ Books).

ROGER WEINGARTEN is the author of numerous collections of poetry, including *Premature Elegy by Firelight* (Longleaf Press, 2007), *Greatest Hits: 1972–2002* (Pudding House Publications, 2003), *Ghost Wrestling* (1997), *Infant Bonds of Joy* (1990), and *Shadow Shadow* (1986). His poems have appeared in *APR*, the *New Yorker*, *Poetry*, the *Paris Review*, the *New Republic*, *Ploughshares*, the *Prague Revue*, and the *Kenyon Review*, among many others. He has co-edited several poetry anthologies, including *Stranger at Home: American Poetry with an Accent* (2008) and *Poets of the New Century* (2001). His awards include a Pushcart Prize, a *Louisville Review* Poetry Prize, a National Endowment for the Arts Award, and an Ingram Merrill Foundation Award in Literature. He founded the MFA in writing and the postgraduate Summer Writers' Conference at Vermont College of the Fine Arts.

JACK WHITE is a musician, record producer, and occasional actor. During the 1990s, White was a part-time musician in various underground bands in Detroit, Michigan, while working by day as an upholsterer. White formed the White Stripes in 1997 with Meg White, his then wife. The band went on to have a string of critically acclaimed albums, with their third, *White Blood Cells*, catapulting them to international stardom. He was ranked #17 on *Rolling Stone's* list of "the 100 Greatest Guitarists of All Time." In 2005, White became a founding member of the rock band the Raconteurs. In 2009, he became a founding member of a third group, the Dead Weather.

XU XI is the author of eight books of fiction and essays, and editor of three anthologies of Hong Kong literature in English. A Chinese-Indonesian native of Hong Kong, the city was home until her mid-twenties, after which she led a peripatetic existence around Europe, America, and Asia. In 2009, she was elected faculty chair of Vermont College of Fine Arts's MFA in writing program, the first woman, ethnic minority, and foreign-born U.S. national to hold the position. In 2010, she became the first writer in residence at the English department of the City University of Hong Kong, overseeing a new MFA program that specializes in Asian writing in English.

AL YOUNG is a poet, novelist, short story writer, screenwriter, editor, essayist, musician, and educator. His volumes of poetry include *Heaven: Collected Poems, 1956–1990* (1992), *The Blues Don't Change: New and Selected Poems* (1982), *Geography of the Near Past* (1976), *Some Recent Fiction* (1974), and *The Song Turning Back into Itself* (1971). His novels include *Snakes: A Novel* (1970) and *Seduction by Light* (1988). His memoirs include *Drowning in the Sea of Love: Musical Memoirs* (1995), *Mingus/Mingus: Two Memoirs* (1989, with Janet Coleman). He is the recipient of several awards, including National Arts Council awards for editing and poetry, the Pushcart Prize, a Guggenheim Memorial Foundation Fellowship, and the Before Columbus Foundation Award, as well as several NEA fellowships. He lives in Palo Alto, California.

Credits

Every attempt was made to contact all authors not in public domain to have their permissions. If we missed or could not contact authors, please notify the press and proper acknowledgements will be made in subsequent editions.

LABOR POEMS AND SONGS

Maggie Anderson: "Spitting in the Leaves" was first published in *Cold Comfort* (University of Pittsburgh Press, 1986). "Closed Mill" was first published in *A Space Filled with Moving* (University of Pittsburgh Press, 1992). Reprinted with the kind permission of the author and The University of Pittsburgh Press. © Maggie Anderson.

Antler: "Factory" was originally published in Lawrence Ferlinghetti's Pocket Poet Series (City Lights Book, San Francisco, 1980). "Written after Learning Slaves in Ancient Greece and Rome Had 115 Holidays a Year" is from *Last Words* (Ballantine Books, NY, 1986). Both poems also appear in *Antler: The Selected Poems* (Soft Skull Press, 2000). Reprinted with the kind permission of the author. © Antler.

Alvin Aubert: "Migration Scene c. 1939." Used with the kind permission of the author. © Alvin Aubert.

Amiri Baraka: "A Poem Some People Will Have to Understand." Reprinted with the kind permission of the author. © Amiri Baraka.

Jan Beatty: "My Father Teaches Me to Dream" and "Poetry Workshop at the Homeless Shelter" are from *The Boneshaker* (University of Pittsburgh Press, 2002). "Mad River" and "A Waitress's Instructions on Tipping, or Get the Cash Up and Don't Waste My Time" are from *Mad River* (University of Pittsburgh Press, 1995). Reprinted with the kind permission of the author and The University of Pittsburgh Press. © Jan Beatty.

Daniel Berrigan: "Prayer from a Picket Line." Reprinted with the kind permission of the author. © Daniel Berrigan.

553

Bret Lott: "Work" is from *A Dream of Old Leaves: Stories* (Washington Square Press, NY, 1999). Reprinted with the kind permission of the author. © Bret Lott.

Colleen J. McElroy: "Sister Detroit." Reprinted with the kind permission of the author. © Colleen J. McElroy. 2005.

Clifford Odets: "I Can't Sleep." Reprinted with the kind permission of the author's Estate and Walter Odets. © Clifford Odets Estate.

John Sayles: "The 7-10 Split" is from *The Anarchists' Convention & Other Stories* (Nation Books, New York, 2005). Reprinted with the kind permission of the author. © 1979 and 2005 John Sayles.

Michael Shay: "The Problem with Mrs. P." Reprinted with the kind permission of the author. © Michael Shay.

Larry Smith: excerpt from *Beyond Rust* (Bottom Dog Press, OH, 1995). Reprinted with the kind permission of the author. © Larry Smith.

Jeff Vande Zande: "Layoff." From the Bottom Dog Press anthology *Our Working Lives: Short Stories of People & Work*. Reprinted with the kind permission of the author. © Jeff Vande Zande.

Xu Xi: "To Body To Chicken." Reprinted with the kind permission of the author. © Xu Xi.

NON-FICTION, HISTORIES, AND MEMOIRS

Rebecca Harding Davis: excerpt from *Life in the Iron Mills*. Public Domain.

Dorothy Day: excerpts from "In Fields and Factories" and "Loaves & Fishes" both from *Dorothy Day: Selected Writings* edited by Robert Ellsberg. © 1983, 1992, and 2005 by Robert Ellsberg and Tamar Hennessey. Anniversary Edition (Orbis Books, Marynoll, NY 10545). Reprinted with the kind permission of Orbis Books. © 2005.

Jennifer Gillan: "Navigating New Jersey." Reprinted with the kind permission of the author. © Jennifer Gillan.

WORKING WORDS

THE COFFEE HOUSES OF SEVENTEENTH-CENTURY ENGLAND WERE PLACES OF fellowship where ideas could be freely exchanged. In the cafés of Paris in the early years of the twentieth century, the surrealist, cubist, and dada art movements began. The coffee houses of 1950s America provided refuge and tremendous literary energy. Today, coffee house culture abounds at corner shops and online.

Coffee House Press continues these rich traditions. We envision all our authors and all our readers—be they in their living room chairs, at the beach, or in their beds—joining us around an ever-expandable table, drinking coffee and telling tales. And in the process of this exchange of stories by writers who speak from many communities and cultures, the American mosaic becomes reinvented, and reinvigorated.

We invite you to join us in our effort to welcome new readers to our table, and to the tales told in the pages of Coffee House Press books.

Please visit www.coffeehousepress.org
for more information.

FUNDER ACKNOWLEDGMENT

Coffee House Press is an independent nonprofit literary publisher. Our books are made possible through the generous support of grants and gifts from many foundations, corporate giving programs, state and federal support, and through donations from individuals who believe in the transformational power of literature. Coffee House Press receives major operating support from the Bush Foundation, the McKnight Foundation, from Target, and from the Minnesota State Arts Board, through an appropriation from the Minnesota State Legislature and from the National Endowment for the Arts. Coffee House also receives support from: three anonymous donors; Allan Appel; Around Town Literary Media Guides; Bill Berkson; the James L. and Nancy J. Bildner Foundation; the Patrick and Aimee Butler Family Foundation; the Buuck Family Foundation; Dorsey & Whitney, LLP; Fredrikson & Byron, P.A.; Sally French; Jennifer Haugh; Anselm Hollo and Jane Dalrymple-Hollo; Jeffrey Hom; Stephen and Isabel Keating; the Kenneth Koch Literary Estate; the Lenfestey Family Foundation; Ethan J. Litman; Mary McDermid; Sjur Midness and Briar Andresen; the Rehael Fund of the Minneapolis Foundation; Deborah Reynolds; Schwegman, Lundberg, Woessner, P.A.; John Sjoberg; David Smith; Mary Strand and Tom Fraser; Jeffrey Sugerman; the Archie D. & Bertha H. Walker Foundation; Stu Wilson and Mel Barker; the Woessner Freeman Family Foundation in memory of David Hilton; and many other generous individual donors.

NATIONAL ENDOWMENT FOR THE ARTS

This activity is made possible in part by a grant from the Minnesota State Arts Board, through an appropriation by the Minnesota State Legislature and a grant from the National Endowment for the Arts. MINNESOTA STATE ARTS BOARD

TARGET.

To you and our many readers across the country,
we send our thanks for your continuing support.

Good books are brewing at www.coffeehousepress.org